1000+ SCIENCE FACTS

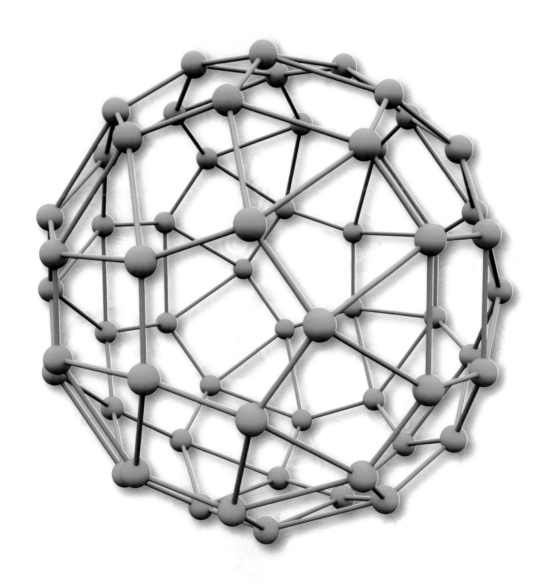

1000+ SCIENCE FACTS

First published in 2012 by Miles Kelly Publishing Ltd
Harding's Barn, Bardfield End Green, Thaxted, Essex, CM6 3PX, UK

Copyright © Miles Kelly Publishing Ltd 2012

This edition published in 2015

2 4 6 8 10 9 7 5 3 1

Publishing Director Belinda Gallagher
Creative Director Jo Cowan
Editorial Director Rosie Neave
Editors Carly Blake, Sarah Parkin, Claire Philip, Amy Johnson
Cover Designer Simon Lee
Designers Kayleigh Allen, Dave and Angela Ball at D&A,
John Christopher, Jo Cowan, Sally Lace, Andrea Slane
Production Elizabeth Collins, Caroline Kelly
Reprographics Stephan Davis, Jennifer Cozens, Thom Allaway
Assets Lorraine King

ISBN 978-1-78209-964-2

Printed in China

Made with paper from a sustainable forest

www.mileskelly.net
info@mileskelly.net

CONTENTS

SCIENCE

GREAT SCIENTISTS

INVENTIONS

SPACE

EXPLORING SPACE

ASTRONOMY

FLIGHT

SPEED

EVOLUTION

PLANT LIFE

ANIMAL LIFE

HUMAN BODY

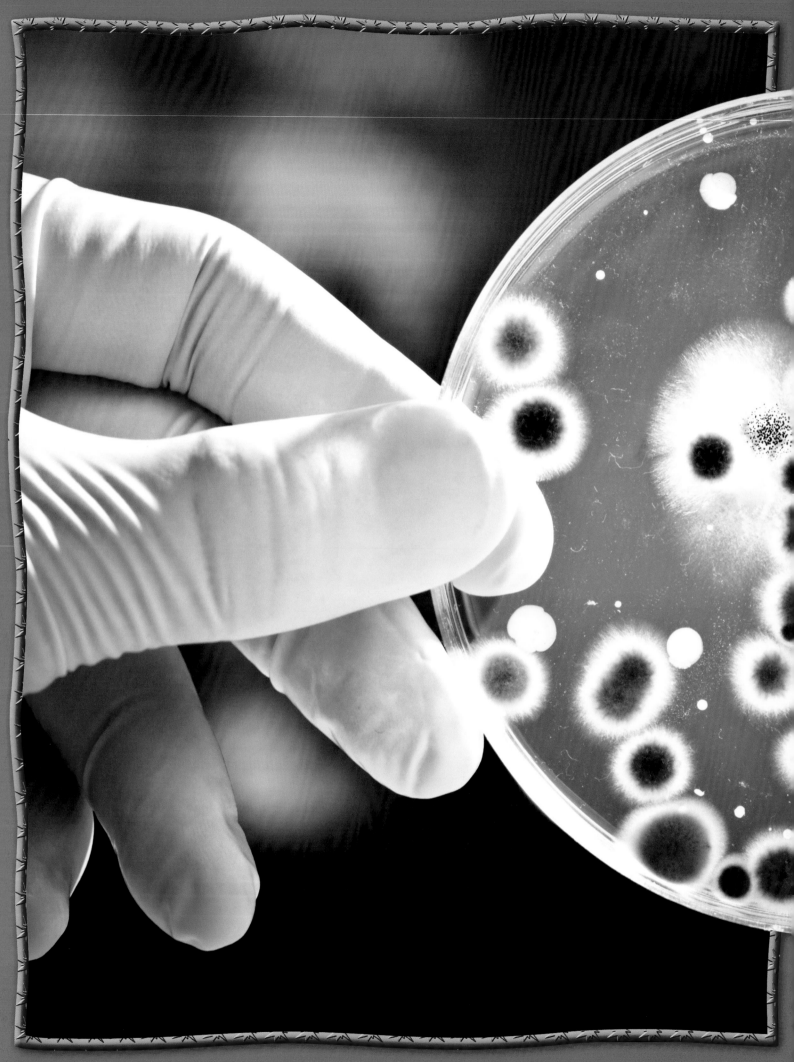

SCIENCE

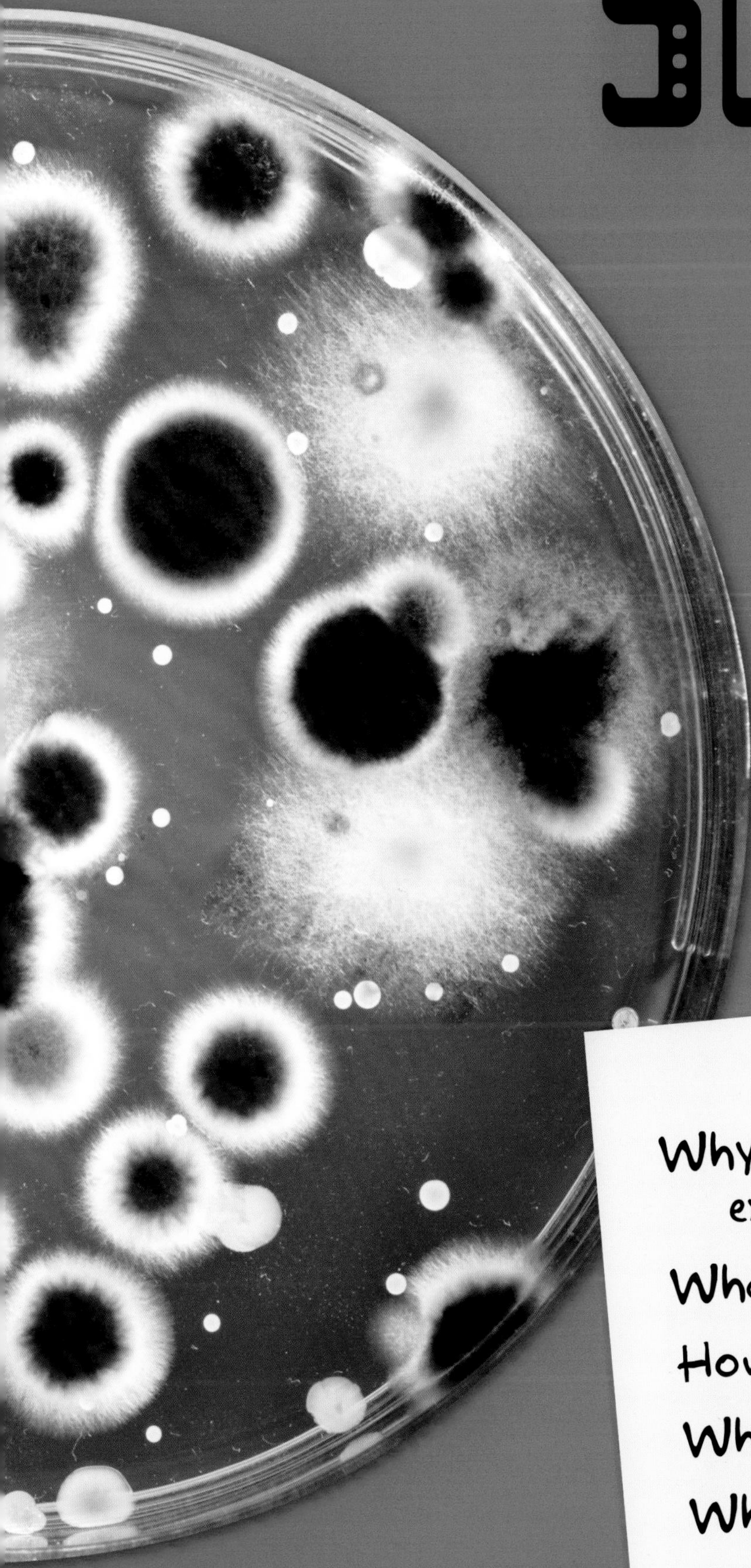

- Powerful machines
- Thermal radiation
- Refraction and reflection
- Laser light
- Generating electricity
- Radio waves
- Acids and bases
- The Periodic Table
- Subatomic particles
- Scientific method

Why do some engines use explosions?

What does "ultrasonic" mean?

How big is a light wave?

What is glass made from?

When is a laser good for your health?

Why do we need science?

1 Even one hundred books like this could not explain all the reasons why we need science. Toasters, bicycles, cell phones, computers, cars, lightbulbs—all the gadgets and machines we use every day are the results of scientific discoveries. Houses, skyscrapers, bridges, and rockets are built using science. Our knowledge of medicines, nature, light, and sound comes from science. Then there is the science of predicting the weather, investigating how stars shine, finding out why carrots are orange…

▼ In a big city, science is all around you—everything from sky-scraping buildings to speedy vehicles and useful gadgets is based on science and technology.

Machines big and small

2 **Machines are everywhere!** They help us do things, or make doing them easier. Every time you play on a seesaw, you are using a machine. A lever is a stiff bar that tilts at a point called the pivot or fulcrum. The pivot of the seesaw is in the middle. Using the seesaw as a lever, a small person can lift a big person by sitting further from the pivot.

▶ On a seesaw lever, the pivot is in the middle. Other levers have pivots at the end.

Thread

▶ Turning a screw moves it along with more force than the effort used to turn it.

3 **The screw is another simple but useful scientific machine.** It is a ridge, or thread, wrapped around a bar or pole. It changes a small turning motion into a powerful pulling or lifting movement. Wood screws hold together furniture or shelves. A car jack lets you lift up a whole car.

4 **Where would you be without wheels?** Not going very far. The wheel is a simple machine, a circular disk that turns around its center on a bar called an axle. Wheels carry heavy weights easily. There are giant wheels on big trucks and trains and small wheels on rollerblades.

Axle

▼ Wheels reduce friction, allowing heavy loads to be carried more easily.

▼ Two pulleys together reduce the force needed to lift a heavy girder by one half.

5 A pulley turns around, like a wheel. It has a groove around its edge for a cable or rope. Lots of pulleys allow us to lift very heavy weights easily. The pulleys on a tower crane can lift huge steel girders to the top of a skyscraper.

▲ Bicycle gears mean you can pedal at the same speed, with the same force, when climbing up a hill or speeding down it.

Reversing gears

Sliding rack

Pinion gear

Bevel gears

Slow pinion gear

Screw-shaped worm gear

▲ Gears change the turning direction of a force. They can slow it down or speed it up —and even convert it into a sliding force (rack and pinion).

Pivot

Lever

I DON'T BELIEVE IT!

A ramp is a simple machine called an inclined plane. It is easier to walk up a ramp than to jump straight to the top.

6 Gears are like wheels, with pointed teeth around the edges. They change a fast, weak turning force into a slow, powerful one—or the other way around. On a bicycle, you can pedal up the steepest hill in bottom (lowest) gear, then speed down the other side in top (highest) gear.

When science is hot!

7 Fire! Flames! Burning! Heat! The science of heat is important in all kinds of ways. Not only do we cook with heat, but we also warm our homes and heat water. Burning happens in all kinds of engines in cars, trucks, planes, and rockets. It is also used in factory processes, from making steel to shaping plastics.

▲ A firework burns suddenly as an explosive, producing heat, light, and sound. The "bang" is the sound made by the paper wrapper as it is blown apart.

Heat from the drink is conducted up the metal spoon

8 Heat can move by conduction. A hot object will pass on, or transfer, some of its heat to a cooler one. Dip a metal spoon in a hot drink and the spoon handle soon warms up. Heat is conducted from the drink, through the metal.

9 Heat moves by invisible "heat rays." This is called thermal radiation and the rays are infrared waves. Our planet is warmed by the Sun because heat from the Sun radiates through space as infrared waves.

TRUE OR FALSE?

1. Burning happens inside the engine of a plane.
2. A device for measuring temperature is called a calendar.
3. Heat rays are known as infrablue waves.

Answers:
1. True 2. False 3. False

◄ Metal is a good conductor of heat. Put a teaspoon in a hot drink and feel how quickly it heats up.

10 Burning, also called combustion, is a chemical process. Oxygen gas from the air joins to, or combines with, the substance being burned. The chemical change releases lots of heat, and usually light too. If this happens really fast, we call it an explosion.

▲ A burner flame makes glass so hot it becomes soft and bendy, so it can be stretched, shaped, and even blown up like a balloon.

11 Temperature is a measure of how hot or cold something is. It is usually measured in degrees Fahrenheit (°F) or Celsius (°C). Water freezes at 32°F (0°C), and boils at 212°F (100°C). We use thermometers to take our temperatures. Your body temperature is about 98.6°F (37°C).

▶ This thermometer contains alcohol colored by a red dye. As it warms, the alcohol expands (takes up more space). It moves up the thin tube, showing the temperature on the scale.

12 Heat moves through liquids and gases by convection. Some of the liquid or gas takes in heat, gets lighter, and rises into cooler areas. Then other cooler liquid or gas moves in to do the same and the process repeats. You can see this as "wavy" hot air rising from a flame.

▶ Hot air shimmering over a candle is a visible sign of the heat being convected away.

Engine power

13 Imagine having to walk or run everywhere, instead of riding in a car. Engines are machines that use fuel to do work for us and make life easier. Fuel is a substance that has chemical energy stored inside it. The energy is released as heat by burning or exploding the fuel in the engine.

▼ A jet engine has sets of angled blades, called turbines, that spin on shafts.

Turbines squash incoming air

Jet fuel is sprayed into the air inside the chamber, creating a small explosion

Burning gases spin exhaust turbines

14 Most cars have gasoline engines. An air and gasoline mixture is pushed into a hollow chamber called a cylinder. A spark from a spark plug makes it explode, which pushes a piston down inside the cylinder. This movement is used by gears to turn the wheels. Most cars have four or six cylinders.

15 A diesel engine doesn't use sparks. The mixture of air and diesel is squashed in the cylinder, becoming so hot it explodes. Diesel engines are used in machines such as tractors that need lots of power.

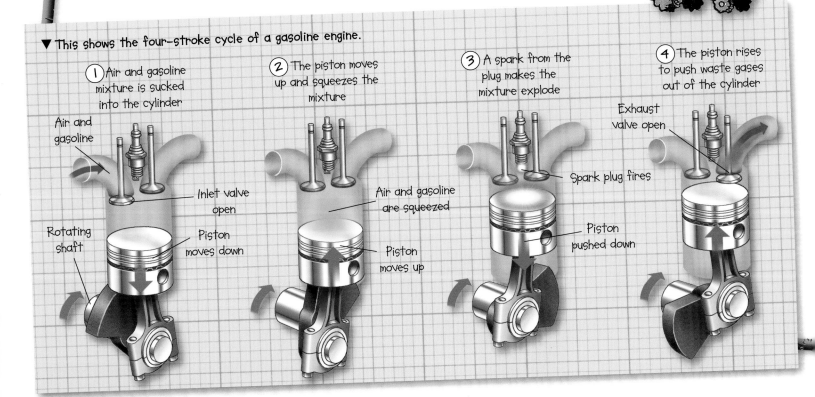

▼ This shows the four-stroke cycle of a gasoline engine.

① Air and gasoline mixture is sucked into the cylinder

② The piston moves up and squeezes the mixture

③ A spark from the plug makes the mixture explode

④ The piston rises to push waste gases out of the cylinder

Air and gasoline

Inlet valve open

Rotating shaft

Piston moves down

Air and gasoline are squeezed

Piston moves up

Spark plug fires

Piston pushed down

Exhaust valve open

▲ On a fast jet plane at full power, the exhaust gases from the engines glow almost white-hot.

16 A jet engine mixes air and kerosene and sets fire to it in one long, continuous, roaring explosion. Incredibly hot gases blast out of the back of the engine. These push the engine forward—along with the plane.

17 An electric motor passes electricity through coils of wire. This makes the coils magnetic, and they push or pull against magnets around them. The push-pull makes the coils spin on their shaft (axle).

▼ Using magnetic forces, an electric motor turns electrical energy into moving or kinetic energy.

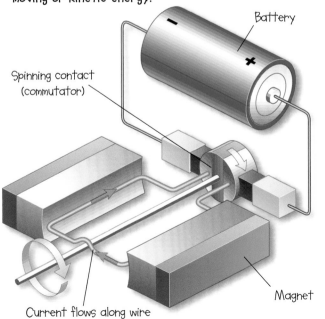

Battery

Spinning contact (commutator)

Current flows along wire

Magnet

18 Engines that burn fuel give out gases and particles through their exhausts. Some of these gases are harmful to the environment. The less we use engines, the better. Electric motors are quiet, efficient, and reliable, but they still need fuel—to make the electricity at the power plant.

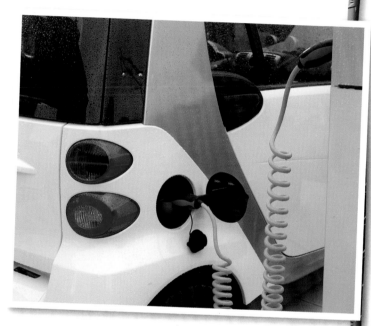

▲ Electric cars have sets of batteries to turn the motor. The batteries are "filled" with electrical energy by plugging into a recharging point.

QUIZ

1. Are exhaust gases good for the environment?

2. Does a diesel engine use sparks?

3. How many cylinders do most cars have?

4. Do electric cars have batteries?

Answers:
1. No, some of them are harmful 2. No 3. Four or six 4. Yes

Science on the move

19 Without science, you would have to walk everywhere, or ride a horse. Luckily, scientists and engineers have developed many methods of transport, most importantly, the car. Lots of people can travel together in a bus, train, plane, or ship. These use less energy and resources, and make less pollution than cars.

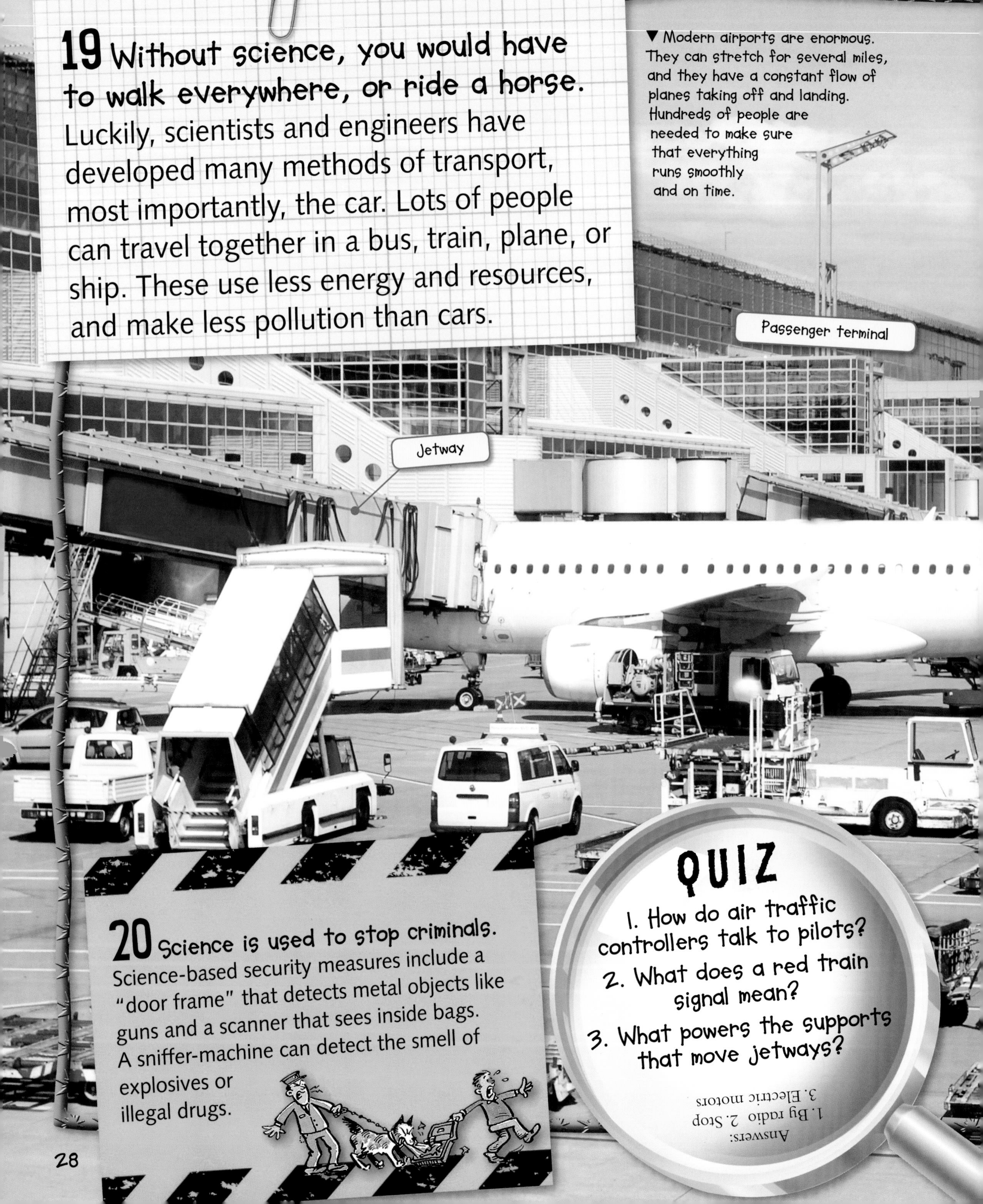

▼ Modern airports are enormous. They can stretch for several miles, and they have a constant flow of planes taking off and landing. Hundreds of people are needed to make sure that everything runs smoothly and on time.

Passenger terminal

Jetway

20 Science is used to stop criminals. Science-based security measures include a "door frame" that detects metal objects like guns and a scanner that sees inside bags. A sniffer-machine can detect the smell of explosives or illegal drugs.

QUIZ
1. How do air traffic controllers talk to pilots?
2. What does a red train signal mean?
3. What powers the supports that move jetways?

Answers:
1. By radio 2. Stop 3. Electric motors

21 Jetways are extending walkways that stretch out from the passenger terminal right to the planes' doors. Their supports move along on wheeled trolleys driven by electric motors.

22 Every method of transport needs to be safe and on time. In the airport control tower, air traffic controllers track planes on radar screens. They talk to pilots by radio. Beacons send out radio signals, giving the direction and distance to the airport.

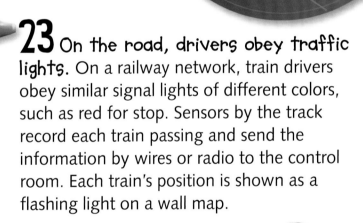

▶ The radar screen shows each aircraft as a blip, with its flight number or identity code.

23 On the road, drivers obey traffic lights. On a railway network, train drivers obey similar signal lights of different colors, such as red for stop. Sensors by the track record each train passing and send the information by wires or radio to the control room. Each train's position is shown as a flashing light on a wall map.

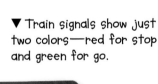

▼ Train signals show just two colors—red for stop and green for go.

D-27

▶ Trackside switches and detectors react to a train going past and automatically change the signals, so that a following train does not get too close.

Noisy science

24 Listening to the radio or television, playing music, shouting at each other—they all depend on the science of sound—acoustics. Sounds are carried by invisible waves in the air. The waves are areas of low pressure, where air particles are stretched farther apart, alternating with areas of high pressure, where they are squashed closer together.

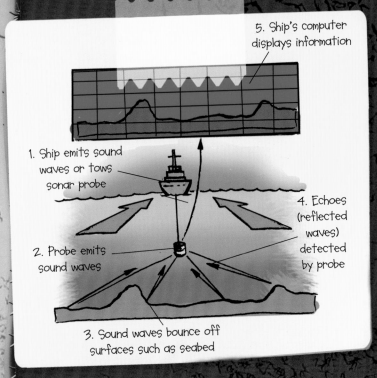

5. Ship's computer displays information

1. Ship emits sound waves or tows sonar probe

2. Probe emits sound waves

3. Sound waves bounce off surfaces such as seabed

4. Echoes (reflected waves) detected by probe

25 Scientists measure the loudness or intensity of sound in decibels, dB. A very quiet sound like a ticking watch is 10 dB. Ordinary speech is 50–60 dB. Loud music is 90 dB. A jet plane taking off is 120 dB. Too much noise damages the ears.

◀ In sonar (echo-sounding), sound waves in the water bounce or reflect off objects, and are detected.

Atomic explosion

26 Whether a sound is high or low is called its pitch, or frequency. It is measured in Hertz, Hz. A singing bird or whining motorcycle has a high pitch. A rumble of thunder or a massive truck has a low pitch. People can hear frequencies from 20 to 20,000 Hz.

Jet plane

Express train

Whisper

▶ The decibel scale measures the intensity, or energy, in sound.

0 dB   40 dB   80 dB   120 dB   180 dB

27 Sound waves spread out from a vibrating object that is moving rapidly to and fro. Stretch an elastic band between your fingers and twang it. As it vibrates, it makes a sound. When you speak, vocal cords in your neck vibrate. You can feel them through your skin.

28 Sound waves travel about 1,080 feet every second. This is fast, but it is one million times slower than light waves. Sound waves also bounce off hard, flat surfaces. This is called reflection. The returning waves are heard as an echo.

29 Loudspeakers change electrical signals into sounds. The signals in the wire pass through a wire coil inside the speaker. This turns the coil into a magnet, which pushes and pulls against another magnet. The pushing and pulling make the cone vibrate, which sends sound waves into the air.

◄ The word "sonic" means making sounds, and the high-pitched noises of bats can be described as "ultrasonic"— too high for us to hear.

Echoes bouncing back off the moth

Sound waves from the bat

▲ Bats make high-pitched sounds. If the sounds hit an insect they bounce back to the bat's ears. The reflected sound (echo) gives the bat information about the size and location of the insect.

BOX GUITAR

You will need:
shoebox   elastic band
split pins   card

Cut a hole about 4 inches across on one side of an empty shoebox. Push split pins through either side of the hole, and stretch an elastic band between them. Pluck the band. Hear how the air and box vibrate. Cover the hole with card.
Is the "guitar" as loud?

Look out—light's about!

30 Almost everything you do depends on light and the science of light, which is called optics. Light is a form of energy that you can see. Light waves are made of electricity and magnetism—and they are tiny. About 2,000 of them laid end to end would stretch across this period.

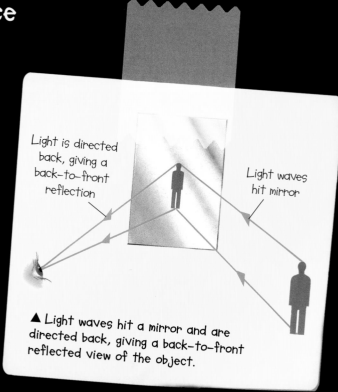

Light is directed back, giving a back-to-front reflection

Light waves hit mirror

▲ Light waves hit a mirror and are directed back, giving a back-to-front reflected view of the object.

▲ A prism of clear glass or clear plastic separates the colors in white light.

32 Like sound, light bounces off surfaces that are very smooth. This is called reflection. A mirror is smooth, hard and flat. When you look at it, you see your reflection.

31 Ordinary light from the Sun or from a lightbulb is called white light. But when white light passes through a prism, a triangular block of clear glass, it splits into many colors. These colors are known as the spectrum. Each color has a different length of wave. A rainbow is made by raindrops, which work like millions of tiny prisms to split up sunlight.

33 **Light passes through certain materials, like clear glass and plastic.** Materials that let light pass through, to give a clear view, are transparent. Those that do not allow light through, like wood and metal, are opaque.

34 **Mirrors and lenses are important parts of many optical (light-using) gadgets.** They are found in cameras, binoculars, microscopes, telescopes, and lasers. Without them, we would have no close-up photographs of tiny microchips or insects or giant planets—in fact, no photos at all.

I DON'T BELIEVE IT!

Light is the fastest thing in the Universe— it travels through space at about 186,000 miles per second. That's seven times around the world in less than one second!

▼ A concave lens, which is thin in the middle, makes things look smaller.

Light rays from object

Eye sees light rays coming from this position

▲ A convex lens, which bulges in the middle, makes things look larger.

35 **Light does not usually go straight through glass.** It bends slightly where it goes into the glass, then bends back as it comes out. This is called refraction. A lens is a curved piece of glass or plastic that bends light to make things look bigger, smaller, or clearer. Spectacle and contact lenses bend light to help people see more clearly.

▲ Glass and water bend, or refract, light waves. This makes a drinking straw look bent where it goes behind the glass and then into the water.

36 Laser light is a special kind of light. Like ordinary light, it is made of waves, but it has three main differences. Ordinary white light is a mixture of colors, while laser light is one pure color. Ordinary light waves have peaks (highs) and troughs (lows), which do not line up—laser light waves line up perfectly. Lastly, ordinary light spreads and fades. A laser beam can travel for thousands of miles as a strong, straight beam.

◀ The narrow horizontal beam from a laser spirit level can shine all the way across a building site.

▼ Waves of light build up and bounce to and fro inside a laser, then emerge at one end.

Silver mirror

Part-silver mirror

Particles in ruby crystal

Laser beam emerges

37 To make a laser beam, energy is fed in short bursts into a substance called the active medium. The energy might be electricity, heat, or ordinary light. In a red ruby laser, the active medium is a rod of ruby crystal. A strong lamp makes the particles in the crystal vibrate. The energy they give off bounces to and fro inside the crystal. Eventually, the rays vibrate with each other and they are all the same length. The energy becomes so strong that it bursts through a mirror at one end of the crystal.

▲ In a spectacular outdoor light show, different colored laser beams sweep to and fro as they pierce the darkness, seemingly all the way into space.

Beam bounces off CD

Laser

Spinning CD

Laser beam bent by prism

Reflected beam passes through prism

Reflected beam detected by sensor

▲ A CD laser detects tiny pits in the disk's underside.

38 **Lasers were invented in 1960.** They are used to play CDs and DVDs for music and movies, and in computers. They cut through thick metal in factories, and carry out delicate eye operations. They carry phone calls and television programs along cables. They even measure movements of the Earth to warn of volcanoes or earthquakes.

◀ An industrial laser has the power to melt metal into gas and cut a neat line.

QUIZ

1. How far can laser beams travel?

2. When were lasers invented?

3. Which everyday machines use lasers?

Answers:
1. Thousands of miles
2. 1960 3. DVD players,
CD players, computers

Mysterious magnets

39 Without magnets there would be no electric motors, computers, or loudspeakers. Magnetism is an invisible force to do with atoms—tiny particles that make up everything. Atoms are made of even smaller particles, including electrons. Magnetism is linked to the way that these line up and move. Most magnetic substances contain iron. As iron makes up a big part of the metallic substance steel, steel is also magnetic.

▶ For metal recycling, an electromagnet lifts out only iron-containing or ferrous metals, such as steel.

40 A magnet is a lump of iron or steel that has all its electrons and atoms lined up. This means that their magnetic forces all add up. The force surrounds the magnet, in a region called the magnetic field. This is strongest at the two parts of the magnet called the poles.

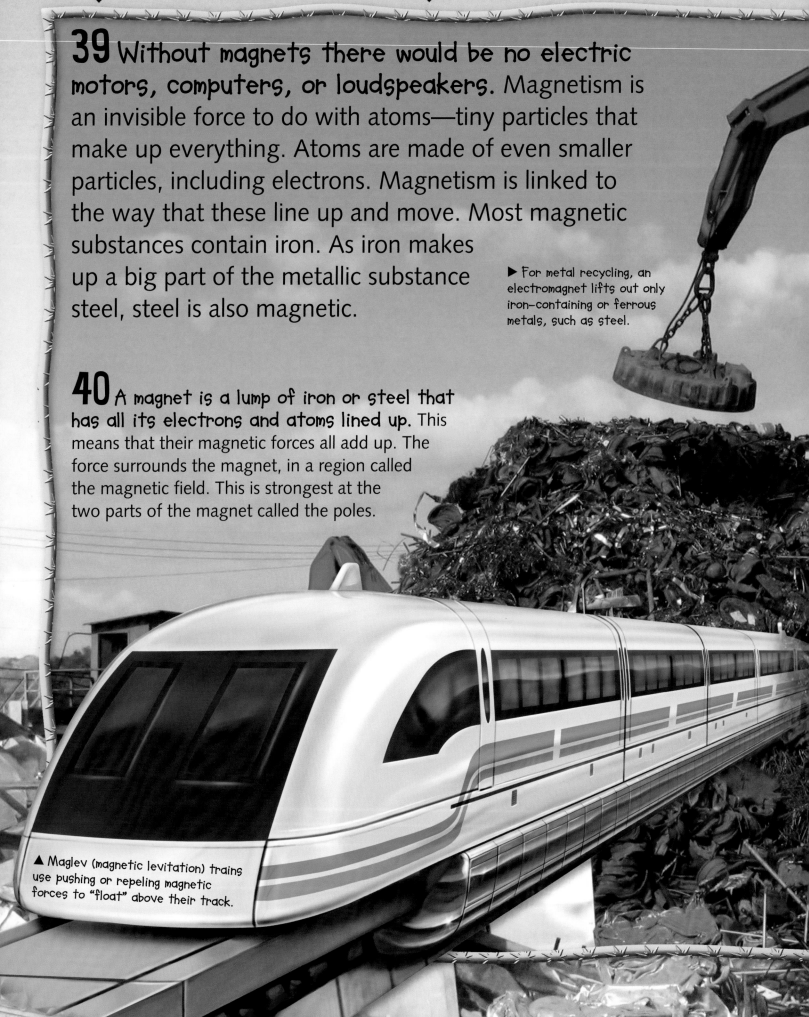

▲ Maglev (magnetic levitation) trains use pushing or repeling magnetic forces to "float" above their track.

41 **A magnet has two different poles—north and south.** A north pole repels (pushes away) the north pole of another magnet. Two south poles also repel each other. But a north pole and a south pole attract (pull together). Both magnetic poles attract any substance containing iron, like a nail or a screw.

42 **When electricity flows through a wire, it makes a weak magnetic field around it.** If the wire is wrapped into a coil, the magnetism becomes stronger. This is called an electromagnet. Its magnetic force is the same as an ordinary magnet, but when the electricity goes off, the magnetism does too. Some electromagnets are so strong, they can lift whole cars.

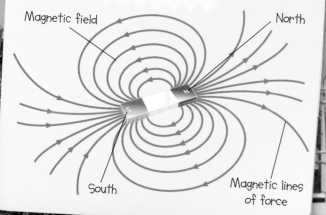

▼ The field around a magnet affects objects that contain iron.

Magnetic field

North

South

Magnetic lines of force

QUIZ

Which of these substances or objects is magnetic?

1. Steel spoon 2. Plastic spoon
3. Pencil 4. Drinks can
5. Food can 6. Screwdriver
7. Cooking foil

Answers:
1.Yes 2.No 3.No 4.No 5.Yes 6.Yes 7.No

43 **Flick a switch and things happen.** The television goes off, the computer comes on, lights shine, and music plays. Electricity is our favorite form of energy. We send it along wires and plug hundreds of machines into it.

▼ When an electric current flows, the electrons (small blue balls) all move the same way, jumping from one atom to the next. (The red balls are the centers or nuclei of the atoms.)

Atom

44 **Electricity depends on electrons.** In certain substances, when electrons are "pushed," they hop from one atom to the next. When billions do this every second, electricity flows. The "push" is from a battery or a generator. Electricity only flows in a complete loop or circuit. Break the circuit and the flow stops.

Electron

▼ Solar panels contain many hundreds of fingernail-sized PV (photovoltaic) cells. These convert light energy ("photo") to electrical energy ("voltaic").

▼ A battery has a chemical paste inside its metal casing.

Positive contact

Negative contact on base

45 **A battery makes electricity from chemicals.** Two different chemicals next to each other, such as an acid and a metal, swap electrons and get the flow going. Electricity's pushing strength is measured in volts. Most batteries are about 1.5, 3, 6, or 9 volts, with 12 volts in cars.

46 **Electricity flows easily through some substances, including water and metals.** These are electrical conductors. Other substances do not allow electricity to flow. They are insulators. Insulators include wood, plastic, glass, card, and ceramics. Metal wires and cables have coverings of plastic, to stop the electricity leaking away.

47 Electricity from power plants is carried along cables on high pylons, or buried underground. This is known as the distribution grid. At thousands of volts, this electricity is extremely dangerous.

▼ Electricity generators are housed in huge casings, some bigger than trucks.

Pylon holds cables off the ground

◄ To check and repair high-voltage cables, the electricity must be turned off well in advance.

48 Mains electricity is made at a power plant. A fuel such as coal or oil is burned to heat water into high-pressure steam. The steam pushes past the blades of a turbine and makes them spin. The turbines turn generators, which have wire coils near powerful magnets, and the spinning motion makes electricity flow in the coils.

MAKE A CIRCUIT
You will need:
lightbulb   battery   wire
plastic ruler   metal spoon   dry card
Join a bulb to a battery with pieces of wire, as shown. Electricity flows round the circuit and lights the bulb. Make a gap in the circuit and put various objects into it, to see if they allow electricity to flow again. Try a plastic ruler, a metal spoon, and some dry card.

49 The air is full of waves we cannot see or hear, unless we have the right machine. Radio waves are a form of electrical and magnetic energy, just like heat and light waves, microwaves, and X-rays. All of these are called electromagnetic waves and they travel at an equal speed —the speed of light.

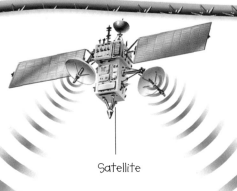

Satellite

Radio waves

51 Radio waves carry their information by being altered, or modulated, in a certain pattern. The height of a wave is called its amplitude. If this is altered, it is known as AM (amplitude modulation). Look for AM on the radio display.

50 Radio waves are used for both radio and television. They travel vast distances. Long waves curve around the Earth's surface. Short waves bounce between the Earth and the sky.

▼ This range of waves, with different wavelengths, are electrical and magnetic energy. They are called the electromagnetic spectrum.

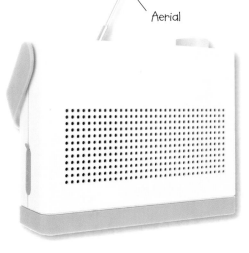

Aerial

▲ A radio set picks up radio waves using its aerial or antenna.

52 The number of waves per second is called the frequency. If this is altered, it is known as FM (frequency modulation). FM radio is clearer than AM, and less affected by weather and thunderstorms.

Long radio waves

Shorter radio waves (TV)

Microwaves

Infrared waves

Light waves (visible light)

Ultraviolet rays

X-rays

Short X-rays

Gamma rays

53 Radio waves are sent out, or transmitted, from antennae on tall masts or on satellites, to reach a very wide area. A radio receiver converts the pattern of waves to sounds. A television receiver or TV set changes them to pictures and sounds.

I DON'T BELIEVE IT!

You could send and receive radio signals on the Moon, but not in the sea. Radio waves travel easily through space, but only a few feet in water.

▼ A dish-shaped receiver picks up radio waves for TV channels.

54 Digital radio uses incredibly short bursts of radio waves with gaps between them—many thousands each second. Each burst represents the digit (number) 1, and a gap is 0. The order of the 1s and 0s carries information in the form of binary code, as in a computer.

▶ A plasma screen has thousands of tiny boxes, or cells, of three colors—red, green, and blue. Electric pulses heat the gas inside for a split second into plasma, which gives out a burst of light. Combinations of these colors gives all the other colors.

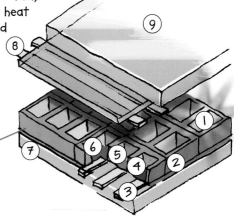

▼ Flatscreen TVs can be LCD or plasma. They use less electricity than cathode-ray TVs and produce a better picture.

KEY

① Glowing "on" cell
② Dark "off" cell
③ Rear grid of electrical contacts
④ – ⑥ Colored phosphors inside cells
⑦ Backing plate
⑧ Front grid of electrical contacts
⑨ Transparent front cover

55 **Computers are amazing machines, but they have to be told exactly what to do.** So we put in instructions and information, by various means. These include typing on a keyboard, inserting a disk or memory stick, downloading from the Internet, using a joystick or games controller, or linking up a camera, scanner, or another computer.

56 Most computers are controlled by instructions from a keyboard and a mouse. The mouse moves a pointer around on the screen and its click buttons select choices from lists called menus.

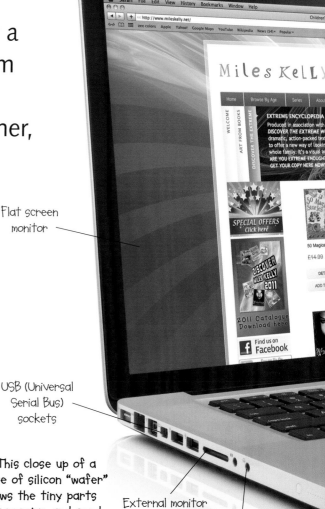

Flat screen monitor

USB (Universal Serial Bus) sockets

External monitor (screen) socket

Headphone socket

Silicon "wafer"

Plastic casing

Wire "feet" link to other part in the computer

◄ This close up of a slice of silicon "wafer" shows the tiny parts that receive and send information in a computer.

57 Some computers are controlled by talking to them! They pick up the sounds using a microphone. This is speech recognition technology.

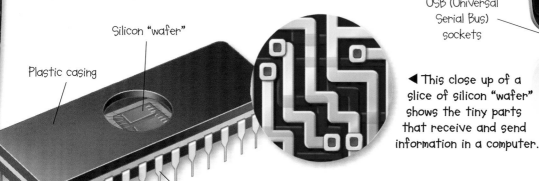

58 The "main brain" of a computer is its Central Processing Unit. It is usually a microchip—millions of electronic parts on a chip of silicon, hardly larger than a fingernail. It receives information and instructions from other microchips, carries out the work, and sends back the results.

QUIZ

You may have heard of these sets of letters. Do you know what they mean? Their full written-out versions are all here on these two pages.

1. RAM   2. ROM
3. CPU

Answers:
1. Random Access Memory
2. Read Only Memory
3. Central Processing Unit

▲ Launched in 2010, the Apple iPad began a new trend in computerized devices called "tablets."

CD or DVD drive reader

Mouse pad

Keyboard

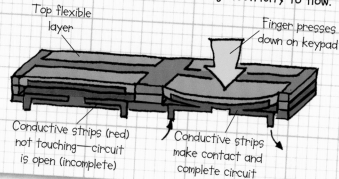

▼ The keys on a keyboard have bendy metal contacts that come together when pressed, allowing electricity to flow.

Top flexible layer

Finger presses down on keypad

Conductive strips (red) not touching—circuit is open (incomplete)

Conductive strips make contact and complete circuit

▲ As well as desktop computers, there are also laptops with a fold-up LCD (liquid crystal display) screen. Touching the mouse pad with a finger controls the cursor or insert point on the screen.

59 **Information and instructions are contained in the computer in memory microchips.** There are two kinds. Random Access Memory is like a jotting pad. It keeps changing as the computer carries out its tasks. Read Only Memory is like an instruction book. It usually contains the instructions for how the computer starts up and how all the microchips work together.

60 **A computer usually displays its progress on a monitor screen.** It feeds information to output devices such as printers, loudspeakers, and robot arms. Information can be stored on CDs, DVDs, memory sticks (chips), external HDs (hard drive disks), or uploaded to the Internet.

Web around the world

61 **The world is at your fingertips—if you are on the Internet.** The Internet is one of the most amazing results of science. It is a worldwide network of computers, linked like one huge electrical spider's web.

62 **Signals travel between computers in many ways.** These include electricity along telephone wires, flashes of laser light along fiber-optic cables, or radio waves between tall towers. Information is changed from one form to another in a split second. It can also travel between computers on different sides of the world in less than a second using satellite links.

First "private" Internet, ARPANET, for the U.S. military

Joint Academic Network (JANET) connects UK universities via their own Internet

Yahoo! Launches as a "Guide to the World Wide Web"—what we now call a browser or search engine

Animation starts to become common on websites

1969 | **1984** | **1994** | **1996**

1961 | **1972** | **1989** | **1995**

First ideas for "packet switching," the basic way the Internet parcels up and sends information in small blocks or packets

First emails, mostly on ARPANET

The birth of the Internet as we know it today, when Tim Berners-Lee and the team at CERN invent the World Wide Web to make information easier to publish and access

eBay and Amazon booksellers begin, and online trade starts to rise

63 **The World Wide Web is public information that anyone can find on the Internet, available for everyone to see.** However, sometimes you have to pay or join a club to get to certain parts of it. A website is a collection of related information, usually made up of text, videos, and pictures. There might be hundreds of web pages within each website. Email is the system for sending private messages from one person to another.

I DON'T BELIEVE IT!

The World Wide Web is the best known and most widely used part of the Internet system. It has billions of pages of information.

▼ Many cell phones can be used to access the Internet, allowing users to browse web pages, send emails, and watch videos.

Half of households in the UK have Internet connections

YouTube is launched, allowing video sharing

The first iPhones bring mobile Internet use for almost anyone

Facebook has fewer new users signing up— is the slower growth temporary, or the beginning of the end for online social networking?

2003 **2005** **2007** **2011**

1998 **2004** **2006** **2010**

Google is launched as a rival to Yahoo!

Facebook is launched, starting the trend for social networking over the Internet

Twitter is launched for posting and sharing text messages, but has a slow start

HD (High Definition) Internet video links become more practical

▲ The Web and the Internet interact with other technologies. Twitter is an online public version of text-only messages called "tweets" developed from mobile phone "texting" (SMS, Short Message Service).

What's it made of?

64 You wouldn't make a bridge out of straw, or a cup out of bubblewrap! Choosing the right substance for the job is important. All the substances in the world can be divided into several groups. For example, metals such as iron, silver, and gold are strong, hard, and shiny, and conduct heat and electricity well. They are used to make things that have to be strong and long-lasting.

65 Plastics are made mainly from the substances in petroleum (crude oil). There are so many kinds—some are hard and brittle while others are soft and flexible. They are usually long-lasting, not affected by weather or damp, and they resist heat and electricity.

KEY

① The front wing is a special shape—this produces a force that presses the car down onto the track

② The main body of the car is made from carbon fiber, a light but very strong material

③ The car's axles are made from titanium— a very strong, light metal

④ The engine is made from various alloys, or mixtures of metals, based on aluminum. It produces up to ten times the power of a family car engine

⑤ Each tire is made of thick, tough rubber to withstand high speeds

⑥ The rear wing is also carbon fiber composite

▼ A racing car has thousands of parts made from hundreds of materials. Each is suited to certain conditions such as stress, temperature, and vibrations.

66 Ceramics are materials based on clay or other substances dug from the Earth. They can be shaped and dried, like a clay bowl. Or they can be fired—baked in a hot oven called a kiln. This makes them hard and long-lasting, but brittle and prone to cracks. Ceramics resist heat and electricity very well.

Metal

Fiber

Ceramic

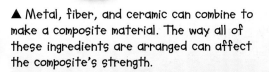

▲ Metal, fiber, and ceramic can combine to make a composite material. The way all of these ingredients are arranged can affect the composite's strength.

◄ In 2007, the Interstate 35W bridge collapsed in Minneapolis killing 13 people. It was due to cracking of small steel connecting plates that were too thin for the weight.

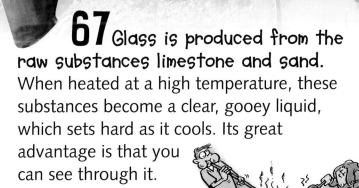

67 Glass is produced from the raw substances limestone and sand. When heated at a high temperature, these substances become a clear, gooey liquid, which sets hard as it cools. Its great advantage is that you can see through it.

68 Composites are mixtures or combinations of different materials. For example, glass strands are coated with plastic to make GRP—glass-reinforced plastic. This composite has the advantages of both materials.

MAKE YOUR OWN COMPOSITE

You will need:
flour newspaper strips
water balloon pin

You can make a composite called pâpier maché from flour, newspaper, and water. Tear newspaper into strips. Mix flour and water into a paste. Dip each strip in the paste and place it around a blown-up balloon. Cover the balloon and allow it to dry. Pop the balloon with a pin, and the composite should stay in shape.

World of chemicals

69 **The world is made of chemical substances.** Some are completely pure. Others are mixtures of substances—such as petroleum (crude oil). Petroleum provides us with thousands of different chemicals and materials, such as plastics, paints, soaps, and fuels. It is one of the most useful, and valuable, substances in the world.

The fumes cool as they rise up the tower, causing them to condense

Fuel gases for burning

Gasoline and vehicle fuels

Kerosene and medium fuels (jet fuel)

Heavy oils for lubrication

Furnace

Waxes, tars, bitumens, asphalts

▼ The biggest offshore oil platforms are more than 490 feet tall above the ocean surface. They drill boreholes into the seabed and pump up the crude oil, or petroleum.

Crude oil is super-heated and some parts turn into fumes

▲ The huge tower (fractionating column) of an oil refinery may be 330 feet high.

70 **In an oil refinery, crude oil is heated in a huge tower.** Some of its different substances turn into fumes and rise up the tower. The fumes condense (turn back into liquids) at different heights inside, due to the different temperatures at each level. Thick, gooey tars, asphalts, and bitumens —used to make road surfaces— remain at the bottom.

71 One group of chemicals is called acids.

They vary in strength from very weak citric acid, which gives the sharp taste to fruits such as lemons, to extremely strong and dangerous sulfuric acid in a car battery. Powerful acids burn and corrode, or eat away, substances. Some even corrode glass or steel.

72 Another group of chemicals is bases.

They vary in strength from weak alkaloids, which give the bitter taste to coffee beans, to strong and dangerous bases in drain cleaners and industrial polishes. Bases feel soapy or slimy and, like acids, they can burn or corrode.

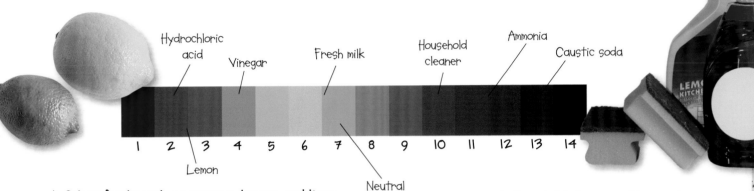

Hydrochloric acid — Vinegar — Fresh milk — Household cleaner — Ammonia — Caustic soda

1 2 3 4 5 6 7 8 9 10 11 12 13 14

Lemon

Neutral

▲ Citrus fruits such as oranges, lemons, and limes have a tart taste because they contain a mild acid, called citric acid. It has a pH of 3.

▲ Household cleaners often contain alkalis to help them break down grease and fat. Some cleaners have a pH of 10.

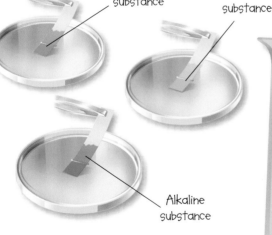

Acidic substance

Neutral substance

Alkaline substance

▶ Indicator paper changes color when it touches different substances. Acids turn it red, alkalis make it bluish-purple. The deeper the color, the stronger the acid or base.

73 Acids and bases are "opposite" types of chemicals.

When they meet, they undergo changes called a chemical reaction. The result is usually a third type of chemical, called a salt. The common salt we use for cooking is one example. Its chemical name is sodium chloride.

FROTHY FUN

You will need:
vinegar   washing soda

Create a chemical reaction by adding a few drops of vinegar to a spoonful of washing soda in a saucer. The vinegar is an acid, the soda is a base. The two react by frothing and giving off bubbles of carbon dioxide gas. What is left is a salt (but not to be eaten).

Pure Science

74 The world seems to be made of millions of different substances—such as soil, wood, concrete, plastics, and air. These are combinations of simpler substances. If you could take them apart, you would see that they are made of pure substances called elements.

1											
1 H Hydrogen											

	2										
3 Li Lithium	4 Be Beryllium										
11 Na Sodium	12 Mg Magnesium										

		3	4	5	6	7	8	9	10	11	12
19 K Potassium	20 Ca Calcium	21 Sc Scandium	22 Ti Titanium	23 V Vanadium	24 Cr Chromium	25 Mn Manganese	26 Fe Iron	27 Co Colbalt	28 Ni Nickel	29 Cu Copper	30 Zn Zinc
37 Rb Rubidium	38 Sr Strontium	39 Y Yttrium	40 Zr Zirconium	41 Nb Niobium	42 Mo Molybdenum	43 Tc Technetium	44 Ru Ruthenium	45 Rh Rhodium	46 Pd Palladium	47 Ag Silver	48 Cd Cadmium
55 Cs Caesium	56 Ba Barium	Elements 57–71	72 Hf Hafnium	73 Ta Tantalum	74 W Tungsten	75 Re Rhenium	76 Os Osmium	77 Ir Iridium	78 Pt Platinum	79 Au Gold	80 Hg Mercury
87 Fr Francium	88 Ra Radium	Elements 89–103	104 Rf Rutherfordium	105 Db Dubnium	106 Sg Seaborgium	107 Bh Bohrium	108 HS Hassium	109 Mt Meitnerium	110 Ds Darmstadtium	111 Rg Roentgenium	112 Cn Copernicum

Atomic number
Chemical symbol

20
Ca
Calcium

Name

57 La Lanthanum	58 Ce Cerium	59 Pr Praseodymium	60 Nd Neodymium	61 Pm Promethium	62 Sm Samarium	63 Eu Europium	64 Gd Gadolinium	65 Tb Terbium
89 Ac Actinium	90 Th Thorium	91 Pa Protactinium	92 U Uranium	93 Np Neptunium	94 Pu Plutonium	95 Am Americium	96 Cm Curium	97 Bk Berkelium

► Stars are made mainly of burning hydrogen, which is why they are so hot and bright.

▲ The Periodic Table is a chart of all the elements. In each row the atoms get heavier from left to right. Each column (up–down) contains elements with similar chemical features. Every element has a chemical symbol, name, and atomic number, which is the number of particles called protons in its central part, or nucleus.

75 Hydrogen is the simplest element and it is the first in the Periodic Table. This means it has the smallest atoms. It is a very light gas, which floats upward in air. Hydrogen was used to fill giant airships. But there was a problem—hydrogen catches fire easily and explodes.

76 About 90 elements are found naturally on and in the Earth. In an element, all of its particles, called atoms, are exactly the same as each other. Just as important, they are all different from the atoms of any other element.

Note: Elements 113–118 are synthetic elements that have only been created briefly, so their properties cannot be known for certain.

18	
2 **He** Helium	

13	14	15	16	17	
5 **B** Boron	6 **C** Carbon	7 **N** Nitrogen	8 **O** Oxygen	9 **F** Fluorine	10 **Ne** Neon
13 **Al** Aluminum	14 **Si** Silicon	15 **P** Phosphorus	16 **S** Sulfur	17 **Cl** Chlorine	18 **Ar** Argon
31 **Ga** Gallium	32 **Ge** Germanium	33 **As** Arsenic	34 **Se** Selenium	35 **Br** Bromine	36 **Kr** Krypton
49 **In** Indium	50 **Sn** Tin	51 **Sb** Antimony	52 **Te** Tellurium	53 **I** Iodine	54 **Xe** Xenon
81 **Ti** Thallium	82 **Pb** Lead	83 **Bi** Bismuth	84 **Po** Polonium	85 **At** Astatine	86 **Rn** Radon
113 **Uut** Ununtrium	114 **Uuq** Ununquadum	115 **Uup** Ununpentium	116 **Uuh** Ununhexium	117 **Uus** Ununseptium	118 **Uuo** Ununoctium

66 **Dy** Dysprosium	67 **Ho** Holmium	68 **Er** Erbium	69 **Tm** Thulium	70 **Yb** Ytterbium	71 **Lu** Lutetium
98 **Cf** Californium	99 **Es** Einsteinium	100 **Fm** Fermium	101 **Md** Mendelevium	102 **No** Nobelium	103 **Lr** Lawrencium

78 Uranium is a heavy and dangerous element. It gives off harmful rays and tiny particles. This process is called radioactivity and it can cause sickness, burns, and diseases such as cancer. Radioactivity is a form of energy and, under careful control, radioactive elements are used as fuel in nuclear power plants.

▶ Aluminum is a strong but light metal that is ideal for forming the body of vehicles such as planes.

77 Carbon is a very important element in living things—including our own bodies. It joins easily with atoms of other elements to make large groups of atoms called molecules. When it is pure, carbon can be two different forms. These are soft, powdery soot, and hard, glittering diamond. The form depends on how the carbon atoms join to each other.

79 Aluminum is an element that is a metal, and it is one of the most useful in modern life. It is light and strong, it does not rust, and it is resistant to corrosion. Saucepans, drinks cans, cooking foil, and jet planes are made mainly of aluminum.

Bond (link)   Atom

◀ Diamond is a form of the element carbon where the atoms are linked, or bonded, in a very strong boxlike pattern.

Small Science

80 Many pages in this book mention atoms. They are the smallest bits of a substance. They are so tiny, even a billion atoms would be too small to see. But scientists have carried out experiments to find out what's inside an atom. The answer is—even smaller bits. These are subatomic particles, and there are three main kinds.

81 At the center of each atom a blob called the nucleus. It conta two kinds of subatomic particles. The are protons and neutrons. Protons ar positive, or plus. The neutron is neith positive nor negative. Around the cer of each atom are subatomic particles called electrons. They whizz round th nucleus. In the same way that a prote the nucleus is positive or plus, an elec is negative or minus. The number of protons and electrons is usually the sa

82 Atoms of the various elements have different numbers of protons and neutrons. An atom of hydrogen has just one proton. An atom of helium, the gas put in party balloons to make them float, has two protons and two neutrons. An atom of the heavy metal called lead has 82 protons and 124 neutrons.

I DON'T BELIEVE IT!

One hundred years ago, people thought the electrons were spread out in an atom, like the raisins in a raisin pudding.

Hydrogen   Helium   Oxygen

▶ The bits inside an atom give each substance its features, from exploding hydrogen to life-giving oxygen.

Electron

Proton

Neutron

83 **It is hard to imagine the size of an atom.** A grain of sand, smaller than this o, contains at least 100 billion billion atoms. If you could make the atoms bigger, so that each one becomes as big as a pin head, the grain of sand would be 1.25 miles high!

Electron

Nucleus made from protons and neutrons

Movement of electrons

▲ The protons and neutrons in the nucleus of an atom are held together by a powerful force.

84 **"Nano" means one-billionth (1/1,000,000,000th), and nanotechnology is science at the smallest level—how atoms join to make molecules.** It is fairly new, but it has already produced many useful products, from stronger materials in jet planes and racing cars, to self-cleaning glass and bouncier tennis balls!

◀ This idea for a nano gear-bearing allows the central axle to spin inside the outer collar. It could be used in micromachines.

▼ Buckyballs are ball-shaped structures made of carbon atoms, used in some types of solar panels and medical research.

▶ Like buckyballs, nanotubes are formed mainly of carbon atoms. They can be combined with plastics in hitech equipment such as racing bicycles.

Scientists at work

85 There are thousands of different jobs and careers in science. Scientists work in laboratories, factories, offices, mines, steelworks, nature parks, and almost everywhere else. They find new knowledge and make discoveries using a process called the scientific method.

86 First comes an idea, called a theory or hypothesis. This asks or predicts what will happen in a certain situation. Scientists continually come up with new ideas and theories to test. One very simple theory is—if I throw a ball up in the air, will it come back down?

▲ Some scientific work involves handling microbes or dangerous chemicals. This means safety precautions such as wearing gloves and a face mask may be necessary.

▶ In scientific terms, throwing a ball into the air is an experiment. What will be the result?

QUIZ
Put these activities in the correct order, so that a scientist can carry out the scientific method.
1. Results   2. Experiment
3. Conclusions   4. Theory
5. Measurements

Answer: 4, 2, 5, 1, 3

87 The scientist carries out an experiment or test, to check what happens. The experiment is carefully designed and controlled, so that it will reveal useful results. Any changes are carried out one at a time, so that the effect of each change can be studied. The experiment for our simple theory is—throw the ball up in the air.

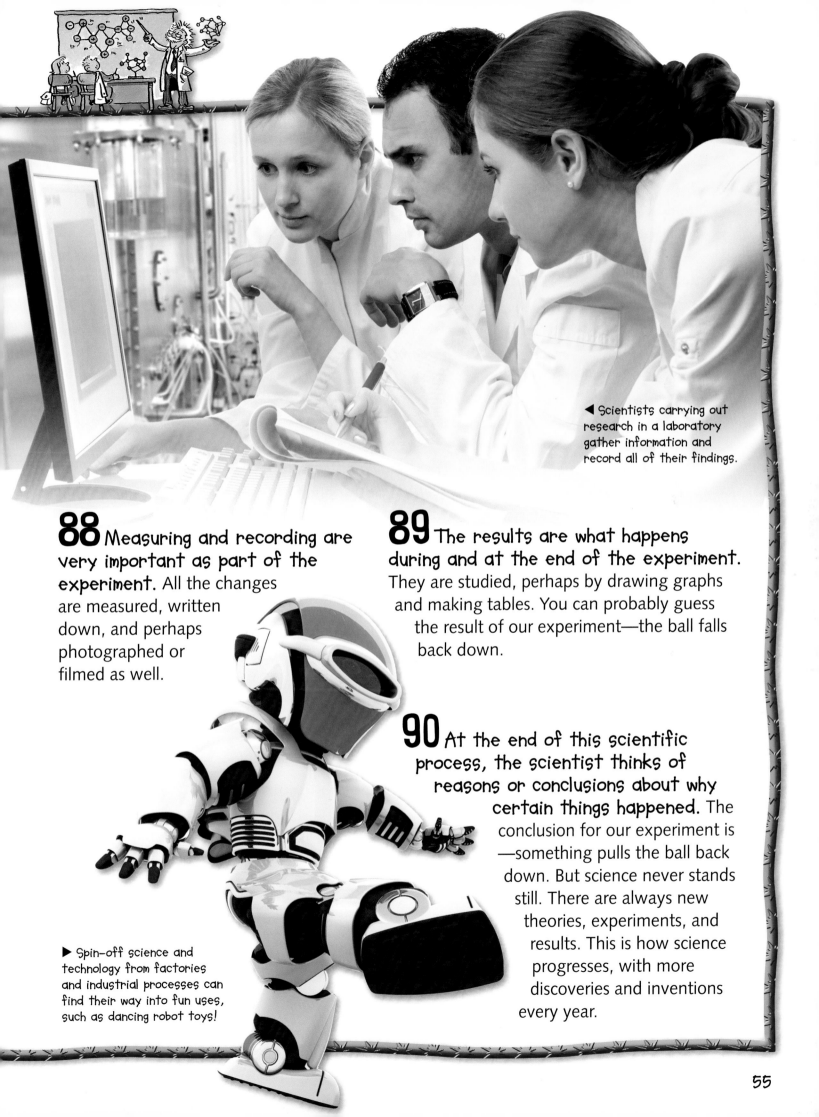

◀ Scientists carrying out research in a laboratory gather information and record all of their findings.

88 Measuring and recording are very important as part of the experiment. All the changes are measured, written down, and perhaps photographed or filmed as well.

89 The results are what happens during and at the end of the experiment. They are studied, perhaps by drawing graphs and making tables. You can probably guess the result of our experiment—the ball falls back down.

90 At the end of this scientific process, the scientist thinks of reasons or conclusions about why certain things happened. The conclusion for our experiment is —something pulls the ball back down. But science never stands still. There are always new theories, experiments, and results. This is how science progresses, with more discoveries and inventions every year.

▶ Spin-off science and technology from factories and industrial processes can find their way into fun uses, such as dancing robot toys!

Science in nature

91 **Science and its effects are found all over the natural world.** Scientists study animals, plants, rocks, and soil. They want to understand nature, and find out how science and its technology affect wildlife.

92 **One of the most complicated types of science is ecology.** Ecologists try to understand how the natural world links together. They study how animals and plants live, what animals eat, and why plants grow better in some soils than others. They count the numbers of animals and plants and may trap animals briefly to study them, or follow the growth of trees in a wood. When the balance of nature is damaged, ecologists can help to find out why.

▼ One of the most important jobs in science is to study damage and pollution in the natural world. Almost everything we do affects wild places and animals and plants. For example, the power plant here may make the river water warmer. This could encourage animals and plants accidentally introduced from tropical areas, which change the balance of nature.

▼ The science of ecology involves long periods of studying nature in all kinds of habitats, from rivers to the seabed. For example, observing birds like herons, and fish such as trout, shows which foods they eat. This helps us to understand how changes to the habitat may affect them.

KEY
① Water beetle
② Rainbow trout
③ Water scorpion
④ Banded demoiselle damselfly
⑤ Heron
⑥ Otter
⑦ Warbler
⑧ Power plant
⑨ Reedmace

◄ Oil spills and leaks cause vast damage to a region's ecology. Scientists advise on the best ways to clear up the pollution.

93 Ecologists use many forms of high-tech science in their studies. They may fit an animal with a radio-collar so that its movements can be tracked. Special cameras see in the dark and show how night hunters catch their prey. Radar used to detect planes can also follow flocks of birds. The sonar (echo-sounding) equipment of boats can track shoals of fish or whales.

◄ Tracking tigers is vital to know the threats faced by these endangered big cats, and help to save them.

Body science

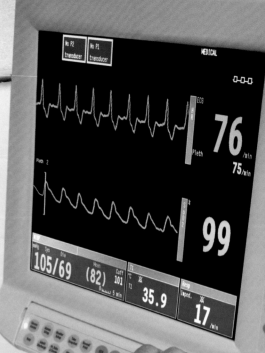

94 One of the biggest areas of science is medicine. Medical scientists work to produce better drugs, more spare parts for the body, and more machines for use by doctors. They also carry out scientific research to find out how people can stay healthy and prevent disease.

▲ Medical technology uses the latest equipment to diagnose illness, treat life-threatening conditions, and cure diseases. This monitoring unit displays heart rate, pulse rate, amounts of oxygen in the blood, breathing speed, blood pressure, and other vital signs.

95 As parts of the body work, such as the muscles and nerves, they produce tiny pulses of electricity. Pads on the skin pick up these pulses, which are displayed as a wavy line on a screen or paper strip. The ECG (electro-cardiograph) machine shows the heart beating. The EEG (electro-encephalograph) shows nerve signals flashing around the brain.

Laser beam hits retina inside eye

► A laser beam shines safely through the front of the eye to mend inner problems such as a detached retina.

96 Laser beams are ideal for delicate operations, or surgery, on body parts such as the eye. The beam makes very small, precise cuts. It can be shone into the eye and made most focused, or strongest, inside. So it can make a cut deep within the eye, without any harm to the outer parts.

► An endoscope is inserted into the body to give a doctor a picture on screen. The treatment can be given immediately.

MAKE A PULSE MACHINE

You will need:

modeling clay   drinking straw

Find your pulse by feeling your wrist, just below the base of your thumb, with a finger of the other hand. Place some modeling clay on this area, and stick a drinking straw into it. Watch the straw twitch with each heartbeat. Now you can see and feel your pulse. Check your pulse rate by counting the number of heartbeats in one minute.

97 The endoscope is like a flexible telescope made of fiber-strands. This is pushed into a body opening such as the mouth, or through a small cut, to see inside. The surgeon looks into the other end of the endoscope, or at a picture on a screen.

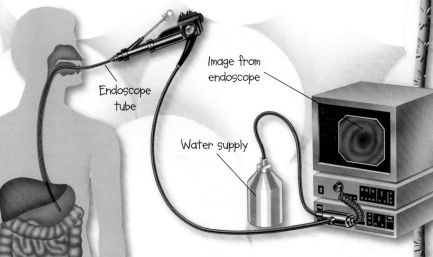

Image from endoscope

Endoscope tube

Water supply

Science in the Future

98 **Many modern machines and processes can cause damage to our environment and our health.** The damage includes acid rain, destruction of the ozone layer, and the greenhouse effect, leading to climate change and global warming. Science can help to find solutions. New filters and chemicals called catalysts can reduce dangerous fumes from vehicle exhausts and power plants, and in the chemicals in factory waste pipes.

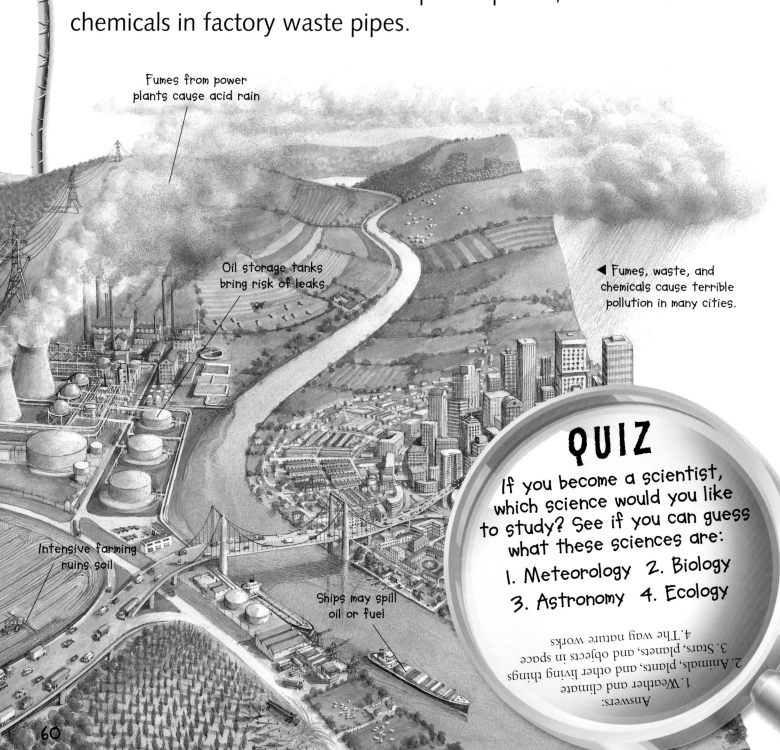

Fumes from power plants cause acid rain

Oil storage tanks bring risk of leaks

◄ Fumes, waste, and chemicals cause terrible pollution in many cities.

Intensive farming ruins soil

Ships may spill oil or fuel

QUIZ

If you become a scientist, which science would you like to study? See if you can guess what these sciences are:

1. Meteorology 2. Biology

3. Astronomy 4. Ecology

Answers:
1. Weather and climate
2. Animals, plants, and other living things
3. Stars, planets, and objects in space
4. The way nature works

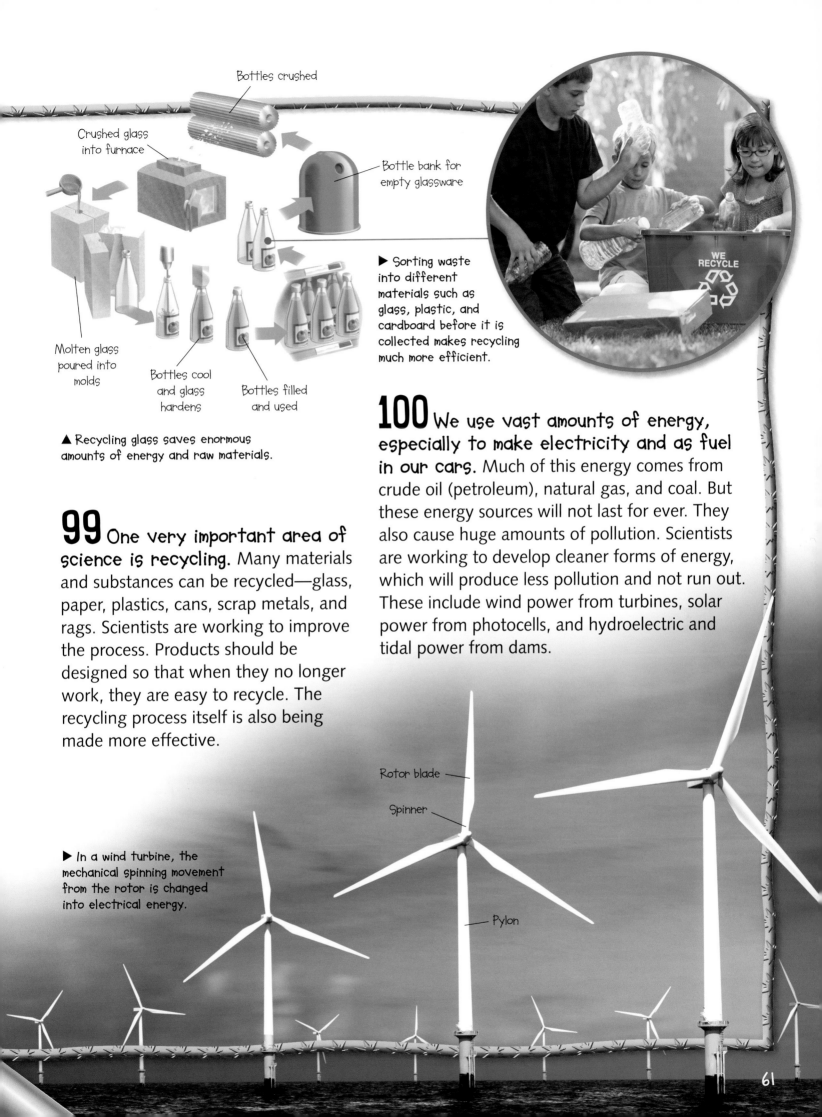

Bottles crushed

Crushed glass into furnace

Bottle bank for empty glassware

Molten glass poured into molds

Bottles cool and glass hardens

Bottles filled and used

► Sorting waste into different materials such as glass, plastic, and cardboard before it is collected makes recycling much more efficient.

▲ Recycling glass saves enormous amounts of energy and raw materials.

100 We use vast amounts of energy, especially to make electricity and as fuel in our cars. Much of this energy comes from crude oil (petroleum), natural gas, and coal. But these energy sources will not last for ever. They also cause huge amounts of pollution. Scientists are working to develop cleaner forms of energy, which will produce less pollution and not run out. These include wind power from turbines, solar power from photocells, and hydroelectric and tidal power from dams.

99 One very important area of science is recycling. Many materials and substances can be recycled—glass, paper, plastics, cans, scrap metals, and rags. Scientists are working to improve the process. Products should be designed so that when they no longer work, they are easy to recycle. The recycling process itself is also being made more effective.

Rotor blade

Spinner

Pylon

► In a wind turbine, the mechanical spinning movement from the rotor is changed into electrical energy.

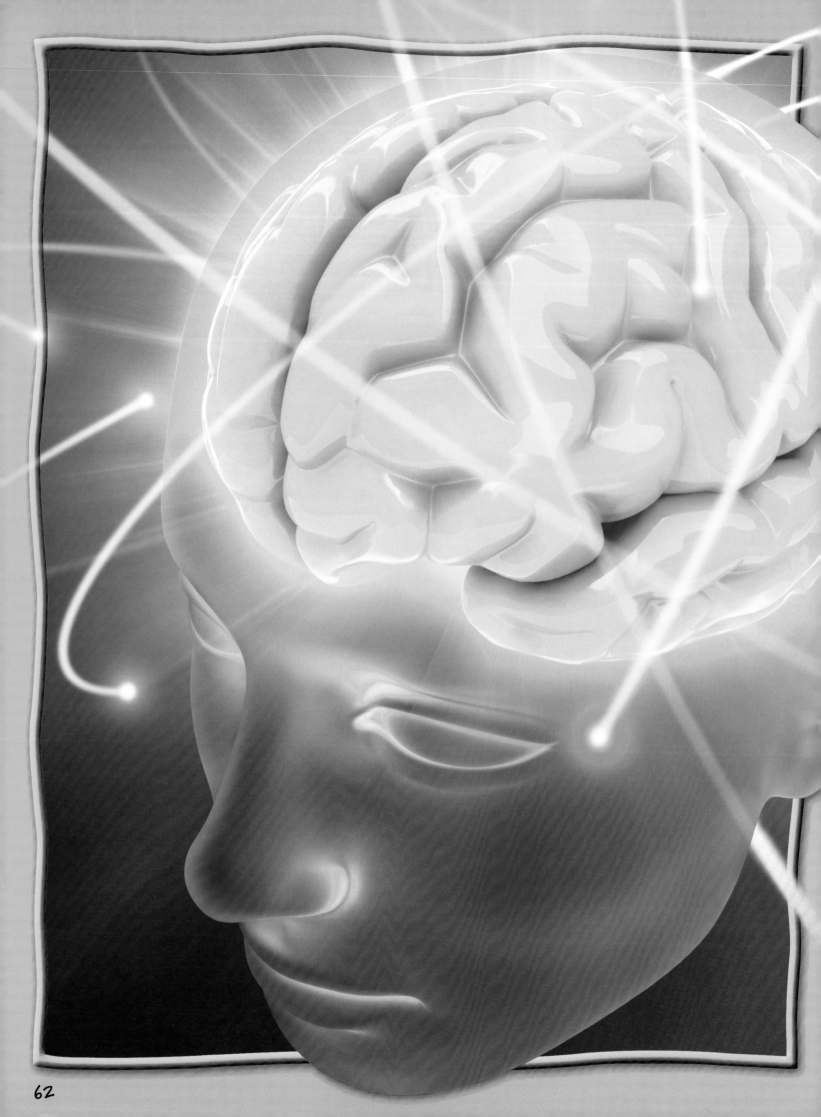

GREAT SCIENTISTS

- Mathematics
- Anatomy
- Microscopic life
- The Laws of Motion
- Natural history
- Chemical elements
- Diseases and cures
- Radiation
- Space and time
- DNA and genetics

Who invented algebra?

What is gravity?

Why do some objects float in water?

Who discovered DNA?

What is at the center of a black hole?

What is a scientist?

101 A scientist is someone who studies the world and how it works. Scientists ask questions then try to answer them with experiments, observations, and mathematical reasoning. They also come up with ideas and theories and try to test them in the same way. This is how we find out about the world—from what atoms are to how the Universe works.

▶ A volcanologist studies volcanoes to find out how and why they erupt. Studying an active volcano can be very dangerous work!

102 Scientific ideas are constantly changing. What scientists think is true in one age may be questioned in the next. Just a century ago, astronomers thought the Universe was no bigger than our Milky Way Galaxy. We now know the Universe is much vaster, with more than 500 billion galaxies.

103 In the past, scientists often studied a wide range of subjects. In fact, the word "scientist" was not widely used until 1830. Most of the great scientists in this book from before that time were called "natural philosophers."

▶ There are many different kinds of scientist. They specialize in different fields, such as particle physicists who study atoms and microbiologists who study microscopic life.

Life Sciences

Botany............... Botanists study plants in nature and the laboratory

Zoology............... Zoologists study animals in nature and the laboratory

Genetics............... Genetics is the science of how living things pass on features to offspring

Medicine............... Medicine is the science of understanding and healing the human body

Physical Sciences

Physics............... Physicists study matter and forces and how they move through space and time

Chemistry............... Chemists study substances and how they react with each other

Astronomy............ Astronomers study space—from moons and planets to stars and galaxies

Earth Sciences

Geology............... Geologists study rocks and minerals and how the Earth works

Oceanography........ Oceanographers study the oceans and ocean currents and tides

Paleontology...... Paleontologists study prehistoric life and fossils

Meteorology......... Meteorologists study the weather, climate, and changes in the atmosphere

Mathematical marvels

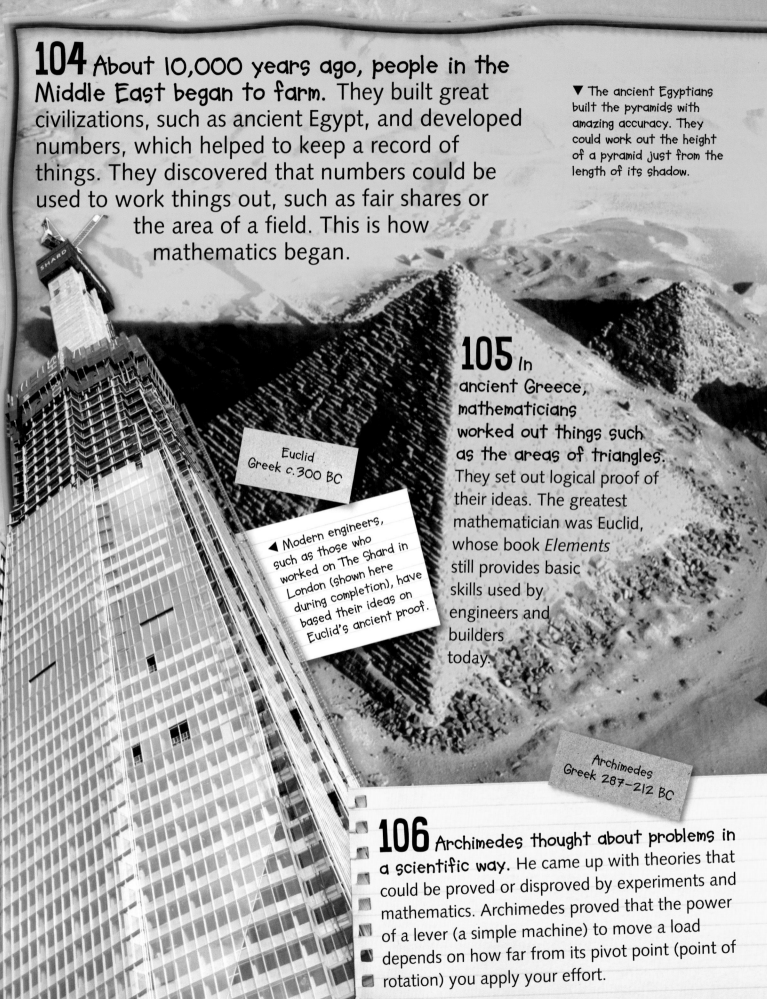

104 About 10,000 years ago, people in the Middle East began to farm. They built great civilizations, such as ancient Egypt, and developed numbers, which helped to keep a record of things. They discovered that numbers could be used to work things out, such as fair shares or the area of a field. This is how mathematics began.

▼ The ancient Egyptians built the pyramids with amazing accuracy. They could work out the height of a pyramid just from the length of its shadow.

Euclid
Greek c.300 BC

◀ Modern engineers, such as those who worked on The Shard in London (shown here during completion), have based their ideas on Euclid's ancient proof.

105 In ancient Greece, mathematicians worked out things such as the areas of triangles. They set out logical proof of their ideas. The greatest mathematician was Euclid, whose book *Elements* still provides basic skills used by engineers and builders today.

Archimedes
Greek 287–212 BC

106 Archimedes thought about problems in a scientific way. He came up with theories that could be proved or disproved by experiments and mathematics. Archimedes proved that the power of a lever (a simple machine) to move a load depends on how far from its pivot point (point of rotation) you apply your effort.

107 A story tells how the king of Syracuse suspected impure gold had been used to make his crown. Archimedes was asked to investigate. But how could he tell without melting the crown? He hit on the solution while in his bath, and was so excited he ran naked through the streets shouting, "Eureka!" (which means, "I've got it!").

108 Archimedes explained how things float. When an object sinks down in water, the water pushes it back up with a force equal to the weight of water displaced (pushed away). The object has a natural upthrust or "buoyancy." He showed that an object sinks until its weight is equal to the weight of water displaced, then it floats.

The weight of the ship is equal to the water is displaces

◀▼ Heavy ships float because they are supported by the weight of water they push out of the way.

When the ships sinks down, the water it displaces thrusts it back up with equal force

109 Archimedes launched a giant ship on his own using levers and pulleys. A pulley turns around like a wheel and has a groove for a cable or rope. Lots of pulleys allow us to lift heavy weights easily.

▼ Archimedes identified three types (classes) of lever, according to where you apply effort in relation to the pivot.

① A **class 1** lever has the load and effort on opposite sides of the pivot or fulcrum, like a seesaw

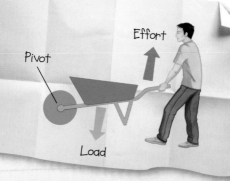

② A **class 2** lever has the load and effort on the same side of the pivot, as in a wheelbarrow

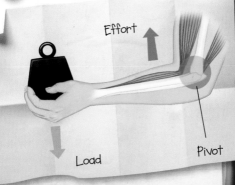

③ A **class 3** lever has the effort between the load and the pivot, like a human elbow

Baghdad brilliance

110 When Muhammad began to teach the religion of Islam in the 600s, he charged followers to search for knowledge. Baghdad and other Islamic cities became centers of learning. Ibn Sina studied everything from philosophy to physics. He not only identified the main forms of energy and the idea of force, he wrote a book, *The Canon of Medicine*, which became the doctors' bible for 600 years.

Ibn Sina Avicenna
Persian c.980–1037

QUIZ

1. What did the astrolabe measure?
2. What is distillation used for today?
3. What does algebra use to replace unknown numbers in calculations?

Answers:
1. Angles 2. For refining oil and alcohol 3. Symbols or letters

Muhammad al-Fazari
Arabic or Persian
Died 796 or 806

111 Muslims needed to know the true direction of Muhammad's birthplace. So scientists developed astronomical instruments to map the stars. The astrolabe was invented by astronomer Muhammad al-Fazari. It measured angles by sight, and skilled users could work out directions from the position of stars alone.

▶ Muslim astronomers mapped the stars and their movements very accurately.

Jabir ibn Hayyan (Geber)
Persian 721–815

112 Jabir ibn Hayyan (Geber) stirred and heated chemicals together in measured quantities to see how they interacted. Jabir also found he could purify liquids by boiling them and collecting the droplets of steam. This is called distillation and is used today for refining oil and alcoholic spirits.

113 Roman numerals were awkward to use for large numbers. So in the 8th century, after studying Indian Hindu numbers, al-Khwarizmi introduced the Arabic numerals we now use around the world. Roman numerals need seven figures to give a number as small as 38 (XXXVIII). With seven figures, Arabic numerals can give nearly ten million!

al-Khwarizmi
Arabic or Persian
c.780–850

▲ As well distillation, Geber discovered acids that were strong enough to dissolve metals.

▶ Roman numerals were built up by adding lines. Arabic numerals use symbols for one to 10, which is simpler.

114 Al-Khwarizmi created the math known as algebra. Algebra uses symbols or letters to replace unknown numbers in calculations. Mathematicians can work out the unknown numbers by putting the symbols in standard "recipes" called equations. Algebra is part of nearly all scientific calculations.

115 When al-Khwarizmi's name was written in Latin it was spelt "Algoritmi." This name has given us the word "algorithms." Algorithms are logical step-by-step mathematical sequences, and it was al-Khwarizmi who first developed the idea. Algorithms are now the basis of all computer programs.

Ancient Roman	Modern Hindu-Arabic
I	1
II	2
III	3
IV	4
V	5
VI	6
VII	7
VIII	8
IX	9
X	10

Thinking again

Leonardo da Vinci
Italian 1452–1519

116 In the 1400s, Islamic science reached Europe. The ideas of ancient Greece and Rome were rediscovered, and people like Leonardo da Vinci were excited. They realized that by studying the world, they might learn how it works.

117 You might think helicopters and cars are modern ideas—but Leonardo drew designs for them 500 years ago. His sketches for a hang glider type flying machine are so detailed that experts recently built one for real—and found that it just about worked.

▼ A scientific genius, Leonardo made brilliant notes and drawings on everything from geology to flying machines.

▼ Leonardo was way ahead of his time, making models to study how rivers flowed.

118 Leonardo wrote to the Duke of Milan offering his services as an engineer. He had an idea for an armored car or tank. Tanks were only first used in World War I (1914–1918). Yet there is a picture of one in Leonardo's notebooks from the 1480s.

119 To draw human figures accurately, artists studied the human body. To show the body's inner layers, Leonardo developed a way of drawing cross-sections and 3D versions of muscles.

▶ Leonardo drew highly accurate diagrams of the human muscular system.

120 Early physicians learned about the body (often wrongly) from ancient books—especially those of Galen (129–199), a Roman doctor. Andreas Vesalius realized the only way to find out was to cut up real corpses (dead bodies). As he did this, he got artist Jan van Calcar to draw what he found. They made the first accurate book of human anatomy (the way the body is put together) in 1543.

▶ As Vesalius carefully cut up bodies, Jan van Calcar made drawings to build up an accurate guide to human anatomy.

Andreas Vesalius
Dutch 1514–1564

121 Many scientists studied in Padua in Italy in the 1500s, including English physician William Harvey. When Harvey returned to England, he studied how blood flowed through the body. He found that it doesn't flow to and fro like tides as Galen said. Instead it is pumped by the heart nonstop around the body through tubes called arteries and veins.

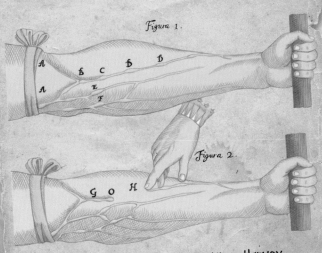

▲ Careful experiments showed William Harvey that blood flowed around the body again and again.

William Harvey
English 1578–1657

Microbes and measures

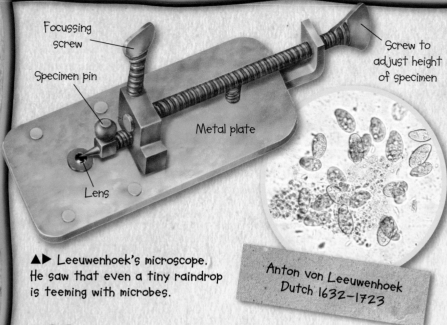

Focussing screw

Screw to adjust height of specimen

Specimen pin

Metal plate

Lens

▲▶ Leeuwenhoek's microscope. He saw that even a tiny raindrop is teeming with microbes.

Anton von Leeuwenhoek Dutch 1632–1723

123 Robert Hooke was another microscope pioneer and saw that living things are made from tiny "parcels." He called them cells, because to him they looked like tiny rows of rooms or cells that monks lived in. Hooke also invented the hearing aid and the anemometer (for measuring wind speed).

▼ Through his microscope, Hooke saw that living things are made up from tiny packages, which he named "cells."

122 No one knew there was life too small to see—until Anton von Leeuwenhoek looked through his microscope in the 1670s. Leeuwenhoek made his own microscope, with lenses that could magnify up to 270 times.

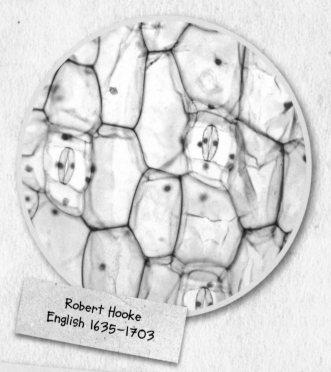

Christiaan Huygens Dutch 1629–1695

Robert Hooke English 1635–1703

124 Before the 1600s, people could only tell the time to within ten minutes. But in 1658 Christiaan Huygens perfected a clock that kept time with a swinging weight, or pendulum. It was the world's first accurate clock, so precise it could keep time to within a minute over a week.

◀ Huygens also worked out the math of pendulums that helps us understand how planets move.

125 Following the pioneering work of Italian astronomer and mathematician Galileo Galilei, Huygens made his own telescope. Through it, he saw that the planet Saturn had a moon, too, later called Titan. He also realized that what had looked to Galileo like ears on Saturn were part of a flat ring running around it.

▼ We now know that Saturn's rings are made up of tiny particles of water, ice, and dust.

René Descartes
French 1596–1650

126 French philosopher René Descartes came up with the idea of graphs. Graphs are a way of looking at things that are changing together. When something accelerates, both speed and time change. On a graph, you draw the changes as a simple line called a curve.

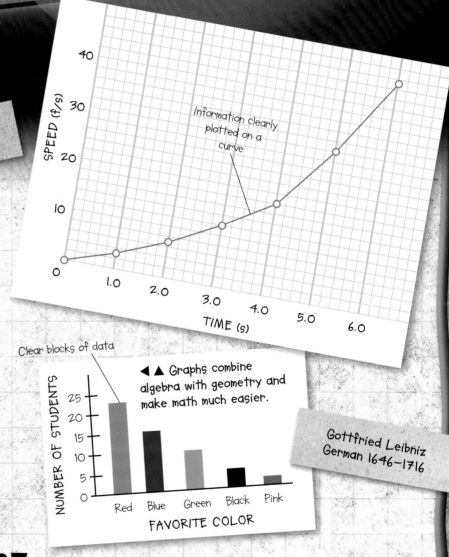

Information clearly plotted on a curve

SPEED (f/s)

TIME (s)

Clear blocks of data

◀▲ Graphs combine algebra with geometry and make math much easier.

NUMBER OF STUDENTS

Red Blue Green Black Pink
FAVORITE COLOR

Gottfried Leibniz
German 1646–1716

I DON'T BELIEVE IT!

There are thought to be millions of types of bacteria, but no one knew they existed until Leeuwenhoek saw them through his microscope.

127 Most things in nature move at varying speeds. To study them, Isaac Newton and Gottfried Leibnitz devised a kind of math called calculus. Calculus helps you find out how fast something is moving at any one instant—a time so short that it seems to move no distance at all.

Motion man

Sir Isaac Newton
English 1643–1727

128 Isaac Newton discovered that every movement in the Universe obeys three rules, known as the Laws of Motion. They sum up what it takes to get something moving or to stop (1st Law), to make something move faster or slower, or change direction (2nd Law), and how the movement of one thing affects another (3rd Law).

LAW 1: An object won't move unless something forces it to. It will go on moving at the same speed and in the same direction unless forced to change. This is called inertia.

▶▲ Scientists can use these laws to work out everything—from the way a diver pushes off from a springboard to the rotation of a galaxy.

LAW 2: The greater the mass of an object, the more force is needed to make it speed up, slow down, or change direction.

129 Newton also discovered gravity—the force of attraction between all matter. He knew that nothing strays from its course without being forced to. So when something starts to fall, it must be forced to. That force is called gravity.

MARBLE MOTION

Demonstrate Newton's Third Law of Motion with marbles or the balls on a pool table. Roll one ball or marble into another—and watch how when they collide, one ball moves one way and the other ball moves the other way.

LAW 3: For every action, there is an equal opposite reaction—in other words, when something pushes off in one direction, the thing it's pushing from is pushed back with equal force in the opposite direction.

130 Sunlight is colorless or white—so where do all the colors come from? Newton realized that sunlight contains all the colors, mixed up. He proved it using a prism, a triangular block of glass.

▲ When sunlight shines through a prism, its rays are bent, each color to a different degree. When the light emerges from the far side of the prism, it splits into a spectrum—all the colors of the rainbow.

131 Newton was the first modern scientist, but he wrote works of alchemy—a mixture of science, magic, and astrology. Alchemists wanted to find the "philosopher's stone" (a substance that could turn metal to gold) and the "elixir of life" (a liquid that keeps you young forever). They wrote in code to keep their work secret, so Newton's notebooks are impossible to understand.

Nature's secrets

132 Today, all living things are organized into clear groups—thanks to biologist Carolus Linnaeus. Before this, animals and plants were listed at best alphabetically. Since creatures have different names in different places, this led to chaos.

PARTS OF A FLOWERING PLANT

Anther (male part)

Stigma (female part)

▲ Linnaeus realized that flowering plants can be classified by the shape of their male and female parts.

Carolus Linnaeus
Swedish 1707–1778

▼ A volcanic eruption is a short, sharp force of nature. James Hutton concluded that the landscape is shaped mostly by more gradual forces such as running rivers.

James Hutton
Scottish 1726–1797

133 People once thought the Earth was just a few thousand years old and the entire landscape was shaped by a few short, huge disasters. But in his book *Theory of the Earth*, published in 1788, James Hutton showed how the Earth has been shaped gradually over millions of years by milder forces, such as running rivers.

HOMEMADE FOSSIL

Make your own fossil by pressing a snail shell or an old bone into tightly compressed fine sand. Take out the shell or bone, then pour runny plaster or wall filler into the mold left behind. Leave the plaster to set, then dig up your fossil!

Charles Lyell
English 1797–1875

134 Charles Lyell showed how rocks tell the story of Earth's past. Rock layers form one on top of the other over time and can be read by a geologist like pages in a book. They contain fossils—the remains of once living things turned to stone—showing what creatures were alive when each layer formed.

▲ The first dinosaur fossils were discovered in rock in Lyell's lifetime.

Mary Anning
English 1799–1847

135 Mary Anning hunted for fossils on the shore at Lyme Regis in England, one of the world's richest fossil sites. At the age of 12, she found the skeleton of an ichthyosaur, a dolphin-shaped creature from the time of the dinosaurs—though no one knew about dinosaurs at the time. She went on to find the first fossils of a giant swimming reptile, *Plesiosaurus*, and the first flying reptiles, or pterosaurs.

▲ Mary Anning discovered fossils of a giant swimming reptile, a plesiosaur, which may have looked like this.

William Buckland
English 1784–1856

136 In 1824, William Buckland wrote the first scientific description of a dinosaur fossil, *Megalosaurus*. This meat-eater was 30 feet long and weighed as much as an elephant. People were astonished such creatures had ever lived, but soon more fossils were found.

▶ Buckland named *Megalosaurus* in 1824. It was not until 1842 that the term "dinosaur" was first used.

It's chemistry

Gas molecules

Plunger squeezes gas

Large volume of gas with low pressure

Medium volume of gas with medium pressure

Small volume of gas with high pressure

▲ When a gas is squeezed, the pressure increases in proportion. The more the gas is squeezed, the higher the pressure.

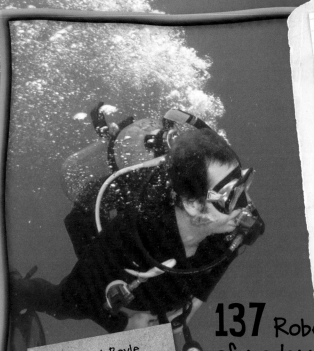

Robert Boyle
Irish 1627–1691

▲ Boyle's Law shows that the pressure of gases in a diver's suit and body rises as he descends, due to the weight of the water.

137 Robert Boyle was the first great chemist of modern times. With Boyle's Law, he showed that when a gas is compressed its pressure increases at the same rate. He also suggested that everything is made up from basic chemicals or "elements," which can join together in different ways.

▼ Lavoisier showed that, like solid elements, two gases can join to make a new substance, or compound. Here he is experimenting with hydrogen and oxygen, to produce water.

138 People once believed air was not a substance. But Antoine Lavoisier realized substances can exist in three different states—solid, liquid, and gas—and if gases are substances, then so is air. He found air is a mix of gases, mostly nitrogen and oxygen.

139 Scientists used to think that everything that burns contained a substance called phlogiston. They thought that as something burned it lost phlogiston. Lavoisier found by careful weighing that tin gains weight when it burns, because it takes in oxygen. So phlogiston couldn't exist. Lavoisier had proved the importance of accurate measurement.

Antoine Lavoisier
French 1743–1794

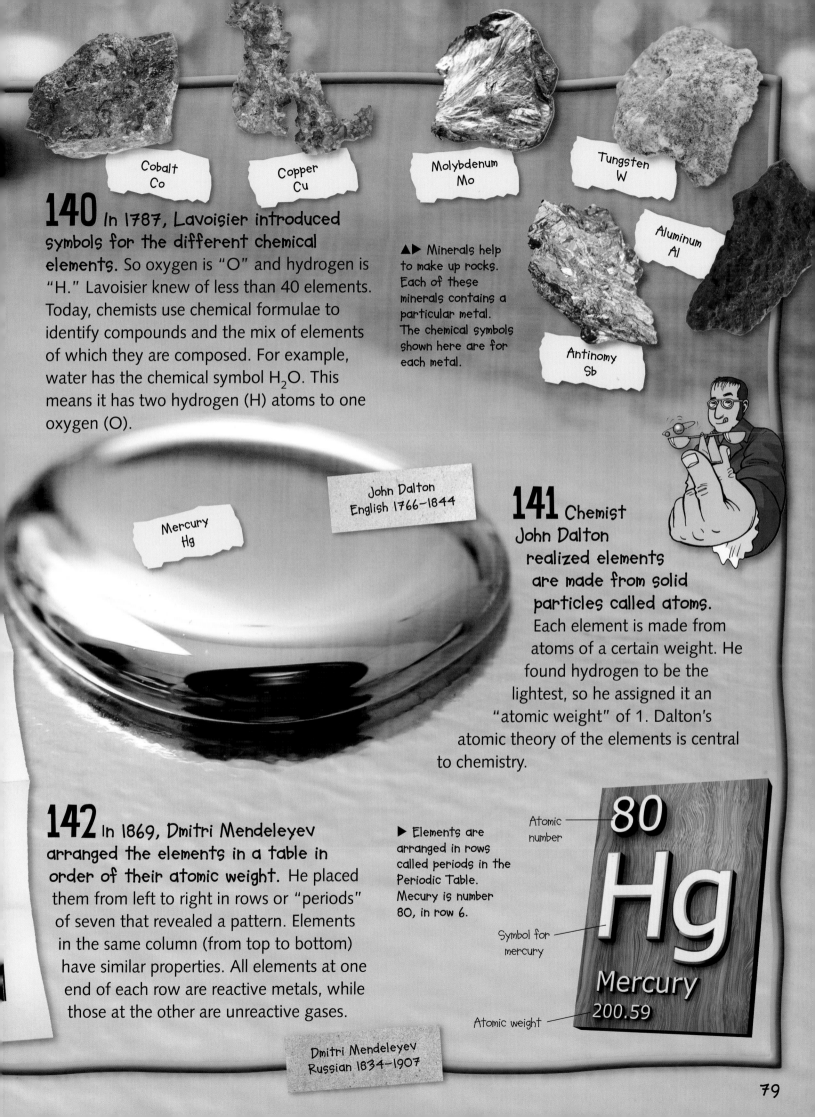

Cobalt
Co

Copper
Cu

Molybdenum
Mo

Tungsten
W

Aluminum
Al

Antinomy
Sb

140 In 1787, Lavoisier introduced symbols for the different chemical elements. So oxygen is "O" and hydrogen is "H." Lavoisier knew of less than 40 elements. Today, chemists use chemical formulae to identify compounds and the mix of elements of which they are composed. For example, water has the chemical symbol H_2O. This means it has two hydrogen (H) atoms to one oxygen (O).

▲▶ Minerals help to make up rocks. Each of these minerals contains a particular metal. The chemical symbols shown here are for each metal.

John Dalton
English 1766–1844

Mercury
Hg

141 Chemist John Dalton realized elements are made from solid particles called atoms. Each element is made from atoms of a certain weight. He found hydrogen to be the lightest, so he assigned it an "atomic weight" of 1. Dalton's atomic theory of the elements is central to chemistry.

142 In 1869, Dmitri Mendeleyev arranged the elements in a table in order of their atomic weight. He placed them from left to right in rows or "periods" of seven that revealed a pattern. Elements in the same column (from top to bottom) have similar properties. All elements at one end of each row are reactive metals, while those at the other are unreactive gases.

▶ Elements are arranged in rows called periods in the Periodic Table. Mecury is number 80, in row 6.

Atomic number

80

Hg

Symbol for mercury

Mercury
200.59

Atomic weight

Dmitri Mendeleyev
Russian 1834–1907

Sparks of genius

143 In the 1700s, scientists discovered that rubbing things together can give an electrical charge and may create a spark. Benjamin Franklin wondered if lightning was electrical too. He attached a key to a kite, which he flew during a thunderstorm, and got a similar spark from the key.

▼ A spark flew from the key on Franklin's kite, showing that lightning was electrical.

Benjamin Franklin
American 1706–1790

Luigi Galvani
Italian 1737–1798

144 Luigi Galvani made a dead frog's legs twitch with electricity. He believed, incorrectly, that electricity was made by animals' bodies. Alessandro Volta believed this was just a chemical reaction. In 1800, he used the reaction between "sandwiches" of disks made of the metals copper and zinc in saltwater to create a battery.

Zinc

Copper

Wire

◄ The Voltaic pile battery was the first plentiful source of electricity.

Alessandro Volta
Italian 1745–1827

Hans Christiaan Øersted
Danish 1777–1851

145 No one realized electricity and magnetism were linked—until physicist Hans Øersted noticed something strange. During a lecture in 1820, he observed that when an electric current was switched on and off, a nearby compass needle swiveled. He went on to confirm with experiments that an electric current creates a magnetic field around it. This effect is known as electromagnetism.

146 Michael Faraday was fascinated by Øersted's discovery. The following year he showed how the interreaction between a magnet and an electrical current can make a wire move. Faraday and others then went on to use this discovery to create the first electric motors.

▼ Faraday found that when a wire moves near a magnet, an electric current is generated in it.

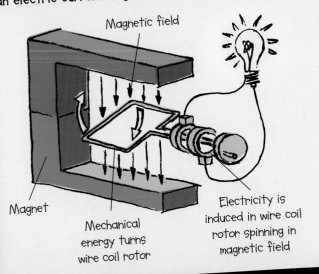

Magnetic field

Magnet

Mechanical energy turns wire coil rotor

Electricity is induced in wire coil rotor spinning in magnetic field

147 In 1830, Faraday in London and Joseph Henry in New York found that magnets create electricity. When a magnet is moved near an electric circuit, it creates a surge of electricity. Using this idea, machines could be built to generate lots of electricity.

148 Faraday's experiments in electricity convinced him that all types of electricity were basically the same. It didn't matter if they were produced naturally in Earth's atmosphere in the form of lightning, artificially by chemical reactions in a battery, or by a rotating copper coil inside a magnetic field.

Faraday showed how a cage of metal wire (known as a Faraday cage) could block electrical discharges and protect a person from lightning.

Cured!

149 People who survived the disease smallpox became immune to a second attack. This meant their bodies could resist the infection. Doctor Edward Jenner injected his gardener's son with cowpox, a milder disease, to see if it gave the same immunity. It did.

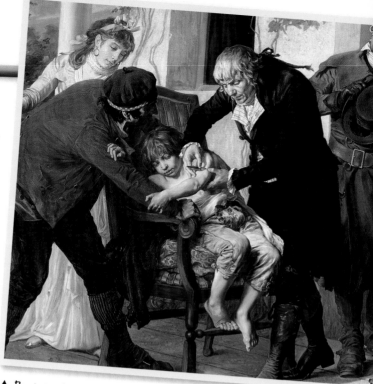

▲ By injecting his gardener's son with cowpox, Edward Jenner had taken the first step toward wiping out the killer disease smallpox.

150 Before 1850, no one knew dirt in hospitals could spread killer germs. Countless patients died of infections. Doctor Ignaz Semmelweiss asked students to wash their hands before dealing with patients. This act of simple hygiene helped reduce the number of deaths.

151 Surgeon Joseph Lister introduced soap to his operations to keep things spotlessly clean. Cleanliness cut infections during surgery dramatically, and antiseptic techniques are now a vital part of every operation.

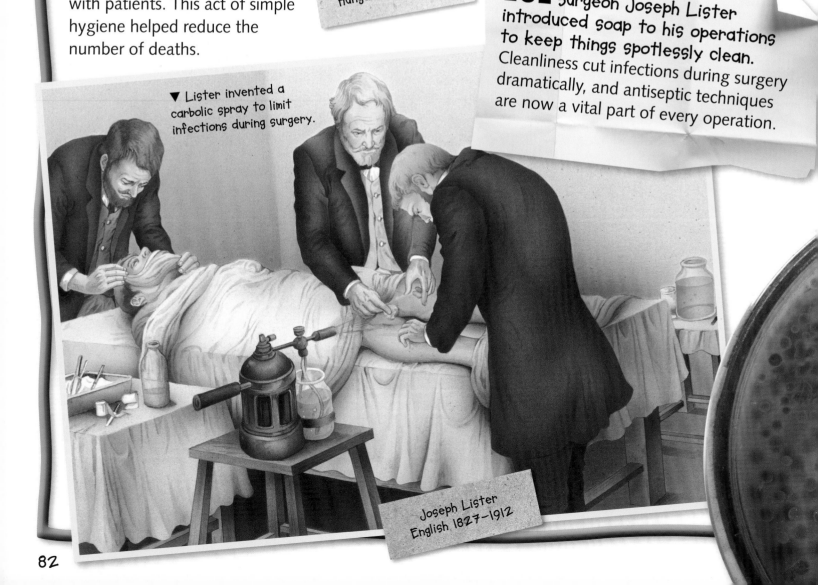

▼ Lister invented a carbolic spray to limit infections during surgery.

152 The idea that germs cause disease has been around for over 400 years. But it was Louis Pasteur who, with Robert Koch, proved the link in the 1870s. They showed how bacteria spread the sheep disease anthrax.

Louis Pasteur
French 1822–1895

▼ We now know many diseases are spread by microbes— mainly bacteria and viruses. In future they may be targeted by tiny "nano-robots" placed inside our bodies.

Robert Koch
German 1843–1910

Paul Ehrlich
German 1854–1915

153 Paul Ehrlich believed diseases might be cured by targeting germs with chemical "magic bullets." He and student Sahachiro Hato searched for a chemical to kill the bacteria that caused the disease syphilis. They found one called arsphenamine, which wiped out the syphilis germ but left the patient almost unharmed.

Sahachiro Hato
Japanese 1873–1938

Alexander Fleming
Scottish 1881–1955

154 In 1928, Alexander Fleming saw a clue that led to the miracle drugs antibiotics. He was culturing (growing) bacteria in dishes in his lab, when he saw that mold growing on one neglected dish had killed the bacteria. Fleming realized that the mold, called *Penicillium notatum*, could be harnessed to fight disease.

◄ Ten years after Fleming discovered the bacteria-killing mold, Howard Florey (1898–1968) and Ernst Chain (1906–1977) created the first antibiotic drug, penicillin.

Dangerous rays

155 In 1886, Heinrich Hertz proved that an electromagnetic current spreads as waves. He made a flickering electric spark jump a gap in an electrical circuit. As the spark flickered, it radiated waves, which set another spark flickering in sync in an aerial receiver. Hertz had discovered radio waves.

Heinrich Hertz
German 1857–1894

② High voltage current jumps a gap in an electric circuit and creates a spark

③ Spark sends out electromagnetic waves

④ Waves induce a tiny spark in aerial receiver

① Coil produces high voltage current

▲ Hertz's experiments with electricity and electromagnetic waves led to the development of the radio.

I DON'T BELIEVE IT!

Before people realized how dangerous it was, radium was added to products such as toothpaste and hair cream to give them a healthy glow.

▼ We now know that the cathode rays in Crookes' glass tube were actually made up of tiny electrical particles.

Cathode terminal

Cathode rays

Anode terminal

Mask

Shadow

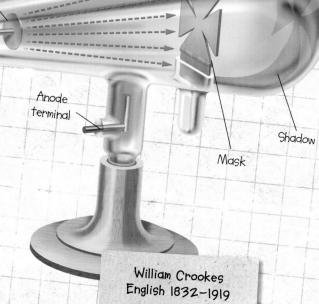

156 In the 1870s, William Crookes made a glass tube with nearly all the air sucked out of it. When connected to an electric current, the glass tube glowed. This was because electric charge flowed between the terminals, sending out electromagnetic radiation, which Crookes called cathode rays. A metal mask inside the tube cast a shadow, showing that the rays traveled in straight lines.

William Crookes
English 1832–1919

Wilhelm Röntgen
German 1845–1923

157 In 1895, Wilhelm Röntgen found that even when he covered a Crookes tube, its rays still made a nearby screen glow. Some rays must be shining through the cover. He tried putting other objects in front of the rays (which he called X-rays) and eventually placed his wife's hand. The rays passed through flesh, but were blocked by bone. Röntgen replaced the screen with photo paper and took the first X-ray photo of his wife's hand.

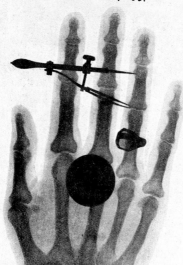

▼ As well as bone, Röntgen discovered that X-rays were blocked by the metal of his wife's jewelry, and a compass!

Henri Becquerel
French 1852–1908

158 Henri Becquerel found that uranium crystals left on photo paper in a drawer made a photo of themselves. They were releasing or "radiating" their own energy. He had discovered radioactivity— radiation so energetic it breaks up atoms. This kind of radiation is quite different from electromagnetic radiation and is used to make nuclear bombs.

◀ Marie Curie was the first woman to be awarded a Nobel Prize, in 1903 for physics. She was awarded it again, this time in chemistry, in 1911.

Pierre Curie
French 1859–1906

159 Pierre and Marie Curie were fascinated by radioactivity. They discovered two new radioactive elements, radium and polonium. In 1903, they were awarded the Nobel Prize for their work. Marie Curie died from cancer caused by exposure to radioactivity.

Marie Curie
Polish 1867–1934

Atomic science

Sir Joseph John (JJ) Thomson
English 1856–1940

160 Scientists once thought atoms were the smallest particles. In 1897, JJ Thomson noticed how magnets bent rays from a cathode ray tube. He realized the rays were streams of particles, much smaller than an atom. Thomson wrongly believed these particles or "electrons" split off from atoms like currants off a bun.

Sir Ernest Rutherford
New Zealand–born British
1871–1937

161 Ernest Rutherford found that radioactivity is the result of atoms breaking up into different atoms, sending out streams of "alpha" and "beta" particles. In 1911, he fired streams of alpha particles at gold foil. Most went straight through, but a few bounced back, pushed by the nuclei inside the gold foil atoms. He realized that atoms aren't solid, but largely empty space with a tiny, dense nucleus (core).

▶ Fortunately, all nuclear explosions since the attack on Japan in 1945 have been tests.

Neils Bohr
Danish 1885–1962

162 In 1912, Niels Bohr suggested that different kinds of atom had a certain number of electrons. He thought they buzzed around an atom's nucleus at varying distances, like planets around the Sun. Atoms give out light and lose energy when electrons fall closer to the nucleus. When atoms absorb light, the electrons jump further out.

▶ We now know that electrons are like fuzzy clouds of energy rather than planets.

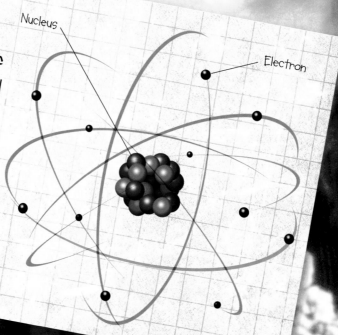

Nucleus

Electron

163 In 1918 Rutherford split atoms for the first time. He fired alpha particles at nitrogen gas and found that hydrogen nuclei chipped off the nitrogen nuclei. He realized that all atomic nuclei are clusters of hydrogen nuclei, which he called protons. Fourteen years later, James Chadwick discovered nuclei also have another kind of particle in the nucleus—the neutron.

James Chadwick
English 1891–1974

164 Enrico Fermi fired neutrons at a uranium atom, to see if they'd stick to form a bigger atom. Instead, the uranium atom split into two smaller atoms and released more neutrons, and heat and light energy. Fermi realized that if these neutrons spun off to split more uranium atoms a "chain reaction" of splitting could occur.

Enrico Fermi
Italian–American
1901–1954

① Neutron fired at nucleus of Uranium atom

◀ Enrico Fermi showed how a chain reaction of an atom splitting could begin with the impact of just a single neutron.

② Nucleus splits in two

④ More neutrons released

Uranium atom

③ Energy released

⑤ Chain reaction occurs

165 During World War II (1939–1945) Fermi created a chain reaction of nuclear splitting, or "fission." This unleashed energy to create an incredibly powerful bomb. At Los Alamo, New Mexico, Robert Oppenheimer used this idea to make the first nuclear bombs, which were dropped on the Japanese cities of Hiroshima and Nagasaki in August 1945, killing thousands of people outright.

Robert Oppenheimer
American 1904–1967

BOWLING REACTION!

Ask an older relative to take you bowling. It's not just fun, it'll show you how a nuclear chain reaction can work, especially if you are lucky enough to strike ten. The ball may only hit one pin directly, but as that pin falls, it can knock down all the rest in turn.

Space and time weirdness

166 In 1900, Max Planck worked out that heat is not radiated in a smooth flow, but in tiny chunks of energy that he called quanta. Albert Einstein realized that all radiation works like this—and that chunks of energy are particles. So a ray of light is streams of particles, not just waves, as everyone thought.

Max Planck
German 1858–1947

TRUE OR FALSE?

1. A ray of light is made up of particles.
2. The speed of light can vary.
3. Gravity bends space and time.
4. Paul Dirac's theory was called quantum engines.

Answers:
1. True 2. False, the speed of light is always the same 3. True 4. False, it was called quantum mechanics

Albert Einstein
German 1879–1955

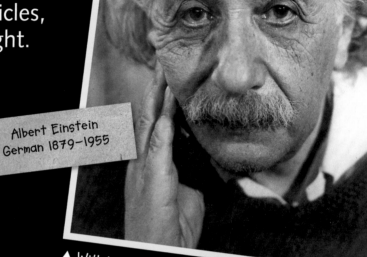

▲ With his theories of relativity, Einstein overturned our understanding of the nature of time and space.

167 Speed is always measured compared to something, so the speed of an object varies depending on what you compare it to. In 1887, Einstein showed that light is special—it travels the same speed no matter how you measure it. Speed is the distance something moves through space in a certain time. If light's speed is fixed, Einstein realized that time and space must vary instead. So time and space are not fixed—they are relative and can be distorted. This is Einstein's theory of special relativity.

168 Einstein's theory of special relativity has weird effects for things traveling near the speed of light. For example, time on board a spacecraft traveling near the speed of light would seem to run slower, and the spacecraft would appear to shrink in length and get heavier.

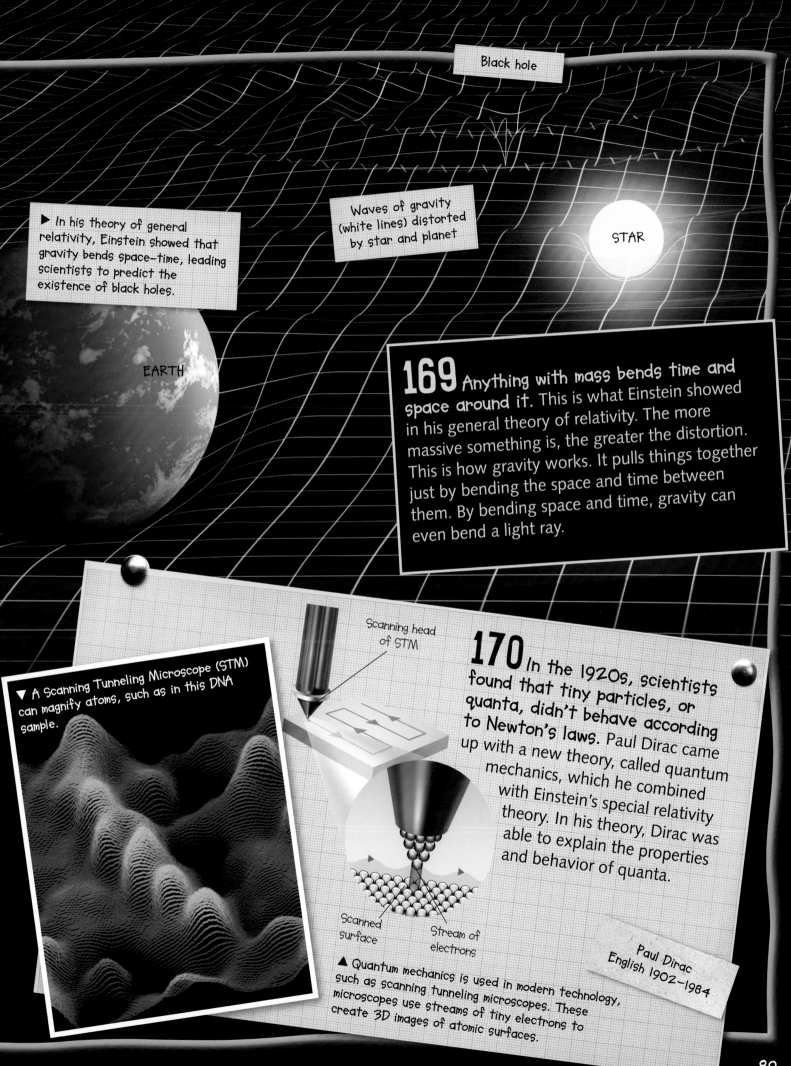

Black hole

Waves of gravity (white lines) distorted by star and planet

STAR

▶ In his theory of general relativity, Einstein showed that gravity bends space-time, leading scientists to predict the existence of black holes.

EARTH

169 **Anything with mass bends time and space around it.** This is what Einstein showed in his general theory of relativity. The more massive something is, the greater the distortion. This is how gravity works. It pulls things together just by bending the space and time between them. By bending space and time, gravity can even bend a light ray.

Scanning head of STM

▼ A Scanning Tunneling Microscope (STM) can magnify atoms, such as in this DNA sample.

170 **In the 1920s, scientists found that tiny particles, or quanta, didn't behave according to Newton's laws.** Paul Dirac came up with a new theory, called quantum mechanics, which he combined with Einstein's special relativity theory. In his theory, Dirac was able to explain the properties and behavior of quanta.

Scanned surface

Stream of electrons

Paul Dirac English 1902–1984

▲ Quantum mechanics is used in modern technology, such as scanning tunneling microscopes. These microscopes use streams of tiny electrons to create 3D images of atomic surfaces.

Star gazers

171 A century ago, astronomers began to wonder if faint clouds in space called nebulae were actually distant galaxies. But were the stars within them really dim or just far away? To find out, astronomers looked for stars of varying brightness called cepheids. Slow varying cepheids are bright, so if they look dim, they must be far away.

► Henrietta Leavitt discovered how the brightest cepheid stars take longest to vary.

Henrietta Swan Leavitt
American 1868–1921

◄ Andromeda was the first galaxy identified using cepheids.

172 In 1923, Edwin Hubble spotted a cepheid in the Andromeda nebula. It took a month to vary in brightness, so by Leavitt's scale it had to be 7,000 times brighter than the Sun—and 6 million trillion miles away. So Andromeda must be a separate galaxy. Astronomers know now it is just one of 500 billion or so!

Edwin Hubble
American 1889–1953

▲ Edwin Hubble making observations at the Mount Wilson telescope in California.

173 In 1931, Hubble found that the further away galaxies are, the redder they are. They are redder or "red-shifted" because light waves are stretched out behind an object that is zooming away from us, just like sound drops in pitch after a car speeds past. So, the further a galaxy is from Earth, the faster it is moving away from us.

Georges Lemaître
Belgian 1894–1966

174 If galaxies are speeding apart now, they must have been closer together in the past. So the Universe is expanding. In the 1920s, Alexander Friedmann and Georges Lemaître suggested that the Universe was once just a tiny point that swelled like a giant explosion. One critic called the idea the Big Bang, and the name stuck.

Arno Penzias
German–American
Born 1933

175 Although the Big Bang theory caught on, there wasn't much proof. Then Arno Penzias and Robert Wilson picked up a faint buzz of radio signals from all over the sky. Astronomers believe that this buzz, called the Cosmic Microwave Background, is the faint afterglow of the Big Bang.

Alexander Friedmann
Russian 1888–1925

Robert Woodrow Wilson
American Born 1936

QUIZ

1. What was the first galaxy to be discovered beyond the Milky Way?
2. What is the theory of the origin of the Universe called?
3. What were pulsars jokingly called?

Answers:
1. The Andromeda Galaxy
2. The Big Bang
3. Little green men

▲ When Burnell first detected the radio pulses from pulsars, the stars were jokingly called "little green men."

176 In 1967, Jocelyn Bell Burnell picked up strange radio pulses from certain stars. These pulsing stars, or pulsars, are actually tiny stars spinning at incredible speeds. They were once giant stars that have since collapsed to make a super-dense star just a few miles across.

Dame Jocelyn Bell Burnell
Northern Irish Born 1943

Plan for life

177 Gregor Mendel wanted to know why some living things look like their parents and why others look different. In the 1860s, he experimented with pea flowers and their pollen to see which ones gave green peas and which ones gave yellow. Characteristics such as color, he suggested, are passed to offspring by factors—which we now call genes.

Gregor Mendel
Austrian 1822–1884

▼ Chromosomes are the X-shaped bundles of DNA coiled up in the nucleus of a living cell.

Cell

178 In the 1900s, Thomas Hunt Morgan experimented with fruit flies. He showed that genes are linked to tiny bundles in living cells called chromosomes. By removing materials from a bacterial cell one by one, Oswald Avery later found the one material it needed to pass on characteristics—DNA.

Thomas Hunt Morgan
American 1866–1945

Oswald Avery
Canadian-American
1877–1955

Cell nucleus contains chromosomes

Rosalind Franklin
English 1920–1958

▲ The characteristics in this family group are clear to see, and have been passed on by DNA.

179 Scientists thought DNA's ability to pass on characteristics lay in its shape. Inspired by X-rays taken by Rosalind Franklin, Francis Crick and James Watson worked out in 1953 that the DNA molecule is a double helix (spiral). It's like a twisted rope ladder with two long strands either side linked by thousands of "rungs."

James Watson
American Born 1928

Francis Crick
English 1916–2004

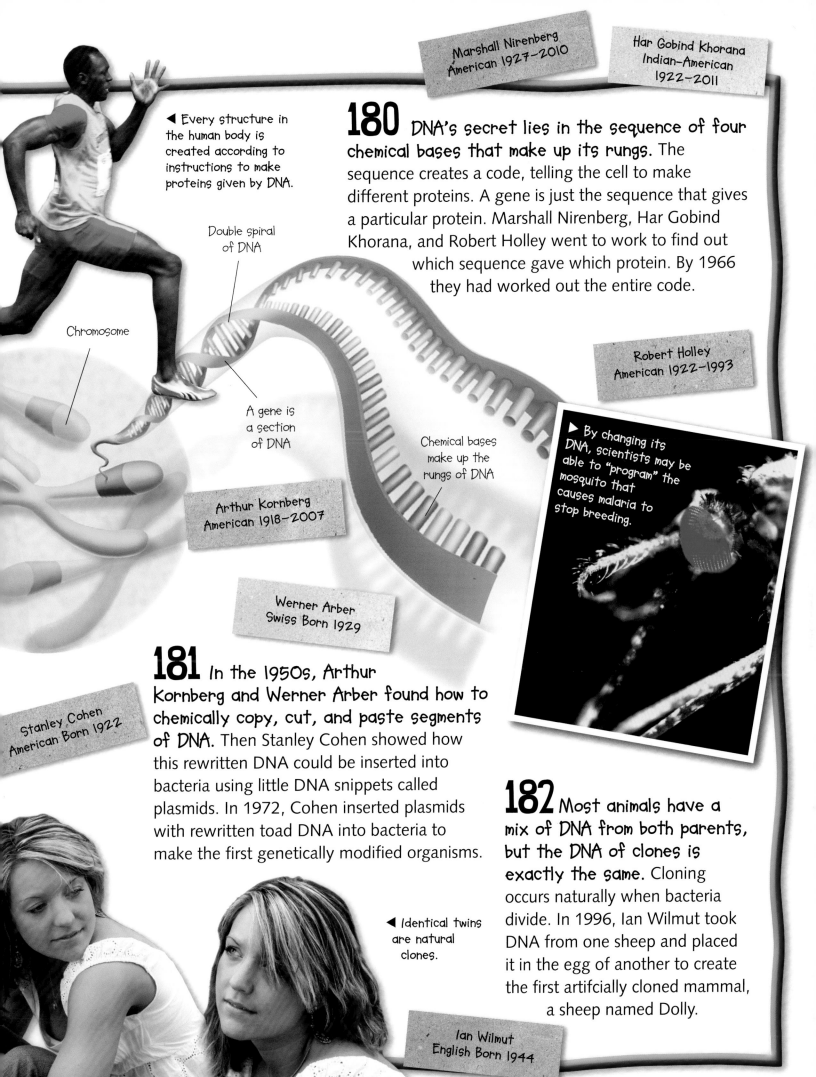

◀ Every structure in the human body is created according to instructions to make proteins given by DNA.

180 DNA's secret lies in the sequence of four chemical bases that make up its rungs. The sequence creates a code, telling the cell to make different proteins. A gene is just the sequence that gives a particular protein. Marshall Nirenberg, Har Gobind Khorana, and Robert Holley went to work to find out which sequence gave which protein. By 1966 they had worked out the entire code.

Double spiral of DNA

Chromosome

A gene is a section of DNA

Chemical bases make up the rungs of DNA

▶ By changing its DNA, scientists may be able to "program" the mosquito that causes malaria to stop breeding.

181 In the 1950s, Arthur Kornberg and Werner Arber found how to chemically copy, cut, and paste segments of DNA. Then Stanley Cohen showed how this rewritten DNA could be inserted into bacteria using little DNA snippets called plasmids. In 1972, Cohen inserted plasmids with rewritten toad DNA into bacteria to make the first genetically modified organisms.

◀ Identical twins are natural clones.

182 Most animals have a mix of DNA from both parents, but the DNA of clones is exactly the same. Cloning occurs naturally when bacteria divide. In 1996, Ian Wilmut took DNA from one sheep and placed it in the egg of another to create the first artifcially cloned mammal, a sheep named Dolly.

Frontiers of science

184 By creating the World Wide Web in 1989, Tim Berners-Lee transformed the way the world communicates. The World Wide Web made the Internet accessible to everyone, anywhere in the world. It worked by turning computer output into web pages that could be read and displayed by any computer.

▲ Hawking suggested that the Big Bang might be a black hole in reverse, expanding from a singularity.

183 Stephen Hawking's work on black holes in space changed our understanding of the Universe. Black holes are places where gravity is so powerful that it draws in even light. At the center is a minute point called a singularity.

185 Light is the fastest thing in the Universe. But in 2001 Lene Vestergaard Hau slowed it to a standstill by shining it through sodium atoms in a special cold state called a Bose-Einstein Condensate (BEC). In a BEC, atoms are so inactive there is nothing for particles of light to interact with, forcing them to slow down.

Brian Greene
American Born 1963

Michio Kaku
American Born 1947

186 Brian Greene and Michio Kaku are working on a theory that ties together all our ideas about the Universe, matter, and energy. They believe everything is made of tiny strings of energy called superstrings. Just as a violin string can make different notes, so a superstring creates particles by vibrating in different ways.

Craig Venter
American Born 1946

▲ In 2010, Venter created the world's first man-made living cell.

187 Craig Venter was one of many scientists involved in mapping the entire sequence of genes in human DNA. He is also sampling the oceans for microorganisms to see just how varied DNA is.

188 Scientists explain how forces such as electromagnetic radiation are transmitted by tiny messenger particles known as bosons. But they don't know why things are heavy and have mass, and why they take force to get going and stop. Peter Higgs suggested it could be down to a mystery particle now called the Higgs boson.

▼ Scientists are trying to find the Higgs boson with a massive underground machine at CERN in Switzerland, where they smash atoms together at incredible speeds.

Peter Higgs
English Born 1929

QUIZ

1. What would you find at the center of a black hole?
2. What's the slowest speed light can travel?
3. Where is CERN?

Answers:
1. A singularity 2. A complete stop 3. Switzerland

INVENTIONS

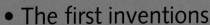

- The first inventions
- Wheels and rails
- Weapons of war
- Exploration by sea
- Renewable energy
- Writing and printing
- Musical instruments
- Communication
- Recording technology
- Inventions at home

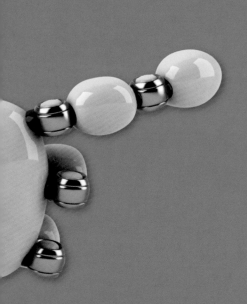

When were tools first made?

What is a boneshaker?

Who invented the compass?

What was the first sound ever recorded?

Why were early refrigerators dangerous?

In the beginning

189 Humans have always been inventors. More than one million years ago, our ancient relatives made simple stone tools. Around 30,000 years ago our more recent ancestors were much more skilled at tool-making (1) and they had worked out how to sew skins together to make clothes (2). The first musical instruments were made from bone more than 20,000 years ago (3). Early humans lived by hunting animals, and invented bows and arrows to which they added tips of sharp stone. Tools, clothes, weapons, dwellings, and other inventions gradually became more complicated and numerous.

▶ Stone Age clothes were made out of animal skins sewn together using a bone needle.

The first inventions

190 The first inventors lived about 2.5 million years ago. They were small, humanlike creatures who walked upright on two legs. Their first inventions were stone tools. They hammered stones with other stones to shape them. These rough tools have been found in Tanzania in Africa. Scientists call this early relative of ours "handy man."

Spear made from wood with tip of sharp flint

191 Stone Age people made really sharp weapons and tools by chipping a stone called flint. They dug pits and tunnels in chalky ground to find the valuable flint lumps. Their digging tools were made from reindeer antlers.

▲ Flint tools were shaped to fit comfortably into the hand, with finely chipped cutting edges that could cut through large bones.

192 Early hunters were able to kill the largest animals. With flint tips on their weapons, they overcame wild oxen and horses and even killed huge, woolly mammoths. They used their sharp flint tools to carve up the bodies. The flint easily sliced through tough animal hides.

▼ Stone Age hunters trapped woolly mammoths in pits and killed them with spears and stones.

Stone

Pit covered with sticks

193 **The ax was a powerful weapon.** A new invention, the ax handle, made it possible to strike very hard blows. Fitted with a sharp stone head, the ax was useful for chopping down trees for firewood and building shelters.

▶ Ax heads were valuable, and were traded with people who had no flint.

MODERN AX

▶ A modern ax is made of steel but it still has a long, sharp cutting edge and wooden handle.

▶ Saws were made from about 12,000 BC, and had flint "teeth" held in place by resin.

MODERN SAW

▲ Today's steel saws also use many small sharp teeth to slice tough materials.

I DON'T BELIEVE IT!

Some Stone Age hunters used boomerangs! They made them out of mammoth tusks thousands of years before Australian boomerangs, and used them for hunting.

194 **Saws could cut through the hardest wood.** Flint workers discovered how to make very small flint flakes. They fixed the flakes like teeth in a straight handle of wood or bone. If the teeth broke, they could add new ones. Saws were used to cut through tough bones as well as wood.

Making fire

195 **People once used fire created by lightning.** The first fire-makers probably lived in East Asia more than 400,000 years ago. As modern humans spread from Africa, over 60,000 years ago, they found that northern winters were very cold, and fire helped them stay warm. They discovered how to twirl a fire stick very fast—by placing the loop of a bowstring around the stick and moving the bow back and forth. After thousands of years, people invented a way to make sparks from steel by hitting it with a flint. Now they could carry their fire-making tinderboxes around with them.

▲ People discovered that very hot flames would harden, or "fire," pottery in ovenlike kilns.

▶ Fire provided early people with warmth, light, and heat to cook food. The temperature deep within a cave stays the same whatever the weather outside.

MAKING HEAT

When your hands are cold you rub them together. Do this slowly. They feel the same. Now rub them together really fast. Feel how your hands get warmer. Rubbing things together is called friction. Friction causes heat.

196 Fire makes food taste good. The invention of cooking made food safer, because cooking kills germs. Cooking roots and meat on a fire makes them more tender as well as tastier. Humans are the only animals that cook food.

▲ Some people like cooking outdoors on a fire, as our relatives did over a quarter of a million years ago.

197 Humans invented lamps to light deep, dark caves. The lamps were saucers of clay or stone that burned animal fat, with moss for a wick. Campfire flames kept wild animals away at night. They also cooked food and kept people warm. People could see to make wall paintings in the caves.

New ways of moving

198 With wheels you can move huge weights. Once, heavy weights were dragged along the ground, sometimes on sledges—parts of 7,000-year-old sledges have been found in Scandinavia. Then, more than 5,500 years ago, the Sumerians of Mesopotamia began to make wheels from carved planks, which they fastened together.

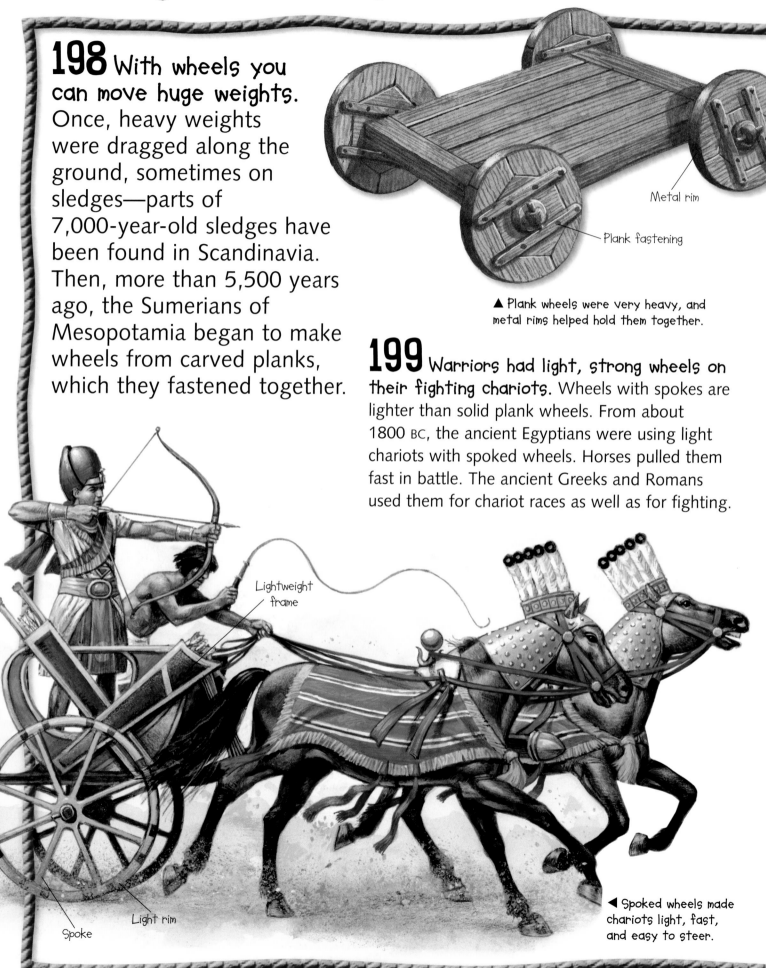

Metal rim

Plank fastening

▲ Plank wheels were very heavy, and metal rims helped hold them together.

199 Warriors had light, strong wheels on their fighting chariots. Wheels with spokes are lighter than solid plank wheels. From about 1800 BC, the ancient Egyptians were using light chariots with spoked wheels. Horses pulled them fast in battle. The ancient Greeks and Romans used them for chariot races as well as for fighting.

Lightweight frame

Light rim

Spoke

◀ Spoked wheels made chariots light, fast, and easy to steer.

TIMELINE OF BICYCLE DESIGN

1818
Hobby

1861
Velocipede (Boneshaker)

Early 1870s
Penny Farthing

1976
Mountain bike

200 Railway lines were once made of wood! Wheels move easily along rails. Horses pulled heavy wagons on these wagonways over 400 years ago. William Jessop invented specially shaped metal wheels to run along metal rails in 1789. Modern trains haul enormous loads at great speed along metal rails.

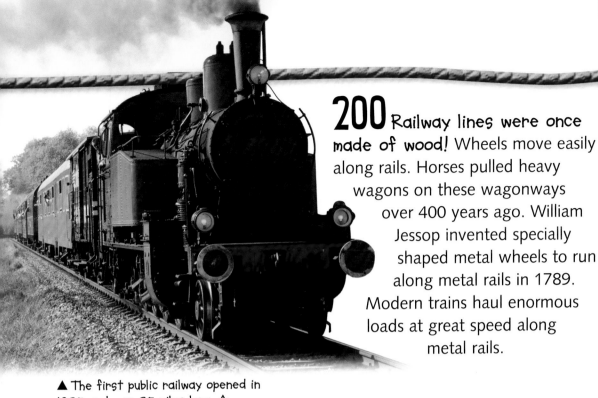

▲ The first public railway opened in 1825 and was 25 miles long. A century later, steam trains like this puffed across whole continents.

201 In 1861, bikes with solid tires were called boneshakers! An even earlier version of the bicycle was sometimes called the "hobby horse." It had no pedals, so riders had to push their feet against the ground to make it move. The invention of air-filled rubber tires made cycling more comfortable.

▲ Bicycle design has come a long way—early designs were very heavy, and had no pedals or way of steering.

QUIZ

Which came first?
1. (a) the chariot, or
   (b) the sledge?
2. (a) solid wheels, or
   (b) spoked wheels?
3. (a) rails, or
   (b) steam engines?

Answers:
1.b 2.a 3.a

▼ Wheels this size are usually only found on giant dump trucks. These carry heavy loads such as rocks or soil that can be tipped out.

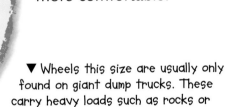

202 Cars with gigantic wheels can drive over other cars! Big wheels give a smooth ride. At some motor shows, trucks with enormous wheels compete to drive over rows of cars. Tractors with huge wheels were invented to drive over very rough ground.

On the farm

203 The first farmers used digging sticks. In the area now called Iraq, about 9000 BC, farmers planted seeds of wheat and barley. They used knives made of flint flakes fixed in a bone or wooden handle to cut the ripe grain stalks. The quern was invented to grind grain into flour between two stones.

▲ Curved knives made of bone or wood were used for harvesting grain.

▼ Plowed furrows made it easier to sow, water, and harvest crops.

204 Humans pulled the first plows. They were invented in Egypt and surrounding countries as early as 4000 BC. Plows broke the ground and turned over the soil faster and better than digging sticks. Later on, oxen and other animals pulled plows. The invention of metal plows made plowing much easier.

I DON'T BELIEVE IT!

Some Stone Age people invented the first fridges! They buried spare food in pits dug in ground that was always frozen.

205 **For thousands of years, farming hardly changed.** Then from about 300 years ago a series of inventions made it much more efficient. One of these was a seed-drill, invented by Englishman Jethro Tull. Pulled by a horse, it sowed seeds at regular spaces in neat rows. It was less wasteful than the old method of throwing grain onto the ground.

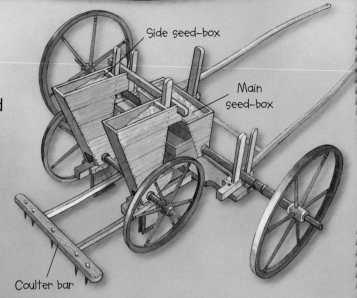

Side seed-box

Main seed-box

Coulter bar

▲ Jethro Tull's seed-drill sowed three rows of seed at a time.

206 **Modern machines harvest huge fields of wheat and other crops in record time.** The combine harvester was invented to cut the crop and separate grain at the same time. Teams of combine harvesters roll across the plains of America, Russia, Australia, and many other places, harvesting the wheat. What were once huge areas of land covered with natural grasses now provide grain for bread.

207 **Scientists are changing the way plants grow.** They have invented ways of creating crop plants with built-in protection from pests and diseases. Other bumper crop plants grow well in places where once they could not grow at all because of the soil or weather.

▼ The latest combine harvesters have air-conditioned, soundproofed cabs and nearly all have sound systems. Some even use satellite navigation (satnav or GPS receivers) to plot their route automatically around fields.

Under attack!

208 Using a spear thrower is like having an arm twice the normal length. They were probably invented over 20,000 years ago. Hunters and warriors used them to hurl spears harder and farther than ever before. People all over the world invented this useful tool, and Australian Aborigines still use it.

▶ One end of the spear thrower is cupped to hold the spear butt.

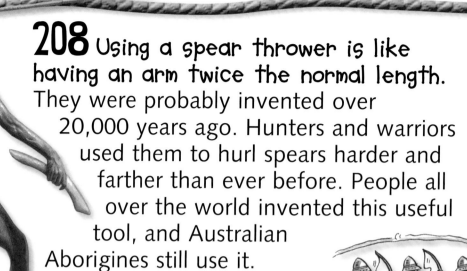

209 Arrows from a longbow could pass through iron armor. Bows and arrows were invented at least 20,000 years ago. More than 900 years ago, the English longbow was made from a yew branch. Archers used it to fire many arrows a long distance in a short time. By law, all Englishmen had to practice regularly with the longbow. It helped them win many famous battles.

▶ Bowmen often stood behind lines of sharpened stakes that protected them from enemies on horseback.

I DON'T BELIEVE IT!

Longbow archers could aim and fire six arrows per minute. The arrow sometimes went straight through an enemy's armor and out the other side.

210 Crossbows had to be wound up for each shot. They were invented over 2,000 years ago in the Mediterranean area, and fired a metal bolt or short arrow. They were powerful and accurate, but much slower than longbows. Soldiers used them in sieges throughout Europe from about AD 1000 onward. But in battles, where speed was important, crossbows were often beaten by longbows.

► Crossbows were the first mechanical hand weapons, and at one time the Church tried to ban them.

211 In the Bible, David killed the giant, Goliath, with a pebble from a sling. The sling is an ancient weapon probably invented by shepherds. They used it when guarding their flocks, and still do in some countries. The slinger holds the two loose ends, and puts a pebble in the pouch. Then he whirls it round his head and lets go of one end. The pebble flies out at the target.

▼ Modern catapults with extra-strong rubber fling stones 650 feet or more.

212 Even a small catapult can do a lot of damage. The rubber strips are like bowstrings, which can fire a pebble from a pouch, like a sling. Some anglers use a catapult to fire food to attract fish to the water's surface.

From stone to metal

213 Sometimes pieces of pure natural gold or copper can be found in the ground. The first people to work metal lived in the eastern Mediterranean around 8000 BC, and beat these metals with stone tools. They made the first copper weapons and gold ornaments.

▶ Bronze ax heads were sharper, and less easily damaged, than stone ones.

▲ Gold is quite a soft metal. Early goldsmiths beat it into a variety of shapes and made patterns of hammered indentations on its surface to create beautiful objects.

214 Blowing air onto flames makes them hotter. About 8,500 years ago people discovered how to melt metals out of the rocks, or ores, containing them. They invented bellows —animal-skin bags, to blow air onto the flames. The hot flames melted the metal out of the ore. We call this "smelting" the metal.

215 Bronze weapons stay sharper for longer than copper ones. About 5,500 years ago, metal workers invented bronze by smelting copper ores and tin ores together. They used the bronze to make hard, sharp swords, spearheads, and ax heads.

Bellows   Heat source

Molten bronze

Stone mold

◀ Molten bronze was poured into molds of stone or clay to make tools.

▲ After smelting, iron was beaten into shape to make strong, sharp weapons.

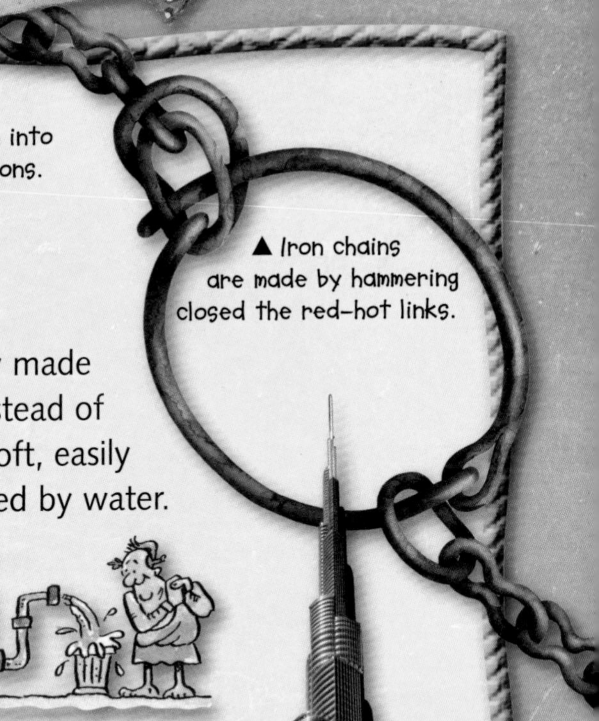

▲ Iron chains are made by hammering closed the red-hot links.

216 Armies with iron weapons can beat armies with bronze weapons. Iron is harder than bronze, but needs a very hot fire to smelt it. About 1500 BC, metal workers began to use charcoal in their fires. This burns much hotter than ordinary wood and is good for smelting iron.

217 The Romans were excellent plumbers. They made water pipes out of lead instead of wood or pottery. Lead is soft, easily shaped, and is not damaged by water.

▼ At a smelting works metal ore is heated past its melting point and the liquid is poured to set in a mold.

218 Some modern steelworks are the size of towns. Steel is made from iron, and was first invented when small amounts of carbon were mixed into molten iron. Steel is very hard, and used to build many things, including ships and skyscrapers.

▶ Burj Khalifa in Dubai is the world's tallest building, at 2,722 ft. It has a steel framework weighing more than 4,000 tons.

Boats and sails

219 Viking explorers reached America 1,000 years ago. The world's first boats were log rafts, useful for carrying heavy loads, but very slow. Viking boats were fast, and could travel far across the open sea. Sails were invented at least 5,000 years ago, and the Vikings used both sails and oars.

▶ Viking boats were made of long planks fitted onto wooden frames, and steered by means of a long oar fastened near the stern (back of the ship). They could be sailed across deep oceans, or rowed up shallow rivers, and made river journeys from the Baltic as far as the Black Sea.

I DON'T BELIEVE IT!

In 450 BC a merchant called Himilco sailed from North Africa to Britain. He ended up in Cornwall and bought Cornish tin!

220 About 300 years ago sailing ships sailed all the world's oceans. Some, like the British man-of-war fighting ships, were enormous, with many sails and large crews of sailors. Countries such as Britain, France, Spain, and Holland had large navies made up of these ships.

221 Some sailing boats race around the world nonstop. Modern sailing boats use many inventions, such as machines to roll up the sails and gears that allow the boat to steer itself. These boats are tough, light, and very fast.

▲ Sailing ships called caravels, designed in the 1400s, were light, easily steered, and ideal for exploring. Early ones had lanteen (triangular) sails, with square ones added later.

▶ Modern ocean-going yachts have a huge balloonlike sail called a spinnaker, invented in the mid-1800s. It is used mainly when heading in the direction the wind is blowing.

Wonderful clay

222 **Stone Age hunters used baked clay to do magic.** At least 30,000 years ago in Central Europe they discovered that some clay went hard in the sun, and even harder in a fire. They made clay figures of animals and humans, and used them in magic spells that they believed helped them catch food. Hardening clay in a fire was the start of the invention of pottery.

◀ By the year 500 AD in South America, Mayan craftsmen were "firing" elaborate clay sculptures to make them hard and shiny.

Clay pot

Heat duct

Fuel

▶ Kilns produced much higher temperatures than open fires, and the heat could be controlled.

MAKE A COILED POT

Roll modeling clay into a long, "snake" shape. Coil some of it into a flat circle. Continue to coil, building the coils upward. Try and make a bowl shape, and finally smooth out the ridges.

223 **Hard clay bowls changed the way people ate.** Early pots were made in China over 15,000 years ago. They were shaped by hand and hardened in fires. They could hold liquid, and were used to boil meat and plants. This made the food tastier and more tender. Around 7000 BC, potters in Southeast Asia used a new invention—a special oven to harden and waterproof clay, called a kiln.

224 Potters' wheels were probably invented before cart wheels. About 3500 BC in Mesopotamia (modern Iraq), potters invented a wheel on which to turn lumps of clay and shape round pots. By spinning the clay, the potter could make smooth, perfectly round shapes quickly.

▲ As the clay turns around on the disk "wheel," the potter applies gentle pressure to shape it into a bowl, vase, urn, or similar rounded item.

225 Brick-making was invented in hot countries without many trees. The first brick buildings were built in 9000 BC in Syria and Jordan. House builders made bricks from clay and straw, and dried them in the hot sun. By 3500 BC, bricks hardened in kilns were used in important buildings in Mesopotamia.

226 Modern factories make thousands of pots at a time. They are "fired" in huge kilns. Wheels with electric motors are used, though much factory pottery is shaped in molds. Teams of workers paint patterns.

Flat roof

Trap door

Ladder

Roof beams

◄ With the invention of bricks, it was possible to construct large buildings. In 6000 BC, the Turkish town of Çatal Hüyük had houses with rooftop openings connected by ladders instead of doors.

Sailing into the unknown

227 Early sailors looked at the stars to find their way about. Around 1000 BC, Phoenician merchants from Syria were able to sail out of sight of land without getting lost. They knew in which direction certain stars lay. The north Pole Star, in the Little Bear constellation (star group), always appears in the north.

▲ Two stars in the Great Bear constellation are called the Pointers. They point to the north Pole Star in the Little Bear constellation.

228 Magnetic compasses always point north and south. They allow sailors to navigate (find their way) even when the stars are invisible. The Chinese invented the magnetic compass about 3,000 years ago. It was first used in Europe about 1,000 years ago.

◄ Compasses have a magnetized needle placed on a pivot so it can turn easily. Beneath this is a card with marked points to show direction.

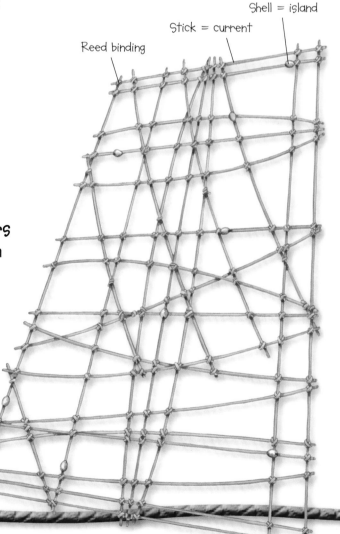

Reed binding

Stick = current

Shell = island

229 Early maps showed where sea monsters lived. The first attempt at a world map was drawn by the Greek Ptolemy in AD 160. Greek maps of around 550 BC showed the known world surrounded by water in which monsters lived. Over 500 years ago, Pacific islanders had maps of sticks and shells, showing islands and currents. The first globe was invented in 1492 by a German, Martin Behaim.

► Using stick and shell maps, Pacific islanders successfully crossed thousands of miles of ocean.

Mirrors

Telescope

Moving arm

▼ The chronometer was invented by Englishman John Harrison in 1735. It was a reliable timepiece, specially mounted to remove the effect of a ship's motion at sea.

► The sextant was developed around 1730 and was an important navigation aid until the 1900s.

Scale

230 Eighteenth-century sailors could work out exactly where they were on the oceans. They used an instrument called a sextant, invented around 1730. The sextant measured the height of the Sun from the horizon. The chronometer was an extremely reliable clock that wasn't affected by the motion of the sea.

USING A COMPASS

Take a compass outside and find out which direction is north. Put a cardboard arrow with "N" on it on the ground pointing in the right direction. Then try to work out the directions of south, west, and east.

▼ Modern navigation instruments use signals from several satellites to pinpoint their position.

Antenna (aerial) detects signals from available satellites

Batteries

Receiver compares the available satellite signals and "locks on" to the three strongest ones

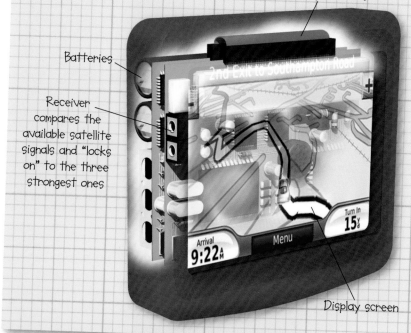

2nd Exit to Southampton Road

Arrival 9:22ᴬᴹ   Menu   Turn In 15¾

Display screen

231 New direction-finding inventions can tell anyone exactly where they are. A hand-held instrument, called a GPS receiver, receives signals from satellites in space. It shows your position to within a few feet. These receivers can be built into cars, ships, planes—even cell phones!

Weapons of war

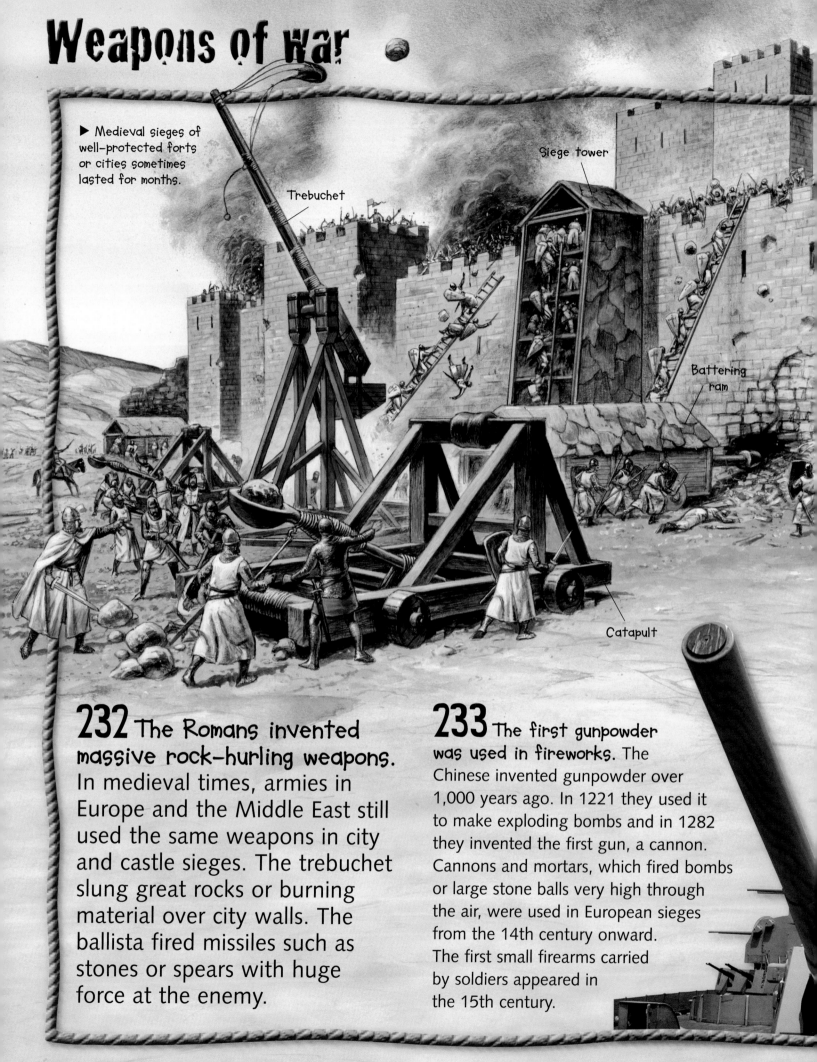

► Medieval sieges of well-protected forts or cities sometimes lasted for months.

Trebuchet

Siege tower

Battering ram

Catapult

232 The Romans invented massive rock-hurling weapons. In medieval times, armies in Europe and the Middle East still used the same weapons in city and castle sieges. The trebuchet slung great rocks or burning material over city walls. The ballista fired missiles such as stones or spears with huge force at the enemy.

233 The first gunpowder was used in fireworks. The Chinese invented gunpowder over 1,000 years ago. In 1221 they used it to make exploding bombs and in 1282 they invented the first gun, a cannon. Cannons and mortars, which fired bombs or large stone balls very high through the air, were used in European sieges from the 14th century onward. The first small firearms carried by soldiers appeared in the 15th century.

234 The battering ram could smash through massive city walls and gates. The Egyptians may have invented it in 2000 BC to destroy brick walls. It was a huge tree-trunk, often with an iron head, swung back and forth in a frame. Sometimes it had a roof to protect the soldiers from rocks and arrows from above.

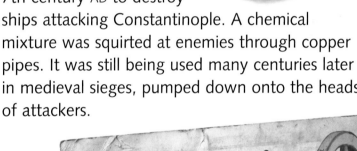

235 Gunpowder was used in tunnels to blow up castle walls. Attackers in a siege dug tunnels under the walls and supported them with wooden props. Then, they blew up or burned away the props so that the walls collapsed.

236 Greek fire was a secret weapon that burned on water. The Greeks invented it in the 7th century AD to destroy ships attacking Constantinople. A chemical mixture was squirted at enemies through copper pipes. It was still being used many centuries later in medieval sieges, pumped down onto the heads of attackers.

▼ The biggest battleship guns can hurl explosive shells more than 25 miles.

▲ The Gatling gun could fire six bullets a second.

237 Modern machine guns can fire thousands of bullets per minute. Richard Gatling, an American, invented a gun that would later lead to the development of the machine gun in 1862. As in all modern guns, each machine-gun bullet has its own metal case packed with deadly explosives.

Harvesting nature's energy

238 **The first inventions to use wind power were sailing boats.** Invented around 3500 BC by the Egyptians, and also by the Sumerians of Mesopotamia, the first sailing boats had a single square sail. By AD 600, windmills for grinding grain had been invented in Arab countries. Some European windmills, in use from about AD 1100 onward, could be turned to face the wind.

239 **The first waterwheels invented were flat, not upright.** The ancient Greeks were using upright wheels more than 2,100 years ago, and the Romans improved the design with bucketlike containers and gears to slow the turning rate. As well as grinding corn, some were used to drive pumps or saws.

Sail

Direction vane

Main drive

Rotation point

Vertical shaft

Gears

Millstones

Flour chute

▶ Many windmills were made entirely of wood apart from the millstones.

◀ In overshot watermills, the water strikes the top of the millwheel.

▲ Hydroelectric dams change the energy of moving water into electrical energy.

240 Early steam engines often threatened to explode. Thomas Savery's 1698 steam pump, invented in Devon, England, wasted fuel and was dangerous. Englishman Richard Trevithick developed a steam engine to move on tracks in 1804.

Generator changes the spinning movement from the rotor into electrical energy

The angle of the blades changes according to the speed of the wind

241 Spinning magnets can create an electric current. Michael Faraday and other scientists invented the first magnetic electricity generators (producers) in the 1830s. Today, huge dams use the power of millions of tons of flowing water to turn electricity generators, which have spinning electromagnets inside them.

Yaw control pod swings around to keep the rotor blades pointing into the wind

242 The strength of the wind usually increases the higher up you are. Some of the largest wind turbines in use today stand as high as a 50-story building, with propellers spanning more than the length of a soccer pitch. They produce enough electricity to power 5,000 homes or more.

▶ An increasing number of wind turbines are being built to make electricity.

Rotor blade

Marks on a page

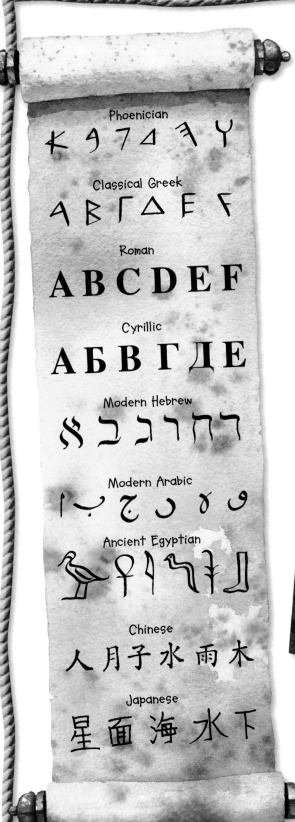

Phoenician

K 9 7 4 7 Y

Classical Greek

A B Γ Γ E F

Roman

A B C D E F

Cyrillic

А Б В Г Д Е

Modern Hebrew

א ב ג ד ה ו

Modern Arabic

ا ب ت ج ح خ

Ancient Egyptian

𓅿 𓏏 𓎡 𓈖 𓆑 𓂋

Chinese

人 月 子 水 雨 木

Japanese

星 面 海 水 下

▲ Ancient picture writing used hundreds of different signs, but most modern alphabets have far fewer letters.

243 The first writing was made up of pictures. Writing was invented by the Sumerians 5,500 years ago. They scratched their writing onto clay tablets. The most famous word pictures are the "hieroglyphs" of ancient Egyptians from about 5,000 years ago. Cuneiform writing was made up of wedge shapes pressed into clay with a reed. It followed the Sumerian picture writing.

▲ Some of the religious books handwritten by monks were decorated with beautiful illustrations.

244 The world's earliest books were rolls of paper made from reeds. The first of this kind was produced in Egypt between 1500 BC and 1350 BC and was called "The Book of the Dead." Christian monks used to write their religious books on sheets of parchment made from animal skins.

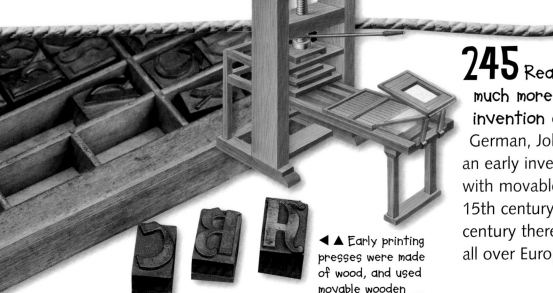

245 Reading suddenly became much more popular after the invention of printing. A German, Johannes Gutenberg, was an early inventor of a printing press with movable letters in the 15th century. By the end of the century there were printing presses all over Europe.

◄▲ Early printing presses were made of wood, and used movable wooden letters.

246 Once, people were expert at doing sums on their fingers. The first written numbers were invented about 3100 BC by Middle Eastern traders. Around AD 300, the Chinese invented a counting machine called an abacus. It was a frame with beads strung on wires. Some people still use them.

Container of ink is punched open to release the ink, and pressurized to get the ink into the nozzle area

▼ Modern home printers build up the image as many tiny dots of ink forming a long row or line, and then another line next to it, and so on.

Print head zooms to and fro along a guide rail, squirting out tiny jets of ink

New sheets of paper are fed from the paper tray through a tiny gap by rubber rollers

Printed sheets pile up in the print tray

Power button

▲ Experts can do complicated sums very fast on an abacus.

247 Computers do sums at lightning speed. Early modern computers were invented in the United States and Europe in the 1930s and 1940s. Today, computers are small, cheap, and extremely powerful. They can store whole libraries of information. The Internet allows everyone to share information and send messages immediately almost anywhere in the world.

I DON'T BELIEVE IT!

Some early Greek writing was called, "the way an ox plows the ground." It was written from right to left, then the next line went left to right, and so on, back and forth.

Making things bigger

▲ Spectacles became important as more people began to read books.

248 Small pieces of glass can make everything look bigger. Spectacle-makers in Italy in the 14th century made their own glass lenses to look through. These helped people to read small writing. Scientists later used these lenses to invent microscopes, to see very small things, and telescopes, to see things that are far away.

249 Scientists saw the tiny bacteria that cause illness for the first time with microscopes. The Dutch invented the first microscopes, which had one lens. In the 1590s Zacharias Janssen of Holland invented the first microscope with two lenses, which was much more powerful.

◀ Early microscopes with two or more lenses, like those of English inventor Robert Hooke (1635–1703), were powerful, but the image was unclear.

250 The Dutch tried to keep the first telescope a secret. Hans Lippershey invented it in 1608, but news soon got out. Galileo, an Italian scientist, built one in 1609. He used it to get a close look at the Moon and the planets.

QUIZ

1. Which came first, (a) the telescope, or (b) spectacles?
2. Do you study stars with (a) a microscope, or (b) a telescope?
3. Which are smaller, (a) bacteria, or (b) ants

Answers:
1.b 2.b 3.a

251 Modern microscopes make things look thousands of times bigger. A German, Ernst Ruska, invented the first electron microscope in 1933. It made things look 12,000 times their actual size. The latest microscopes can magnify things millions of times.

◀ An electron microscope shows a tiny parasite in monstrous detail, but this tick is actually less than 0.6 inches long.

252 You cannot look through a radio telescope. An American, Grote Reber, invented the first one and built it in his backyard in 1937. Radio telescopes pick up radio signals from space with a dish-shaped receiver. The signals come from distant stars, and, more recently, from space probes.

▶ Most radio telescope dishes can be moved to face in any direction.

Making music

253 Humans are the only animals that play tunes on musical instruments. Stone Age people made the first percussion instruments, such as rattles, from bones and tusks. Modern versions of these instruments are still used in orchestras today.

▼ The instruments of the modern orchestra are grouped into sections according to type— usually string, woodwind, brass, and percussion.

GUIDE TO THE ORCHESTRA

■ **Percussion** instruments, such as drums, produce sound when they are made to vibrate by being hit, rubbed, shaken, or scraped.

■ **Brass** instruments, such as horns, are made of curled brass tubes. Sound is produced by blowing into a cup-shaped mouthpiece.

■ **Woodwind** instruments produce sound when a player blows against an edge (as in flutes) or through a wooden reed (as in clarinets).

■ **String** instruments have strings. They produce sound when their strings are plucked or bowed.

254 Over 20,000 years ago Stone Age Europeans invented whistles and flutes. They made them out of bones or antlers. Modern flutes still work in a similar way—the player covers and uncovers holes in a tube while blowing across it.

255 The earliest harps were made from tortoise shells. They were played in Sumeria and Egypt about 5,000 years ago. Modern harps, like most ancient harps, have strings of different lengths.

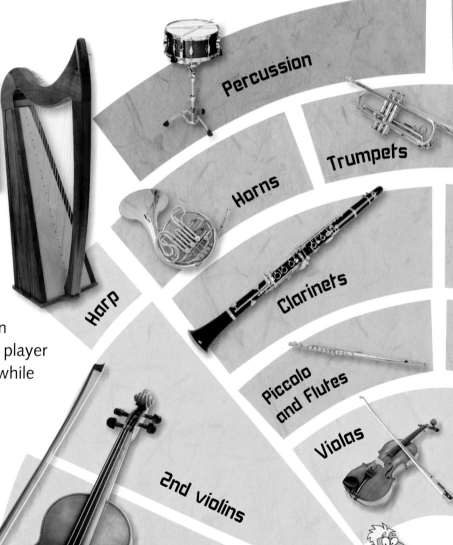

Percussion

Trumpets

Horns

Clarinets

Piccolo and Flutes

Harp

Violas

2nd violins

1st violins

Conductor

▲ The grand piano's strings are laid out horizontally in a harp-shaped frame.

256 Pianos have padded hammers inside, which strike the strings. The first piano-like instrument was invented in about 1480 and its strings were plucked, not struck, when the keys were pressed. It made a softer sound than a modern piano.

257 The trumpet is among the loudest instruments in the orchestra. A trumpetlike instrument was found in Tutankhamen's tomb in Egypt dating back to 1320 BC. Over 2,000 years ago, Celtic warriors in northern Europe blew bronze trumpets shaped like mammoth tusks to frighten their enemies.

Timpani

Trombones

Tubas

Bassoons

Oboes

Double basses

Cellos

◀ The trumpet, played here by award-winning Alison Balsom, has a total tubing length of about 58 inches as well as three moveable valves.

258 Bagpipes sound as strange as they look. They were invented in India over 2,000 years ago. The Roman army had bagpipe players. In the Middle Ages, European and Middle Eastern herdsmen sometimes played bagpipes while they looked after their animals.

▶ Some modern bagpipes still have a bag of sewn animal skins.

Keeping in touch

259 Some African tribes used to use "talking drums" to send messages. Native Americans used smoke signals, visible several miles away. Before electrical inventions such as the telephone, sending long-distance messages had to be a simple process.

260 Wooden arms on tall poles across the country sent signals hundreds of miles in 18th-century France. Claude Chappe invented this system, now called semaphore, in 1797. Until recently, navies used semaphore flags to signal from ship to ship. In 1838 American Samuel Morse invented a code of short and long bursts of electric current or light, called dots and dashes. It could send messages along a wire, or could be flashed with a light.

◀ Skilled morse code operators could send 30 words per minute.

▼ Each position of the semaphore signaler's arms forms a different letter. What does this message say?

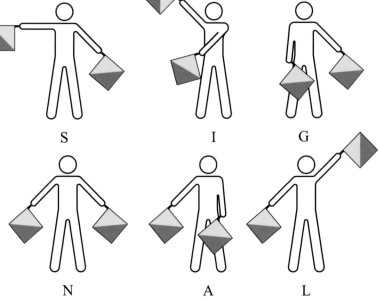

S   I   G

N   A   L

261 The telephone can send your voice around the world. A Scotsman, Alexander Graham Bell, invented it in the 1870s. When you speak, your voice is changed into electric signals that are sent along to a receiver held by the other user. Within 15 years there were 140,000 telephone owners in the United States.

Transmitter   Receiver

▶ Bell's early telephone (top) in 1876 had one of the first electrical loudspeakers. The modern moving-coil design was invented in 1898 by Oliver Lodge.

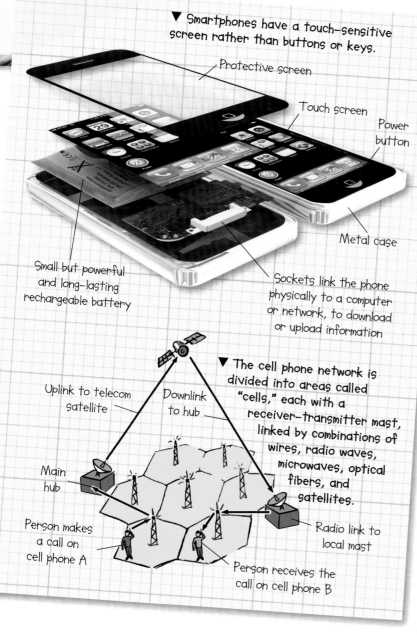

▼ Smartphones have a touch-sensitive screen rather than buttons or keys.

Protective screen

Touch screen

Power button

Metal case

Small but powerful and long-lasting rechargeable battery

Sockets link the phone physically to a computer or network, to download or upload information

▼ The cell phone network is divided into areas called "cells," each with a receiver-transmitter mast, linked by combinations of wires, radio waves, microwaves, optical fibers, and satellites.

Uplink to telecom satellite

Downlink to hub

Main hub

Person makes a call on cell phone A

Radio link to local mast

Person receives the call on cell phone B

262 With a cell phone you can talk to practically anyone wherever you are. Your voice is carried on radio waves or microwaves and passed from antenna to antenna until it reaches the phone you are calling. Some of the antennas are on space satellites.

263 Radio signals fly through the air without wires. An Italian, Guglielmo Marconi, invented the radio or "wireless" in 1899. Radio stations send signals, carried on invisible radio waves, which are received by an antenna. A Scotsman, John Logie Baird, invented an early TV system in 1926. TV pictures can travel through the air or along wires.

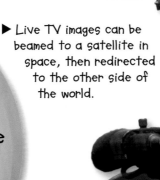

I DON'T BELIEVE IT!

Early TV performers had to wear thick, clownlike makeup. The pictures were so fuzzy that viewers could not make out their faces otherwise.

▶ Live TV images can be beamed to a satellite in space, then redirected to the other side of the world.

TV camera

Keeping a record

▼ Thomas Edison produced many important inventions, including sound recording, electric lightbulbs and an early film-viewing machine.

264 The first sound recording was the nursery rhyme, "Mary had a little lamb." In 1877 an American, Thomas Edison, invented a way of recording sounds by using a needle to scratch marks on a cylinder or tube. Moving the needle over the marks again repeated the sounds. Performers spoke or sang into a horn, and the sounds were also played back through it.

265 To play the first disk records, you had to keep turning a handle. Emile Berliner, a German, invented disk recording in 1887. The disks were played with steel needles, and soon wore out. They also broke easily if you dropped them. Long-playing disks appeared in 1948. They had 20 minutes of sound on each side and were made of flexible plastic, which didn't break so easily.

MODERN MUSIC PLAYER

▲ Digital music players can hold over two weeks of sound recording, played through earphones or a dock with speakers.

▼ Early record players had to be wound up between records, and the loudspeaker was a large horn.

QUIZ
1. Were the first recordings on (a) disks, or (b) cylinders?
2. Which came first, (a) films, or (b) long-playing records?
3. Was the first photograph of (a) flowers, or (b) rooftops?
4. The first films were viewed through a hole in a box—true or false?

Answers:
1.b 2.a 3.b 4.True

266 It took eight hours to take the world's first photograph in 1826. Frenchman Joseph Nicéphore Niépce was the inventor, and the first photograph was of rooftops. Early cameras were huge, and the photos were on glass plates. In 1881 Peter Houston invented rolls of film, which George Eastman developed for the company Kodak, making photography much easier.

▲ Digital cameras have a display screen that shows the view the lens sees, which is the image that will be stored.

▲ The Lumière brothers, who invented the movie projector, also made films and opened the first public cinema.

267 Only one person at a time could watch the first films. The viewer peered through a hole in a box. Thomas Edison's company invented films in 1888. The invention of a projector in 1895 by the French Lumière brothers allowed a whole audience to watch the film on a screen.

▶ Launched in 2001, the iPod took little more than one year to develop.

268 The forerunner of the MP3 player was the portable laser-based CD player. It was more than ten times bigger and heavier than an iPod. Moving it often made the compact disk (CD) skip.

Round the house

269 **A horse and cart were needed to move the first successful vacuum cleaner around.** An English engineer, Hubert Cecil Booth, invented it in 1902. The first "Hoover" electric vacuum cleaner was built from a wooden box, an electric fan, and an old sack in 1907 in America.

▼ Refrigerators were once large, noisy, and had little food space.

▲ Early vacuum cleaners worked by opening and closing a bellows with a handle.

270 **Early refrigerators, invented in the 19th century, killed many people.** They leaked the poisonous gas that was used to cool them. In 1929 the gas was changed to a nonpoisonous one called freon. We now know that freon causes damage to the planet's atmosphere, so that has been changed too.

QUIZ

1. Did the first "Hoover" need (a) a horse, or (b) an electric fan?

2. Were early refrigerators dangerous because (a) they blew up, or (b) they leaked poison gas?

3. The Cretans had china toilets 4,000 years ago —true or false?

Answers:
1.b 2.b 3.False

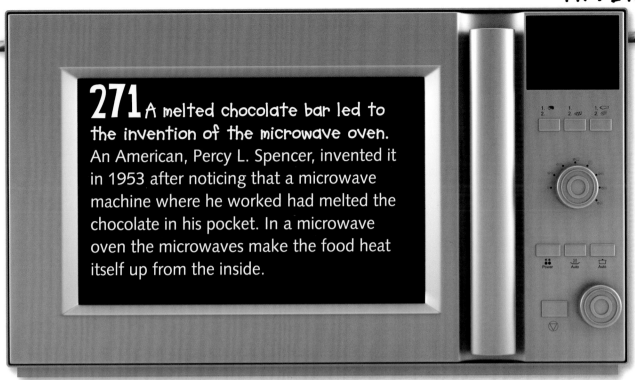

271 A melted chocolate bar led to the invention of the microwave oven. An American, Percy L. Spencer, invented it in 1953 after noticing that a microwave machine where he worked had melted the chocolate in his pocket. In a microwave oven the microwaves make the food heat itself up from the inside.

▲ In a microwave oven the microwaves are deflected by metal vanes down onto the food below.

272 There is no air inside a lightbulb. If there was, it would burn out in no time. The first lightbulbs failed because air could get in. American Thomas Edison invented an air-tight lightbulb in 1879 that could burn for a long time. He opened the first electric light company in 1882.

Vacuum bulb

◀ In a lightbulb, electricity causes a wire filament to glow brightly in the airless bulb.

Filament

▲ Energy-saving bulbs make light using fluorescence, where a chemical substance called phosphor lining the tube glows.

Screw thread

Power contact

273 Four thousand years ago in Crete in Greece the king's palaces had flushing lavatories. They used rainwater. In England, lavatories that flushed when you pulled a handle were invented in the 18th century. In 1885 Thomas Twyford invented the first all-china flushing lavatory.

SPACE

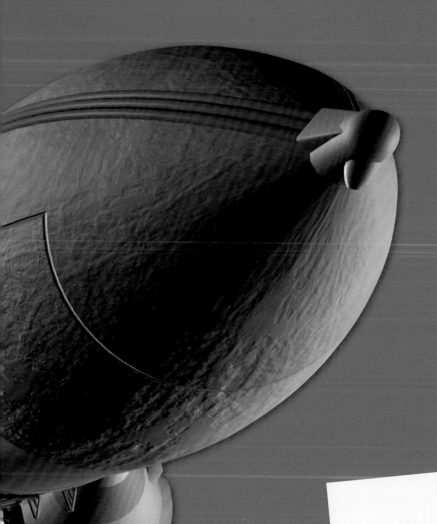

What is a solar flare?

Why are there craters on the Moon?

Where is the largest volcano in the Solar System?

What is it like on Mercury?

Why does Saturn have rings?

274 Space is all around the Earth, high above the air. Here on the Earth we are surrounded by air. If you go upward, up a mountain or in an aircraft, the air grows thinner until there is none at all. Space officially begins 62 miles up from sea level. It is mostly empty, but there are many exciting things such as planets, stars, and galaxies. People who travel in space are called astronauts.

▶ In space, astronauts wear spacesuits to go outside a space station or a spacecraft, such as a space shuttle, as it circles the Earth. Much farther away are planets, stars, and galaxies.

Our life-giving star

275 **The Sun is our nearest star.** It does not look like other stars because it is so much closer to us. Most stars are so far away they look like points of light in the sky. The Sun is not solid like the Earth, but is a giant ball of superhot gases, so hot that they glow like the flames of a bonfire.

SOLAR FLARE

◄ The Sun's hot, glowing gas is always on the move, bubbling up to the surface and sinking back down again.

276 Very little could live on Earth without the Sun. Deep in its center the Sun is constantly making energy that keeps its gases hot and glowing. This energy works its way to the surface where it escapes as heat and light. Without it, the Earth would be cold and dark with hardly any life at all.

SUNSPOT

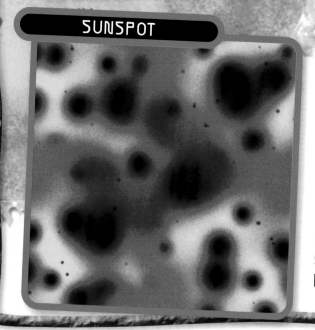

277 The Sun is often spotty. Sunspots appear on the surface, some wider than the Earth. They look dark because they are cooler than the rest of the Sun. Solar flares—explosions of energy—suddenly shoot out from the Sun. The Sun also throws huge loops of gas called prominences out into space.

278 When the Moon hides the Sun there is a solar eclipse. Every so often, the Sun, Moon, and Earth line up in space so that the Moon comes directly between the Earth and the Sun. This stops the sunlight from reaching a small area on Earth. This area grows dark and cold, as if night has come early.

▶ When there is an eclipse, we can see the corona (glowing gas) around the Sun.

Sun

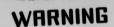

Moon

Total eclipse

Earth

Shadow of eclipse

▲ When the Moon casts a shadow on the Earth, there is a solar eclipse.

I DON'T BELIEVE IT!
The surface of the Sun is nearly 60 times hotter than boiling water. It is so hot it would melt a spacecraft flying near it.

A family of planets

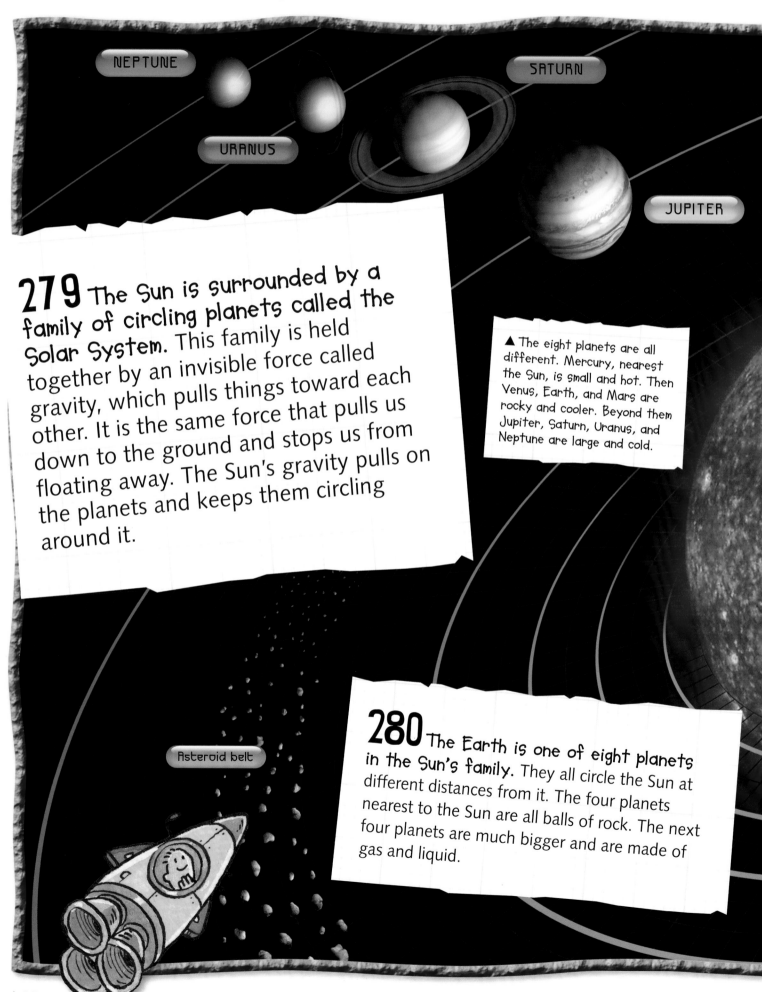

NEPTUNE

URANUS

SATURN

JUPITER

279 The Sun is surrounded by a family of circling planets called the Solar System. This family is held together by an invisible force called gravity, which pulls things toward each other. It is the same force that pulls us down to the ground and stops us from floating away. The Sun's gravity pulls on the planets and keeps them circling around it.

▲ The eight planets are all different. Mercury, nearest the Sun, is small and hot. Then Venus, Earth, and Mars are rocky and cooler. Beyond them Jupiter, Saturn, Uranus, and Neptune are large and cold.

Asteroid belt

280 The Earth is one of eight planets in the Sun's family. They all circle the Sun at different distances from it. The four planets nearest to the Sun are all balls of rock. The next four planets are much bigger and are made of gas and liquid.

281 Moons circle the planets, traveling with them round the Sun. Earth has one moon. It circles the Earth while the Earth circles round the Sun. Mars has two tiny moons, but Mercury and Venus have none at all. There are large families of moons, like miniature solar systems, around all the large gas planets.

I DON'T BELIEVE IT!
If the Sun was the size of a large beach ball, the Earth would be as small as a pea, and the Moon would look like a pinhead.

SUN

MARS

Earth's moon

EARTH

VENUS

MERCURY

282 There are millions of smaller members in the Sun's family. Some are tiny specks of dust speeding through space between the planets. Larger chunks of rock, many as large as mountains, are called asteroids. Comets come from the edge of the Solar System, skimming past the Sun before they disappear again.

Planet of life

283 **The planet we live on is called Earth.** It is a round ball of rock. On the outside, where we live, the rock is hard and solid. But deep below our feet, inside the Earth, the rock is hot enough to melt. You can sometimes see this hot rock showering out of an erupting volcano.

284 **Earth is the only planet with life.** From space the Earth is a blue-and-white planet, with huge oceans and wet masses of cloud. People, animals, and plants can live on Earth because of all this water.

285 **Sunshine gives us daylight when it is night on the other side of the Earth.** When it is daytime, your part of the Earth faces toward the Sun and it is light. At night, your part faces away from the Sun and it is dark. Day follows night because the Earth is always turning.

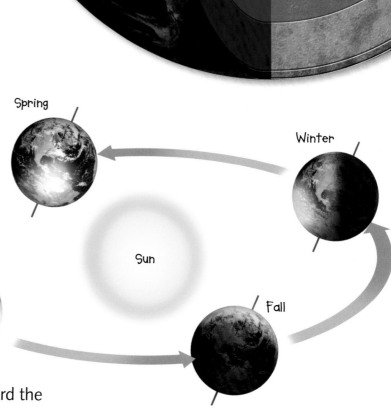

Spring

Winter

Summer

Sun

Fall

▲ The Earth tilts, so we have different seasons as it moves around the Sun. These are the seasons for the northern half of the Earth.

◀ The inner core at the center of the Earth is made of iron. It is very hot and keeps the outer core as liquid. Outside this is the mantle, made of thick rock. The thin surface layer that we live on is called the crust.

KEY

1 Inner core

2 Outer core

3 Mantle

4 Crust

286 Craters on the Moon are scars from space rocks crashing into the surface. When a rock smashes into the Moon at high speed, it leaves a saucer-shaped dent, pushing some of the rock outward into a ring of mountains.

Crater

287 Look for the Moon on clear nights and watch how it seems to change shape. Over a month it changes from a thin crescent to a round shape. This is because sunlight is reflected by the Moon. We see the full Moon when the sunlit side faces the Earth and a thin, crescent shape when most of the sunlit side is facing away from us.

I DON'T BELIEVE IT!

The Moon has no air. When astronauts went to the Moon they had to take air with them in their spacecraft and spacesuits.

The Earth's neighbors

288 Venus and Mars are the nearest planets to the Earth. Venus is closer to the Sun than the Earth while Mars is farther away. Each takes a different amount of time to circle the Sun and we call this its year. A year on Venus is 225 days, on Earth 365 days, and on Mars 687 days.

▲ All we can see of Venus from space are the tops of its clouds. They take just four days to race right around the planet.

289 Venus is the hottest planet. It is hotter than Mercury, although Mercury is closer to the Sun and gets more of the Sun's heat. Heat builds up on Venus because it is completely covered by clouds that trap the heat, like the glass in a greenhouse.

290 Venus has poisonous clouds with drops of acid that would burn your skin. They are not like clouds on Earth, which are made of droplets of water. These thick clouds do not let much sunshine reach the surface of Venus.

▼ Under its clouds, Venus has hundreds of volcanoes, large and small, all over its surface. We do not know if any of them are still erupting.

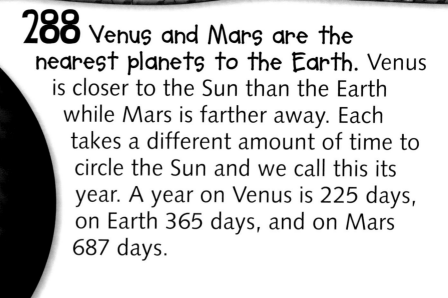

Radio aerial

Solar panel

Camera

▲ *Mariner 9* was the first space probe to circle another planet. Since that time more than 30 other crafts have traveled there and several have soft-landed.

292 Winds on Mars whip up huge dust storms that can cover the whole planet. Mars is very dry, like a desert, and covered in red dust. When a space probe called *Mariner 9* arrived there in 1971, the whole planet was hidden by dust clouds.

291 Mars has the largest volcano in the Solar System. It is called Olympus Mons and is three times as high as Mount Everest, the tallest mountain on Earth. Olympus Mons is an old volcano and it has not erupted for millions of years.

PLANET-SPOTTING

See if you can spot Venus in the night sky. It is often the first bright "star" to appear in the evening, just above where the Sun has set. Because of this we sometimes call it the "evening star."

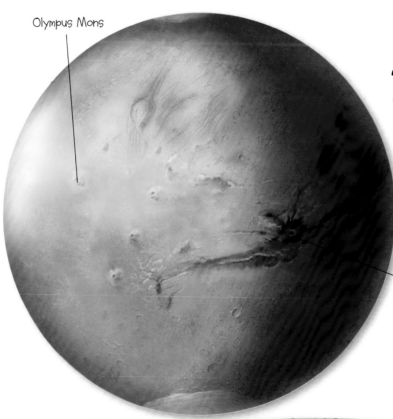

Olympus Mons

Valles Marineris

293 There are plans to send astronauts to Mars but the journey would take six months or more. The astronauts would have to take with them everything they need for the journey there and back and for their stay on Mars.

◀ An enormous valley seems to cut Mars in half. It is called Valles Marineris. To the left is a row of three huge volcanoes and beyond them you can see the largest volcano, Olympus Mons.

The smallest of all

294 Tiny Pluto is so far away, it was not discovered until 1930. In 2006, Pluto was classed as a dwarf planet. It is less than half the width of the smallest planet, Mercury. In fact Pluto is smaller than our Moon.

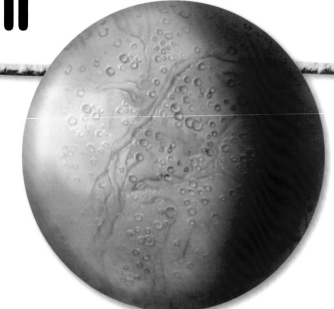

▲ Pluto is too far away to see any detail on its surface, but it might look like this.

295 Pluto is further from the Sun than the eight main planets. It is so far from the Sun that if you stood on its surface, the Sun would not look much brighter than the other stars. Pluto gets little heat from the Sun and is completely covered with ice.

297 The first space probe to visit Pluto will be *New Horizons*. It blasted off in 2006 and is due to reach the dwarf planet by 2015. If all goes well it will then carry on to the outer region of the Solar System, called the Kuiper Belt.

296 No one knew Pluto had a moon until 1978. An astronomer noticed what looked like a bulge on the side of the dwarf planet. It turned out to be a moon half the width of Pluto, called Charon. In 2005 two more tiny moons were found, Nix and Hydra.

▼ If you were on Pluto, its moon Charon would look much larger than our Moon does, because Charon is so close to Pluto.

298 Mercury looks like our Moon.
It is a round, cratered ball of rock. Although
a little larger than the Moon, like the Moon
it has no air.

◀ Mercury's many
craters show how often
it was hit by space rocks.
One was so large that it
shattered rocks on the
other side of the planet.

▼ The Sun looks huge as
it rises on Mercury. A
traveler to Mercury
would have to keep out
of its heat.

299 The sunny side of Mercury is boiling hot but
the night side is freezing cold. Being the nearest planet
to the Sun, the sunny side can get twice as hot as an oven.
But Mercury spins round slowly so the night side has time
to cool down, and there is no air to trap the heat.
The night side becomes more than
twice as cold as the coldest
place on Earth—Antarctica.

The biggest of all

300 Jupiter is the biggest planet, more massive than all the other planets in the Solar System put together. It is 11 times as wide as the Earth although it is still much smaller than the Sun. Saturn, the next largest planet, is more than nine times as wide as the Earth.

301 Jupiter and Saturn are gas giants. They have no solid surface for a spacecraft to land on. All that you can see are the tops of their clouds. Beneath the clouds, the planets are made mostly of gas (like air) and liquid (water is a liquid).

302 The Great Red Spot on Jupiter is a 300-year-old storm. It was first noticed about 300 years ago and is at least twice as wide as the Earth. It rises above the rest of the clouds and swirls around like storm clouds on Earth.

▼ Jupiter's fast winds blow the clouds into colored bands around the planet.

▼ There are many storms on Jupiter but none as large or long lasting as the Great Red Spot.

▼ Jupiter's Moon Io is always changing because its many volcanoes throw out new material from deep inside it.

JUPITER'S MOON IO

THE GREAT RED SPOT

CLOUDS

▶ Although Saturn's rings are very wide, they stretch out in a very thin layer around the planet.

303 The shining rings around Saturn are made of millions of chunks of ice.
These circle the planet like tiny moons and shine by reflecting sunlight from their surfaces. Some are as small as ice cubes while others can be as large as a car.

I DON'T BELIEVE IT!
For its size, Saturn is lighter than any other planet. If there was a large enough sea, it would float like a cork.

304 Jupiter and Saturn spin round so fast that they bulge out in the middle.
This can happen because they are not made of solid rock. As they spin, their clouds are stretched out into light and dark bands around them.

305 Jupiter's moon Io looks a bit like a pizza.
It has many active volcanoes that throw out huge plumes of material, making red blotches and dark marks on its orange-yellow surface.

So far away

▼ There is very little to see on Uranus, just a few wisps of cloud above the greenish haze.

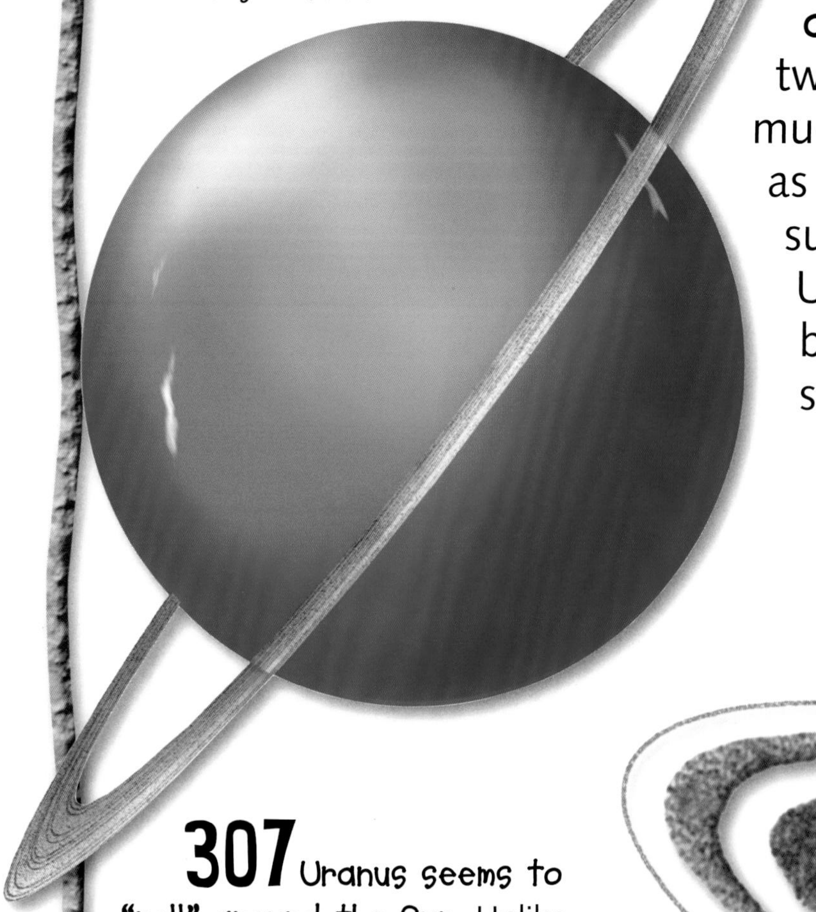

306 Uranus and Neptune are gas giants like Jupiter and Saturn. They are the next two planets beyond Saturn but are much smaller, being less than half as wide. They too have no hard surface. Their cloud tops make Uranus and Neptune both look blue. They are very cold, being so far from the Sun.

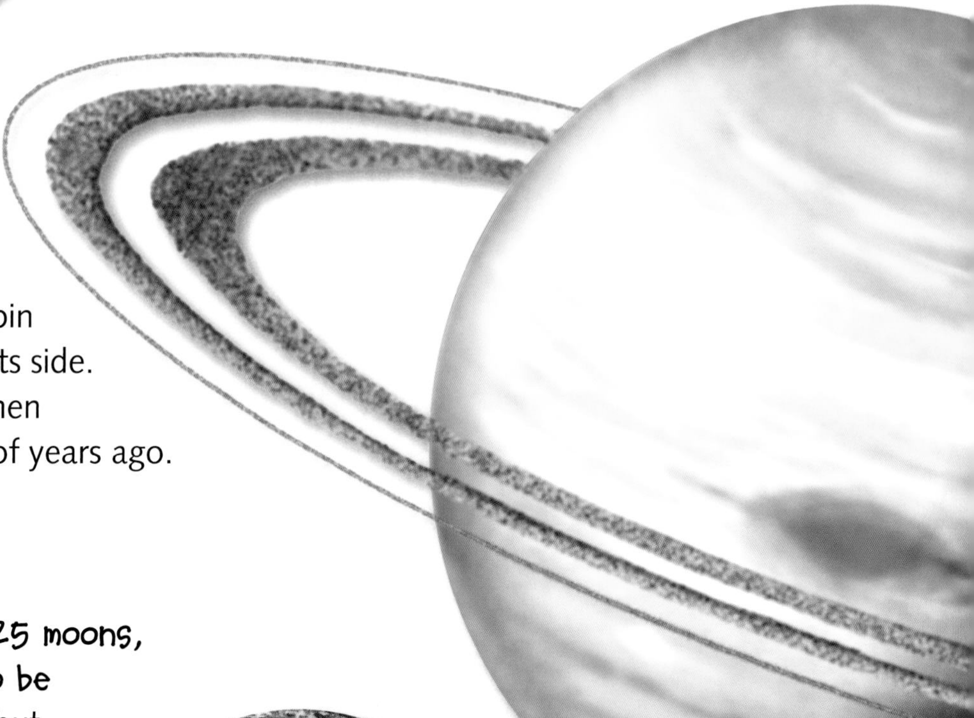

307 Uranus seems to "roll" around the Sun. Unlike most of the other planets, which spin upright like tops, Uranus spins on its side. It may have been knocked over when something crashed into it millions of years ago.

308 Uranus has more than 25 moons, and there are probably more to be discovered. Most are very small, but Titania, the largest, is 978 miles across, which makes it the eighth largest moon in the Solar System.

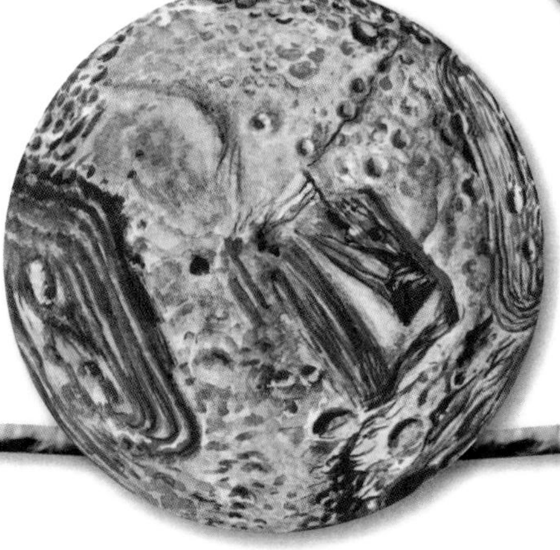

► Miranda is one of Uranus' moons. It looks as though it has been split apart and put back together again.

309 Neptune had a storm that disappeared. When the *Voyager 2* space probe flew past Neptune in 1989 it spotted a huge storm like a dark version of the Great Red Spot on Jupiter. When the Hubble Space Telescope looked at Neptune in 1994, the storm had gone.

311 Neptune has bright blue clouds that make the whole planet look blue. Above these clouds are smaller white streaks. These are icy clouds that race around the planet. One of the white clouds seen by the *Voyager 2* space probe was called "Scooter" because it scooted around the planet so fast.

310 Neptune is sometimes farther from the Sun than Pluto. Planets and dwarf planets go around the Sun on orbits (paths) that look like circles, but Pluto's path is more squashed. This sometimes brings it closer to the Sun than Neptune.

▼ Several dwarf planets orbit farther away than Neptune and Pluto. Eris is probably 1,430 miles across, about the same size as Pluto.

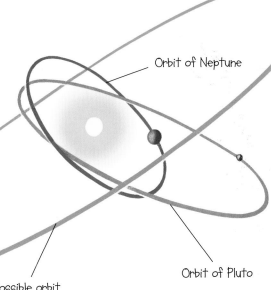

Orbit of Neptune

Possible orbit of Eris

Orbit of Pluto

▲ Like all the gas giant planets, Neptune has rings, although they are much darker and thinner than Saturn's rings.

QUIZ

1. How many moons does Uranus have?
2. Which is the biggest planet in our Solar System?
3. Which planet seems to "roll" around the Sun?
4. What color are Neptune's clouds?

Answers:
1. More than 25 2. Jupiter 3. Uranus 4. Blue

312 There are probably billions of tiny comets at the edge of the Solar System. They circle the Sun far beyond Neptune and even Pluto. Sometimes one is disturbed and moves inward toward the Sun, looping around it before going back to where it came from. Some comets come back to the Sun regularly, such as Halley's comet, which returns every 76 years.

313 A comet is often called a dirty snowball because it is made of dust and ice mixed together. Heat from the Sun melts some of the ice. This makes dust and gas stream away from the comet, forming a huge tail that glows in the sunlight.

▲ The solid part of a comet is hidden inside a huge, glowing cloud that stretches into a long tail.

314 Comet tails always point away from the Sun. Although it looks bright, a comet's tail is extremely thin so it is blown outward, away from the Sun. When the comet moves away from the Sun, its tail goes in front of it.

315 Asteroids are chunks of rock that failed to stick together to make a planet. Most of them circle the Sun between Mars and Jupiter where there would be room for another planet. There are millions of asteroids, some the size of a car, and others as big as mountains.

ASTEROIDS

Asteroids travel in a ring around the Sun. This ring is called the Asteroid belt and can be found between Mars and Jupiter.

316 Meteors are sometimes called shooting stars. They are not really stars, just streaks of light that flash across the night sky. Meteors are made when pebbles racing through space at high speed hit the top of the air above the Earth. The pebble gets so hot it burns up. We see it as a glowing streak for a few seconds.

▼ At certain times of year there are meteor showers, when you can see more shooting stars than usual.

QUIZ

1. Which way does a comet tail always point?
2. What is another name for a meteor?
3. Where is the asteroid belt?

Answers:
1. Away from the Sun
2. Shooting star
3. Between Mars and Jupiter

A star is born

317 Stars are born in clouds of dust and gas called nebulae. Astronomers can see these clouds as shining patches in the night sky, or dark patches against the distant stars. These clouds shrink as gravity pulls the dust and gas together. At the center, the gas gets hotter and hotter until a new star is born.

318 Stars begin their lives when they start making energy. When the dust and gas pulls tightly together it gets very hot. Finally it gets so hot in the middle that it can start making energy. The energy makes the star shine, giving out heat and light like the Sun.

KEY

❶ Clumps of gas in this nebula start to shrink into the tight round balls that will become stars.

❷ The gas spirals round as it is pulled inward. Any left over gas and dust may form planets around the new star.

❸ Deep in its center, the new star starts making energy, but it is still hidden by the cloud of dust and gas.

❹ The dust and gas are blown away and we can see the star shining. Maybe it has a family of planets like the Sun.

319 Young stars often stay together in clusters. When they start to shine they light up the nebula, making it glow with bright colors. Then the starlight blows away the remains of the cloud and we can see a group of new stars, called a star cluster.

STAR CLUSTER

This cluster of young stars, with many stars of different colors and sizes, will gradually drift apart, breaking up the cluster.

QUIZ

1. What is a nebula?
2. How long has the Sun been shining?
3. What color are large hot stars?
4. What is a group of new young stars called?

Answers:
1. A cloud of dust and gas in space 2. About 4.5 billion years 3. Bluish-white 4. Star cluster

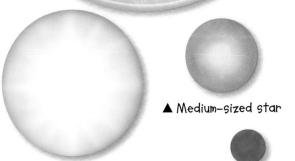

▲ Large white star

▲ Medium-sized star

▲ Small red star

320 Smaller stars live much longer than huge stars. Stars use up their gas to make energy, and the largest stars use up their gas much faster than smaller stars. The Sun is about halfway through its life. It has been shining for about 4.5 billion years and will go on shining for another 4.5 billion years.

BUTTERFLY NEBULA

At the end of its life a red giant star threw out this glowing cloud of gas.

321 Large stars are very hot and white, smaller stars are cooler and redder. A large star can make energy faster and get much hotter than a smaller star. This gives them a very bright, bluish-white color. Smaller stars are cooler. This makes them look red and shine less brightly. Ordinary in-between stars like our Sun look yellow.

Death of a star

322 Stars begin to die when they run out of gas to make energy. The middle of the star begins to shrink but the outer parts expand, making the star much larger.

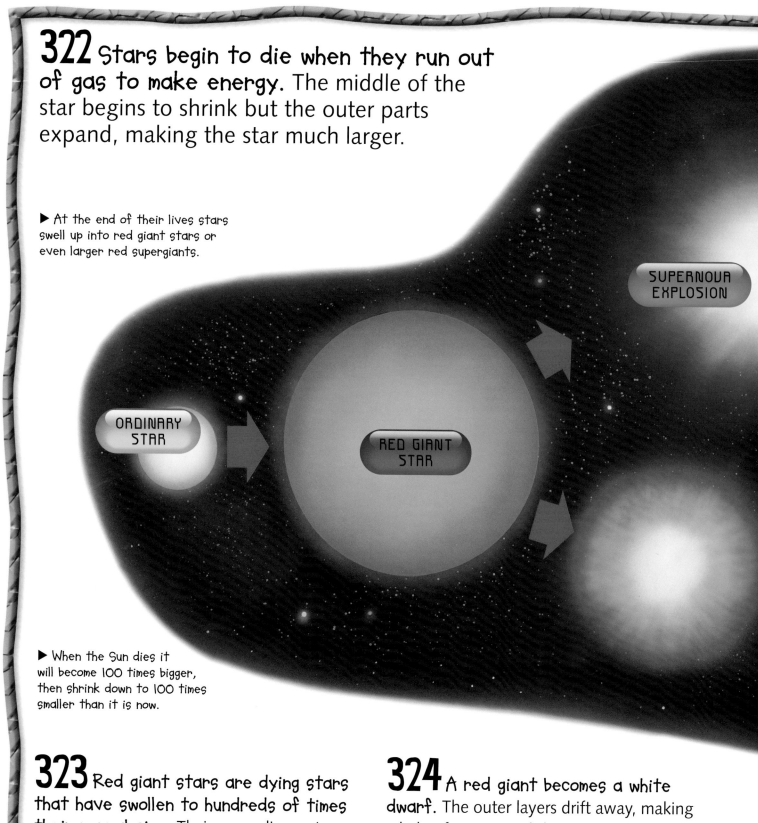

▶ At the end of their lives stars swell up into red giant stars or even larger red supergiants.

ORDINARY STAR

RED GIANT STAR

SUPERNOVA EXPLOSION

▶ When the Sun dies it will become 100 times bigger, then shrink down to 100 times smaller than it is now.

323 Red giant stars are dying stars that have swollen to hundreds of times their normal size. Their expanding outer layers get cooler, making them look red. When the Sun is a red giant it will be large enough to swallow up the nearest planets, Mercury and Venus, and perhaps Earth.

324 A red giant becomes a white dwarf. The outer layers drift away, making a halo of gas around the star. The starlight makes this gas glow and we call it a planetary nebula. All that is left is a small, hot star called a white dwarf, which cannot make energy and gradually cools and dies.

BLACK HOLE

WHITE DWARF STAR

BLACK DWARF STAR

325 Very heavy stars end their lives in a huge explosion called a supernova. This explosion blows away all the outer parts of the star. All that is left is a tiny hot star in the middle of the shell.

◄ After a supernova explosion, a giant star may end up as a very tiny hot star or even a black hole.

I DON'T BELIEVE IT!
One of the main signs of a black hole is flickers of very hot gases near one just before they are sucked in.

SUPERNOVA

326 After a supernova explosion the largest stars may end up as black holes. The remains of the star fall in on itself. As it shrinks, its gravity gets stronger. Eventually the pull of its gravity can get so strong that nothing near it can escape. This is called a black hole.

When a supernova occurs gas rushes outward in all directions, making a glowing shell.

327 The Sun is part of a huge family of stars called the Milky Way Galaxy. There are billions of other stars in our Galaxy, as many as the grains of sand on a beach. We call it the Milky Way because it looks like a very faint band of light in the night sky, as though someone has spilt some milk across space.

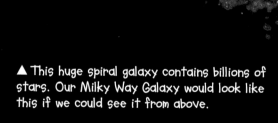

▲ This huge spiral galaxy contains billions of stars. Our Milky Way Galaxy would look like this if we could see it from above.

328 Curling arms give some galaxies their spiral shape. The Milky Way has arms made of bright stars and glowing clouds of gas that curl round into a spiral shape. Some galaxies, called elliptical galaxies, have a round shape like a squashed ball. Other galaxies have no particular shape.

I DON'T BELIEVE IT!
If you could fit the Milky Way onto these two pages, the Sun would be so tiny, you could not see it.

329 There are billions of galaxies outside the Milky Way. Some are larger than the Milky Way and many are smaller, but they all have more stars than you can count. The galaxies tend to stay together in groups called clusters.

330 There is no bump when galaxies collide. A galaxy is mostly empty space between the stars. But when galaxies get very close they can pull each other out of shape. Sometimes they look as if they have grown a huge tail stretching out into space, or their shape may change into a ring of glowing stars.

A CLUSTER OF GALAXIES

Astronomers have nicknamed this interesting cluster of galaxies the "Bullet Cluster." It is made up of two colliding groups of galaxies.

▲ These two galaxies are so close that each has pulled a long tail of bright stars from the other.

▼ From left to right these are spiral, irregular, and elliptical galaxies, and a spiral galaxy with a bar across the middle.

What is the Universe?

331 The Universe is the name we give to everything we know about. This means everything on Earth, from tiny bits of dust to the highest mountain, and everything that lives here, including you. It also means everything in space—all the billions of stars in the billions of galaxies.

332 The Universe started with a massive explosion called the Big Bang. Astronomers think that this happened about 13.7 billion years ago. A huge explosion sent everything racing outward in all directions. To start with, everything was packed incredibly close together. Over time it has expanded (spread out) into the Universe we can see today, which is mostly empty space.

333 The Universe's matter includes planets, stars, and gas, and its energy includes light and heat. Scientists suspect that it also contains unknown dark matter and dark energy, which we are unable to detect. These may affect what finally happens to the Universe.

▼ Astronomers suspect that the universe is primarily made up of dark matter (purple)—a mysterious and unproven substance.

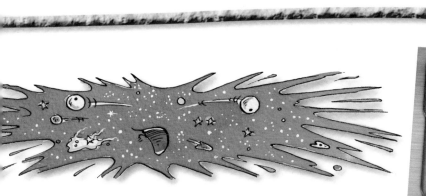

334 **The galaxies are still racing away from each other.** When astronomers look at distant galaxies they can see that other galaxies are moving away from our galaxy, and the more distant galaxies are moving away faster. In fact all the galaxies are moving apart from each other. We say that the Universe is expanding.

DOTTY UNIVERSE

You will need:
balloon   pen
Blow up a balloon a little, holding the neck to stop air escaping. Mark dots on the balloon with a pen, then blow it up some more. Watch how the dots move apart from each other. This is like the galaxies moving apart as the Universe expand.

335 **We do not know what will happen to the Universe billions of years in the future.** It may keep on expanding. If this happens, old stars will gradually die and no new ones will be born. Everywhere will become dark and cold.

KEY

1 All the parts that make up the Universe were once packed tightly together. No one knows why the Universe started expanding with a Big Bang.

2 As everything moved apart in all directions, stars and galaxies started to form.

3 Today there are galaxies of different shapes and sizes, all moving apart. One day they may start moving toward each other.

4 The Universe could stop expanding and stay the same, or shrink and end with a Big Crunch.

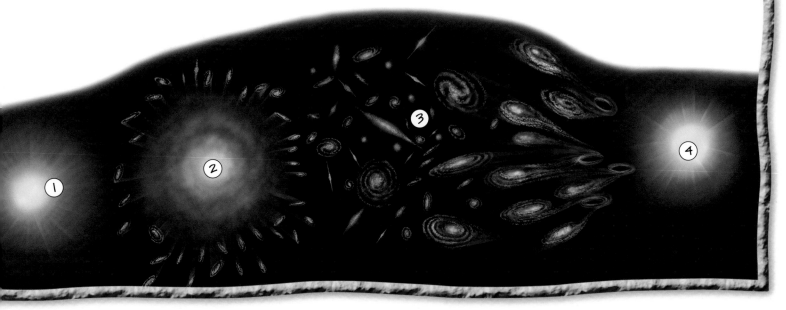

Three, two, one...Liftoff!

336 To blast into space, a rocket has to travel nearly 40 times faster than a jumbo jet. If it goes any slower, gravity pulls it back to Earth. Rockets are powered by burning fuel, which makes hot gases. These gases rush out of the engines, shooting the rocket forward.

▼ In 2007, the Dawn spacecraft started its journey to the asteroid belt tucked inside the nose cone at the top of a Delta II rocket.

Satellite goes into space

Third stage

First stage

Second stage

Booster rockets drop away

▲ Each stage fires its engine to make the rocket go faster and faster until it puts the satellite into space.

337 A single rocket is usually not powerful enough to launch a satellite or spacecraft. So most have two or three stages, which are really separate rockets mounted on top of each other, each with its own engines. When the first stage has used up its fuel it drops away, and the second stage starts. Finally the third stage takes over to go into space.

United State

▼ The shuttle is blasted into space by three rocket engines and two huge booster rockets.

QUIZ

1. Do shuttles use parachutes to stop or to start?
2. How many times faster than a jet does a rocket have to travel to blast into space?
3. How many booster rockets does a shuttle have?

Answers:
1. To stop
2. Forty times faster 3. Two

338 The space shuttles were spaceplanes that could be used over and over again. The first was launched in 1981 and there have been more than 130 missions since. The shuttle took off straight up like a rocket, carrying a load of up to 24 tons. To land it swooped down to glide onto a runway.

▼ The shuttle puts down its wheels and lands on the runway. A parachute and speed brake bring the shuttle to a standstill.

Living in space

339 Space is a dangerous place for astronauts. It can be boiling hot in the sunshine or freezing cold in the Earth's shadow. There is also dangerous radiation from the Sun. Dust, rocks, and bits from other rockets race through space at such speed, they could easily make a small hole in a spacecraft, letting the air leak out.

MANNED MANEUVERING UNIT (JET PACK)

VISOR

CAMERA

JOY STICK CONTROL

▶ Astronauts need advanced spacesuits to protect them from a number of dangers in space.

KEY

❶ Outer layers protect the wearer from the fierce heat of the Sun

❷ Soft lining goes next to the skin

❸ This layer seals the suit from the vacuum of space

❹ Tubes carrying water

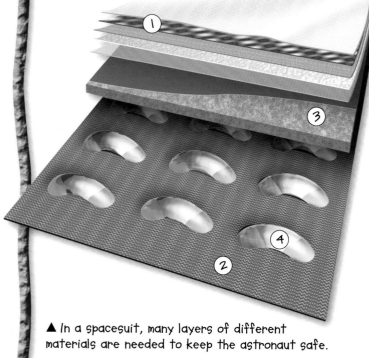

▲ In a spacesuit, many layers of different materials are needed to keep the astronaut safe.

340 Spacesuits protect astronauts when they are out in space. They are very bulky because they are made of many layers to make them strong. They must hold the air for astronauts to breathe and protect them against speeding dust and harmful radiation. To keep the astronauts cool while they work outside the spacecraft, tubes of water under the spacesuit carry away heat.

SPACE MEALS

You will need:

dried noodles   boiling water

Buy a dried snack such as noodles, which just needs boiling water added. This is the kind of food astronauts eat. Most of their meals are dried so they are not too heavy to launch into space.

GLOVE

SPACESUIT

341 Everything floats around in space as if it had no weight. So all objects have to be fixed down or they will float away. Astronauts have footholds to keep them still while they are working. They strap themselves into sleeping bags so they don't bump into things when they are asleep.

342 Astronauts must take everything they need into space with them. Out in space there is no air, water, or food so all the things that astronauts need to live must be packed into their spacecraft and taken with them.

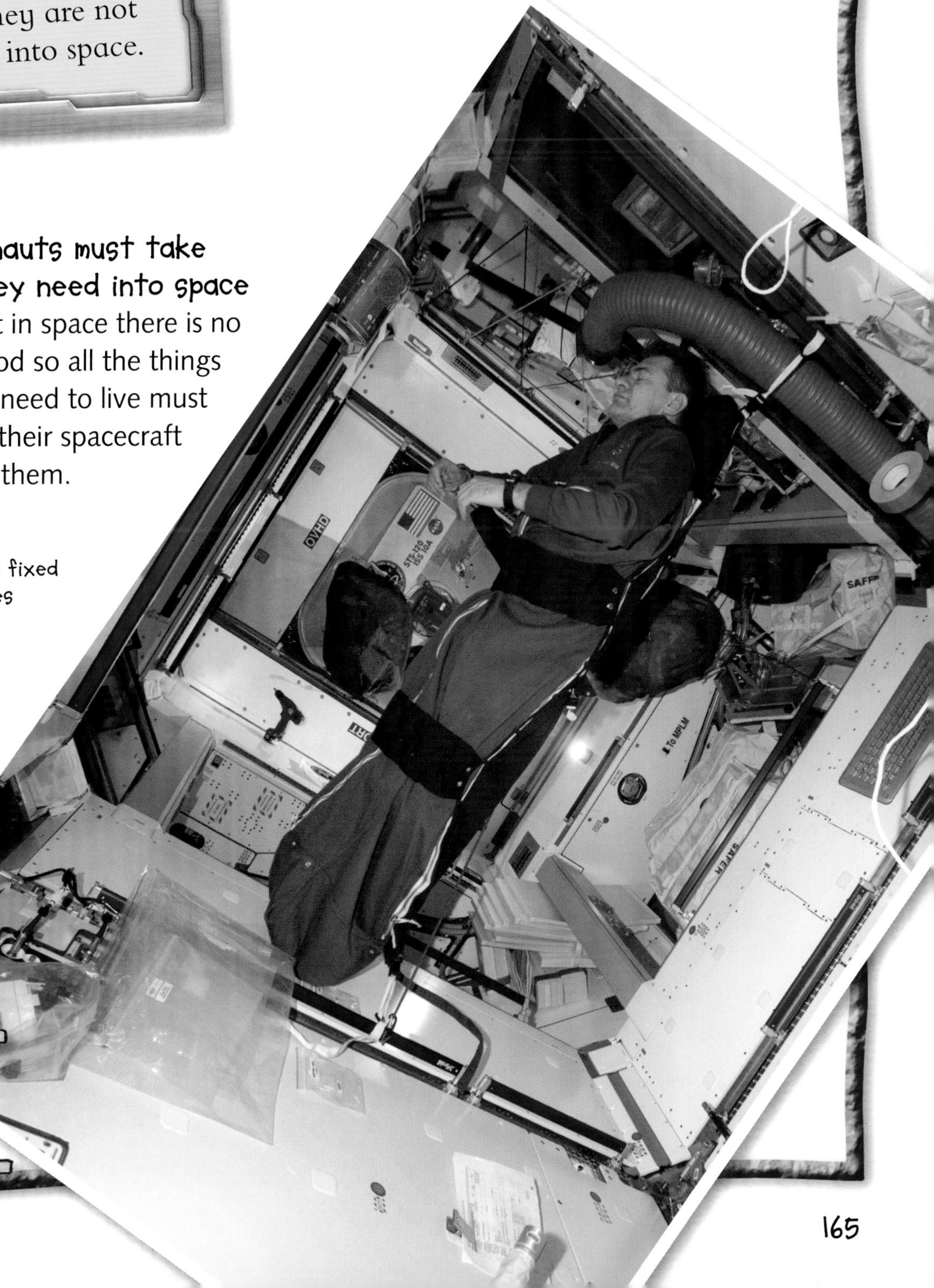

▶ Sleeping bags are fixed to walls so sometimes astronauts look as though they are asleep standing up.

Home from home

343 A space station is a home in space for astronauts and cosmonauts (Russian astronauts). It has a kitchen for making meals, and cabins with sleeping bags. There are lavatories, wash basins, and sometimes showers. There are places to work, and controls where astronauts can check that everything is working properly.

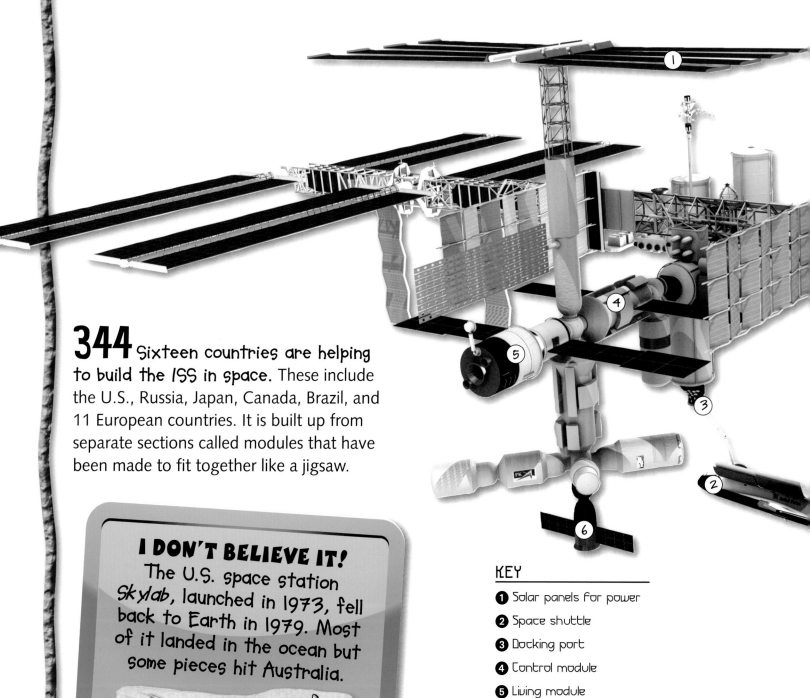

344 Sixteen countries are helping to build the ISS in space. These include the U.S., Russia, Japan, Canada, Brazil, and 11 European countries. It is built up from separate sections called modules that have been made to fit together like a jigsaw.

I DON'T BELIEVE IT!
The U.S. space station *Skylab*, launched in 1973, fell back to Earth in 1979. Most of it landed in the ocean but some pieces hit Australia.

KEY
1 Solar panels for power
2 Space shuttle
3 Docking port
4 Control module
5 Living module
6 Soyuz ferry

345 Each part is launched from Earth and added to the ISS in space. There they are fitted by astronauts at the ISS using the shuttle's robot arm. Huge panels of solar cells have been added. These turn sunlight into electricity to provide a power supply for the space station.

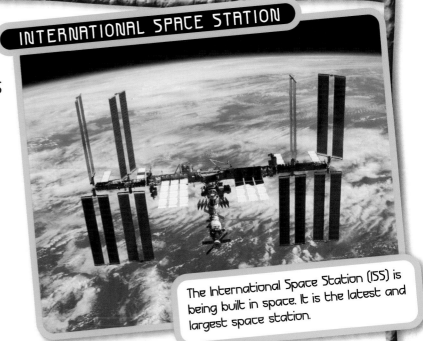

INTERNATIONAL SPACE STATION

The International Space Station (ISS) is being built in space. It is the latest and largest space station.

▼ The International Space Station provides astronauts with a home in space. It is still being constructed while in orbit.

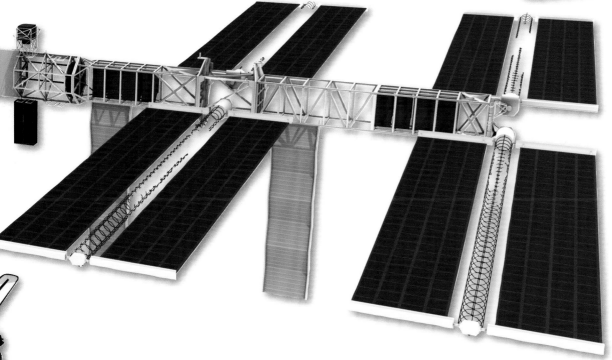

346 The crew live on board the ISS for several months at a time. The first crew of three people arrived at the space station in November 2000 and stayed for over four months. When the space station is finished there will be room for seven astronauts and they will have six modules where they can live and work.

347 Most people and supplies travel to the ISS in Russian *Soyuz* spacecraft. There are also robot ferries with no crew, including Russian *Progress* craft and European ATVs (Automated Transfer Vehicles). In 2001, American Dennis Tito became the first space tourist, staying on the ISS for eight days.

348 Hundreds of satellites circle the Earth in space. They are launched into space by rockets and may stay there for ten years or more.

▼ Weather satellites look down at the clouds and give warning when a violent storm is approaching.

349 Communications satellites carry TV programs and telephone messages around the world. Large aerials on Earth beam radio signals up to a space satellite that then beams them down to another aerial, half way round the world. This lets us talk to people on the other side of the world, and watch events such as the Olympics Games while they are happening in faraway countries.

▼ Communications satellites can beam TV programs directly to your home through your own aerial dish.

350 Weather satellites help the forecasters tell us what the weather will be like. These satellites can see where the clouds are forming and which way they are going. They watch the winds and rain and measure how hot the air and the ground are.

▶ The different satellites each have their own job to do, looking at the Earth, or the weather, or out into space.

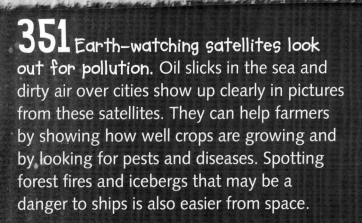

351 Earth-watching satellites look out for pollution. Oil slicks in the sea and dirty air over cities show up clearly in pictures from these satellites. They can help farmers by showing how well crops are growing and by looking for pests and diseases. Spotting forest fires and icebergs that may be a danger to ships is also easier from space.

▶ Satellite telescopes let astronomers look far out into the Universe and discover what is out there.

▼ Pictures of the Earth taken by satellites can help make very accurate maps.

352 Satellite telescopes let astronomers look at exciting things in space. They can see other kinds of radiation, such as X-rays, as well as light. X-ray telescopes can tell astronomers where there may be a black hole.

I DON'T BELIEVE IT!
Spy satellites circling the Earth take pictures of secret sites around the world. They can listen to secret radio messages from military ships or aircraft.

353 The first men landed on the Moon in 1969. They were two astronauts from the U.S. *Apollo 11* mission. Neil Armstrong was the first person to set foot on the Moon. Only five other *Apollo* missions have landed on the Moon since then.

354 The giant *Saturn 5* rocket launched the astronauts on their journey to the Moon. It was the largest rocket that had ever been built. Its three huge stages lifted the astronauts into space, and then the third stage gave the spacecraft an extra boost to send it to the Moon.

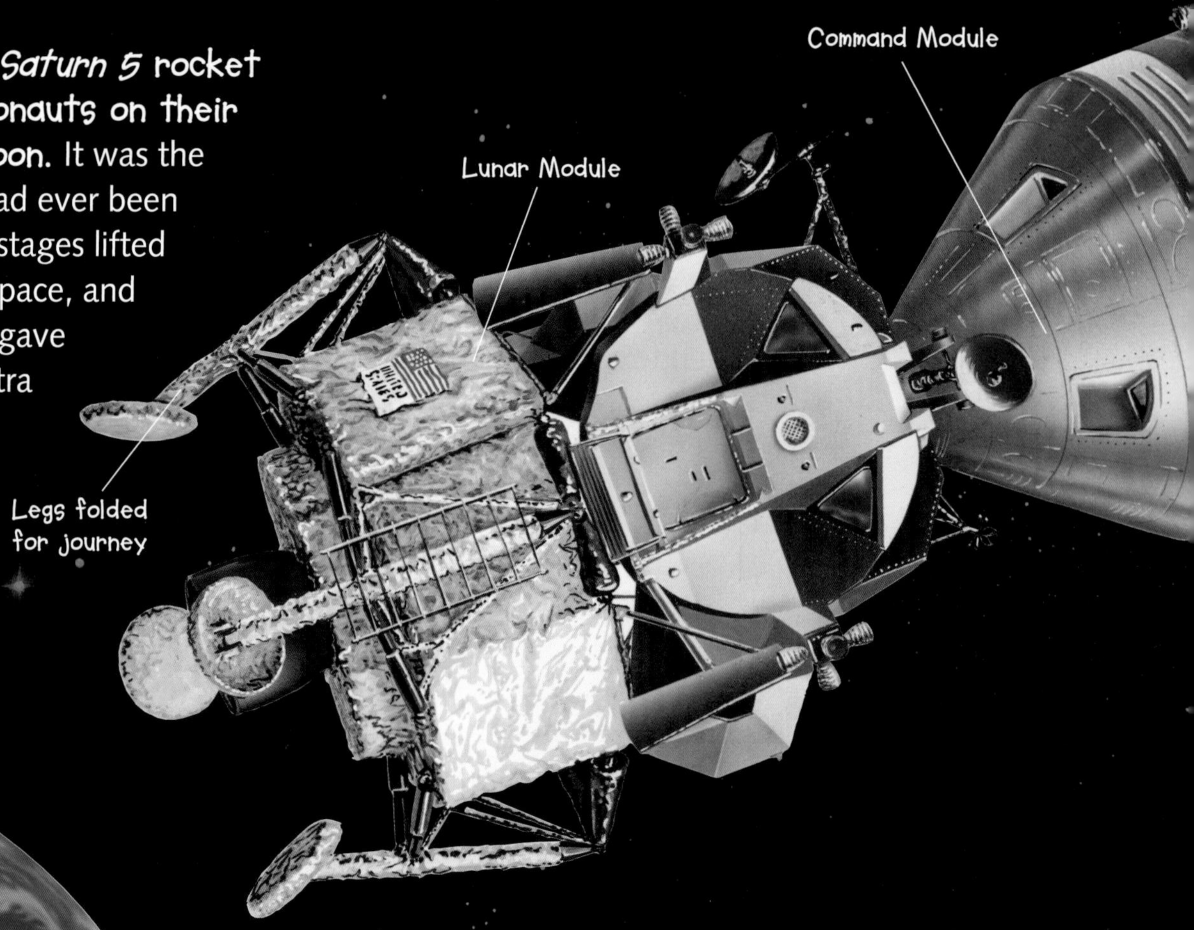

Command Module

Lunar Module

Legs folded for journey

◄ The distance from the Earth to the Moon is nearly 250,000 miles. That is about as far as traveling round the Earth ten times.

355 The Command Module that carried the astronauts to the Moon had no more room than an estate car. The astronauts were squashed inside it for the journey, which took three days to get there and another three to get back. On their return, the Command Module with the astronauts inside, splashed down in the sea.

▼ The Lunar and Command Modules traveled to the Moon fixed together, then separated for the Moon landing.

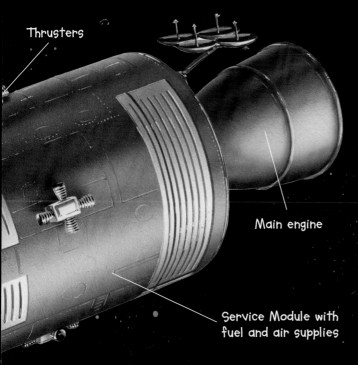

Thrusters

Main engine

Service Module with fuel and air supplies

▲ The longest time that any of the *Apollo* missions stayed on the Moon was just over three days.

356 No one has been back to the Moon since the last *Apollo* mission left in 1972. Maybe one day people will return to the Moon and build bases where they can live and work.

357 The Lunar Module took two of the astronauts to the Moon's surface. Once safely landed they put on spacesuits and went outside to collect rocks. Later they took off in the Lunar Module to join the third astronaut who had stayed in the Command Module, circling above the Moon on his own.

358 The Lunar Rover was a moon car for the astronauts to ride on. It looked like a buggy with four wheels and two seats. It could only travel about as fast as you can run. The astronauts drove for up to 12 miles at a time, exploring the Moon's hills, valleys, flat plains, and cliffs.

I DON'T BELIEVE IT!
On the way to the Moon an explosion damaged the *Apollo 13* spacecraft, leaving the astronauts with little heat or light.

Are we alone?

359 **The only life we have found so far in the Universe is here on Earth.** Everywhere you look on Earth from the frozen Antarctic to the hottest, driest deserts, on land and in the sea, there are living things. Some are huge, such as whales and elephants, and others are much too small to see. But they all need water to live.

▼ On Earth, animals can live in many different habitats, such as in the sea, the air, in deserts and jungles, and icy lands. Try and list as many animals as you can that live in the habitats below.

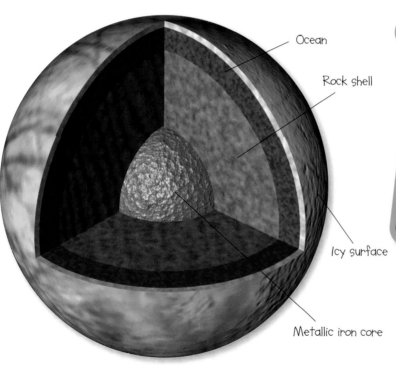

Ocean

Rock shell

Icy surface

Metallic iron core

▲ Deep beneath the cracked, icy surface of Europa, it may be warm enough for the ice to melt into water.

360 **There may be an underground ocean on Europa, one of Jupiter's moons.** Europa is a little smaller than our Moon and is covered in ice. However, astronomers think that there may be an ocean of water under the ice. If so, there could be strange living creatures swimming around deep underground.

DESERT

SEA

POLAR LANDS

RAIN FOREST

362 Astronomers have found planets circling other stars, called exoplanets. Most of them are large, like Jupiter. But perhaps some could be smaller, like Earth. They could have a rocky surface that is not too hot or too cold, and suitable for liquid water—known as "Goldilocks planets" after the fairytale character who tried the three bears' porridge. These planets could support some kind of life.

▲ No one knows what other exoplanets would be like. They could have strange moons or colorful rings. Anything that lives there might look very strange to us.

361 Mars seems to have had rivers and seas billions of years ago. Astronomers can see dry riverbeds and ridges that look like ocean shores on its surface. This makes them think Mars may have been warm and wet long ago and something may once have lived there. Now it is very cold and dry with no sign of life.

I DON'T BELIEVE IT!
It would take thousands of years to get to the nearest stars with our present spacecraft.

▲ This message could tell people living on distant planets about the Earth, and the people who live here.

363 Scientists have sent a radio message to a distant group of stars. They are hoping that anyone living there will understand the message about life on Earth. However, it will take 25,000 years to get to the stars and another 25,000 years for a reply to come back to Earth!

EXPLORING SPACE

- The first satellites
- Apollo Moon landings
- Planning a mission
- Escape velocity
- Flyby missions
- Engines and fuel
- Orbiters
- Landing on a new world
- Exploring Mars
- Missions to the Sun

Where are spacecraft tested?
What does a spectrometer do?
How far is it to Mars?
Where did Voyager 2 go?
Why are some crafts designed to crash?

364 For thousands of years people gazed up at the night sky and wondered what it would be like to explore space. This became a reality around 50 years ago, and since then humans have been to the Moon, and unmanned spacecraft have visited all of the planets in the Solar System. Spacecraft have also explored other planets' moons, asteroids, and glowing comets. These amazing discoveries help us to understand the Universe.

▶ ESA's *Integral* satellite (launched in 2002) is deployed from a Proton rocket to observe invisible gamma rays in space. Since 1957, humans have sent spacecraft to all eight planets in the Solar System, as well as more than 50 moons, asteroids, and comets.

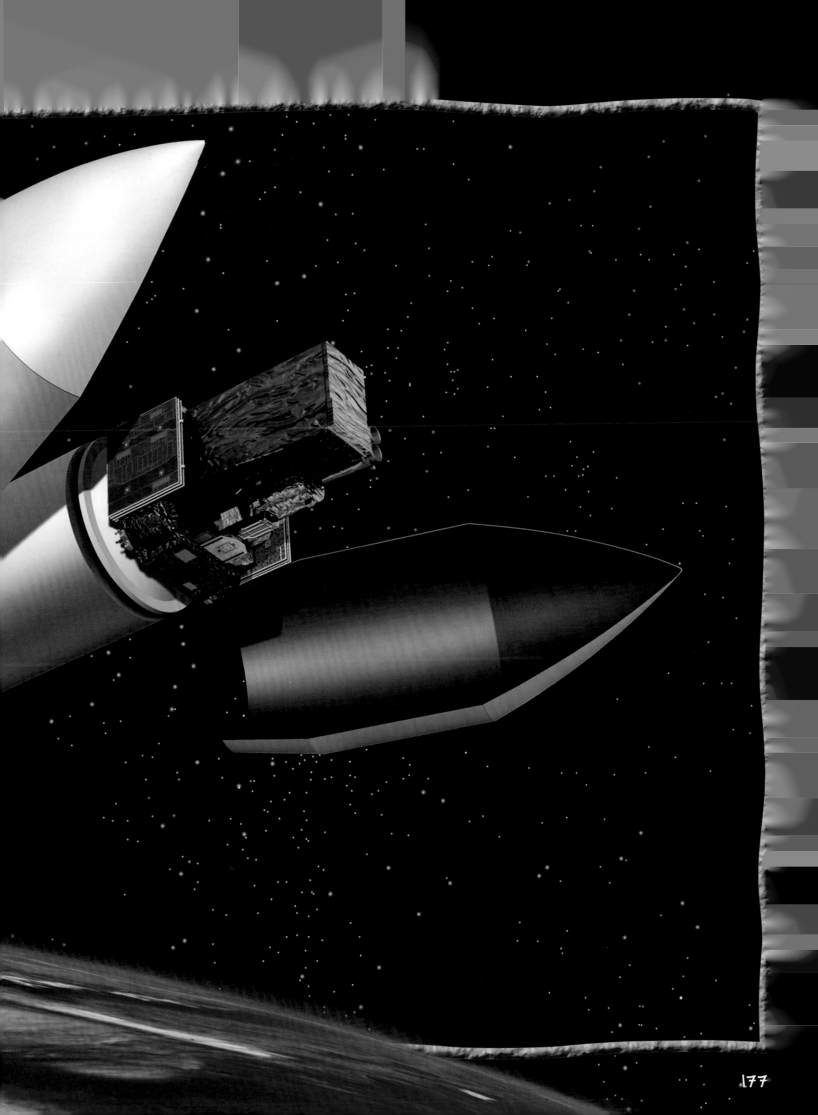

Who explores, and why?

365 Exploring space involves sending craft, robots, equipment, and sometimes people to planets, moons, asteroids, and comets. Some craft fly near to their targets, while others land. As they explore, they gather information to send back to Earth.

366 Space exploration is different from other space sciences. For example, astronomy is the study of objects in space including planets, stars, and galaxies, as well as the Universe as a whole. Much of this is done using telescopes, rather than traveling out into space.

Vandenberg Air Force Base and Spaceport, California

NORTH AMERICA

NASA Headquarters, Washington D.C.

Kennedy Space, Center, Florida

Alcantara Launch Center, Sao Luis, Brazil

Guiana Space Centre, Kourou, French Guiana

SOUTH AMERICA

▼ Astronomers use huge, extremely powerful telescopes to observe outer space from Earth.

▲ Space mission headquarters and launch sites are spread across the world.

367 Space exploration is complicated and expensive. Generally, only large nations, such as the USA, Russia, Japan, and Europe, send craft into space. Recently, China and India have also launched exploratory missions.

368 Sending even a small spacecraft into space costs vast amounts of money. The Japanese *Hayabusa* mission to bring back samples of the comet Itokawa began in 2003. It lasted seven years and cost around $170 million. Sending the *Phoenix* lander to Mars in 2008 was even more expensive, at $450 million dollars.

▶ The comet-visiting *Hayabusa* spacecraft blasted off from Uchinoura Space Center, Japan, in 2003. It returned to Earth in 2010, carrying samples of comet dust.

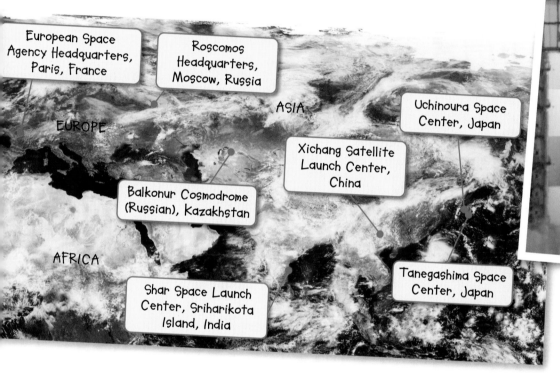

European Space Agency Headquarters, Paris, France

Roscomos Headquarters, Moscow, Russia

ASIA

EUROPE

Uchinoura Space Center, Japan

Xichang Satellite Launch Center, China

Balkonur Cosmodrome (Russian), Kazakhstan

AFRICA

Tanegashima Space Center, Japan

Shar Space Launch Center, Sriharikota Island, India

▼ Recent observations in space suggest faraway stars could have planets forming around them from bits of gas, dust, and rock—similiar to our own Solar System.

369 If the costs are so great, why do we explore space? Exploring the unknown has long been a part of human nature. Space exploration provides clues that may help us to understand how the Universe formed. Progress in space technology can also help advances on Earth.

179

Early explorers

370 The Space Age began in 1957 when Russia launched Sputnik 1, the first Earth-orbiting satellite. It was a metal, ball-shaped craft that could measure pressure and temperature, and send radio signals back to Earth.

371 In 1958, the U.S. launched the satellite *Explorer 1*. As it orbited the Earth it detected two donut-shaped belts of high-energy particles, known as the Van Allen Belts. They can damage spacecraft and interfere with radio signals.

◀ The Van Allen belts are made up of particles, trapped by Earth's natural magnetic field.

Inner belt

Outer belt

▼ Tracking *Sputnik 1*'s orbit showed how the upper atmosphere of the Earth fades into space.

Heat-resistent outer casing

Inner casing

Batteries

372 In 1959, Russia's *Luna 1* spacecraft was aiming for the Moon, but it missed. Later that year, *Luna 2* crashed into the Moon on purpose, becoming the first craft to reach another world. On its way down the craft measured the Moon's gravity and magnetism.

Antennas

Ventilation fan

QUIZ

Early exploration was a "Space Race" between the U.S. and the Soviet Union. Which had these "firsts?"
1. First satellite in space
2. First person in space
3. First craft on the Moon
4. First person on the Moon

Answers:
1,2,3 – Russia 4 – U.S.

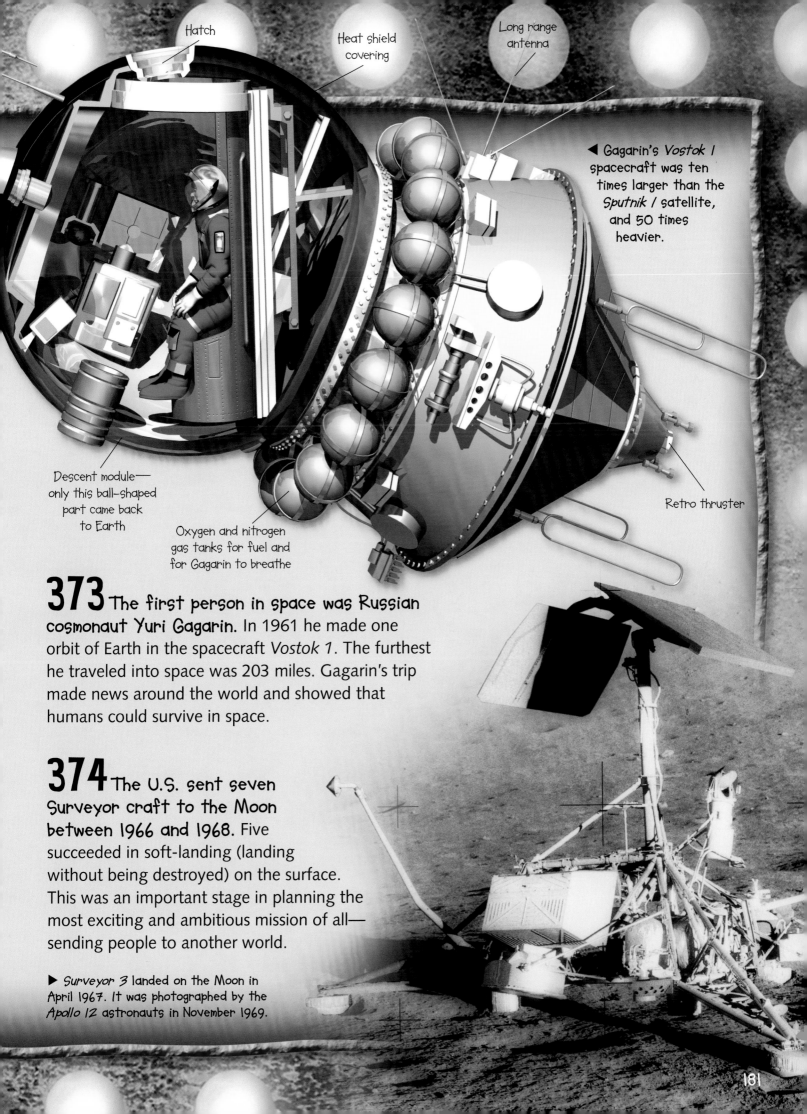

Hatch

Heat shield covering

Long range antenna

◀ Gagarin's *Vostok 1* spacecraft was ten times larger than the *Sputnik 1* satellite, and 50 times heavier.

Descent module—only this ball-shaped part came back to Earth

Oxygen and nitrogen gas tanks for fuel and for Gagarin to breathe

Retro thruster

373 The first person in space was Russian cosmonaut Yuri Gagarin. In 1961 he made one orbit of Earth in the spacecraft *Vostok 1*. The furthest he traveled into space was 203 miles. Gagarin's trip made news around the world and showed that humans could survive in space.

374 The U.S. sent seven Surveyor craft to the Moon between 1966 and 1968. Five succeeded in soft-landing (landing without being destroyed) on the surface. This was an important stage in planning the most exciting and ambitious mission of all—sending people to another world.

▶ *Surveyor 3* landed on the Moon in April 1967. It was photographed by the *Apollo 12* astronauts in November 1969.

181

Man on the Moon!

375 The only humans to have explored another world are 12 U.S. astronauts that were part of the Apollo program. Six Apollo missions landed on the Moon between 1969 and 1972, each with two astronauts. First to step onto the surface were Neil Armstrong and Buzz Aldrin from *Apollo 11*, on July 20, 1969.

376 Each Apollo lunar lander touched down on a different type of terrain. The astronauts stayed on the Moon for three or four days. They explored, carried out experiments, and collected samples of Moon dust and rocks to bring back to Earth.

377 The last three Apollo missions took a Lunar Roving Vehicle (LRV), or "Moon buggy." The astronauts drove for up to 12 miles at a time, exploring the Moon's hills, valleys, flat plains, and cliffs.

378 Since the Apollo missions, more than 50 unmanned spacecraft have orbited or landed on the Moon. In 1994, U.S. orbiter *Clementine* took many photographs, gravity readings, and detailed maps of the Moon's surface.

◀ *Apollo 15*'s Lunar Module pilot James Irwin salutes the U.S. flag and his Commander David Scott, in 1971. Their Lunar Module lander is behind and the Moon buggy is to the right.

MISSION	DATE	CREW	ACHIEVEMENT
Apollo 11	July 1969	Neil Armstrong (C) Buzz Aldrin (LMP) Michael Collins (CMP)	First humans on another world
Apollo 12	November 1969	Pete Conrad (C) Alan Bean (LMP) Richard Gordon (CMP)	First color television pictures of the Moon returned to Earth
Apollo 13	April 1970	James Lovell (C) Fred Haise (LMP) Ken Mattingly (CMP)	*Apollo 13* turned back after launch because of an explosion. It never reached the Moon, but returned safely to Earth
Apollo 14	January–February 1971	Alan Shepard (C) Edgar Mitchell (LMP) Stuart Roosa (CMP)	Longest Moon walks in much improved spacesuits
Apollo 15	July–August 1971	David Scott (C) James Irwin (LMP) Alfred Worden (CMP)	First use of a Moon buggy allowed astronauts to explore a wider range
Apollo 16	April 1972	John Young (C) Charles Duke (LMP) Thomas Mattingly (CMP)	First and only mission to land in the Moon's highlands
Apollo 17	December 1972	Eugene Cernan (C) Harrison Schmitt (LMP) Ronald Evans (CMP)	Returned a record 108 pounds of rock and dust samples

379 In 2009, the *Lunar Reconnaissance Orbiter* began mapping the Moon's surface in detail. Its pictures showed parts of the Apollo craft left by the astronauts. In the same year the Indian orbiter *Chandrayaan 1* discovered ice on the Moon.

◀ On each mission, the Commander (C) and the Lunar Module pilot (LMP) landed on the Moon, while the Command Module pilot (CMP) stayed in the orbiting craft.

380 Planning a mission takes many years. Scientists suggest places to explore, what might be discovered, and the cost. Their government must agree for the mission to go ahead.

▲ In 1961 U.S. space engineer John Houbolt developed the idea of using a three-part spacecraft for the Apollo Moon missions.

381 There are many types of exploratory missions. A flyby takes the spacecraft near to its target world, and past. An orbiter circles around the target. A lander mission touches down on the surface. A lander may release a rover, which can travel around on the surface.

▲ For worlds with an atmosphere, parachutes are used to lower a lander gently. This parachute design for a planned mission to Mars is being tested in the world's biggest wind tunnel in California.

382 The constantly changing positions of Earth and other objects in space mean there is a limited "launch window" for each mission. This is when Earth is in the best position for a craft to reach its target in the shortest time. If the launch window is missed, the distances may become too massive.

▼ The *New Horizons* spacecraft was assembled and checked in perfectly clean, dust-free conditions before being launched to Pluto in 2006.

383 In space, repairs are difficult or impossible. Exploring craft must be incredibly reliable, with tested and proven technology. Each piece of equipment needs a backup, and even if this fails, it should not affect other parts.

384 A spacecraft must be able to cope with the conditions in space and on other worlds. It is incredibly cold in space, but planets such as Venus are hotter than boiling water. Other planets have hazards such as clouds made of tiny drops of acid.

▶ The spacecraft *Galileo* was tested in ultra-bright light of the same level that it would receive as it flew nearer the Sun in 1990 on its way to Jupiter.

385 A test version of the spacecraft is tried on Earth. If successful, the real craft is built in strict conditions. One loose screw or speck of dust could cause disaster. There's no second chance once the mission begins.

I DON'T BELIEVE IT!

The robot submarine *Endurance*, which may one day explore oceans on distant planets or moons, has been tested in frozen lakes in Antarctica and near-boiling pools in New Zealand.

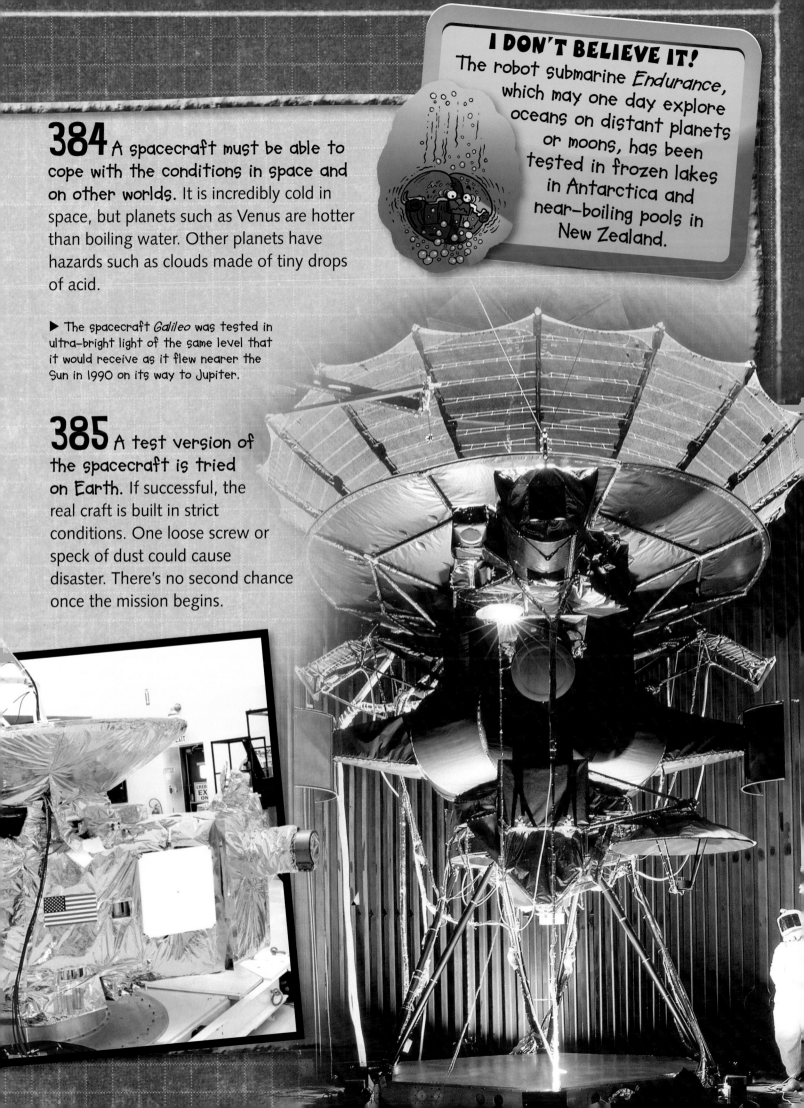

Blastoff!

386 A spacecraft is blasted into space by its launch vehicle, or rocket. The rocket is the only machine powerful enough to reach "escape velocity"—the speed needed to break free from the pull of Earth's gravity. The spacecraft is usually folded up in the nose cone of the rocket.

387 Spacecraft and other objects carried by the rocket are called the "payload." Most rockets take their payload into orbit around the Earth. The nose cone opens to release the craft stored inside. Parts of it unfold, such as the solar panels that turn sunlight into electricity.

388 Different sizes of rockets are used for different sizes of spacecraft. One of the heaviest was the *Cassini-Huygens* mission to Saturn. At its launch in 1997, with all its fuel and equipment on board, it weighed 6.3 tons—almost as much as a school bus. It needed a huge *Titan IV* rocket launcher to power it into space.

Launch point

Escape velocity

Orbit bound by Earth's gravity

◄ Launch vehicles must quickly reach escape velocity—36,700 feet per second—to shrug off Earth's gravitational pull.

SECOND STAGE (S-II)
The middle section of the launcher had five J-2 rocket engines. It was 82 feet tall, and like the first stage, was 33 feet wide.

FIRST STAGE (S-IC)
The bottom part of *Saturn V* was 138 feet tall. The F-1 rocket engines propelled the entire launch vehicle for the first 37 miles.

J-2 rocket engines

F-1 rocket engines

▲ The biggest launchers were the three-stage *Saturn V* rockets used to launch the Apollo missions. Each stage fell away after using up its fuel.

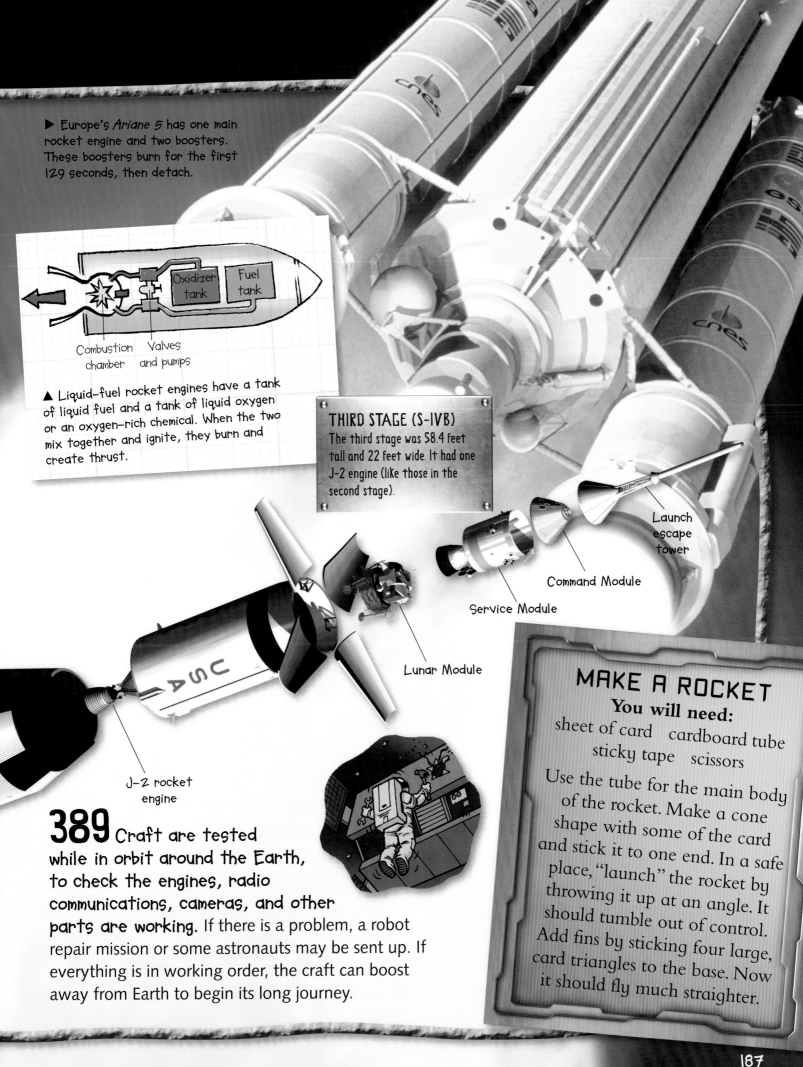

► Europe's *Ariane 5* has one main rocket engine and two boosters. These boosters burn for the first 129 seconds, then detach.

Combustion chamber   Valves and pumps

Oxidizer tank   Fuel tank

▲ Liquid-fuel rocket engines have a tank of liquid fuel and a tank of liquid oxygen or an oxygen-rich chemical. When the two mix together and ignite, they burn and create thrust.

THIRD STAGE (S-IVB)
The third stage was 58.4 feet tall and 22 feet wide. It had one J-2 engine (like those in the second stage).

Launch escape tower

Command Module

Service Module

Lunar Module

J-2 rocket engine

389 Craft are tested while in orbit around the Earth, to check the engines, radio communications, cameras, and other parts are working. If there is a problem, a robot repair mission or some astronauts may be sent up. If everything is in working order, the craft can boost away from Earth to begin its long journey.

MAKE A ROCKET
You will need:
sheet of card   cardboard tube
sticky tape   scissors

Use the tube for the main body of the rocket. Make a cone shape with some of the card and stick it to one end. In a safe place, "launch" the rocket by throwing it up at an angle. It should tumble out of control. Add fins by sticking four large, card triangles to the base. Now it should fly much straighter.

390 Most spacecraft travel for months, even years, to their destinations. The fastest journey to Mars took just over six months, by *Mars Express* in 2003. *Pioneer 10* took 11 years to reach Neptune in 1983.

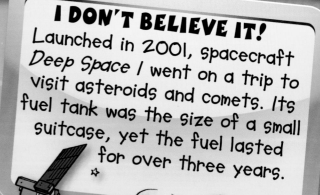

I DON'T BELIEVE IT!

Launched in 2001, spacecraft *Deep Space 1* went on a trip to visit asteroids and comets. Its fuel tank was the size of a small suitcase, yet the fuel lasted for over three years.

◀ *Mars Express* cruised at a speed of 6,700 miles an hour on its way to Mars.

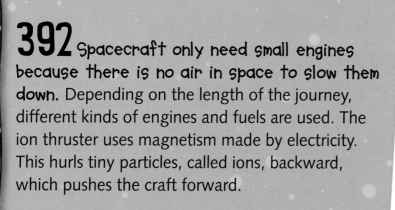

391 Guiding the craft on its course is vital. A tiny error could mean that it misses its distant target by millions of miles. Mission controllers on Earth regularly check the craft's position with radio signals using the Deep Space Network (DSN). The DSN is made up of three huge radio dishes located in California, Madrid in Spain, and Canberra, Australia.

▼ This ion thruster is being tested in a vacuum chamber. The blue glow is the beam of charged atoms being thrown out of the engine.

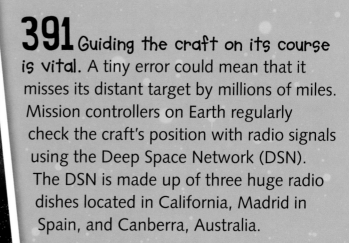

392 Spacecraft only need small engines because there is no air in space to slow them down. Depending on the length of the journey, different kinds of engines and fuels are used. The ion thruster uses magnetism made by electricity. This hurls tiny particles, called ions, backward, which pushes the craft forward.

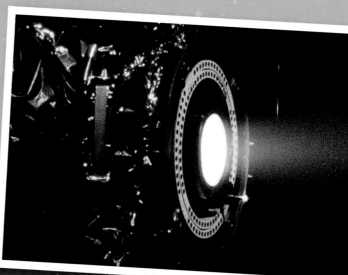

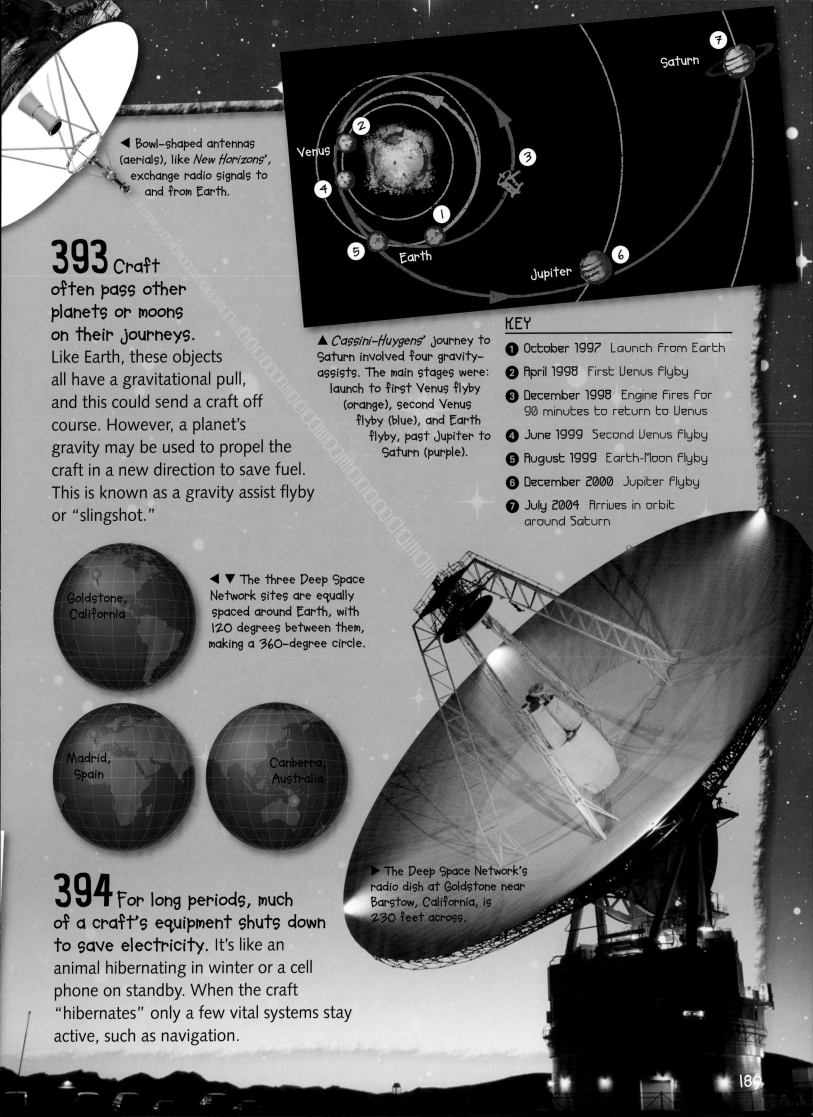

◀ Bowl-shaped antennas (aerials), like *New Horizons'*, exchange radio signals to and from Earth.

393 Craft often pass other planets or moons on their journeys. Like Earth, these objects all have a gravitational pull, and this could send a craft off course. However, a planet's gravity may be used to propel the craft in a new direction to save fuel. This is known as a gravity assist flyby or "slingshot."

▲ *Cassini-Huygens'* journey to Saturn involved four gravity-assists. The main stages were: launch to first Venus flyby (orange), second Venus flyby (blue), and Earth flyby, past Jupiter to Saturn (purple).

Venus

Saturn

Earth

Jupiter

KEY

❶ October 1997 Launch from Earth

❷ April 1998 First Venus flyby

❸ December 1998 Engine fires for 90 minutes to return to Venus

❹ June 1999 Second Venus flyby

❺ August 1999 Earth-Moon flyby

❻ December 2000 Jupiter flyby

❼ July 2004 Arrives in orbit around Saturn

Goldstone, California

◀▼ The three Deep Space Network sites are equally spaced around Earth, with 120 degrees between them, making a 360-degree circle.

Madrid, Spain

Canberra, Australia

394 For long periods, much of a craft's equipment shuts down to save electricity. It's like an animal hibernating in winter or a cell phone on standby. When the craft "hibernates" only a few vital systems stay active, such as navigation.

▶ The Deep Space Network's radio dish at Goldstone near Barstow, California, is 230 feet across.

Ready to explore

395 As the spacecraft approaches its target, its systems power up and it "comes to life." Controllers on Earth test the craft's radio communications and other equipment. At such enormous distances, radio signals can take minutes, even hours, to make the journey.

396 Other kinds of camera can "see" types of waves that are invisible to the human eye. These include infrared or heat rays, ultraviolet rays, radio waves, and X-rays. These rays and waves provide information about the target world, such as how hot or cold it is.

▼ *Mars Reconnaissance Orbiter*'s photograph of the 2,400-foot-wide Victoria Crater was captured by its high-resolution camera and shows amazing detail.

397 Among the most important devices onboard a craft are cameras. Some work like telescopes to take a close-up or magnified view of a small area. Others are wide-angle cameras, which capture a much greater area without magnifying.

The Mars Climate Sounder records the temperature, moisture, and dust in the Martian atmosphere

The high-resolution camera captures close-up, detailed photographs of the surface

QUIZ

Spacecraft have many devices, but rarely microphones to detect sound. Why?

A. The chance of meeting aliens who can shout loudly is very small.

B. Sound waves do not travel through the vacuum of space.

C. It's too difficult to change sound waves into radio signals.

Answer: B

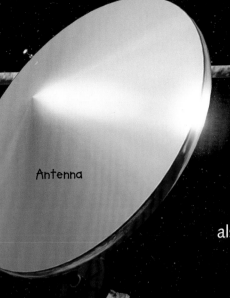

Antenna

398 Magnetometers detect magnetic fields, which exist naturally around some planets, including Earth. Gravitometers measure the target object's pull of gravity. This is especially important in the final stage of the journey—the landing. Some spacecraft also have space dust collectors.

Solar panel

◀ *Mars Reconnaissance Orbiter*, launched in 2005, carries a telescopic camera, wide-angle cameras, sensors for infrared and ultraviolet light, and a radar that "sees" below the surface.

The spectrometer identifies different substances on the surface by measuring how much light is reflected

The subsurface radar can see up to 0.6 miles below the planet's surface

399 The information from the cameras and sensors is turned into radio signal codes and beamed back to Earth. To send and receive these signals, the craft has one or more dish-shaped antennas. These must be in the correct position to communicate with the dishes located on Earth.

Flyby, bye-bye

400 On a flyby mission, a spacecraft comes close to its target. It does not go into orbit around it or land—it flies onward and away into deep space. Some flybys are part of longer missions to even more distant destinations. In these cases the flyby may also involve gravity assist.

LAUNCH FROM EARTH
August 20, 1977

401 A flyby craft may pass its target several times on a long, lopsided path, before leaving again. Each pass gives a different view of the target object. The craft's cameras, sensors, and other equipment switch on to take pictures and record measurements, then turn off again as it flies away.

JUPITER

Flyby on July 9, 1979

402 The ultimate flyby craft was *Voyager 2*. It made a "Grand Tour" of the four outermost planets, which are only suitably aligned every 175 years. *Voyager 2* blasted off in 1977 and flew past Jupiter in 1979, Saturn in 1981, Uranus in 1986, and Neptune in 1989. This craft is still sending back information from a distance twice as far as Pluto is from Earth.

I DON'T BELIEVE IT!
When *Pioneer 11* zoomed to within 27,000 miles of Jupiter in 1974, it made the fastest ever flyby at 31 miles per second.

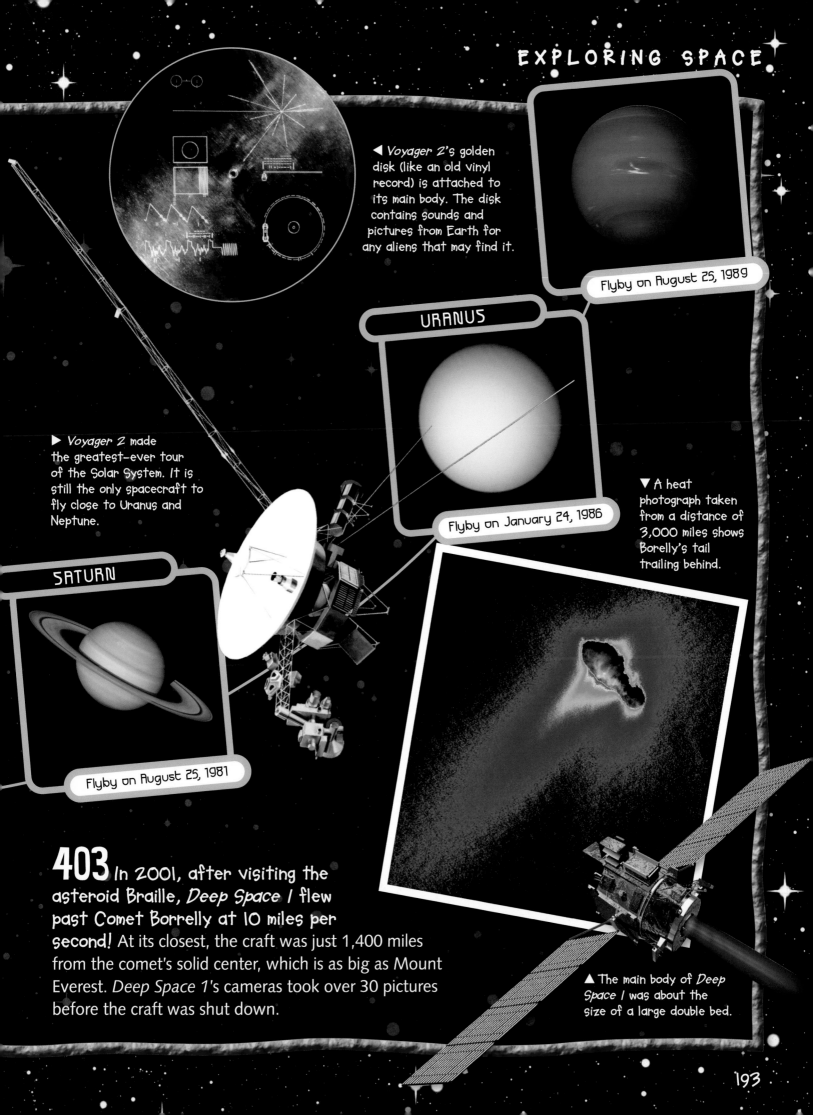

◀ *Voyager 2*'s golden disk (like an old vinyl record) is attached to its main body. The disk contains sounds and pictures from Earth for any aliens that may find it.

Flyby on August 25, 1989

URANUS

▶ *Voyager 2* made the greatest-ever tour of the Solar System. It is still the only spacecraft to fly close to Uranus and Neptune.

Flyby on January 24, 1986

▼ A heat photograph taken from a distance of 3,000 miles shows Borelly's tail trailing behind.

SATURN

Flyby on August 25, 1981

403 In 2001, after visiting the asteroid Braille, *Deep Space 1* flew past Comet Borrelly at 10 miles per second! At its closest, the craft was just 1,400 miles from the comet's solid center, which is as big as Mount Everest. *Deep Space 1*'s cameras took over 30 pictures before the craft was shut down.

▲ The main body of *Deep Space 1* was about the size of a large double bed.

Into orbit

404 On many exploring missions the craft is designed to go into orbit around its target world. Craft that do this are called orbiters, and they provide a much longer, closer look than a flyby mission.

▶ There are several different types of orbit that craft can make around their targets. Here, they are shown around Earth.

A polar orbit passes over the North and South Poles

An equatorial orbit goes around the middle (Equator)

Most orbits are elliptical, with low and high points

405 One of the most elliptical orbits was made by *Mars Global Surveyor*. At its closest, it passed Mars at a distance of 106 miles, twice in each orbit. The craft's furthest distance away was more than ten times greater.

◀ In 2006, two twin STEREO-craft went into orbit around the Sun. With one in front and one behind Earth, the craft made the first 3D observations of the Sun.

Antenna

ORBITER
You will need:
sock   tennis ball   string (3 feet long)
Put the ball in the sock and tie up the top with the string. Go outside. Holding the string half way along its length, whirl the sock above your head so that it "orbits" you. Gradually lengthen the string— does the "orbit" take longer?

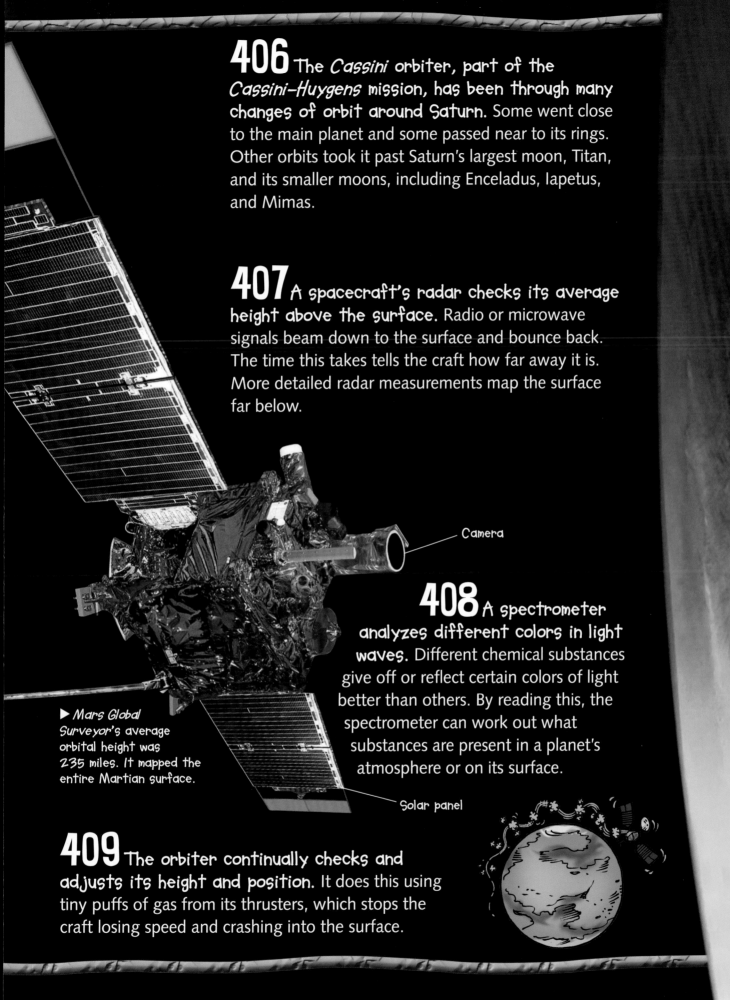

406 The *Cassini* orbiter, part of the *Cassini-Huygens* mission, has been through many changes of orbit around Saturn. Some went close to the main planet and some passed near to its rings. Other orbits took it past Saturn's largest moon, Titan, and its smaller moons, including Enceladus, Iapetus, and Mimas.

407 A spacecraft's radar checks its average height above the surface. Radio or microwave signals beam down to the surface and bounce back. The time this takes tells the craft how far away it is. More detailed radar measurements map the surface far below.

Camera

408 A spectrometer analyzes different colors in light waves. Different chemical substances give off or reflect certain colors of light better than others. By reading this, the spectrometer can work out what substances are present in a planet's atmosphere or on its surface.

▶ *Mars Global Surveyor's* average orbital height was 235 miles. It mapped the entire Martian surface.

Solar panel

409 The orbiter continually checks and adjusts its height and position. It does this using tiny puffs of gas from its thrusters, which stops the craft losing speed and crashing into the surface.

Landers and impactors

410 Some missions have landers that touch down onto the surface of their target world. Part of the spacecraft may detach and land while the other part stays in orbit, or the whole spacecraft may land.

① Spacecraft in orbit

② Landing module separates from orbiter

③ First parachute opened, then detached

▶ The later landers of the Russian *Venera* program (1961–1983) used parachutes to slow down in the thick, hot, cloudy atmosphere of Venus.

411 The journey down can be hazardous. If the planet has an atmosphere (layer of gas around it) there may be strong winds that could blow the lander off course. If the atmosphere is thick, there may be huge pressure pushing on the craft.

④ Main parachutes opened at a height of 30 miles above the surface

412 If there is an atmosphere, the lander may use parachutes, or inflate its own balloons or air bags, to slow its speed. On the *Cassini-Huygens* mission, the *Huygens* lander used two parachutes as it descended for touchdown on Saturn's moon, Titan.

⑤ Ring-shaped shock absorber filled with compressed gas lessened the impact at touchdown

413 If there is no atmosphere, retro thrusters are used to slow the craft down. These puff gases in the direction of travel. Most landers have a strong, bouncy casing for protection as they hit the surface, or long, springy legs to reduce the impact.

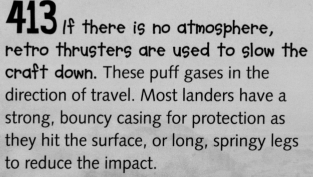

▲ A photograph taken by *Deep Impact* 67 seconds after its impactor crashed into Comet Tempel I, shows material being thrown out.

▲ This image shows how *Beagle 2*'s solar panels were designed to fold out. However contact with the lander was lost soon after it detached from its orbiter in 2003.

414 After touchdown, the lander's solar panels and other parts fold out. Its equipment and systems switch on, and it tests its radio communications with the orbiter and sometimes directly with Earth.

Impactor

415 Some craft are designed to smash into their target, and these are called impactors. The crash is observed by the orbiter and may also be watched by controllers on Earth. The dust, rocks, and gases given off by an impact provide valuable information about the target object.

Camera

▶ In 2005, *Deep Impact* released its impactor, watched it strike Comet Tempel I, and studied the resulting crater.

◀ *Mars Pathfinder* lander being tested on Earth. It used a parachute, retro thrusters, and multi-bubble airbags to land on Mars.

Robotic rovers

416 After touchdown, some landers release small, robotic vehicles called rovers. They have wheels and motors so they can move around on the surface to explore. So far rovers have explored on the Moon and Mars.

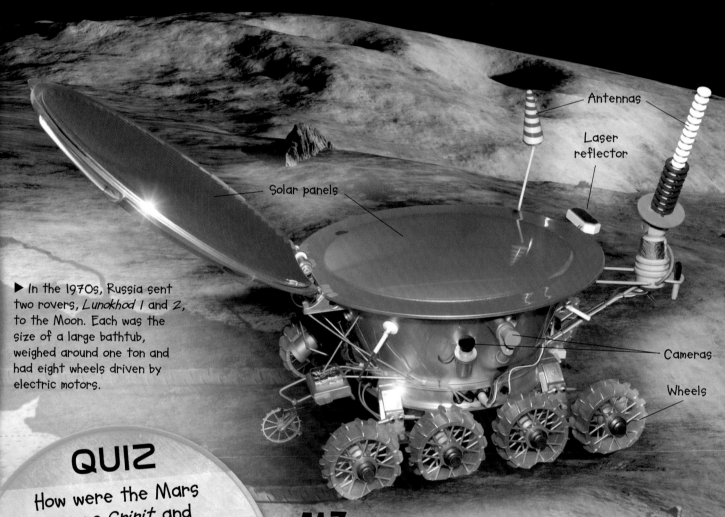

Antennas

Laser reflector

Solar panels

Cameras

Wheels

▶ In the 1970s, Russia sent two rovers, *Lunokhod 1* and *2*, to the Moon. Each was the size of a large bathtub, weighed around one ton and had eight wheels driven by electric motors.

QUIZ

How were the Mars rovers *Spirit* and *Opportunity* named?

1. Words chosen at random.
2. By a group of space experts.
3. By a 9-year-old girl, who won a competition.

Answer:
3. Siberian-born American schoolgirl Sofi Collis won the 2003 'Name the Rovers' competition.

417 Modern rovers are mostly robotic—self-controlled using onboard computers. This is because of the time delay of radio signals. Even when Earth and Mars are at their closest distance to each other, radio signals take over three minutes to travel one way. If a rover was driven by remote control from Earth, it could have fallen off a cliff long before its onboard cameras relayed images of this.

418 Rovers are designed and tested to survive the conditions on their target world. Scientists know about these conditions from information collected from observations on Earth, and from previous missions. Test rovers are driven on extreme landscapes on Earth to make sure they can handle tricky terrain.

▲ A test version of a new rover destined for Mars, here being tested on the slippery rocks of a beach in Wales, UK.

419 The *Spirit* and *Opportunity* rovers landed on Mars in 2004. They are equipped with cameras that allow them to navigate around obstacles. Heat-sensitive cameras detect levels of heat soaked up by rocks, giving clues to what the rocks are made of. Onboard microscopes and magnets gather and study dust particles containing iron.

Navcam

Antenna

Main antenna

Solar panels

Mobile arm carries five gadgets including a camera, rock grinder, and magnets

▶ Twin rovers *Spirit* and *Opportunity* are each about the size of an office desk.

Each wheel has an electric motor

420 A rover for Venus is planned, but its surface temperature is over 750°F. Plastics and some metals would melt there. A Venus rover would have to be made out of metals such as titanium, which have high melting points. Its inner workings would need to be continually cooled.

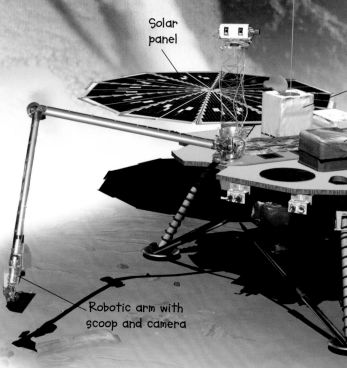

▶ In the late 1970s the U.S.'s two *Viking* landers photographed their robotic sampler arms digging into Mars' surface.

Solar panel

Robotic arm with scoop and camera

421 Some landers and rovers have robot arms that extend from the main body. These scoop or drill into the surface to collect samples, which are then tested in the craft's onboard science laboratory. Samples are tested for chemical reactions, such as bubbling or changing color.

Spheres of minerals containing iron, known as "blueberries"

Circular area ground by tool is 1.8 inches across

422 Most rovers have six wheels. This design allows them to move quickly around sharp corners, without tipping over. Each wheel has an electric motor, powered by onboard batteries that are charged by the solar panels. If the batteries run down, the rover "sleeps" until light from the Sun recharges them.

◀ Mars rovers *Spirit* and *Opportunity* are both equipped with a rock-grinding tool. They use it to grind into rocks and gather dust samples.

423 The *Phoenix* Mars lander had several devices on its robotic arm to measure features of Martian soil. It measured how easily it carried (conducted) heat and electricity, and if it contained any liquids. *Phoenix* also had microscopes for an ultra-close view of the surface samples.

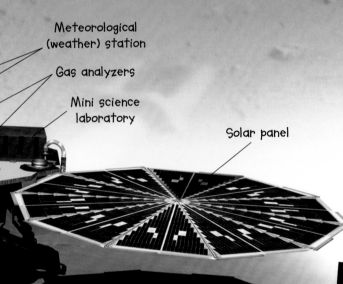

Meteorological (weather) station

Gas analyzers

Mini science laboratory

Solar panel

424 Most landers and rovers have mini weather stations. Sensors measure temperatures and pressures through the day and night and record the Sun's brightness. They also take samples of gases if there is an atmosphere, and record weather, such as wind and dust storms.

◄ The *Phoenix* Mars lander of 2008 had a robotic arm, on the left, and a small weather station.

425 The orbiting craft acts as a relay station to receive signals from its lander and send them on to Earth. A lander can in turn be a relay station for a rover. A rover has a small radio set to communicate with the lander and the lander has a slightly larger one to communicate with the orbiter. The orbiter has the biggest radio set to communicate with Earth.

▲ In the 1960s five U.S. Surveyor landers sent back separate close-up photographs of the Moon's surface. These were joined together to make larger scenes.

Exploring Mars

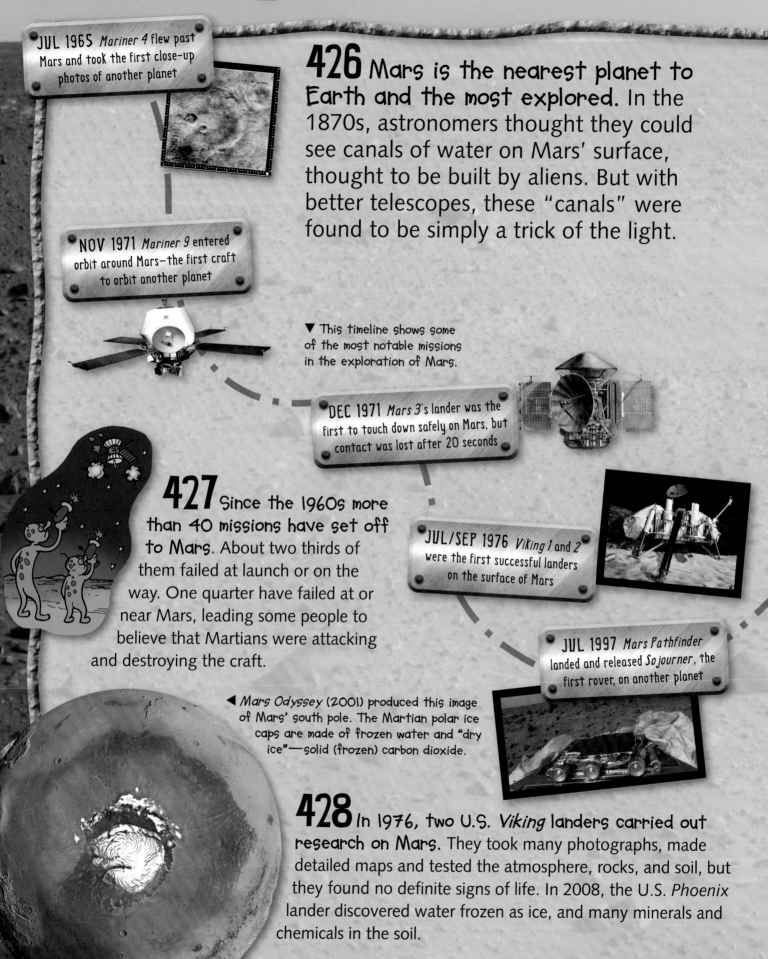

JUL 1965 *Mariner 4* flew past Mars and took the first close-up photos of another planet

426 Mars is the nearest planet to Earth and the most explored. In the 1870s, astronomers thought they could see canals of water on Mars' surface, thought to be built by aliens. But with better telescopes, these "canals" were found to be simply a trick of the light.

NOV 1971 *Mariner 9* entered orbit around Mars—the first craft to orbit another planet

▼ This timeline shows some of the most notable missions in the exploration of Mars.

DEC 1971 *Mars 3*'s lander was the first to touch down safely on Mars, but contact was lost after 20 seconds

427 Since the 1960s more than 40 missions have set off to Mars. About two thirds of them failed at launch or on the way. One quarter have failed at or near Mars, leading some people to believe that Martians were attacking and destroying the craft.

JUL/SEP 1976 *Viking 1* and *2* were the first successful landers on the surface of Mars

JUL 1997 *Mars Pathfinder* landed and released *Sojourner*, the first rover, on another planet

◄ *Mars Odyssey* (2001) produced this image of Mars' south pole. The Martian polar ice caps are made of frozen water and "dry ice"—solid (frozen) carbon dioxide.

428 In 1976, two U.S. *Viking* landers carried out research on Mars. They took many photographs, made detailed maps and tested the atmosphere, rocks, and soil, but they found no definite signs of life. In 2008, the U.S. *Phoenix* lander discovered water frozen as ice, and many minerals and chemicals in the soil.

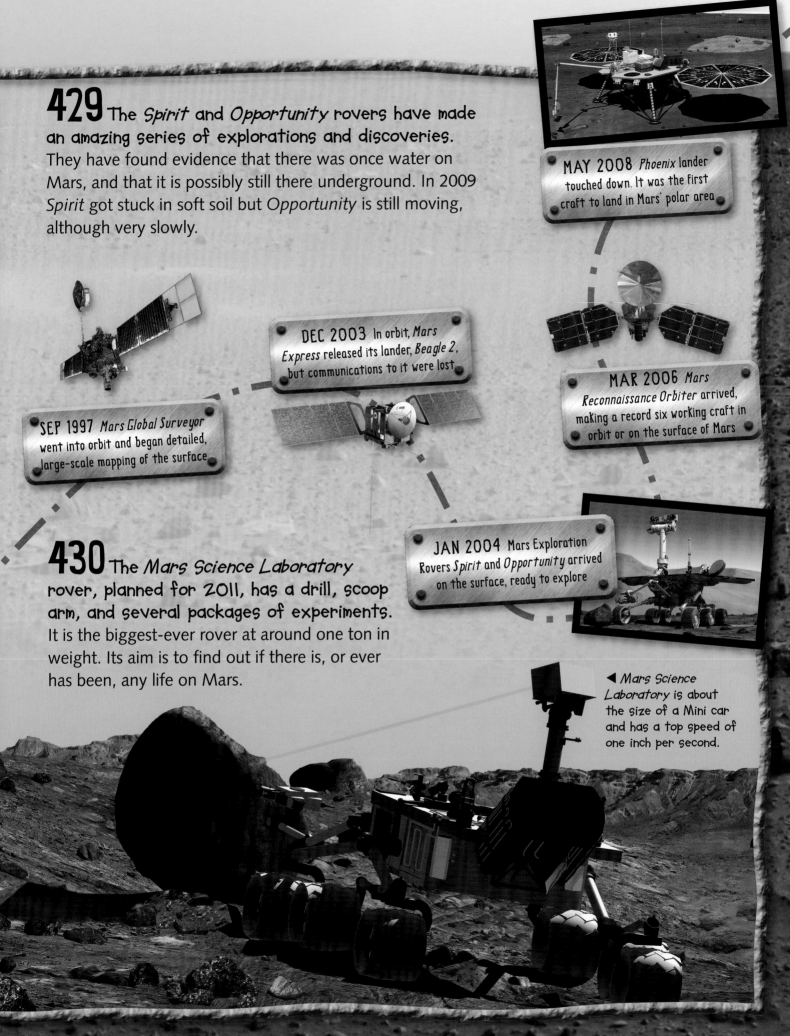

429 The *Spirit* and *Opportunity* rovers have made an amazing series of explorations and discoveries. They have found evidence that there was once water on Mars, and that it is possibly still there underground. In 2009 *Spirit* got stuck in soft soil but *Opportunity* is still moving, although very slowly.

MAY 2008 *Phoenix* lander touched down. It was the first craft to land in Mars' polar area

DEC 2003 In orbit, *Mars Express* released its lander, *Beagle 2*, but communications to it were lost

SEP 1997 *Mars Global Surveyor* went into orbit and began detailed, large-scale mapping of the surface

MAR 2006 *Mars Reconnaissance Orbiter* arrived, making a record six working craft in orbit or on the surface of Mars

430 The *Mars Science Laboratory* rover, planned for 2011, has a drill, scoop arm, and several packages of experiments. It is the biggest-ever rover at around one ton in weight. Its aim is to find out if there is, or ever has been, any life on Mars.

JAN 2004 *Mars Exploration Rovers* Spirit and *Opportunity* arrived on the surface, ready to explore

◀ *Mars Science Laboratory* is about the size of a Mini car and has a top speed of one inch per second.

431 All spacecraft have a mission control center on Earth. Expert teams monitor a craft's systems, including radio communications, and the data a craft collects from its cameras and instruments.

▲ Mission controllers at NASA's Jet Propulsion Laboratory in California celebrate as the first images from rover *Opportunity* reach Earth.

432 Missions often run into problems. Controllers must work out how to keep a mission going when faults occur. If power supplies fail, the teams may have to decide to switch off some equipment so that others can continue working.

433 Sample return missions bring items from space back to Earth. In 2004, the *Genesis* craft dropped off its return container. It was supposed to parachute down to Earth's surface, but it crash-landed in Utah. Luckily, some of its samples of solar wind survived for study.

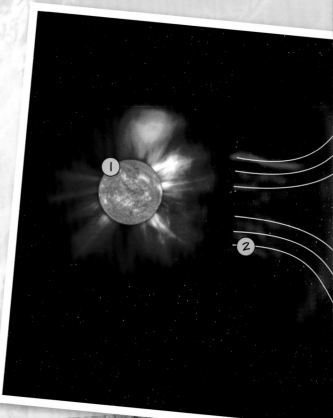

434 Gases, dust, rocks, and other items are brought back to Earth to be studied. In the early 1970s the six manned Apollo missions brought a total of 841.5 pounds of Moon material back to Earth.

▲ This piece of basalt Moon rock, brought back by *Apollo 15*, is being studied by *Apollo 17* astronaut and geologist (rock expert) Jack Schmitt.

435 Samples returned from space must not be contaminated with material from Earth. Keeping samples clean allows scientists to find out what they contain, and stops any dangerous substances being released on Earth. Spacecraft are ultra-clean at launch to prevent them spreading chemicals or germs from Earth to other worlds.

I DON'T BELIEVE IT!

Moon rocks don't look very special, yet over 100 small ones brought back by the Apollo missions have been stolen. More than ten people have been caught trying to sell them.

▼ *Genesis* collected high-energy particles from the Sun's solar wind, which distorts Earth's magnetic field.

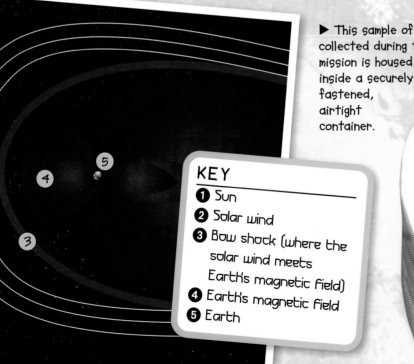

▶ This sample of Moon rock collected during the *Apollo 11* mission is housed inside a securely fastened, airtight container.

KEY
① Sun
② Solar wind
③ Bow shock (where the solar wind meets Earth's magnetic field)
④ Earth's magnetic field
⑤ Earth

Toward the Sun

◀ This photograph taken by *SOHO* uses a disk with a hole to block out some of the Sun's glare. This reveals vast streaming clouds of superheated matter called plasma.

Corona

Coronal mass ejection (CME) of superheated plasma

436 Missions to the Sun encounter enormous heat. In the 1970s the U.S.-German craft *Helios 2* flew to within 27 million miles of the Sun. From 1990, the *Ulysses* probe traveled on a huge orbit, passing near the Sun and as far out as Jupiter.

▶ The Helios mission was featured on stamps worldwide.

1c

HELIOS MISSION

GRENADA

437 In 1995, the *SOHO* satellite began studying the Sun from near Earth. Since then, it has found many new comets. In 2018, *Solar Probe Plus* will orbit to within 3.8 million miles of the Sun, with a shieldlike "sunshade" of heat-resistant, carbon-composite material for protection.

▲ *Messenger* had a "sunshade" made out of a ceramic–composite material to protect it from the Sun's heat.

439 Mercury, the nearest planet to the Sun, has been visited by two spacecraft, *Mariner 10* in 1974, and *Messenger* in 2004. *Messenger* made flybys in 2008 and 2009 and is due in orbit in 2011. These craft measured Mercury's surface temperature at 790°F—twice as hot as a home oven.

438 Missions to Venus include Russia's Venera series (1961 to 1984), U.S. Mariner probes (1962 to 1973), and *Pioneer Venus* (1978). From 1990 to 1994, *Magellan* used radar to map the surface in amazing detail. In 2006, Europe's *Venus Express* began more mapping. Its instruments also studied Venus' extreme global warming.

440 More than 20 craft have visited Venus, the second planet from the Sun. Its atmosphere of thick clouds, extreme pressures, temperatures over 840°F and acid chemicals, pose huge challenges for exploring craft.

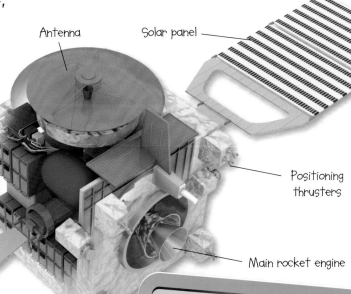

Antenna

Solar panel

Positioning thrusters

Main rocket engine

◀ Studying Venus' atmosphere may help us understand similar climate processes happening on Earth.

Gold coating helps to keep out the Sun's heat

▲ *Venus Express* orbits as low as 155 miles above the poles of Venus.

I DON'T BELIEVE IT!
The fastest spacecraft, and the fastest man-made object ever, was *Helios 2*. It neared the Sun at 42 miles per second!

Asteroids near and far

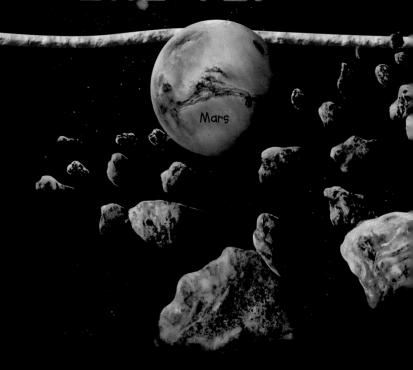
Mars

441 Asteroids orbit the Sun but are far smaller than planets, so even finding them is a challenge. Most large asteroids are in the main asteroid belt between Mars and Jupiter. Much closer to us are Near Earth Asteroids (NEAs), and more than 20 have been explored in detail by flyby craft, orbiters, and landers.

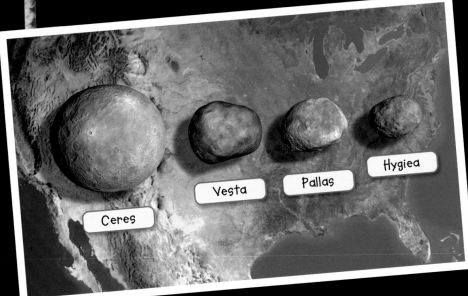
Ceres
Vesta
Pallas
Hygiea

442 Orbiting and landing on asteroids is very difficult. Many asteroids are oddly shaped, and they roll and tumble as they move through space. A craft may only discover this as it gets close.

◀ Dwarf planet Ceres and the three largest asteroids in our Solar System, seen against North America for scale. Vesta, the biggest asteroid, is about 330 miles across.

443 In 1996, the probe NEAR–Shoemaker launched towards NEA Eros. On the way it flew past asteroid Mathilde in the main belt. Then in 2000 it orbited 21-mile-long Eros, before landing. The probe discoverd that the asteroid was peanut-shaped, and also gathered information about Eros' rocks, magnetism, and movement. In 2008, spacecraft *Rosetta* passed main belt asteroid Steins, and asteroid Lutetia in 2010.

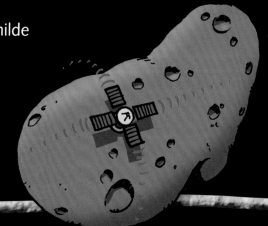

Jupiter

▲ In the main belt there are some dense "asteroid swarms." But most larger asteroids are tens of thousands of miles apart.

444 In 2010 Japan's *Hayabusa* brought back samples of asteroid Itokawa after touching down on its surface in 2005. This information has helped our understanding of asteroids as "leftovers" from the formation of the Solar System 4600 million years ago.

445 *Dawn* was launched in 2007, to explore Vesta—the biggest asteroid—in 2011 and the dwarf planet Ceres in 2015. Vesta may be rocky, while Ceres is thought to be icier, with various chemicals frozen as solids. *Dawn* aims to find out for sure.

▲ The *Dawn* mission badge shows its two main targets.

▶ *Hayabusa* was designed to gather samples of the asteroid Itokawa by firing a metal pellet towards the surface. It could then collect the dust thrown up by the impact.

Comet mysteries

446 Comets travel to and from the edges of the Solar System and beyond as they orbit the Sun. Unlike long-period comets, which may take thousands of years to orbit, short-period comets orbit every 200 years or less and so can be explored.

▶ The Oort cloud surrounds the Solar System and is made up of icy objects. It may be the source of some Sun-orbiting comets.

Sun

Kuiper belt

▶ The Kuiper belt lies beyond Neptune's orbit and is about twice the size of the Solar System. It consists of lots of cometlike objects.

Neptune

447 Like asteroids, comets are difficult to find. Comets warm up and glow only as they near the Sun. Their tails are millions of miles long, but consist only of faint gases and dust. The center, or nucleus, of a comet may give off powerful jets of dust and gases that could blow a craft off course.

▶ A typical comet is mostly dust and ice. It has a glowing area, or coma, around it, and a long tail that points away from the Sun.

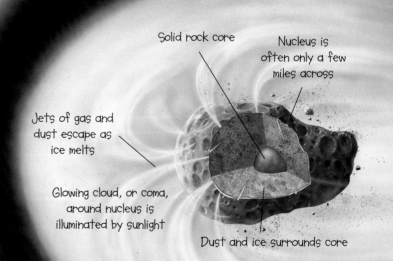

Solid rock core

Nucleus is often only a few miles across

Jets of gas and dust escape as ice melts

Glowing cloud, or coma, around nucleus is illuminated by sunlight

Dust and ice surrounds core

448 The famous Halley's Comet last appeared in 1986. Several exploring craft, known as the "Halley Armada," went to visit it. This included Europe's *Giotto* probe, which flew to within 370 miles of the comet's nucleus. There were also two Russian-French Vega probes, and *Sakigake* and *Suisei* from Japan.

▶ *Stardust* collected comet dust using a very lightweight foam, called aerogel, in a collector shaped like a tennis bat. The collector folded into the craft's bowl-like capsule for return to Earth.

449 In 2008, the *Stardust* probe returned a capsule of dust collected from the comet Wild 2. In 2005, *Deep Impact* visited Comet Tempel 1 and released an impactor to crash into its nucleus and study the dust and gases given off. These craft increase our knowledge of comets as frozen balls of icy chemicals, rock, and dust.

DUST COLLECTED FROM COMET WILD 2

Comet dust particles

▲ Under the microscope, a piece of *Stardust's* aerogel (half the size of this "o") is revealed to have minute dust particles embedded within it.

STARDUST APPROACHING COMET WILD 2

Glowing dust tail illuminated by sunlight

Ion (gas) tail appears bluish

SAMPLE CAPSULE RETURNS TO EARTH

Gas giants

I DON'T BELIEVE IT!
A craft entering Neptune's atmosphere would be hit by the fastest winds in the Solar System—ten times stronger than a hurricane on Earth!

450 The four furthest planets from Earth—Jupiter, Saturn, Uranus, and Neptune—are "gas giants." These are large planets composed mainly of gases. It takes at least two years to reach Jupiter by the most direct route. But craft usually take longer because they use gravity assist.

▼ *Galileo* orbited Jupiter for more than seven years. It released an atmosphere probe to study the gases that make up almost the whole planet.

451 There have been seven flybys of Jupiter and each one discovered more of the planet's moons. The two U.S. Voyager missions, launched in 1977, discovered that Jupiter has rings like Saturn. U.S. spacecraft *Galileo* arrived in orbit around Jupiter in 1995 and released a probe into the planet's atmosphere.

ON TITAN'S SURFACE

▲ *Huygens'* pictures from the surface of Titan, Saturn's largest moon, show lumps of ice and a haze of deadly methane gas.

452 The ringed planet Saturn had flybys by *Pioneer 11* (1979) and *Voyagers 1* and *2* (1980–1981). In 2004 the huge *Cassini-Huygens* craft arrived after a seven-year journey. The orbiter *Cassini* is still taking spectacular photographs of the planet, its rings, and its moons.

▼ The *Huygens* lander separated from *Cassini* and headed for Titan. It sent back more than 750 images from the surface.

TITAN

A heat shield prevented burnup on entry

Parachutes slowed the lander's descent

Huygens lands on Titan

453 The only exploring craft to have visited Uranus and Neptune is *Voyager 2*. During its flyby of Uranus in 1986, *Voyager 2* discovered ten new moons and two new rings. In 1989, the craft passed the outermost planet, Neptune, and discovered six new moons and four new rings.

▼ The four gas giants have many moons—some large, and some very small. This list includes the five largest moons for each (not to scale).

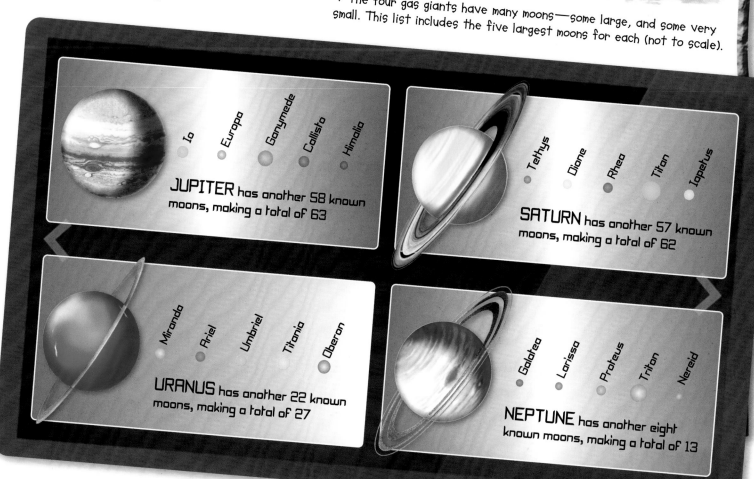

Io Europa Ganymede Callisto Himalia

JUPITER has another 58 known moons, making a total of 63

Tethys Dione Rhea Titan Iapetus

SATURN has another 57 known moons, making a total of 62

Miranda Ariel Umbriel Titania Oberon

URANUS has another 22 known moons, making a total of 27

Galatea Larissa Proteus Triton Nereid

NEPTUNE has another eight known moons, making a total of 13

Into the future

454 Sending craft to the edges of the Solar System takes many years. U.S. spacecraft *New Horizons* set out in 2006 to study the dwarf planet Pluto by performing a flyby. Photos from the craft have revealed Pluto's complex and varied surface, which has bright and dark regions.

455 *New Horizons'* immense nine-year journey was complicated to plan. It included a flyby of tiny asteroid 132534 APL, then a swing around Jupiter for gravity assist and a speed boost. Flybys of Jupiter's moons followed, before the long cruise to tiny Pluto. Without Jupiter's gravity assist, the trip would take five years longer.

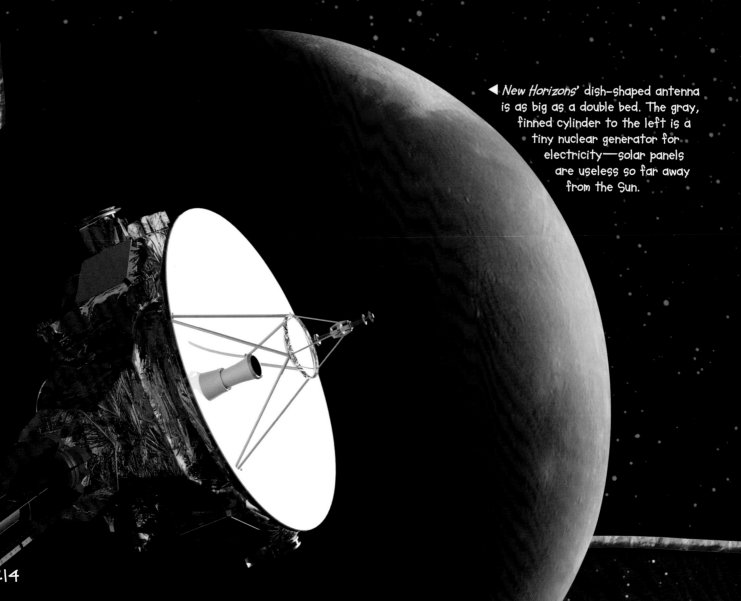

◄ *New Horizons'* dish-shaped antenna is as big as a double bed. The gray, finned cylinder to the left is a tiny nuclear generator for electricity—solar panels are useless so far away from the Sun.

456 Several major explorations are planned for the coming years. The *ExoMars* mission consists of a lander and a rover, due to launch in 2016 and 2018. They will look for signs of life on Mars, using a 6.5-feet-deep drill. The *BepiColombo* mission aims to orbit Mercury and measure the Sun's power.

Drill

◄ The *BepiColombo* mission is planned for launch in 2017. The six-year trip will take the craft past the Moon, Earth, and Venus before reaching Mercury—the closest planet to the Sun.

457 What happens to exploring spacecraft? Some are deliberately crashed into other worlds, so that the impact can be observed by other spacecraft or from Earth. Others burn up as they enter the atmosphere of a planet or large moon.

▲ The drill on *ExoMars* rover will pass soil samples to the mini laboratory on board for analysis.

458 Many exploring spacecraft are still traveling in space, and will be for thousands of years. As they run out of power they become silent, either sitting on their target worlds or drifting though empty space—unless they crash into an object.

► The "Pale Blue Dot" photograph captured in 1990 by *Voyager 1*, was taken from 3.7 billion miles away. Earth is a tiny speck.

FAR-AWAY EARTH

Earth

459 The most distant craft is *Voyager 1*, launched in 1977. It is now more than 11.3 billion miles from Earth, and is still being tracked.

Space magic and myth

▲ H. G. Wells' original story is brought to life in the 1953 movie *War of the Worlds*, in which martians invade Earth and destroy city after city. Humans can't stop them, but instead, germs eventually wipe out the alien invaders.

460 Exploring space has long been a favorite subject for storytelling. Even before rockets, there were theories about space travel and aliens. One of the first was *War of the Worlds*, written in 1898 by H. G. Wells.

◀ The mission statement of *Star Trek*'s starship *Enterprise* was: "To explore strange new worlds, to seek out new life and new civilizations, to boldly go where no one has gone before."

461 In the 1950s, as humans began to explore space, tales of sightings of "flying saucers" and U.F.O.s (Unidentified Flying Objects) soared. Some of these may be explained by secret aircraft or spacecraft being tested by governments. A few people claimed that aliens visited Earth and left signs, such as strange patterns in fields called crop circles.

462 The *Star Wars* (1977–2005) and *Alien* movies (1979–2007) are all about adventures in space. This genre grew in popularity at the same time that space exploration was becoming a reality. The *Star Trek* movies (1979 onward) had several spin off television series, including *Voyager* and *Deep Space Nine*.

463 In the future, scientists may discover a form of ultra-fast travel involving black holes and wormholes (tunnels through space and time). This could allow humans to travel to distant galaxies to look for other "Goldilocks" planets similar to Earth. Like the third bowl of porridge in the nursery story, the conditions on a Goldilocks planet are not too hot and not too cold, but "just right" for life to exist. As yet, no others have been discovered.

QUIZ

1. What was the name of the story written by H. G. Wells about an alien invasion of Earth?
2. What does U.F.O. stand for?
3. What is a "Goldilocks" planet?

Answers:
1. *War of the Worlds*
2. Unidentified Flying Object
3. A planet that has the perfect conditions for life to exist—not too hot, not too cold, but "just right."

464 Space scientists have suggested new kinds of rockets and thrusters for faster space travel. These could reduce the journey time to the next-nearest star, Proxima Centauri, to about 100 years. But one day we may be beaten to it— aliens from a distant galaxy could be exploring space right now and discover us first!

▼ Virgin Galactic will soon be offering space travel to the general public. A ticket for a flight on *SpaceShipTwo* (below) will cost $200,000!

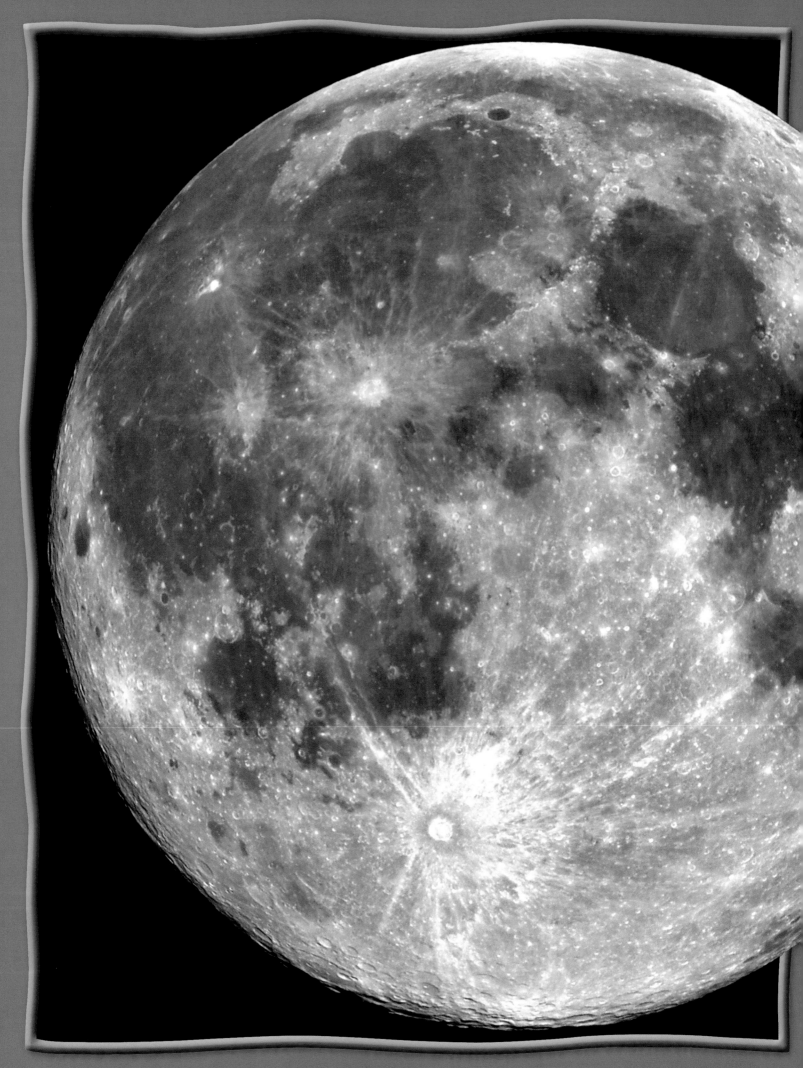

ASTRONOMY

How hot are stars?

Where is the best place to build an observatory?

Why do the planets orbit the Sun?

What does the Big Bang look like?

What is astronomy?

465 Astronomy is the study of everything you can see in the night sky and many other things out in space. Astronomers try to find out all about stars and galaxies. They look for planets circling around stars, and at mysterious explosions far out in space. Telescopes help them to see further, spotting things that are much too faint to see with just their eyes.

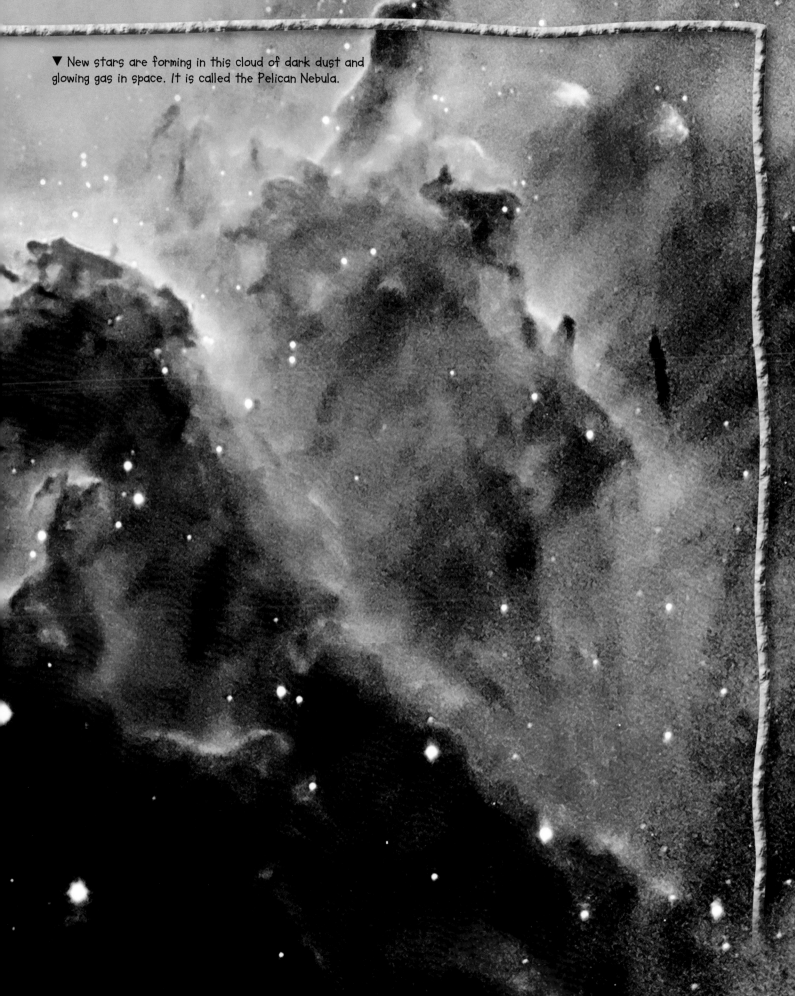

▼ New stars are forming in this cloud of dark dust and glowing gas in space. It is called the Pelican Nebula.

Starry skies

466 People have always been fascinated by the stars and Moon. Ancient people watched the Sun cross the sky during the day and disappear at night. Then when it got dark they saw the Moon and stars move across the sky. They wondered what caused these things to happen.

467 Sometimes the Sun goes dark in the middle of the day due to a solar eclipse. This is caused by the Moon moving in front of the Sun, blocking its light. People in the past did not know this, so eclipses were scary. In ancient China, people thought they were caused by a dragon eating the Sun.

468 In ancient times people did not know what the Sun, Moon, and stars were. Many thought the Sun was a god. The ancient Egyptians called this god Ra. They believed he rode across the sky in a boat each day and was swallowed by the sky goddess, Nut, every evening and then born again the next morning.

▲ The Egyptians pictured their sky goddess Nut with a starry body and their sun god Ra sitting on a throne.

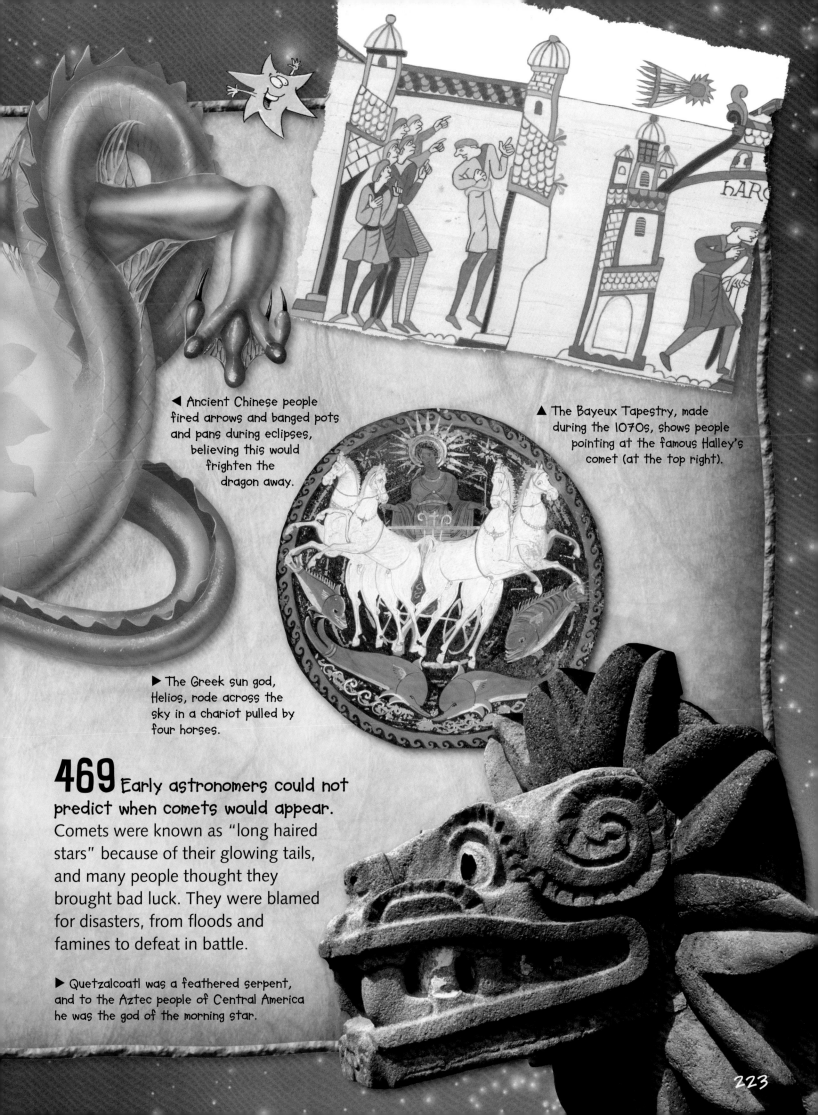

◀ Ancient Chinese people
fired arrows and banged pots
and pans during eclipses,
believing this would
frighten the
dragon away.

▲ The Bayeux Tapestry, made
during the 1070s, shows people
pointing at the famous Halley's
comet (at the top right).

▶ The Greek sun god,
Helios, rode across the
sky in a chariot pulled by
four horses.

469 Early astronomers could not
predict when comets would appear.
Comets were known as "long haired
stars" because of their glowing tails,
and many people thought they
brought bad luck. They were blamed
for disasters, from floods and
famines to defeat in battle.

▶ Quetzalcoatl was a feathered serpent,
and to the Aztec people of Central America
he was the god of the morning star.

223

Mapping the stars

470 Ancient astronomers made maps of star patterns, dividing them into groups called constellations. People around the world all grouped the stars differently. Today, astronomers recognize 88 constellations that cover the whole sky.

▼ The northern half of the Earth has different constellations from the southern half, but all the star patterns stay the same night after night.

▼ Old star maps showed the constellations as animals such as Draco the Dragon and Ursa Minor the Little Bear.

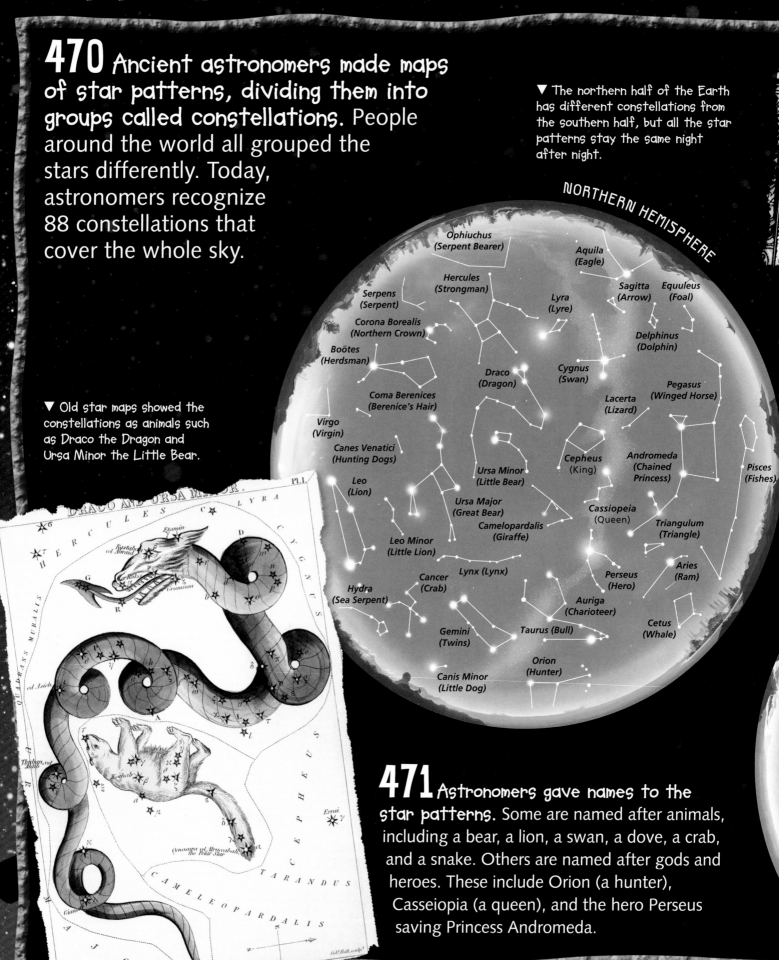

NORTHERN HEMISPHERE

Ophiuchus (Serpent Bearer)
Aquila (Eagle)
Hercules (Strongman)
Serpens (Serpent)
Sagitta (Arrow)
Equuleus (Foal)
Lyra (Lyre)
Corona Borealis (Northern Crown)
Delphinus (Dolphin)
Boötes (Herdsman)
Draco (Dragon)
Cygnus (Swan)
Pegasus (Winged Horse)
Coma Berenices (Berenice's Hair)
Lacerta (Lizard)
Virgo (Virgin)
Cepheus (King)
Andromeda (Chained Princess)
Pisces (Fishes)
Canes Venatici (Hunting Dogs)
Ursa Minor (Little Bear)
Leo (Lion)
Ursa Major (Great Bear)
Cassiopeia (Queen)
Triangulum (Triangle)
Camelopardalis (Giraffe)
Leo Minor (Little Lion)
Aries (Ram)
Lynx (Lynx)
Perseus (Hero)
Cancer (Crab)
Hydra (Sea Serpent)
Auriga (Charioteer)
Cetus (Whale)
Gemini (Twins)
Taurus (Bull)
Orion (Hunter)
Canis Minor (Little Dog)

DRACO AND URSA MINOR

471 Astronomers gave names to the star patterns. Some are named after animals, including a bear, a lion, a swan, a dove, a crab, and a snake. Others are named after gods and heroes. These include Orion (a hunter), Casseiopia (a queen), and the hero Perseus saving Princess Andromeda.

◄ Here an ancient astronomer (bottom left) is pictured comically looking through the starry celestial sphere to see how it moves.

473 Stars appear to move across the sky at night. This is because the Earth is spinning all the time, but in the past people thought the stars were fixed to the inside of a huge hollow ball called the celestial sphere, which moved slowly around the Earth.

472 Over 2,000 years ago, the Greek astronomer Hipparchus made a catalog of over 850 stars. He listed their brightness and positions, and called the brightest ones first magnitude stars. Astronomers still call the brightness of a star its magnitude.

SPOT A STAR PATTERN

You will need:

clear night   warm clothes   dark place
good view of the sky

If you live in the North, look for the saucepan-shape of the Big Dipper—four stars for the bowl and three for the handle.

If you live in the South, look overhead for four stars in the shape of a cross—the Southern Cross.

474 Ancient astronomers noticed that one star seems to stay still while the others circle around it. This is the Pole Star. It is above the North Pole and shows which direction is north.

The ancient Egyptians used this knowledge to align the sides of the pyramids exactly.

SOUTHERN HEMISPHERE

Lepus (Hare)
Canis Major (Great Dog)
Columba (Dove)
Eridanus (River Eridanus)
xtans (xtant)
Puppis (Stern), Carina (Keel) and Vela (Sail)
Caelum (Chisel)
Pictor (Painter's Easel)
Fornax (Furnace)
Hydra (Sea Serpent)
Recticulum (Net)
Dorado (Goldfish)
Phoenix (Phoenix)
Cetus (Whale)
Volans (Flying Fish)
Crater (Cup)
Crux (Southern Cross)
Chamaeleon (Chameleon)
Grus (Crane), Tucana (Toucan), and Pavo (Peacock)
Centaurus (Centaur)
Musca (Fly)
Apus (Bird of Paradise)
vus ow)
Indus (Indian)
Aquarius (Water Carrier)
Triangulum Australe (Southern Triangle)
Corona Australis (Southern Crown)
Piscis Austrinus (Southern Fish)
Ara (Altar)
Virgo (Virgin)
Scorpius (Scorpion)
Capricornus (Sea Goat)
Libra (Scales)
Serpens (Serpent) and Ophiuchus (Serpent Bearer)
Sagittarius (Archer)

Keeping time

475 The Sun, Moon, and stars can be used to measure time. It takes a day for the Earth to spin round, and a year for it to circle the Sun. By observing changes in the positions of constellations, astronomers worked out the length of a year so they could make a calendar.

Day 1

Day 3
Crescent
Moon

Day 5

Day 7
Half Moon

Day 10

Day 14
Full Moon

Day 17

Day 19

Day 21
Half Moon

Day 24

Day 26
Crescent
Moon

Day 28
New Moon

▲ The Moon's changing shapes are called the phases of the Moon. It doesn't really change shape—it is always a round ball of rock.

476 It takes 29.5 days for the Moon to circle the Earth. The Moon seems to change shape because we see different amounts of its sunlit side as it goes round the Earth. When the sunlit side faces Earth we see a Full Moon. When it faces away, we see only a thin crescent shape.

477 Ancient people used sundials to tell the time. A sundial consists of an upright rod and a flat plate. When the Sun shines, the rod casts a shadow on the plate. As the Sun moves across the sky, the shadow moves round the plate. Marks on the plate indicate the hours.

478 As the Earth circles the Sun, different stars appear in the sky. This helped people predict when seasons would change. In ancient Egypt the bright star Sirius showed when the river Nile would flood, making the land ready for crops.

MAKE A SUNDIAL
You will need:
short stick   modeling clay
card   pencil   clock
1. Stand the stick upright on the card using the modeling clay. Put it outside on a sunny day.
2. Every hour, make a pencil mark on the card where the shadow ends.
3. Leave the card where it is and the shadow will point to the time whenever the Sun is out.

▼ The shadow made by this sundial points to the time, which is marked on the round dial.

◄ Stonehenge's huge upright stones are lined up with sunrise on the longest day in midsummer and on the shortest day in midwinter.

479 Stonehenge is an ancient monument in England that is lined up with the Sun and Moon. It is a circle of giant stones over 4,000 years old. It may have been used as a calendar, or an observatory to predict when eclipses would happen.

Wandering stars

480 When people began to study the stars they spotted five that were unlike the rest. Instead of staying in fixed patterns, they moved across the constellations, and did not twinkle. Astronomers called them planets, which means "wandering stars."

481 The planets are named after ancient Roman gods. Mercury is the messenger of the gods, Venus is the god of love, Mars is the god of war, Jupiter is king of the gods, and Saturn is the god of farming. Later astronomers used telescopes to find two more planets, and named them Uranus and Neptune after the gods of the sky and the sea.

482 At first people thought that the Earth was at the center of everything. They believed the Sun, Moon, and planets all circled the Earth. The ancient Greek astronomer Ptolemy thought the Moon was nearest Earth, then Mercury and Venus, then the Sun, and finally Jupiter and Saturn.

▼ Ptolemy's picture of the Solar System shows the Earth in the middle and the Sun and planets moving round it in circles.

DRAW AN ELLIPSE

You will need:
two thumbtacks   paper   thick card   pencil   string

1. Place the paper on the card. Push the thumbtacks into the paper, a little way apart.
2. Tie the string into a loop that fits loosely round the thumbtacks.
3. Using the pencil point, pull the string tight into a triangle shape.
4. Move the pencil round on the paper, keeping the string tight to draw an ellipse.

483 Astronomers measured the positions and movements of the planets. What they found did not fit Ptolemy's ideas. In 1543, the Polish astronomer Nicolaus Copernicus suggested that the planets circled the Sun. This explained much of what the astronomers saw, but still didn't fit the measurements exactly.

◄ Nicolaus Copernicus' view placed the Sun in the middle with the Earth moving round it with the other planets.

▲ Kepler's drawing shows how he worked out that the planets move along ellipses, not circles.

484 German astronomer Johannes Kepler published his solution to this problem in 1609. He realized that the orbits of Earth and the planets were not perfect circles, but ellipses (slightly squashed circles). This fitted all the measurements and describes the Solar System as we know it today.

① From above, Ptolemy's plan shows everything (from inside to outside: Earth's Moon, Mercury, Venus, Sun, Mars, Jupiter, Saturn) moving round the Earth.

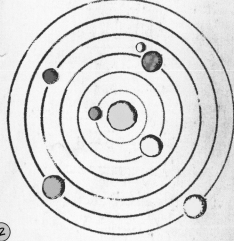

② Copernicus' view changes this to show everything moving round the Sun.

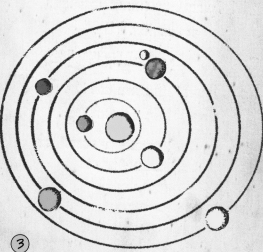

③ Kepler changes the circular paths of the planets into ellipses.

First telescopes

485 The telescope was invented in about 1608. Telescopes use two lenses (disks of glass that bulge out in the middle, or curve inward)—one at each end of a tube. When you look through a telescope, distant things look nearer and larger.

486 Italian scientist Galileo built a telescope in 1609. He was one of the first people to use the new invention for astronomy. With it, Galileo observed craters and mountains on the Moon, and discovered four moons circling the planet Jupiter. He was also amazed to see many more stars in the sky.

▲ Galileo shows a crowd of people the exciting new things he can see through his telescope.

Mirror

JUPITER

IO

EUROPA

▲ Jupiter's four largest moons are called the Galilean moons, because Galileo was the first person to see them using his telescope.

CALLISTO

GANYMEDE

487 When Galileo looked at the planet Venus through his telescope he saw that it sometimes appeared to be crescent shaped, just like the Moon. This meant that Venus was circling the Sun and not the Earth and helped to prove that Copernicus was right about the planets circling the Sun. Galileo described his amazing discoveries in a book called *The Starry Messenger*.

488 Other astronomers were soon trying to build more powerful telescopes. In 1668, English scientist Isaac Newton made one in which he replaced one of the lenses with a curved mirror, shaped like a saucer. He had invented the reflecting telescope. Large modern telescopes are based on Newton's invention.

I DON'T BELIEVE IT!
According to legend, Newton began to think about gravity when he saw an apple fall from a tree, and wondered why the apple fell to the ground instead of floating up.

Eyepiece

Sliding focus

Ball mounting

489 Newton also worked out why the planets orbit the Sun. He realized that something was pulling the planets toward the Sun—a pulling force called gravity. The pull of the Sun's gravity keeps the planets in their orbits, and the Earth's gravity holds the Moon in its orbit. It also prevents everything on Earth from floating off into space.

◄ The mirror in Newton's telescope gave a clearer image of the stars than telescopes with lenses.

Discoveries with telescopes

490 Astronomers made many new discoveries with their telescopes. The English astronomer Edmund Halley was interested in comets. He thought that a bright comet seen in 1682 was the same as one that was seen in 1607, and predicted that it would return in 1758. His prediction was right and the comet was named after him—Halley's Comet.

▲ Halley's comet was last seen in 1986 and will return again in 2061.

◄ Halley also mapped the stars and studied the Sun and Moon.

▼ The Orion Nebula, a huge glowing cloud of gas, is Messier's object number 42.

491 The French astronomer Charles Messier was also a comet hunter. In 1781 he tried to make his search easier by listing over 100 fuzzy objects in the sky that could be mistaken for comets. Later astronomers realized that some of these are glowing clouds of dust and gas and others are distant galaxies.

▲ Messier's object number 16 is the Eagle Nebula, a dusty cloud where stars are born.

▼ Messier's object number 31 is a giant spiral galaxy called Andromeda.

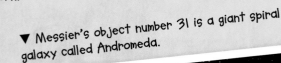

492 William Herschel, a German astronomer living in England, discovered a new planet in 1781. Using a reflecting telescope he had built himself, he spotted a star that seemed to move. It didn't look like a comet, and Herschel realized that it must be a new planet. It was the first planet discovered with a telescope and was called Uranus.

▲ William Herschel worked as astronomer for King George III of England.

493 Astronomers soon discovered that Uranus was not following its expected orbit. They thought another planet might be pulling it off course. Following predictions made by mathematicians, astronomers found another planet in 1846. It was called Neptune. It is so far away that it looks like a star.

494 The discovery of Neptune didn't fully explain Uranus' orbit. In 1930 an American astronomer, Clyde Tombaugh, found Pluto. It was the ninth planet from the Sun and much smaller than expected. In 2006 astronomers decided to call Pluto a dwarf planet.

▲ Herschel's great telescope was the largest telescope in the world at the time and its mirror measured 3.9 feet across.

QUIZ

1. Who discovered the planet Uranus?
2. When was Halley's Comet last seen?
3. Which was the ninth planet from the Sun until 2006?

Answers:
1. William Herschel 2. 1986 3. Pluto

How telescopes work

495 Telescopes make distant things look nearer. Most stars are so far away that even with a telescope they just look like points of light. But the Moon and planets seem much larger through a telescope—you can see details such as craters on the Moon and cloud patterns on Jupiter.

496 A reflecting telescope uses a curved mirror to collect light. The mirror reflects and focuses the light. A second, smaller mirror sends the light out through the side of the telescope or back through a hole in the big mirror to an eyepiece lens. Looking through the eyepiece lens you see a larger image of the distant object.

▶ Starlight bounces off the main mirror of a reflecting telescope back up to the eyepiece lens near the top.

Eyepiece lens

Reflected light

Secondary mirror

Light enters

Primary mirror

497 A telescope that uses a lens instead of a mirror to collect light is called a refracting telescope. The lens focuses the light and it goes straight down the telescope tube to the eyepiece lens at the other end. Refracting telescopes are not as large as reflecting ones because large lenses are very heavy.

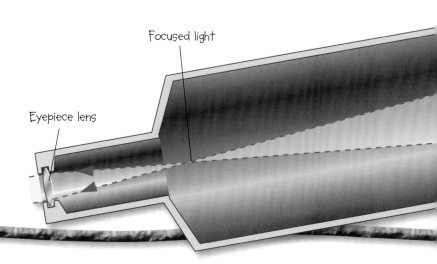

Focused light

Eyepiece lens

498 Astronomers are building telescopes with larger and larger mirrors. Bigger mirrors reveal fainter objects so telescopes can see further and further into the Universe. They also show more details in the distant galaxies and the wispy glowing clouds between the stars.

499 Today, professional astronomers don't look through their telescopes. They use cameras to capture the images. A camera can build up an image over a long time. The light adds up to make a brighter image, showing things that could not be seen by just looking through the telescope.

▲ A telescope reveals round craters on the Moon and large dark patches called "seas" although the Moon is completely dry.

▼ In a refracting telescope the main lens at the top bends the light, making an image near the bottom of the telescope.

Primary lens

Light enters

▲ The mirror from the Rosse Telescope in Ireland is 6 feet across and is kept in the Science Museum in London, UK. One hundred years ago it was the largest telescope in the world.

I DON'T BELIEVE IT!
The Liverpool telescope on the island of La Palma in the Atlantic Ocean is able to automatically observe a list of objects sent to it via the Internet.

Telescopes today

500 **All large modern telescopes are reflecting telescopes.** To make clear images, their mirrors must be exactly the right shape. The mirrors are made of polished glass, covered with a thin layer of aluminum to reflect as much light as possible. Some are made of thin glass that would sag without supports beneath to hold it in exactly the right shape.

501 **Large telescope mirrors are often made up of many smaller mirrors.** The mirrors of the Keck telescopes in Hawaii are made of 36 separate parts. Each has six sides, which fit together to make a mirror 30 feet across—about the width of a tennis court. The small mirrors are tilted to make exactly the right shape.

502 **The air above a telescope is constantly moving.** This can make their images blurred. Astronomers reduce this by using an extra mirror that can change shape. A computer works out what shape this mirror needs to be to remove the blurring effect and keeps changing it every few seconds. This is called adaptive optics.

▶ A huge frame holds the mirrors of a large reflecting telescope in position while tilting and turning to point at the stars.

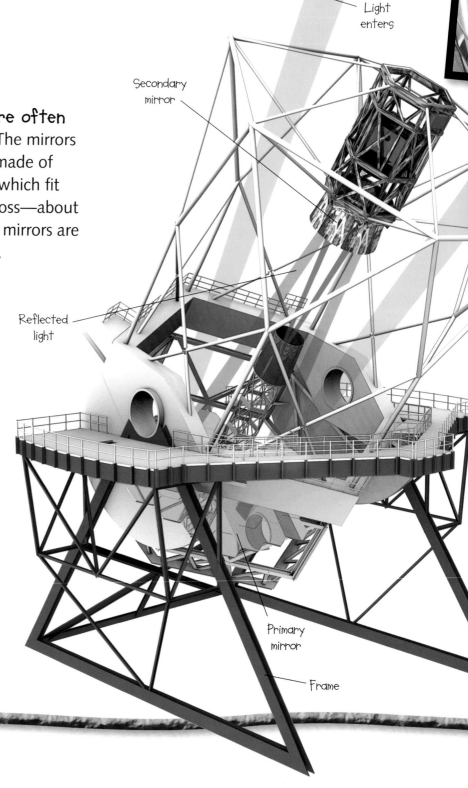

Light enters

Secondary mirror

Reflected light

Primary mirror

Frame

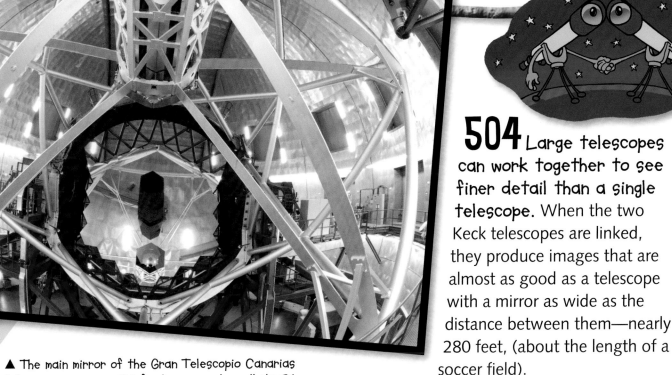

▲ The main mirror of the Gran Telescopio Canarias telescope measures 34 feet across when all its 36 separate parts are fitted together.

504 Large telescopes can work together to see finer detail than a single telescope. When the two Keck telescopes are linked, they produce images that are almost as good as a telescope with a mirror as wide as the distance between them—nearly 280 feet, (about the length of a soccer field).

503 Telescopes must be able to move to track the stars. It may take hours to make an image of a very faint, distant target and during this time the target will move gradually across the sky. Motors drive the telescope at just the right speed to keep it pointing at the target. All the time the image is being recorded using CCDs like those in an ordinary digital camera.

QUIZ

1. What are telescope mirrors made of?
2. How many sides does each piece of a Keck telescope mirror have?
3. Why do telescopes have to move?

Answers:
1. Glass 2. 6
3. To track the stars

▶ This picture of Saturn was taken by one of the Keck telescopes. The orange colors have been added to show the different temperatures in its clouds and rings.

Observatories

505 Observatories are places for watching the skies, often where telescopes are built and housed. There are usually several telescopes of different sizes at the same observatory. Astronomers choose remote places far away from cities, as bright lights would spoil their observations.

506 Observatories are often on the tops of mountains and in dry desert areas. This is because the air close to the ground is constantly moving and full of clouds and dust. Astronomers need very clear, dry, still air so they build their telescopes as high as possible above most of the clouds and dust.

▶ The Gemini North telescope is one of the telescopes at the Mauna Kea Observatories in Hawaii. It has a twin called Gemini South in Chile, South America.

507 A desert is a good place to build an observatory. The high mountains in the Atacama Desert, in Chile, South America, are among the driest places on Earth, and night skies there are incredibly dark. Several large telescopes have been built there including the Very Large Telescope (VLT).

▲ The Very Large Telescope is really four large telescopes and four smaller ones. The large telescopes are inside the square domes.

508 Some famous observatories are on top of a dormant volcano called Mauna Kea, on the island of Hawaii. It is the highest mountain on an island in the world—most clouds are below it. It is a good place for astronomy because the air is very clean and dry. It has more clear nights than most other places on Earth. It has 13 telescopes, four of them very large.

Telescope inside

Raised shutter

Rotating dome

Building linking telescopes

▲ The two Keck telescopes at the Mauna Kea Observatories each have their own round dome with shutters that open to let in the starlight.

▼ Observatories on Mauna Kea, Hawaii.

The Keck telescopes

509 Domes cover the telescopes to protect them and keep the mirrors clean. The domes have shutters that open when the telescopes are operating to let in the starlight. They also turn round so that the telescope can point in any direction and can move to track the stars.

Splitting light

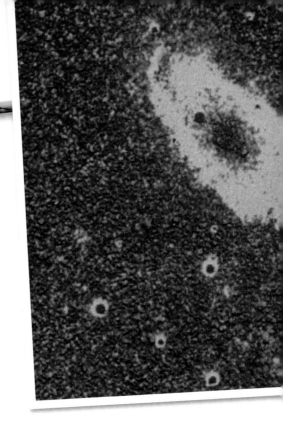

510 Astronomers find out about distant stars by studying the starlight that reaches Earth. They can get more data from the light by splitting it into its different colors—like a rainbow that forms when raindrops split up sunlight. These colors are called a spectrum.

RAINBOW SPECTRUM

You will need:
drinking glass   small mirror
water   flashlight   card

1. Put the mirror in the glass so that it faces upward.
2. Pour water into the glass to cover the mirror.
3. In a dark room, shine the flashlight onto the mirror.
4. Hold the card to catch the reflected light from the mirror and see a rainbow—the water and mirror have split the light into a spectrum.

511 Astronomers can tell how hot a star is from its spectrum. The hottest are blue-white, the coolest are red, and in between are yellow and orange stars. The spectrum also shows how big and bright the star is so astronomers can tell which are ordinary stars and which are red giants or supergiants.

512 A star's spectrum can show what gases the star is made of. Each gas has a different pattern of lines in the spectrum. Astronomers can also use the spectrum to find out which different gases make up a cloud of gas, by looking at starlight that has traveled through the cloud.

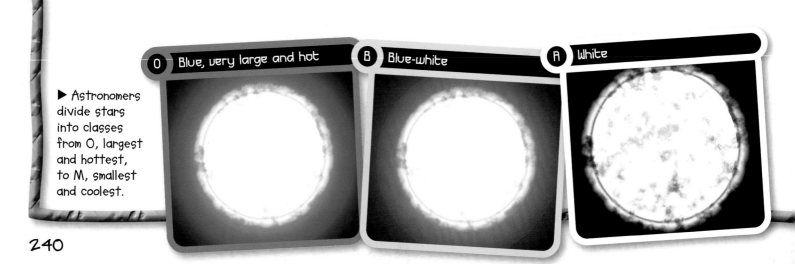

▶ Astronomers divide stars into classes from O, largest and hottest, to M, smallest and coolest.

O Blue, very large and hot

B Blue-white

A White

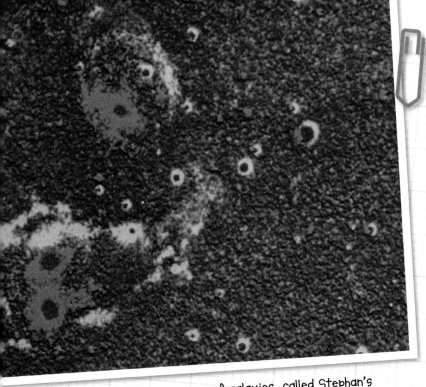

513 If a star or galaxy is moving away from Earth, its light is stretched out. This shows up in its spectrum and astronomers call it red shift. They use it to work out how fast a galaxy is moving and how far away it is. If the galaxy is moving toward Earth, the light gets squashed together and shows up in its spectrum as blue shift.

▲ In this group of galaxies, called Stephan's Quintet, the ones that have been colored red are moving away very quickly.

▼ This diagram shows the light waves coming to Earth from a distant galaxy as a wiggly line.

EARTH

DISTANT GALAXY

LIGHT WAVES

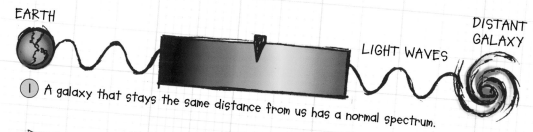

① A galaxy that stays the same distance from us has a normal spectrum.

② If the galaxy is moving away the light is stretched out and the spectrum shifts toward the red end.

③ If the galaxy is moving nearer the light is squashed up and the spectrum shifts toward the blue end.

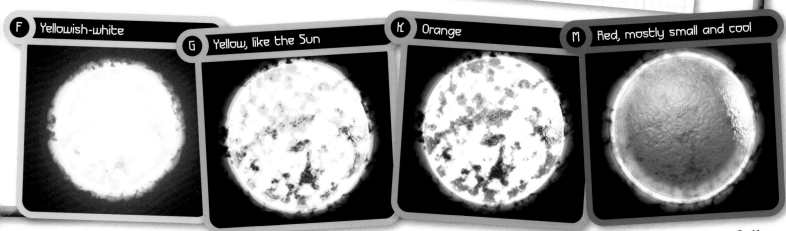

F Yellowish-white

G Yellow, like the Sun

K Orange

M Red, mostly small and cool

Space telescopes

514 Galaxies and stars send out other kinds of radiation, as well as light. Some send out radio waves like the ones that carry TV signals. There are also X-rays, like the kind that hospitals use to show broken bones, infrared light, gamma rays, and ultraviolet light. They all carry information.

515 The Hubble space telescope is like a normal telescope, but it is above the air. Its images are much clearer than if it were on the ground. It has produced images of distant gas clouds showing star birth, and looked deep into space at galaxies that have never been seen before.

▶ The Hubble space telescope was launched into orbit around the Earth in 1990 and is still sending astronomers amazing images from space.

516 Some kinds of radiation are detected more easily by telescopes in space. This is because the air around Earth stops most radiation from reaching the ground, which is good, because it would be harmful to life on Earth. Space telescopes orbit Earth to collect the radiation and send the information down to Earth.

QUIZ

1. What kind of radiation can spot newborn stars?
2. Which space telescopes collect gamma rays from space?
3. What kind of radiation can spot black holes?

Answers:
1. Infrared radiation
2. The Fermi and Integral Gamma-ray Telescopes 3. X-rays and gamma rays

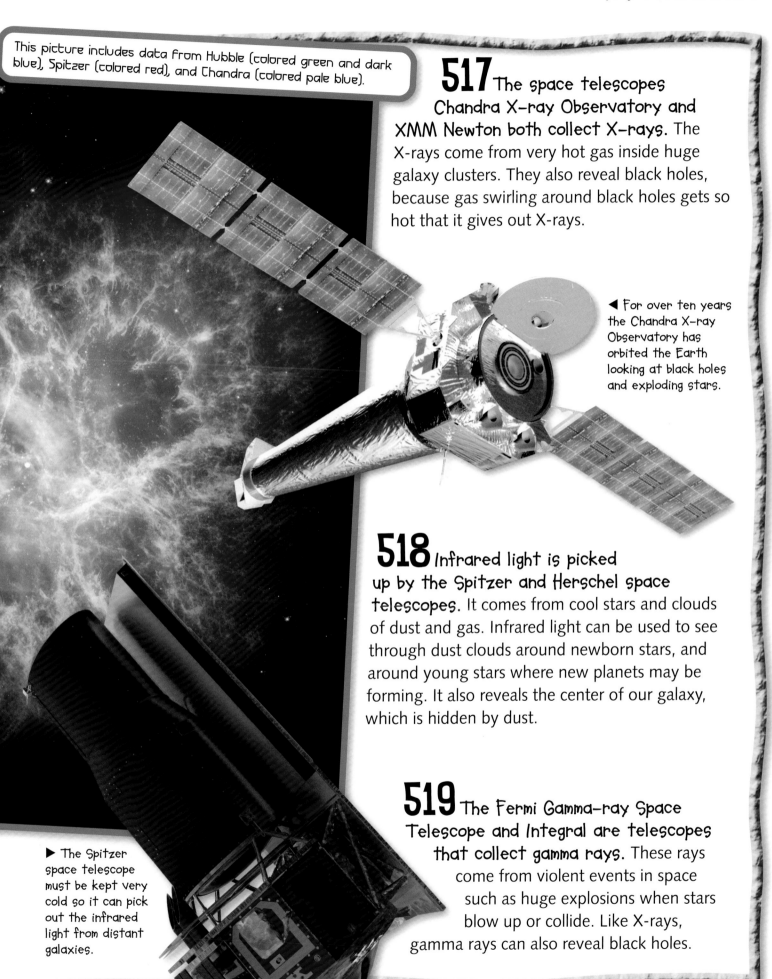

This picture includes data from Hubble (colored green and dark blue), Spitzer (colored red), and Chandra (colored pale blue).

517 The space telescopes Chandra X-ray Observatory and XMM Newton both collect X-rays. The X-rays come from very hot gas inside huge galaxy clusters. They also reveal black holes, because gas swirling around black holes gets so hot that it gives out X-rays.

◀ For over ten years the Chandra X-ray Observatory has orbited the Earth looking at black holes and exploding stars.

518 Infrared light is picked up by the Spitzer and Herschel space telescopes. It comes from cool stars and clouds of dust and gas. Infrared light can be used to see through dust clouds around newborn stars, and around young stars where new planets may be forming. It also reveals the center of our galaxy, which is hidden by dust.

▶ The Spitzer space telescope must be kept very cold so it can pick out the infrared light from distant galaxies.

519 The Fermi Gamma-ray Space Telescope and Integral are telescopes that collect gamma rays. These rays come from violent events in space such as huge explosions when stars blow up or collide. Like X-rays, gamma rays can also reveal black holes.

Radio telescopes

520 Radio waves from space are collected by radio telescopes. Most radio waves can travel through the air, so these telescopes are built on the ground. But there are lots of radio waves traveling around the Earth, carrying TV and radio signals, and phone calls. These can all interfere with the faint radio waves from space.

521 Radio telescopes work like reflecting telescopes, but instead of using a mirror, waves are collected by a big metal dish. They look like huge satellite TV aerials. Most dishes can turn to point at targets anywhere in the sky, and can track targets moving across the sky.

▶ Each radio telescope dish in the Very Large Array measures 82 feet across and can tilt and turn to face in different directions.

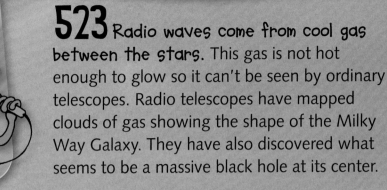

523 Radio waves come from cool gas between the stars. This gas is not hot enough to glow so it can't be seen by ordinary telescopes. Radio telescopes have mapped clouds of gas showing the shape of the Milky Way Galaxy. They have also discovered what seems to be a massive black hole at its center.

522 We can't see radio waves, but astronomers turn the signals into images we can see. The images from a single radio telescope dish are not very detailed but several radio telescopes linked together can reveal finer details. The Very Large Array (VLA) in New Mexico has 27 separate dishes arranged in a "Y" shape, all working together as though it was one huge dish 22 miles across.

524 Radio waves reveal massive jets of gas shooting out from distant galaxies. The jets are thrown out by giant black holes in the middle of some galaxies, which are gobbling up stars and gas around them.

▶ These two orange blobs are clouds of hot gas on either side of a galaxy. They are invisible to ordinary telescopes but radio telescopes can reveal them.

525 The Sun is our closest star and astronomers study it to learn about other stars. Without the Sun's light and heat nothing could live on the Earth, so astronomers keep a close eye on it. Tongues of very hot gas called flares and prominences often shoot out from the Sun.

▼ Wispy gas surrounds the Sun (colored blue) in this image from the SOHO spacecraft.

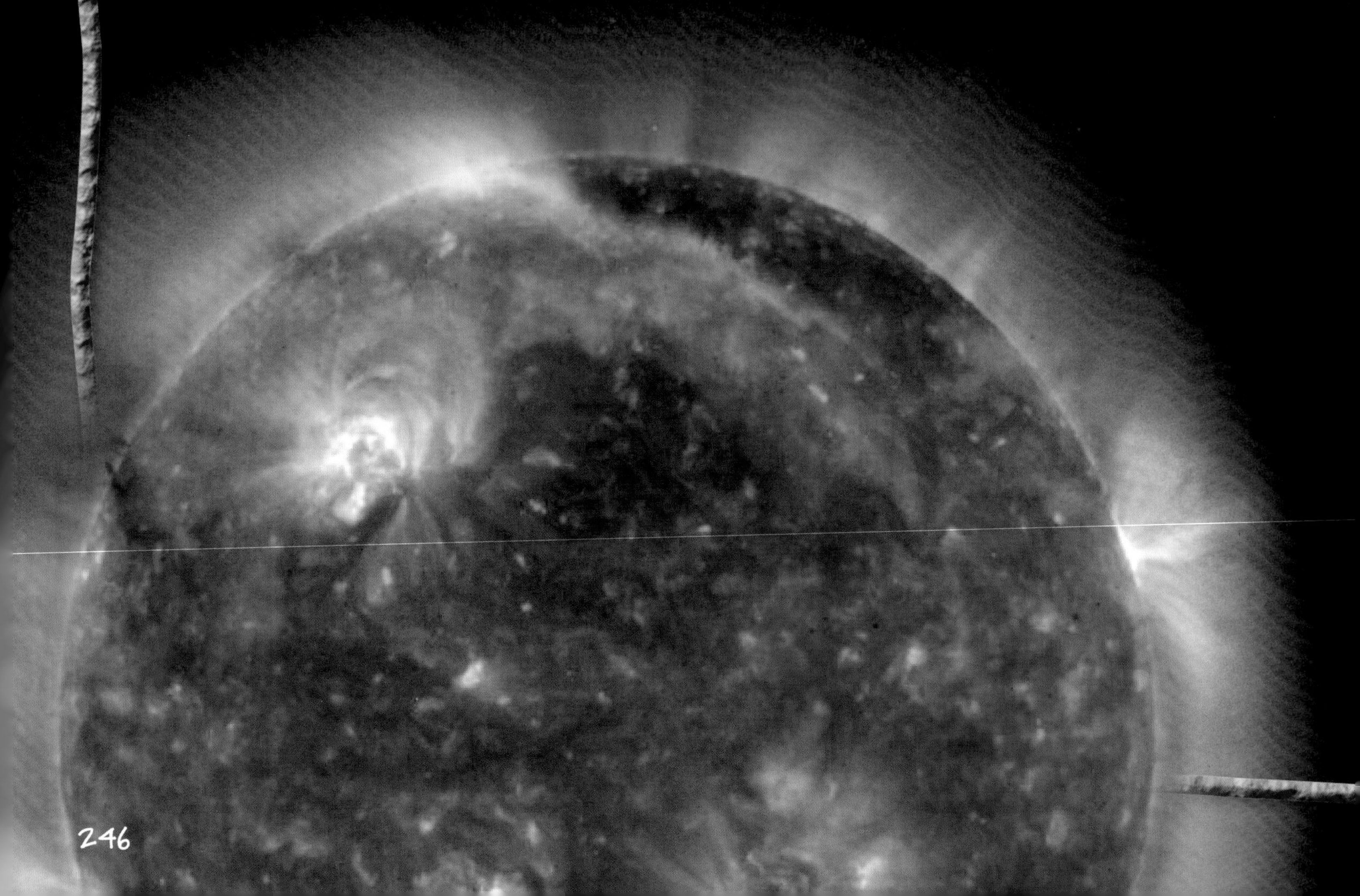

526 Particles constantly stream out from the surface of the Sun in all directions. This is called the solar wind. Sometimes a huge burst of particles, called a Coronal Mass Ejection (CME), breaks out. If one comes toward Earth it could damage satellites and even telephone and power lines. CMEs can be dangerous for astronauts in space.

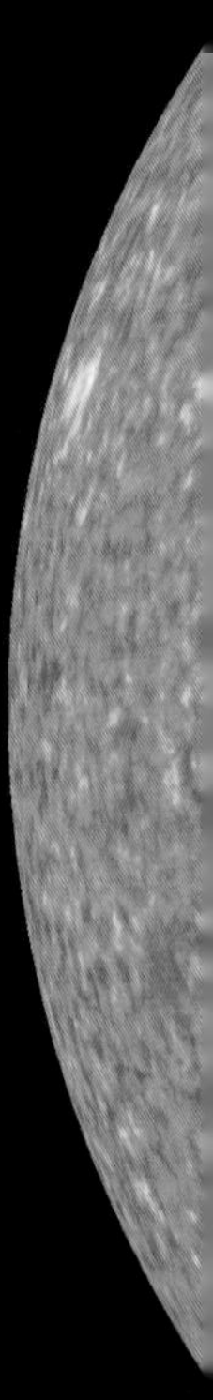

527 A spacecraft called SOHO has been watching the Sun since 1995. It orbits the Sun between the Earth and the Sun, sending data and images back to Earth. It warns of changes in solar wind and of CMEs that could hit Earth, and has spotted many comets crashing into the Sun.

◀ This image, captured in February 2011 by STEREO, shows the world's first ever view of the far side of the Sun.

WARNING
Never look directly at the Sun, especially not through a telescope or binoculars. It is so bright it will harm your eyes and could even make you blind.

I DON'T BELIEVE IT!
The Sun is losing weight! Every second about 4 million tons of its gas is turned into energy and escapes as light and heat. The Sun is so big that it can continue losing weight at this rate for about another 5 billion years.

528 STEREO are a pair of spacecraft that look at the Sun. They orbit the Sun, one each side of the Earth, to get a 3D view. Like SOHO, they are looking for storms on the Sun that could affect the Earth. Information from STEREO is helping astronomers to work out why these storms happen.

▶ This illustration shows the two Stereo spacecraft soon after they were launched in 2006. They moved apart until they were on either side of the Earth.

The edge of the Universe

529 Astronomers think that the Universe started in a huge explosion they call the Big Bang, which sent everything flying apart. As astronomers look into the Universe they are looking back in time. This is because light takes time to travel across the vast distances in space. It takes over four years for light to reach Earth from the second nearest star (after the Sun), so we see this star as it was when the light left it four years ago.

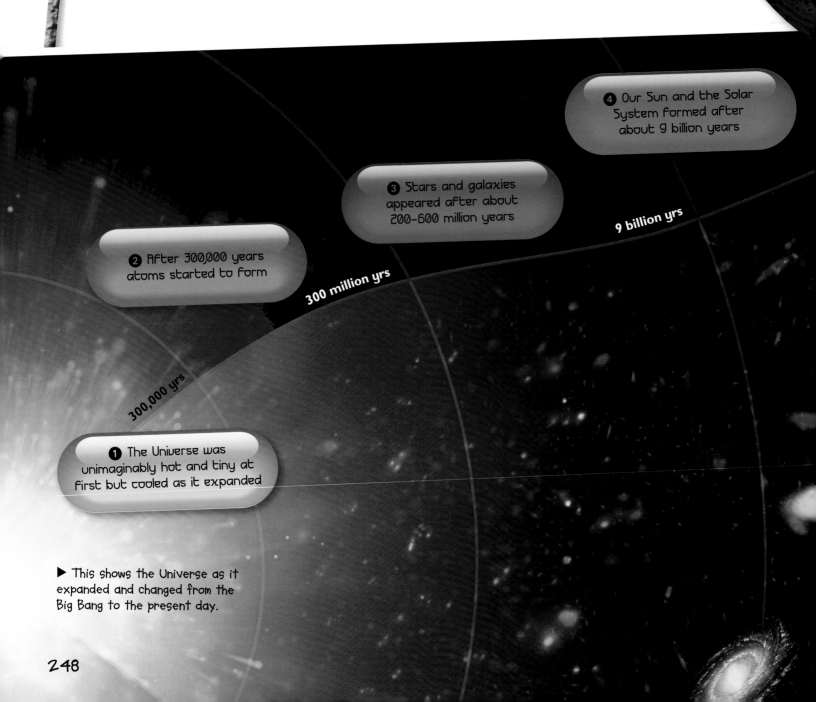

④ Our Sun and the Solar System formed after about 9 billion years

③ Stars and galaxies appeared after about 200–600 million years

9 billion yrs

② After 300,000 years atoms started to form

300 million yrs

300,000 yrs

① The Universe was unimaginably hot and tiny at first but cooled as it expanded

▶ This shows the Universe as it expanded and changed from the Big Bang to the present day.

◄ A map of the Cosmic Background Radiation shows tiny differences in temperature, the red areas are slightly warmer and the blue areas cooler.

530 Astronomers have found faint radiation coming from all over the sky. They call this the Cosmic Background Radiation. It is the remains of radiation left by the Big Bang explosion and helps to prove that the Big Bang really happened. Astronomers send satellites up to map this radiation and find out more about the Universe when it was very young.

13.7 billion yrs

5 The Universe is now about 13.7 billion years old

▲ These galaxies are so far away that we are seeing them as they were billions of years ago when the Universe was much younger.

531 Astronomers use their biggest telescopes and space telescopes to try and find the most distant galaxies. They do not know how soon after the Big Bang the first stars and galaxies appeared and whether they were different from the stars and galaxies they see today. The Hubble space telescope has taken images of very faint faraway galaxies showing astronomers what the early Universe was like.

Up close

532 The planets and our Moon have all been explored by space probes. These travel through space carrying cameras and other instruments with which they can gather data. They then send all the information and images back to astronomers on Earth.

533 Some space probes fly past planets, gathering information. The *Voyager 2* space probe flew past the four giant planets (Jupiter, Saturn, Uranus, and Neptune) in turn between 1979 and 1989. Astronomers now know much more about these planets from the detailed information and images *Voyager 2* sent back.

VOYAGER 2

▶ *Voyager 2* sent back this picture of Callisto, one of Jupiter's large moons.

Launch date: August 20, 1977
Mission: Flew past Jupiter in 1979, Saturn in 1981, Uranus in 1986, and Neptune in 1989. Now flying out of the Solar System into deep space.

534
Space probes can orbit a planet to study it for longer. The probe *Cassini* went into orbit round Saturn. It carried a smaller probe that dropped onto Saturn's largest moon, Titan, to look at its surface, which is hidden by cloud. The main probe circled Saturn, investigating its moons and rings.

535
Venus is hidden by clouds, but the *Magellan* probe was able to map its surface. The probe sent radio signals through the clouds to bounce off the surface. It then collected the return signal. This is called radar. It revealed that Venus has many volcanoes.

CASSINI

▶ Saturn and its rings, taken by the *Cassini* spacecraft as it approached the planet.

Launch date: October 15, 1997
Mission: Arrived at Saturn in 2004. Dropped Huygens probe onto Saturn's largest moon, Titan, then went into orbit to explore Saturn, its rings and moons.

SPIRIT AND OPPORTUNITY

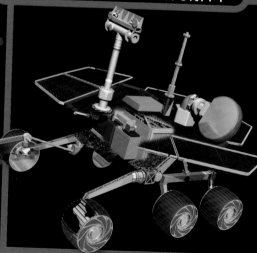

▲ Among the many rocks scattered across the dusty Martian landscape *Spirit* found a rock that could have crashed down from space.

536
Some probes land on a planet's surface. The probes *Spirit* and *Opportunity* explored the surface of Mars. They moved slowly, stopping to take pictures and analyze rocks. They have discovered that although Mars is very dry now, there may have once been water on the surface.

Launch date: June 10, 2003 (Spirit) and July 7, 2003 (Opportunity)
Mission: After landing on Mars in January 2004 the two rovers drove across the surface testing the rocks and soil and sending back images and data.

Astronomy from home

537 Many people enjoy astronomy as a hobby. You need warm clothes and somewhere dark, away from street and house lights, and a clear night. After about half an hour your eyes adjust to the dark so you can see more stars. A map of the constellations will help you find your way around the night sky.

538 Binoculars reveal even more stars and show details on the Moon. It is best to look at the Moon when it is half full. Craters, where rocks have crashed into the Moon, show up along the dark edge down the middle of the Moon. Binoculars also show Jupiter's moons as spots of light on or either side of the planet.

539 Telescopes are usually more powerful than binoculars and show fainter stars. They also show more detail in faint gas clouds called nebulae. Amateurs use reflecting and refracting telescopes, mounted on stands to keep them steady.

540 A camera can be fixed to a telescope to photograph the sky. A camera can build up an image over time if the telescope moves to follow the stars. The images show details that you could not see by just looking through the telescope.

KIT LIST

* Star map
* Red light torch
* Deck chair
* Warm clothes
* Pencil and notebook
* Blanket or sleeping bag
* Binoculars
* Telescope

SPOT VENUS

Venus is the brightest planet and easy to spot— it is known as the "evening star." Look toward the west in the twilight just after the Sun has set. The first bright "star" to appear will often be Venus.

▼ In November each year amateur astronomers look out for extra shooting stars during the Leonid meteor shower.

▲ In 1997 the bright Comet Hale Bopp could be seen easily without a telescope or binoculars.

541 Meteors, also called shooting stars, look like streaks of light in the sky. They are made when tiny pieces of space rock and dust hit the air around the Earth and burn up. Several times during the year there are meteor showers when many shooting stars are seen. You can spot meteors without a telescope or binoculars.

▶ An amateur astronomer uses binoculars to see the many stars in the Milky Way.

542 Amateurs can collect useful information for professional astronomers. They are often the first to spot a new comet in the sky. Comets are named after the person who found them and some amateur astronomers even specialize in comet spotting. Others watch variable stars and keep records of the changes in their brightness.

What lies ahead?

543 Kepler is a new satellite built specially to look for stars that might have planets where there could be life. So far, astronomers have not found life anywhere else in the Solar System. Kepler was launched in 2009 and is looking at stars to see if any of them have any planets like Earth.

▶ A Delta II rocket launches the Kepler spacecraft in March 2009 on its mission to hunt for distant planets.

I DON'T BELIEVE IT!

Astronomers are planning a new radio telescope, to be built in either Australia or South Africa. It is called the Square Kilometer Array and will have at least 3,000 separate radio telescopes. It should start working in 2020.

544 ALMA (short for Atacama Large Millimeter Array) is a powerful new radio telescope being built high up in the Atacama Desert in Chile. It consists of 66 radio dishes linked together to make one huge radio telescope.

545 The James Webb Space Telescope will replace the Hubble Space telescope in 2018. Its mirror will be 21 feet across, nearly three times wider than Hubble's main mirror. This will not fit in a rocket so it will be made of 18 separate mirrors that will unfold and fit together once the telescope is in space.

▲ A large sunshield will keep the mirrors of the James Webb telescope cool so it can make images using infrared light.

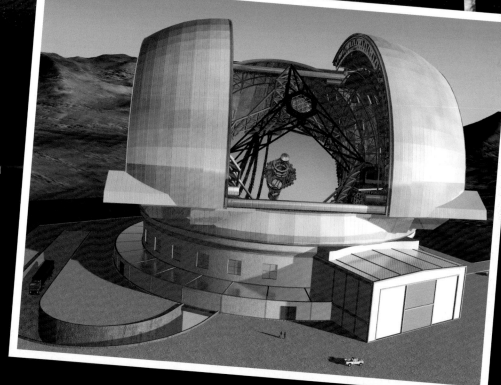

546 Several new giant telescopes are being planned. The Thirty Meter Telescope will have a mirror almost 100 feet across—about the length of three houses. This will be made of 492 smaller mirrors. The European Extremely Large Telescope will have an even larger mirror, 138 feet across, made of 984 separate mirrors. Both should be ready to use in the early 2020s.

▲ The European Extremely Large Telescope will be the largest optical telescope in the world when it is built in the Atacama Desert in Chile.

547 The European Space Agency (ESA) is planning to launch a new X-ray telescope in the future. It will investigate the gases in groups of galaxies, as well as the formation of black holes and how they grow.

FLIGHT

- Early flying
- The first fighter planes
- Getting airborne
- Engines and propellers
- Controlling a plane
- Passenger planes
- Helicopters
- Balloons and airships
- Supersonic aircraft
- Unusual planes

What was the name of the first jet fighter plane?

Why don't helicopters need runways?

What is an airfoil?

How many wheels are there on a jumbo jet?

Where is the cockpit?

Flying machines

▶ Modern fighter planes such as these Eurofighter Typhoons speed through the skies to attack an enemy.

548 People first tried to fly hundreds of years ago. They made wings from different materials and invented machines to take to the air, but nothing seemed to work. Then it was discovered that a curved wing moving through the air lifted upward—and the age of flight began. Now huge airliners carry hundreds of passengers halfway around the world, high above the clouds every day—and in the future, passengers may be able to travel into space.

The first flights

549 **The first humans to fly went up in a balloon, not a plane.** In 1783 in France, the Montgolfier brothers made a large balloon and heated the air inside it by lighting a fire underneath. The balloon rose into the air carrying two passengers who floated over Paris for 25 minutes. They carried a small fire to heat the air and keep the balloon afloat.

▲ In 1783 two volunteers flew to a height of 2,950 feet in the Montgolfier brothers' balloon.

550 **The first planes were gliders with no engines.** In the 1890s, a German called Otto Lilienthal experimented with flying by building small gliders that would carry him into the air. He tried using different wing shapes to see which worked best. To become airborne, he launched himself from the top of a hill and glided downward.

I DON'T BELIEVE IT!

Before letting people fly in their balloon, the Montgolfier brothers tried it out with a duck, a sheep, and a chicken!

▶ To test his flying machines Otto Lilienthal practised jumping from cliffs, hills, and rooftops.

551 The first real plane with an engine flew at a place called Kitty Hawk in North Carolina in 1903. It was built by Wilbur and Orville Wright and called the *Wright Flyer*. It had two wings, one above the other, and was driven by two propellers behind the wings.

552 The first helicopter looked like a plane with whirling wings. It was built in the 1930s. It had a body like a plane but with no wings. Two rotors were fixed on top, each with blades that whirled round in a circle. They lifted the helicopter straight up so it could hover in the air and move backward and forward.

553 The first nonstop flight across the Atlantic from the U.S. to Europe was in 1919. Two British airmen called John Alcock and Arthur Brown flew a Vickers Vimy, a type of bomber aircraft. The journey took 16.5 hours and they flew through terrible storms. The Vimy had an open cockpit, so gave little protection from the weather.

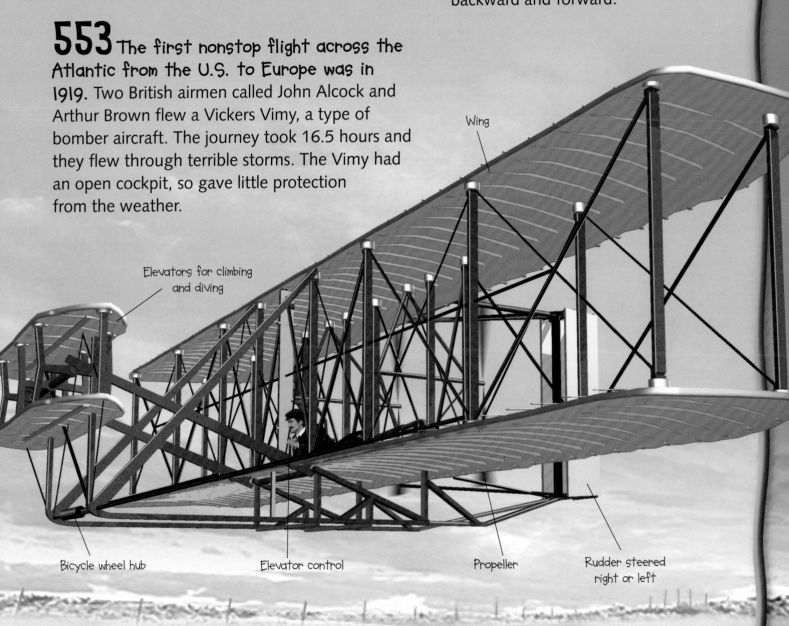

Wing

Elevators for climbing and diving

Bicycle wheel hub

Elevator control

Propeller

Rudder steered right or left

▲ To fly their plane, the Wright brothers had to lie on the lower wing.

Early days of flying

554 During World War I, planes were used in battle. Many were biplanes with double wings such as the Sopwith Camel. Fighter planes were built with machine guns to shoot down enemy planes. They could also fire at soldiers on the ground, while larger planes and airships dropped bombs.

▲ A British pilot in his Sopwith Camel watches a burning German plane. The plane got its name from the hump over its guns.

The *Hindenburg*

555 In the 1920s and '30s huge airships carried people between Europe and the U.S. These giant oval machines had engines and propellers to push and steer them along. Passengers traveled in cabins below the airship. However the light gas used to lift the airship was often hydrogen, which easily catches fire. In May 1937, the airship *Hindenburg* burst into flames. This put an end to travel by airship.

◀ Thirty-six people died when the *Hindenburg* airship crashed in flames in 1937.

TRUE OR FALSE?

1. A fight between two planes was called a catfight.
2. Jet airliners can fly higher than propeller aircraft.
3. Airships are filled with heavy gas.

Answers:
1. False 2. True 3. False

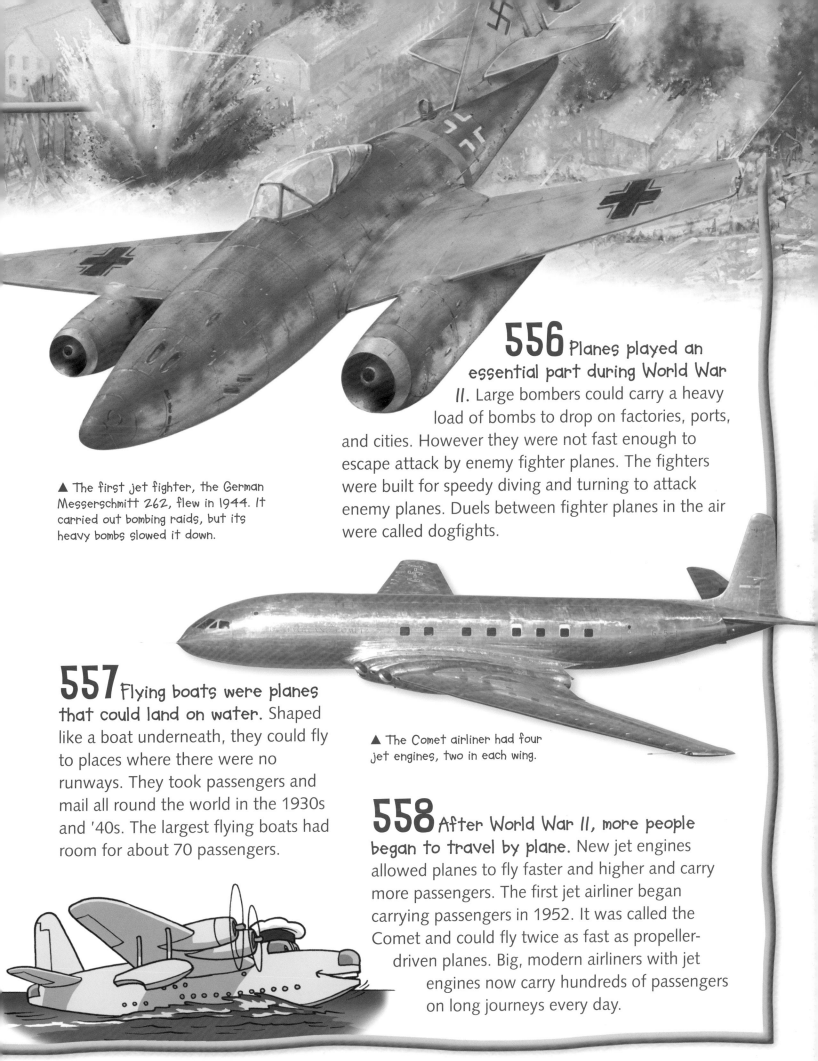

▲ The first jet fighter, the German Messerschmitt 262, flew in 1944. It carried out bombing raids, but its heavy bombs slowed it down.

556 Planes played an essential part during World War II. Large bombers could carry a heavy load of bombs to drop on factories, ports, and cities. However they were not fast enough to escape attack by enemy fighter planes. The fighters were built for speedy diving and turning to attack enemy planes. Duels between fighter planes in the air were called dogfights.

557 Flying boats were planes that could land on water. Shaped like a boat underneath, they could fly to places where there were no runways. They took passengers and mail all round the world in the 1930s and '40s. The largest flying boats had room for about 70 passengers.

▲ The Comet airliner had four jet engines, two in each wing.

558 After World War II, more people began to travel by plane. New jet engines allowed planes to fly faster and higher and carry more passengers. The first jet airliner began carrying passengers in 1952. It was called the Comet and could fly twice as fast as propeller-driven planes. Big, modern airliners with jet engines now carry hundreds of passengers on long journeys every day.

Parts of a plane

559 The main body of a plane is usually long and thin, with a pointed nose and smooth shape to cut through the air easily. This is called the fuselage. At the front is the cockpit, or flight deck, where the pilot controls the plane. In a passenger plane, most of the remaining body is taken up by a cabin with seats for passengers. Under the cabin floor is a hold to store luggage.

▶ An Airbus A380 passenger liner. A typical airliner such as this has a smooth, streamlined body.

Tail

Fuselage

Engine

Cockpit (flight deck)

560 The wings keep the plane up in the air and stick out on either side of the fuselage. They are long and thin with a curved top surface. Engines are usually attached to the wings. Fuel tanks are inside the wings. Along the front and back edges of the wings are moving parts called control surfaces, which can be tilted up or down to steer the plane.

I DON'T BELIEVE IT!

A 747 Jumbo Jet has 18 wheels in total—a set of two wheels under the nose and four sets of four wheels under the body and wings.

◀ The fins on a MiG fighter plane provide extra stability and allow the pilot to control the plane more easily.

Fin

Jet engine

Wing

561 A tail at the back of the fuselage gives the plane stability. It looks like a fin pointing upward with two small wings on either side. These help to stop the plane swaying from side to side. Control surfaces called elevators move up or down and the rudder moves left or right.

562 Planes have wheels for takeoff and landing and for moving on the ground. Legs with wheels, called landing gear, are fixed to the underside of the fuselage. During flight, the landing gear fold up into the fuselage. Big, heavy planes need more wheels to soften the landing.

563 Engines provide power to push the plane forward. Some small planes have only one engine but most airliners have at least two. They are mounted on the wings or attached to the body. An airliner is designed so that if one engine stops working, the plane can go on flying using the other engines.

▼ A plane's wheels, or landing gear, lock into place for takeoff and landing.

Landing gear

How planes fly

564 A plane flies by moving through the air. The engines drive the plane forward with a force called thrust. However, air pushes in the opposite direction and slows the plane down. This is called drag. Weight is the force that tries to pull the plane down. When moving through the air, the wings give an upward force called lift.

Direction of air flow around wing

▲ As the wing moves forward, air streams under and over it, lifting it up.

565 Air flowing over the wings gives an upward lift. The wings are a special shape called an airfoil. The top curves upward while the bottom is flatter. As the plane moves forward, air flowing over the top has further to go and is more spread out than the air beneath. The air beneath pushes the wing harder than the air above it, so the wing lifts, taking the plane with it.

LIFTING FORCE

Wrap a strip of narrow paper around a pencil. Holding one end of the strip, blow hard over the top of it. Watch the free end of the paper lift upward. This shows how an aircraft wing lifts as it moves through the air, keeping the heavy aircraft in the air. The faster you blow, the higher the paper lifts.

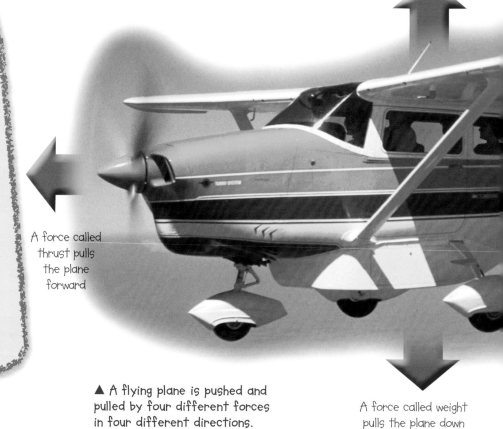

A force called lift pulls the plane up

A force called thrust pulls the plane forward

A force called weight pulls the plane down

▲ A flying plane is pushed and pulled by four different forces in four different directions.

► Flaps on the wings, called ailerons, direct the air flow up or down.

Aileron

567 As the plane moves forward it pushes against the air. The air pushes back, which slows the plane down and makes it use more fuel. Aircraft builders try to make the drag as minimal as possible by designing the plane to be smooth and streamlined so it cuts cleanly through the air.

566 The engines give the thrust that drives the plane forward in the air. As the plane travels faster, the lifting force grows stronger. This force must be equal to the weight of the plane before it can rise into the air and fly. This means that the thrust from the engines must drive the plane quickly to give it enough lift to fly.

568 The weight of a plane is always trying to pull it down. For this reason, planes are built to be as light as possible, using light but strong materials. Even so, a Boeing 747 jumbo jet with all its passengers and luggage can weigh as much as 360 tons and still take off.

▼ Jet engines or propellers thrust a plane forward.

Propeller engine

A force called drag pulls the plane back

569 Planes get thrust from jet engines or propellers. Jet engines are more powerful and better for flying high up where the air is thinner. Airliners and fighter planes have jet engines. Propellers are more useful for planes that fly slower and nearer the ground. Most small private planes and some large planes that carry heavy cargo use propeller engines.

Jet engine

Powerful engines

570 A jet engine thrusts a plane forward by shooting out a jet of hot gases. A turbojet engine uses spinning blades called a compressor to suck air into the front of the engine and squeeze it tightly. This air is then mixed with fuel inside the engine, as the fuel requires air to burn. The burning fuel creates hot gases that shoot out of a nozzle at the back of the engine.

BALLOON JET

Blow up a balloon then let it go. Watch the balloon shoot away as the air rushes out. In the same way, a plane shoots forward when gases rush out of its jet engines.

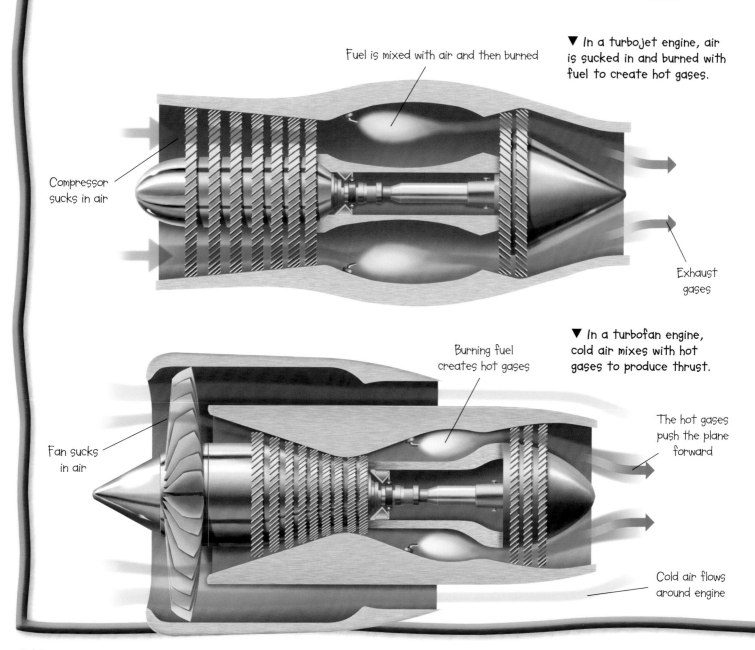

Fuel is mixed with air and then burned

▼ In a turbojet engine, air is sucked in and burned with fuel to create hot gases.

Compressor sucks in air

Exhaust gases

▼ In a turbofan engine, cold air mixes with hot gases to produce thrust.

Burning fuel creates hot gases

The hot gases push the plane forward

Fan sucks in air

Cold air flows around engine

571 A turbofan engine is another type of jet engine used by modern airliners. These are less noisy than turbojet engines and cheaper to run. A large fan at the front sucks in air, but not all of it is squeezed and mixed with fuel. Some of the air flows around the outside of the engine and mixes with the hot gases shooting out of the back.

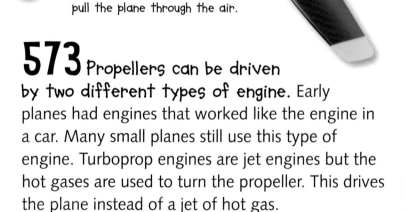

Propeller blade

Hub

▲ When the propellers spin, they pull the plane through the air.

572 Propellers whiz round at high speed, pulling the plane through the air. The propeller has two or more blades sticking out from the center. Each blade is like a small wing and as it spins, it pushes the air backward so the plane moves forward. Small planes have just one propeller at the front, but larger planes may have two or more propellers, each driven by its own engine.

573 Propellers can be driven by two different types of engine. Early planes had engines that worked like the engine in a car. Many small planes still use this type of engine. Turboprop engines are jet engines but the hot gases are used to turn the propeller. This drives the plane instead of a jet of hot gas.

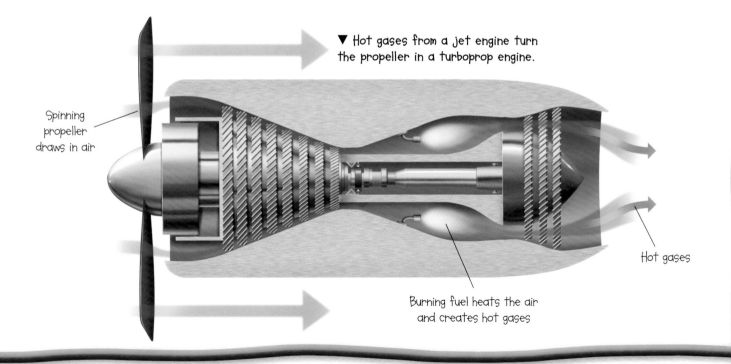

▼ Hot gases from a jet engine turn the propeller in a turboprop engine.

Spinning propeller draws in air

Hot gases

Burning fuel heats the air and creates hot gases

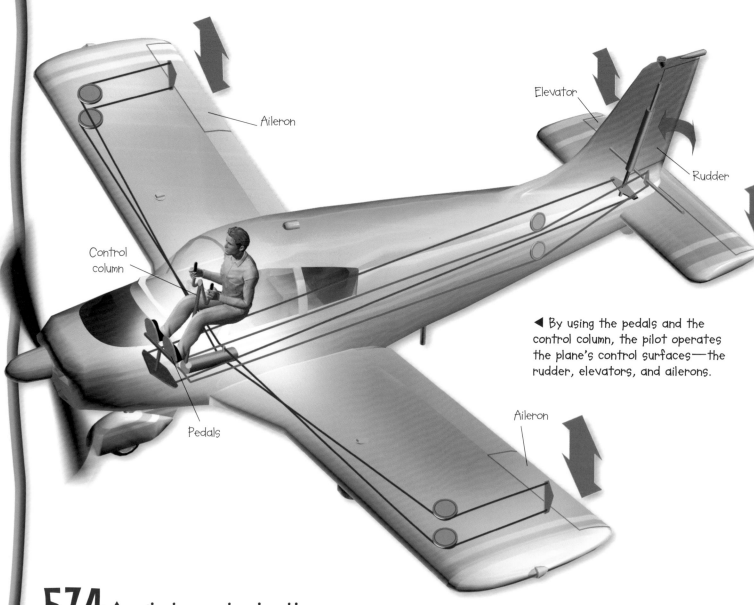

Aileron

Elevator

Rudder

Control column

Pedals

◀ By using the pedals and the control column, the pilot operates the plane's control surfaces—the rudder, elevators, and ailerons.

Aileron

574 A pilot controls the plane, making it climb, dive, or turn. He uses foot pedals and the control column. These are connected to the control surfaces on the wings and tail, which steer the plane. A plane moves in three directions. "Yaw" means to turn to the right or left. "Pitch" tilts the nose up or down and "roll" is simply to roll from side to side.

575 To make the plane climb higher the pilot pulls the control column toward him. This makes the elevators, the flaps attached to the back of the tail, tilt upward. The air flowing over the elevators now pushes the tail down and so the nose goes up and the plane climbs up at an angle. To dive, the pilot pushes the control column forward, tilting the elevators down.

576 Moving the control column to the left or right moves flaps called ailerons on the wings. Pushing to the left makes the left aileron go up and the one on the right go down. This lowers the left wing and lifts the right wing so the plane rolls over to the left. Pushing the control column to the right rolls the plane over to the right.

▲ By operating the control surfaces, a pilot is making this small plane turn in the air.

Roll
Wing tilts up or down

▶ Once in the air, a plane can move in three ways—roll, pitch, and yaw.

577 The pedals turn the plane to the right or left. These are connected to the rudder on the fin. Pushing the left pedal swings the rudder to the left. This turns the tail to the right and the nose toward the left, so the plane makes a left turn. The right pedal swings the rudder to the right, and the plane makes a right turn.

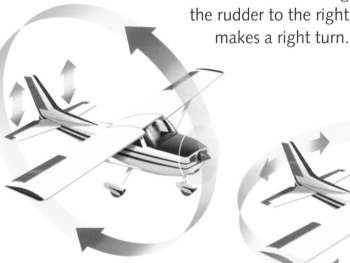

Pitch
Nose tilts up or down

Yaw
Turns left or right

578 When the plane turns in the air it must roll at the same time. This is called banking and is similar to a bike tilting over when turning a corner. For a right turn, the control column is moved to the right while the right pedal is pushed, turning and rolling the plane to the right at the same time.

Taking off and landing

579 **Planes take off by speeding along a runway.** The pilot sets the engines for maximum power. He travels down the runway until the plane has enough speed for the wings to lift it and fly. Planes usually take off facing into the wind. This gives a faster air flow over the wings and more lift.

▶ After takeoff, a plane climbs steeply until it reaches its cruising height.

Wheels for moving on runway

I DON'T BELIEVE IT!

The enormous cargo plane the Antonov AN-225 is so heavy that it needs a run of 2 mi to get up enough speed to takeoff when fully loaded. It has 32 wheels to cushion its landing.

580 When the plane has enough speed, the pilot pulls the control column back, raising the elevators on the tail. This lifts the nose and the plane starts to climb into the air. As soon as the plane is climbing steadily the pilot folds the wheels up into the body. This reduces drag and allows the plane to speed up more quickly. It climbs to its cruising height then levels off for the journey. Airliners fly above the clouds where the air is thinner and there is less drag.

◀ This plane has just taken off from an airport close to a holiday resort. Takeoff is an impressive sight—but it can be very noisy.

581 Air traffic controllers give the pilot instructions and information so that the plane can take off and land safely. The pilot must always follow the instructions of the air traffic controllers and he cannot land or take off until he has their permission to do so.

▲ In the control tower, computers show air traffic controllers which planes are ready for takeoff and landing.

582 Near the end of the journey, the pilot pushes the control column forward to point the nose down and descend. The pilot lines up the plane along the runway. He slows the engines and lowers the flaps on the wings to help slow the plane. When the wheels touch the ground, the plane may reverse its engines to stop.

583 In fog, when the pilot cannot see very far, planes can land automatically. The plane picks up radio signals from beacons beside the runway. The plane's computers use these signals to line the plane up with the runway and land safely on the runway.

▼ When landing, the wheels under the plane's fuselage touch down on the runway first, followed by the nose wheels.

JORDAN AVIATION

www.jordanaviation.jo

The flight deck

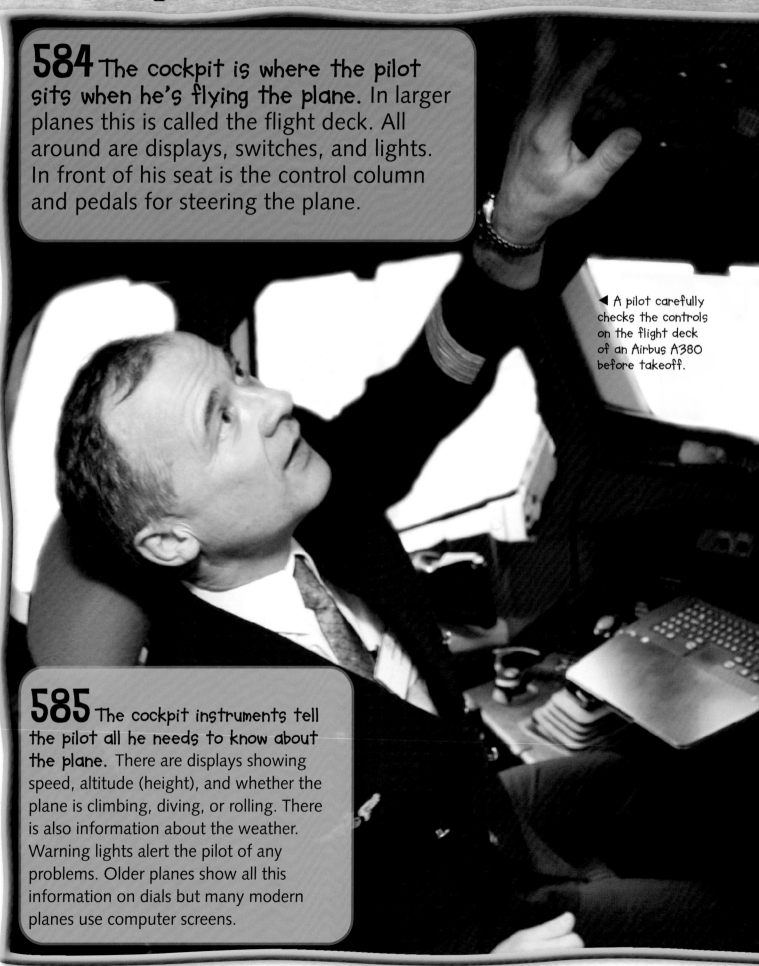

584 The cockpit is where the pilot sits when he's flying the plane. In larger planes this is called the flight deck. All around are displays, switches, and lights. In front of his seat is the control column and pedals for steering the plane.

◀ A pilot carefully checks the controls on the flight deck of an Airbus A380 before takeoff.

585 The cockpit instruments tell the pilot all he needs to know about the plane. There are displays showing speed, altitude (height), and whether the plane is climbing, diving, or rolling. There is also information about the weather. Warning lights alert the pilot of any problems. Older planes show all this information on dials but many modern planes use computer screens.

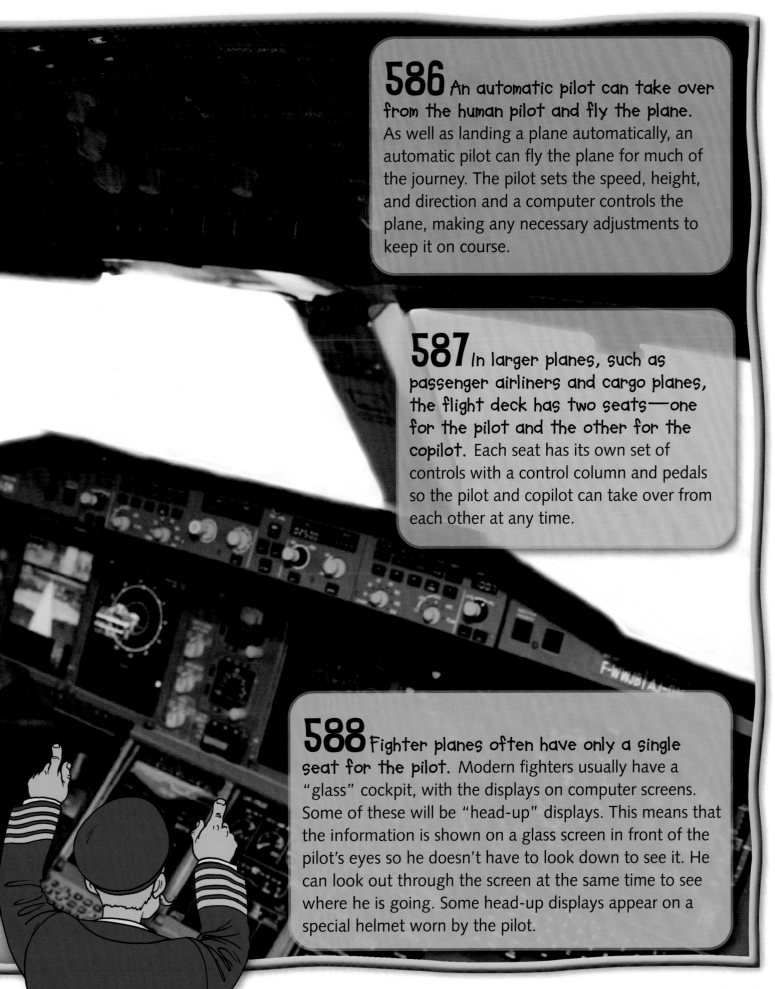

586 An automatic pilot can take over from the human pilot and fly the plane. As well as landing a plane automatically, an automatic pilot can fly the plane for much of the journey. The pilot sets the speed, height, and direction and a computer controls the plane, making any necessary adjustments to keep it on course.

587 In larger planes, such as passenger airliners and cargo planes, the flight deck has two seats—one for the pilot and the other for the copilot. Each seat has its own set of controls with a control column and pedals so the pilot and copilot can take over from each other at any time.

588 Fighter planes often have only a single seat for the pilot. Modern fighters usually have a "glass" cockpit, with the displays on computer screens. Some of these will be "head-up" displays. This means that the information is shown on a glass screen in front of the pilot's eyes so he doesn't have to look down to see it. He can look out through the screen at the same time to see where he is going. Some head-up displays appear on a special helmet worn by the pilot.

A passenger jet airliner

589 **In a passenger jet airliner, the cabin takes up almost all of the body.** It has seats for the passengers, usually between 200 and 400 altogether. At high altitude, the air outside is too thin for people to breathe. This means that the cabin and cockpit are sealed and filled with air for the passengers and crew to breathe.

► A Boeing 747 jumbo jet has wide wings that provide enormous lift. Its four powerful engines push the plane forward at cruising speeds of 620 miles an hour.

▼ Inside the cabin of a Boeing 747 jumbo jet. There is seating capacity for up to 400 passengers.

Upper deck and lounge

Windshield

Galley

Porthole

Landing gear

Oxygen cylinders

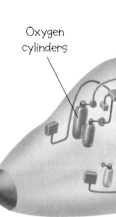

590 **Under the floor of the main cabin is the hold, where most of the luggage is stored.** As well as the passengers' baggage, planes often carry cargo in the hold. There is also room inside the cabin for smaller bags. These can go under the seats or in overhead lockers above the seats. Passengers cannot take a lot of very heavy luggage because the plane cannot fly if it is too heavy.

591 In the cabin there are small kitchens called galleys. Here the cabin staff store food and drink for the journey. Meals are prepared beforehand and delivered to the airport ready to serve. At mealtimes the cabin staff serve food from a trolley.

Tail fin

Rudder

Elevator

Fuselage

Washrooms

Tailplane

Baggage hold

Flap

592 Although flying accidents are rare, safety is very important. Passengers wear seat belts, especially for takeoff and landing. Each seat has a mask that supplies oxygen in case the cabin loses air. There are life jackets under the seats in case the plane has to land on water. There are special exit doors for an emergency landing.

Fuel tanks within wing

Aileron

Jet engine

Oxygen pipes

◀ Because the air is too thin for people to breathe when an airliner is at high altitude, the plane is sealed airtight and carries extra oxygen for emergencies.

Backup oxygen cylinders

I DON'T BELIEVE IT!
The Airbus A380 is a giant airliner. It can carry up to 853 passengers in two decks, one above the other!

At the airport

593 The most obvious parts of an airport are the terminals and the runways. Most big airports have at least two runways over 2 miles long. These allow the largest jets to take off and land. Lights and markings along the runway show the pilot where to touch down.

594 Passengers arrive at the terminal building for their flights. Tickets and passports are checked and luggage is left with the airline staff. Then passengers and their hand luggage are checked by security officers for dangerous objects such as knives. The luggage is also checked. People wait to board their plane in the departure lounge.

Passenger boarding bridge

▶ Airports can be huge and stretch for several miles. They have a constant flow of planes that are taking off and landing.

595 The area around the terminal where the planes park is called the **apron**. In large airports, the passengers walk through a closed bridge directly onto the plane. When everyone is on board and settled in their seats, the doors close and the bridge pulls away. Then the plane moves slowly toward the runway along paths called taxiways. Sometimes a truck called a tug may tow a plane into position on the runway.

596 The control tower ensures planes move safely around the airport. Air traffic controllers keep track of all planes, both on the ground and when they take off and land. Their job is to make sure the planes are far enough apart to avoid accidents. The controller and pilots talk to each other by radio. The pilots wait for the controllers to give permission to take off or land.

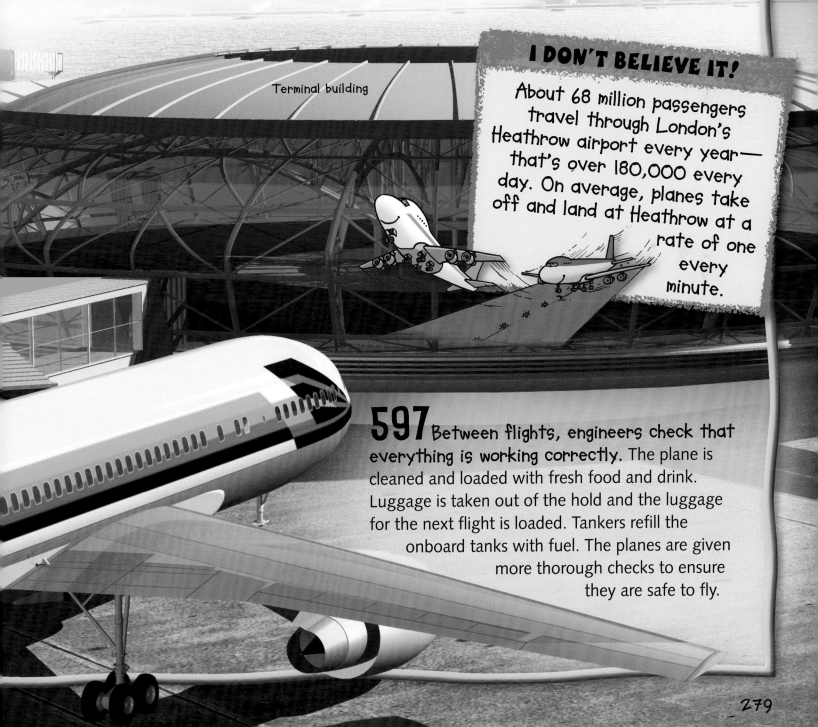

Terminal building

I DON'T BELIEVE IT!

About 68 million passengers travel through London's Heathrow airport every year— that's over 180,000 every day. On average, planes take off and land at Heathrow at a rate of one every minute.

597 Between flights, engineers check that everything is working correctly. The plane is cleaned and loaded with fresh food and drink. Luggage is taken out of the hold and the luggage for the next flight is loaded. Tankers refill the onboard tanks with fuel. The planes are given more thorough checks to ensure they are safe to fly.

Helicopters

Forward tilt

Backward tilt

Sideways tilt

Move up

Move down

▲ Because they can move in any direction, helicopters are extremely useful. The pilot tilts the blades to change direction.

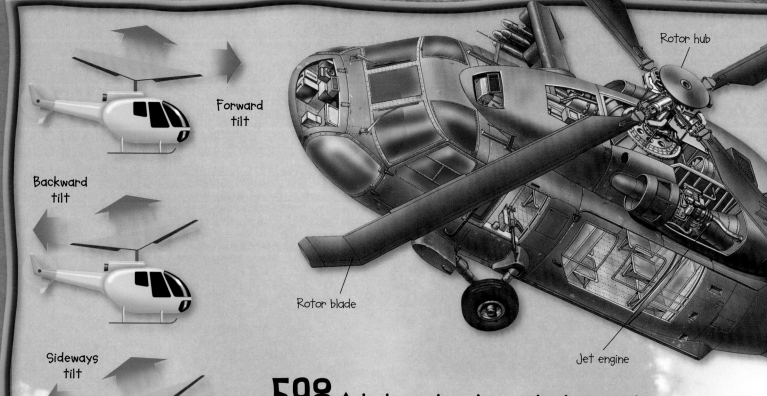

Rotor hub

Rotor blade

Jet engine

598 A helicopter has whirling rotors to lift it into the air. The rotors have blades that are shaped like long, narrow wings. The engine spins the blades. This lifts the helicopter in the same way as the wings on a plane. A tail rotor stops the helicopter spinning in the opposite direction to the main rotor.

599 Helicopters can move in any direction—up, down, right, left, forward, or backward. This is done by changing the tilt of the rotor blades. To go forward, the blades twist as they turn to give more lift at the back. This tilts the tail up and the helicopter moves forward. It can also spin on the spot using the tail rotor. All this movement makes helicopters very difficult to fly.

600 Helicopters do not need a runway and can land anywhere as long as there is enough room. This makes them very useful, especially for rescuing people from the sea or mountains as they can hover in one place. While hovering, injured or stranded people can be lifted into the helicopter then carried to safety.

▲ A helicopter can hover in one place to enable emergency workers to be lowered to accident scenes to help sick or injured people.

Tail rotor

Tailplane and fin

▲ The Black Hawk military helicopter is used to carry troops and supplies during times of combat.

601 Some helicopters have double rotors to lift heavy loads. The Chinook helicopter has one rotor at the front and one at the back. One is slightly above the other and they turn in opposite directions. These helicopters can carry up to 55 soldiers or heavy military equipment slung underneath the helicopter.

▼ Two large rotors give the Chinook helicopter extra lifting power to carry more people.

MAKE A WHIRLING ROTOR

Take a piece of paper 8 in by 2 in and fold it in half. Unfold it then cut from one short edge to the fold to make two strips. Fold these in opposite directions and put a paper clip on the other end. Watch it whirl like a helicopter rotor when you drop it.

Lighter than air

602 Balloons and airships can fly because they are lighter than air. They are filled with a very light gas that tries to rise above the heavier air around it. If there is enough gas, it can lift the weight of the balloon or airship so that it floats up into the air.

▲ The gas from a burner heats up the air inside a balloon, making the balloon float upward.

▶ Hot air balloons are flown for fun and are spectacular to watch. There are competitions held around the world where balloonists can compete in races.

LOOK FOR RISING HOT AIR

Watch the smoke from a BBQ or a bonfire. It always drifts upward. This is because the hot coal heats the air, which rises up above the surrounding colder air. The tiny smoke particles let us see the air rising.

603 The air inside a hot air balloon is heated to make it lighter than the cool air around it. Burners under the balloon heat the air inside, which spreads out and becomes lighter than the air outside. When the burners are turned on, the balloon rises. With the burners off, the balloon gradually falls as the air inside it cools. To fall more quickly, the pilot opens a vent (hole) and lets out some of the hot air. A balloon can't be steered, it goes where the wind blows it.

◀ The first balloon to fly nonstop around the world was Breitling Orbiter 3.

605 Weather balloons use a light gas called helium to go much higher than hot air balloons. They measure temperatures and winds high above the clouds and send the information back by radio. Helium balloons have also broken records. In 1999 Bertrand Piccard and Brian Jones were the first people to fly a balloon around the world without stopping. It took them nearly 20 days in the Breitling Orbiter 3.

604 Airships are also filled with light gas, but unlike balloons they have engines to steer them. Modern airships use helium gas, which does not burn. The engines and propellers drive the airship and steer it with the help of rudders. There is a cabin for the pilot and passengers called a gondola. Airships are often seen hovering above events such as the Olympic Games, carrying TV cameras to give a view from the air.

▶ This airship has been fitted with radar and tied to a ship. It will be used to spot icebergs beneath the water, and warn passing ships to steer clear of them.

Taking off vertically

▼ The American V-z22 Osprey takes off like a helicopter, using its two rotors.

606 Vertical takeoff planes do not need a long runway—they take off upward. There are two main types—planes that use propellers called tiltrotor planes and those that have jet engines and are often called jump jets. These aircraft are mostly used as military planes. They can land on ships at sea and carry troops and equipment to army bases without a runway.

607 The V-22 Osprey is a plane with two large propellers at the ends of its wings. These lift the Osprey straight up into the air just like helicopter rotor blades. Then the engines swivel round at the ends of the wings so the propellers are tilted upright. The Osprey then flies like a normal plane. The propellers can also be tilted to allow the V-22 Osprey to hover like a helicopter.

▶ A spinning fan inside the F-35B acts like a helicopter rotor.

◀ Harrier jump jets operate mainly from aircraft carriers at sea.

608 The new F-35B plane uses a spinning fan and the blast from its jet engines to take off. It needs a short runway. It starts by moving forward then directs the jet from its engine downward. With the help of a large fan in the middle of the plane, it lifts up off the runway. Then the plane swivels backward and flies at supersonic speed. The fan also lets the plane hover in the air and land straight downward.

609 The Harrier jump jet uses its jet engines to take off upward. The jet of gas from the engines is directed downward, pushing the plane up into the air. For normal flight the jets of gas are directed backward and it flies like any other jet plane. Like the Osprey it can hover in the air and land without a runway. A British plane, the Harrier was first introduced in 1969.

I DON'T BELIEVE IT!

In 1954 a strange experimental object took off vertically. It was nicknamed the Flying Bedstead because that is exactly what it looked like—a metal frame with four legs and two engines. It could take off upward, hover, and move backward and forward.

285

Planes for war

610 In war, planes are used to attack the enemy, drop bombs, and carry troops and equipment. Modern military planes often act as both fighter and bomber. They fly fast enough to attack and escape from danger while carrying bombs and missiles. Large bombers can usually fly longer distances than fighter planes.

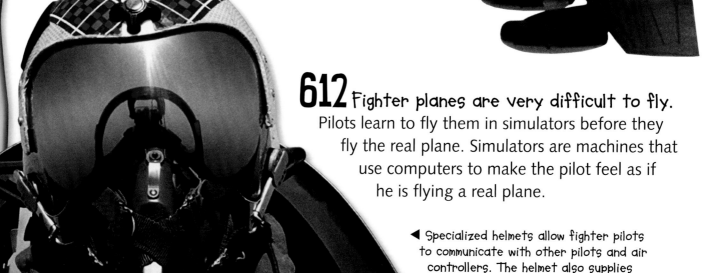

▲ After dropping its bombs a fighter plane speeds away. Fighters are usually small and agile.

611 Military planes have different weapons depending on the mission. They carry rockets, missiles, and bombs as well as guns. Many missiles and bombs can find their own way to the target. Missiles have a rocket engine to home in on the target. "Smart" bombs have no engine. Instead they glide down using fins to steer onto the target. Pilots can fire their weapons at more than one target at the same time.

▼ A fighter plane (far right) flies next to a bigger tanker plane (below) for refuelling.

612 Fighter planes are very difficult to fly. Pilots learn to fly them in simulators before they fly the real plane. Simulators are machines that use computers to make the pilot feel as if he is flying a real plane.

◀ Specialized helmets allow fighter pilots to communicate with other pilots and air controllers. The helmet also supplies the pilot with air to breathe.

613 The armed forces use huge cargo planes to carry troops and heavy equipment. They deliver tanks and all the other supplies and equipment needed by an army wherever it is fighting. Cargo planes need a runway to land on, so helicopters take over from planes to carry men and equipment around the battlefield.

▲ *Global Hawk* spy plane is a robot that operates without a pilot.

614 Planes can spy on the enemy. From the air, spy planes use cameras and spying equipment to give a picture of what is happening on the ground and where enemy planes are. A control center on the plane keeps its own forces informed and tells them what and where to attack. Spy planes also fly over the ocean to spot submarines and warn naval ships.

615 Many military planes can refuel while flying. They often have to fly long distances and there may not be anywhere they can land to refuel. Large tanker planes carrying fuel fly alongside. A pipe links the two planes and delivers fuel from the tanker. This allows the fighter or bomber to fly much further.

I DON'T BELIEVE IT!

Most military planes have ejection seats so the pilot can escape if the aircraft is hit. The whole seat with the pilot sitting in it is catapulted out of the cockpit. A rocket shoots it upward, then a parachute opens to lower it gently to the ground.

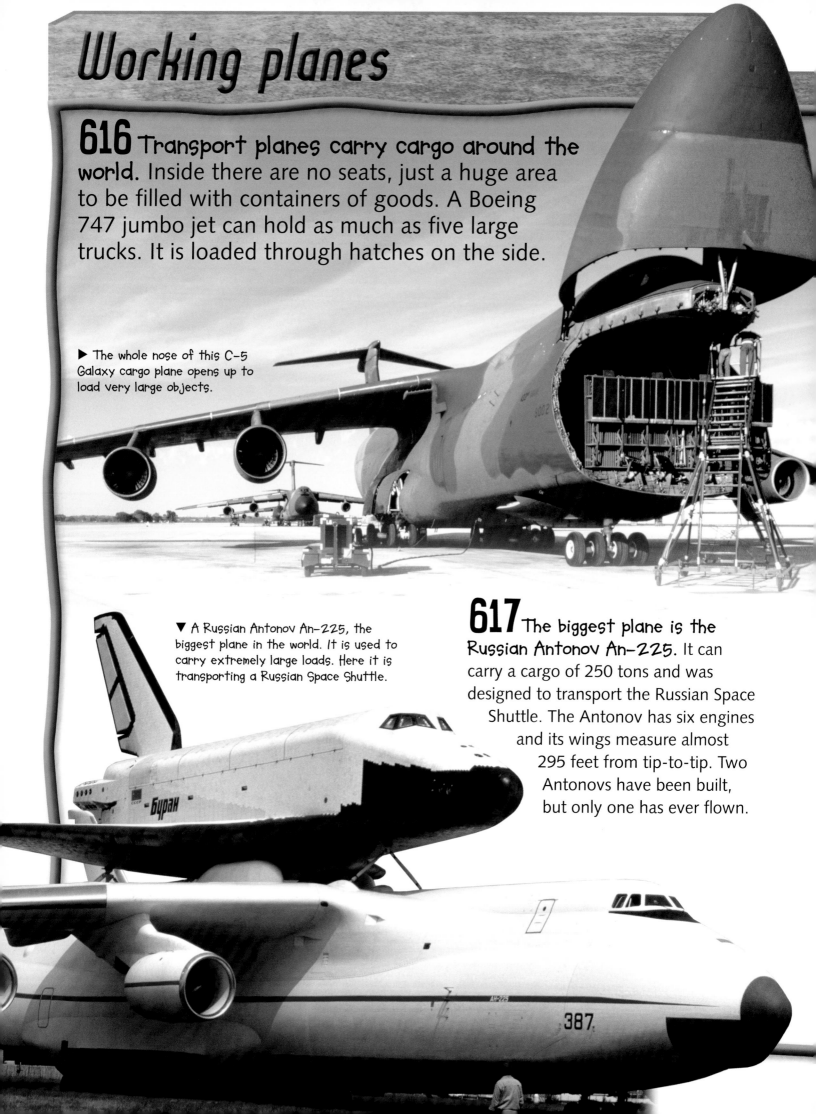

Working planes

616 Transport planes carry cargo around the world. Inside there are no seats, just a huge area to be filled with containers of goods. A Boeing 747 jumbo jet can hold as much as five large trucks. It is loaded through hatches on the side.

▶ The whole nose of this C-5 Galaxy cargo plane opens up to load very large objects.

▼ A Russian Antonov An-225, the biggest plane in the world. It is used to carry extremely large loads. Here it is transporting a Russian Space Shuttle.

617 The biggest plane is the Russian Antonov An-225. It can carry a cargo of 250 tons and was designed to transport the Russian Space Shuttle. The Antonov has six engines and its wings measure almost 295 feet from tip-to-tip. Two Antonovs have been built, but only one has ever flown.

▶ A firefighting plane dumps its load of red fire retardant in an attempt to put out a forest fire. This is a special substance that will stop the fire spreading.

620 Photographs taken from a flying plane give a good view of the ground. These photos can help people to draw maps. They also help historians by finding forgotten villages and roads. Slight bumps left by the burial of old ruins show up more clearly from the air than from the ground.

618 Planes and helicopters can help put out forest fires by dropping water on the fire. Special water-bombing planes fly very low over the sea or a lake and scoop up water. They then fly over the fire and drop the water. Helicopters carry a large bucket underneath and use this to scoop up and drop the water.

619 Helicopters and small planes can act as ambulances. If a person is badly injured in a road accident, an air ambulance helicopter may be called. The patient is put on a stretcher and whisked away to hospital in the helicopter. In Australia, doctors use small planes to visit remote farms and villages—it would take too long by car.

621 The police use helicopters to watch the traffic and chase criminals. Police in a helicopter can spot an escaping criminal and guide the police on the ground to help catch him, particularly in a car chase. The helicopters also fly over busy roads, reporting back on accidents and traffic jams.

Planes for fun

622 **Some people fly planes just for fun or sport.** They use small planes or gliders that take off from small airfields. They do not need a long concrete runway—a strip of mown grass is often good enough. Most small planes can only carry a few passengers and some only have a seat for the pilot.

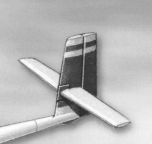

▶ The UK Air Force Red Arrows aerobatic team has been giving displays since 1965.

▲ Gliders are made from light materials. They can stay in the air for hours if conditions are right.

623 **The smallest kind of plane is called a microlight.** This plane is very light, with just a wing, a propeller engine, and one or two seats in an open cockpit. Some look like very small planes but others look more like large kites, with wings that fold up. A pilot has to pass a test to fly a microlight just like they would for any other sort of plane.

624 **Gliders are planes with no engines.** The shape of a glider is long and thin to slice through the air, with long wings for lift. To become airborne, they are towed along the ground until they are moving fast enough to take off. Some are towed into the air by a plane, which takes off pulling the glider behind it. In the air, the plane drops the tow rope and the glider flies on its own gradually dropping to the ground.

▶ A small propeller behind the pilot drives this microlight.

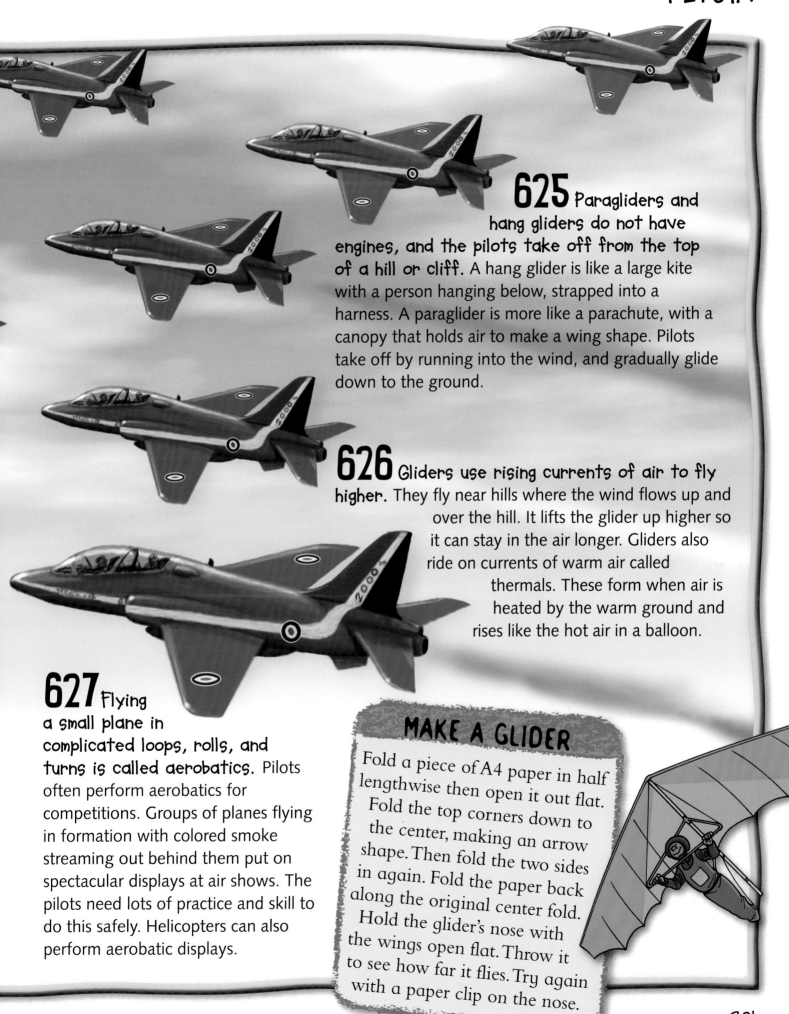

625 Paragliders and hang gliders do not have engines, and the pilots take off from the top of a hill or cliff. A hang glider is like a large kite with a person hanging below, strapped into a harness. A paraglider is more like a parachute, with a canopy that holds air to make a wing shape. Pilots take off by running into the wind, and gradually glide down to the ground.

626 Gliders use rising currents of air to fly higher. They fly near hills where the wind flows up and over the hill. It lifts the glider up higher so it can stay in the air longer. Gliders also ride on currents of warm air called thermals. These form when air is heated by the warm ground and rises like the hot air in a balloon.

627 Flying a small plane in complicated loops, rolls, and turns is called aerobatics. Pilots often perform aerobatics for competitions. Groups of planes flying in formation with colored smoke streaming out behind them put on spectacular displays at air shows. The pilots need lots of practice and skill to do this safely. Helicopters can also perform aerobatic displays.

MAKE A GLIDER

Fold a piece of A4 paper in half lengthwise then open it out flat. Fold the top corners down to the center, making an arrow shape. Then fold the two sides in again. Fold the paper back along the original center fold. Hold the glider's nose with the wings open flat. Throw it to see how far it flies. Try again with a paper clip on the nose.

Planes at sea

628 Military aircraft go to sea on board huge ships called aircraft carriers. These can take planes as close as possible to war zones. The planes use the aircraft carrier like an airport, taking off for a mission then returning to land and refuel. Many planes can fold their wings up when not flying so that more can fit onboard.

629 Vertical takeoff planes can operate from smaller aircraft carriers. They do not need a runway, just enough space on the deck to take off and land again. These smaller carriers often have a ramp at the end of the deck for planes that need a short runway to help them take off.

630 The top deck of an aircraft carrier is the flight deck where the planes take off and land. It is like a runway but not as long, so a catapult shoots the planes forward, giving them extra speed to fly from the deck. After landing, the plane is brought to a standstill by a wire hooked across the deck. Below the flight deck is a hangar deck where planes are stored. They go up and down between the decks in a huge elevator.

TRUE OR FALSE?

1. Seaplanes can land on land.

2. On an aircraft carrier, planes have wings that fold up.

3. A helipad is an area for planes and helicopters to land and take off.

Answers:
1. False 2. True 3. True

▼ Planes park on the flight deck of an aircraft carrier between flights.

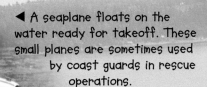

◄ A seaplane floats on the water ready for takeoff. These small planes are sometimes used by coast guards in rescue operations.

632 Seaplanes can land on water. These small planes have floats instead of wheels. The floats rest on the surface so the plane is out of the water. Seaplanes can only land and take off if the water is calm. They are sometimes used for flying between islands, or in remote areas where there are lakes to land on but few runways.

631 Helicopters are also used on ships. They only need a small platform called a helipad for taking off and landing. They cannot travel as far or as fast as a plane, but they can ferry people and equipment and act as look outs. Oil rigs out at sea often depend on helicopters to bring new crews and supplies from the mainland.

▶ Helipads provide a landing place at sea.

Flying faster than sound

633 Supersonic planes fly faster than sound. Sound travels extremely fast—when you clap your hands the sound moves out in all directions and people hear it almost immediately. Supersonic planes travel faster than this. When a plane starts to travel faster than sound, we say it is breaking the sound barrier.

▶ An American F-16 Fighting Falcon can fly twice as fast as sound.

634 Many military fighter planes are built to fly faster than sound. Their engines often have afterburners for more power and speed. These burn extra fuel in the stream of hot gas coming out of the engine. This gives a plane more power for takeoff, or for a short burst of extra speed, and allows it to fly for longer at supersonic speeds.

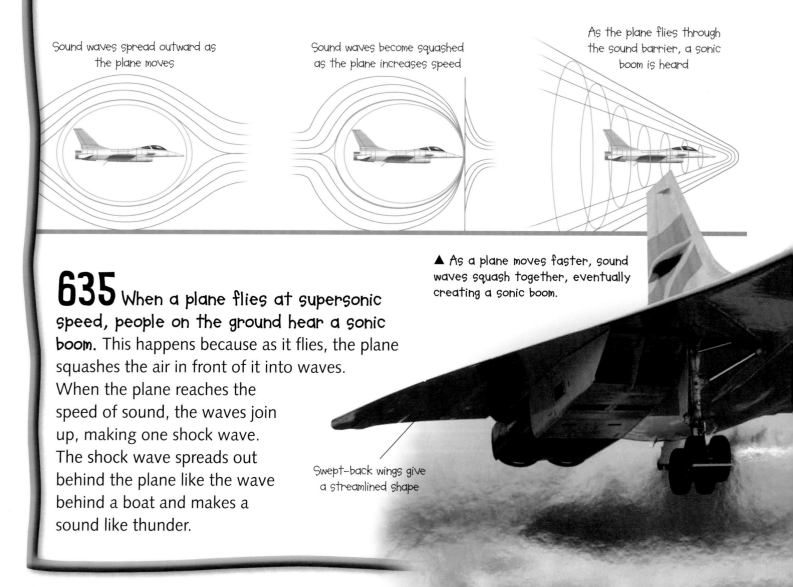

Sound waves spread outward as the plane moves

Sound waves become squashed as the plane increases speed

As the plane flies through the sound barrier, a sonic boom is heard

635 When a plane flies at supersonic speed, people on the ground hear a sonic boom. This happens because as it flies, the plane squashes the air in front of it into waves. When the plane reaches the speed of sound, the waves join up, making one shock wave. The shock wave spreads out behind the plane like the wave behind a boat and makes a sound like thunder.

▲ As a plane moves faster, sound waves squash together, eventually creating a sonic boom.

Swept-back wings give a streamlined shape

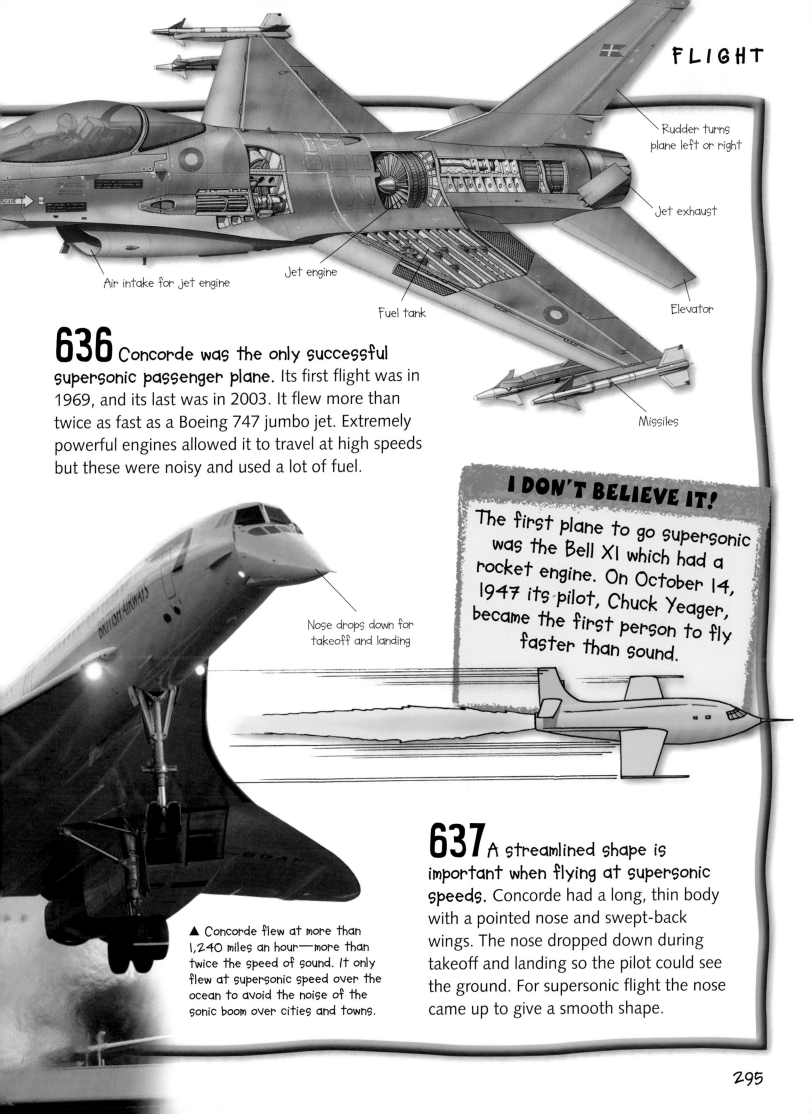

Rudder turns plane left or right

Jet exhaust

Air intake for jet engine

Jet engine

Fuel tank

Elevator

Missiles

636 Concorde was the only successful supersonic passenger plane. Its first flight was in 1969, and its last was in 2003. It flew more than twice as fast as a Boeing 747 jumbo jet. Extremely powerful engines allowed it to travel at high speeds but these were noisy and used a lot of fuel.

Nose drops down for takeoff and landing

I DON'T BELIEVE IT!

The first plane to go supersonic was the Bell XI which had a rocket engine. On October 14, 1947 its pilot, Chuck Yeager, became the first person to fly faster than sound.

▲ Concorde flew at more than 1,240 miles an hour—more than twice the speed of sound. It only flew at supersonic speed over the ocean to avoid the noise of the sonic boom over cities and towns.

637 A streamlined shape is important when flying at supersonic speeds. Concorde had a long, thin body with a pointed nose and swept-back wings. The nose dropped down during takeoff and landing so the pilot could see the ground. For supersonic flight the nose came up to give a smooth shape.

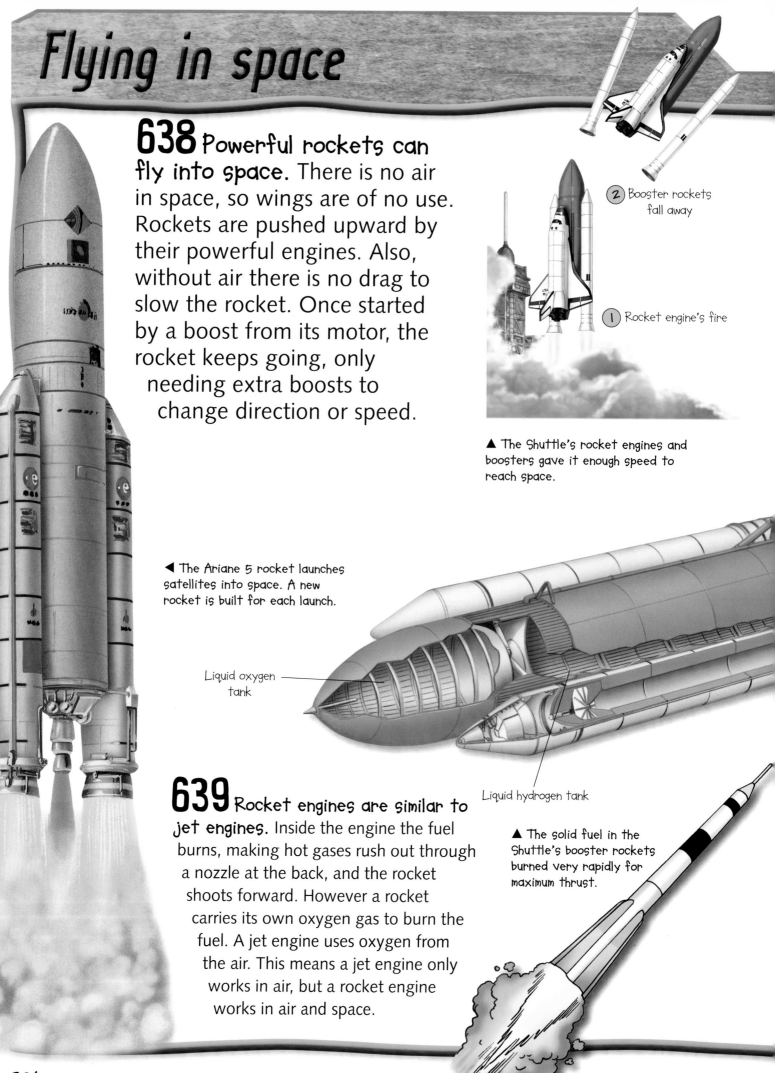

Flying in space

638 **Powerful rockets can fly into space.** There is no air in space, so wings are of no use. Rockets are pushed upward by their powerful engines. Also, without air there is no drag to slow the rocket. Once started by a boost from its motor, the rocket keeps going, only needing extra boosts to change direction or speed.

② Booster rockets fall away

① Rocket engine's fire

▲ The Shuttle's rocket engines and boosters gave it enough speed to reach space.

◄ The Ariane 5 rocket launches satellites into space. A new rocket is built for each launch.

Liquid oxygen tank

Liquid hydrogen tank

▲ The solid fuel in the Shuttle's booster rockets burned very rapidly for maximum thrust.

639 **Rocket engines are similar to jet engines.** Inside the engine the fuel burns, making hot gases rush out through a nozzle at the back, and the rocket shoots forward. However a rocket carries its own oxygen gas to burn the fuel. A jet engine uses oxygen from the air. This means a jet engine only works in air, but a rocket engine works in air and space.

(3) Fuel tank separates

640 The Space Shuttle took off as a rocket. It had three rocket engines, but it also used two huge booster rockets. These only fired for two minutes before dropping back to Earth. The engines used fuel from a separate tank that also fell away when the Shuttle reached space. The booster rockets landed in the sea to be used again, but the tank burned up as it dropped into the atmosphere.

(4) Return to Earth

(5) Touch down

641 The Shuttle landed on a runway like a huge glider. When the Shuttle returned to Earth it did not use its rocket engines. It swooped gently downward and used its wings and tail to slow and guide it toward its long runway. It touched down much faster than an airliner and used a parachute to help it slow down and stop.

— Exhaust nozzle

▶ Orion does not need wings like the Shuttle because it will not land on a runway.

Solid fuel booster

QUIZ

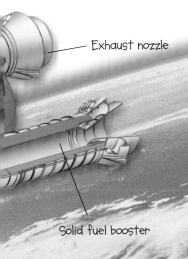

1. How many booster rockets did the Shuttle need to reach space?

2. Will a jet engine work in space?

3. Does a rocket need wings to fly in space?

Answers:
1. Two 2. No 3. No

642 A new spacecraft called Orion will replace the Shuttle. It will be launched by a rocket called Ares, which is similar to the Shuttle's boosters. Four to six astronauts will travel in the cone-shaped capsule. They will be able to go to the International Space Station, or the Moon—or even the planet Mars. When they return to Earth they will float down using parachutes and land in the sea.

Strange planes

643 The Airbus Super Transporter Beluga is a huge transport plane. It is named after a whale and looks as if it has been blown up like a balloon. The lower half of the Beluga is like an ordinary airliner. The top half bulges out to hold large objects. The nose hinges open for loading and unloading. Belugas carry the parts for planes that are being built.

▶▲ The B2 Stealth Bomber (right). It is painted in radar–absorbing coatings that can only be applied in an air–conditioned hangar (above).

644 The Stealth fighter plane looks like a huge flying wing. It is built so it can't be spotted by radar—radio waves that keep track of planes in the air. The Stealth is built with a flat, smooth shape and with special materials that don't reflect radio waves, so it doesn't show up on radar screens.

◀ Bulky cargo is lifted into a Beluga transport plane. Its oddly shaped nose makes it look like a beluga whale.

645 The Sun can provide enough power to fly a plane.

The Solar Challenger plane had long wings covered in more than 16,000 solar cells. These used sunlight to make electricity and drive a propeller. It flew from France to England in 1981. *Helios* was a strange-looking plane—just a huge wing with 14 propellers along the front. These ran on electricity from solar cells covering the wings.

646 The Gossamer *Albatross* flew using human power.

It was a very light plane with long, thin wings—just a flimsy frame wrapped in plastic. The pilot sat inside a tiny cabin pedalling (like a bicycle) to turn a propeller that pushed the plane forward. It flew across the English Channel from England to France in 1979.

▼ *Helios* was a simple wing covered in solar panels, which powered its 14 propellers. It reached a top speed of 20 miles an hour and was made by NASA.

I DON'T BELIEVE IT!

The Gossamer *Albatross* weighed less than its pilot. Together they weighed 220 pounds but only 70 pounds of that was the actual plane. It flew only 5 feet above the ground—just above your head!

647 *Predator* is a robot spy plane.

It is the same size as a small plane but with no cabin or pilot. It flies by remote control like a model plane. Cameras show its controllers a view of the enemy. It can also carry missiles to attack enemy targets.

SPEED

- Measuring speed
- Velocity
- Energy
- Speedy animals
- Racing
- Streamlined design
- The land speed record
- Speed machines
- Acceleration and deceleration
- Light speed

Why do racing bikes slow down when cornering?

What is the fastest reptile?

How fast do galaxies move?

What is velocity?

Who holds the world water speed record?

How fast?

648 Speed is how far (the distance) something goes in a certain time. If a jet plane travels 1,800 miles in three hours, its speed is 600 miles per hour. We describe speed as distance covered—such as feet or miles—in one unit or "piece" of time, such as one minute, one hour, or one year.

649 We describe something as "high speed" if it is very fast, but what we think of as high speed has changed over time. In 1972 the fastest sailing craft was *Crossbow*, a catamaran (yacht with two hulls), at 30.2 miles per hour. Just 30 years later the record was 64 miles per hour, due to the invention of kitesurfing, in which the sailor rides a modified surfboard while holding on to a special kind of kite.

650 Whether something is "speedy" or fast depends on what, where, and when. Cars on a freeway might travel at 70 miles per hour. A garden snail crawls along at 7 inches per minute. The snail is 10,000 times slower than the car—but speedy compared to other kinds of snails.

SPEED

Units for speed

651 Speed is the distance covered in a set time. A racing car might have a speed of 100 miles per hour for one lap of its course, but it might go at 190 miles per hour on straights and 30 miles per hour around bends. The 100 miles per hour is the average speed—total distance divided by total time.

$$\text{SPEED} = \frac{\text{DISTANCE}}{\text{TIME}}$$

652 The knot is used to measure how fast something goes on water. Its name comes from the fact that ships used to measure their speed by letting a rope out into the water. The rope had knots at regular intervals and a float at one end. The more knots that passed over the ship's side in 30 seconds, the faster the speed. One knot is equal to 1.14 miles per hour.

Knots

▶ Sailing speeds are still often measured in knots—as are wind speeds.

653 Throughout history, people have measured distance, time, and speed in lots of different ways. Long ago, the time for a journey by sailing ship was measured to the nearest day, or even the nearest week! Today, modern jet planes mean the journeys are measured in miles or kilometers per hour.

Miles
per hour
(mph)

▶ The speed indicator dial on fast cars may go up to 200 miles per hour.

Feet
per
minute

▶ For a snail or a slug, 3 feet is a very long distance.

654 Even today there are many different ways to describe speed around the world. In most of Europe, road speed is measured in kilometers per hour (km/h). In the UK and U.S. it is measured in miles per hour (mph).

Feet per second

▲ Comets travel through space at more than 218,000 feet per second, but seen from Earth, they appear to be hardly moving.

▶ Most passenger jet planes have a cruising speed of around 560–590 miles per hour.

Miles per hour (mph)

655 To describe and imagine very fast or slow speeds, we have to change the measuring units we use. A rocket must reach more than 25,000 miles per hour to blast away from Earth into space. This is known as escape velocity. It may be easier to imagine as 7 miles per second, or even 36,750 feet per second.

656 Special units can help us when comparing speeds. A cheetah is much faster than a cockroach, but this is mainly because it is much bigger. However, if we compare each animal's speed to its size, things are rather different. A cockroach covers 50 of its own body lengths per second, but the cheetah covers just 12 of its own body lengths per second.

It's all relative

657 All speeds are relative. This is because nothing in the Universe is completely still. Even someone measuring speed is moving! So you can only measure something's speed "relative" to something else—that is, by how fast it goes past.

659 Usually we measure speed as the distance traveled here on Earth, along the surface or through the air—but this is also relative. The Earth's surface is moving as the planet spins once each day. If you could stay put in space, high above the Earth, someone standing still at the Equator (an imaginary line drawn around the midpoint of the Earth) would be moving at 1,516 feet each second.

658 A single object has many different speeds. A train goes at 60 miles per hour relative to its tracks and stations. For a person in a car traveling alongside the track at 40 miles per hour, the train's speed is 20 miles per hour. For a passenger on a train traveling toward the first train at 60 miles per hour, the combined speed is 120 miles per hour.

60 / 0

① To a person standing still at a station, the passing train's speed would be 60 miles per hour.

60 / 40

② For a driver in a car traveling alongside the train, its relative speed is 20 miles per hour.

60 / 60

③ For passengers in an oncoming second train, the combined speed is 120 miles per hour.

▼ ② The Equator is the fastest-moving place on Earth, being the widest part, in the middle of the direction of spin.

EQUATOR

◄ ① This person is standing still at the Equator. But is he moving? Not relative to the Earth's surface. But if seen from space, then yes—as fast as a jet fighter plane.

660 As well as constantly spinning, the Earth travels on its yearly orbit around the Sun. This makes working out speed even more complicated, since Earth's average orbital speed is about 19 miles each second.

▼ ③ Like the other planets, Earth zooms at huge speed around the Sun.

▲ ④ The Sun and millions of other stars are flying in space at gigantic speed, as the whole Galaxy swirls around.

661 Added to this is the speed of the whole Solar System (the Sun and all its planets). It is whirling around the center of our massive group of stars, the Milky Way Galaxy. This speed is even faster—about 160 miles each second.

QUIZ

1. Is someone standing at the North Pole moving faster than someone standing at the South Pole?

2. What is Earth's average orbital speed?

3. Where should you stand to measure "true" speed?

Answers:
1. No—they're equal (both spin around once every 24 hours) 2. 19 miles per second 3. There is nowhere you can stand.

662 Even if you went into deepest space, there is still nowhere that you can stand to measure "true" speed. All the galaxies are flying away from each other, some at more than 190 miles per second. The whole Universe is moving faster and getting bigger.

Measuring speed

663 Long ago, there were no standard ways of measuring speed because there was no accurate way to measure time. People used devices such as sand clocks (in which sand poured through a small hole) to measure time, and methods such as counting their own steps to measure distance. The only way of comparing the speed of two or more things, such as horses, was a head-to-head race.

▼ The Olympics showcase the world's fastest humans in direct competition. Here Vomma Iso-Hollo wins 1932's 3,000 meters steeplechase.

664 Gradually, measuring devices became more accurate. The first stopwatch was developed in the 1850s, and by the 1910s it was accurate to 1/100th of one second. During the 1970s, digital stopwatches increased this to 1/1,000th of one second.

665 To measure distance, people once used lengths of wood. This gave rise to units of length such as the pole or rod, equivalent to 16.5 feet. Tape measures arrived in the 1700s, and by 1970 laser beams could measure distances more accurately.

▼ Stopwatches used clockwork springs and measured to 1/100th of one second. Electronic timing devices use vibrating crystals to measure to 1/1,000th of one second.

▲ A race result may be so close the human eye cannot see who has won. A photo finish uses a sequence of pictures, 1,000 or more each second, to pick out the winner, as in this 100 meters sprint.

666 For distance and speed over long distances, such as across seas, people relied on maps and charts. They measured the distance on the map and multiplied it by the scale of the map. But this was not very accurate—a very thin line on the map could be hundreds of feet wide in the real world.

667 From the 1990s the "satnav" system GPS (which stands for Global Positioning System) meant speed over long distances could be measured much more precisely. GPS satellite clocks are accurate to 14 billionths of one second, and the best GPS receivers can pinpoint position to within 4 inches.

Each satellite transmits its identity and position

Some satellites are farther away, so signals arrive at the GPS unit at different times

GPS unit in vehicle is "tuned in" to the signals from the satellites

▲ A "satnav" receiver compares the times taken for signals to arrive from at least three GPS satellites.

668 Some sports have special ways to measure speed. The Hawk-Eye system uses several video cameras to record a ball's path from different angles. A computer compares the pictures and calculates the ball's speed and direction. A fast cricket bowl is 100 miles per hour, and a tennis serve can be 155 miles per hour—230 feet in one second!

▼ In tennis, the Hawk-Eye tracking system shows the ball's speed, position, and direction, and also if it landed on, in, or outside the line.

OFFICIAL
REVIEW

What is velocity?

669 Speed is distance covered with time—but it has no direction. To describe speed in a certain direction, we use the term "velocity." A swan might have a speed of 40 miles an hour when it migrates to its breeding area, but its velocity is 40 miles per hour due north.

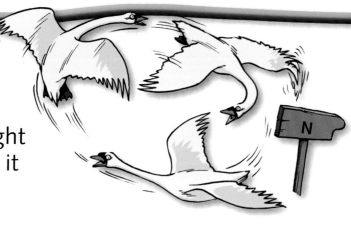

670 Measuring velocity means measuring time and distance (as for speed), and also position. For long distances this can be done using GPS or "satnav" equipment. In smaller areas it can be done with a map, perhaps using local landmarks, or with short-range radio signals such as radio beacons used by aircraft.

◀ This gray reef shark's radio tracker gives its position at different times, showing its overall velocity on longer journeys between reefs, and how, for example, ocean currents affect its movements.

671 Velocity gives much more information than speed. It shows changes in speed, direction, and location, and how fast and how often they happen. This helps aircraft pilots to work out the fuel needed to climb to cruising height, go around storms, and circle or "stack" waiting to land.

▶ As the plane passes through each crisscross radio "grid," the pilots work out its velocity to land safely.

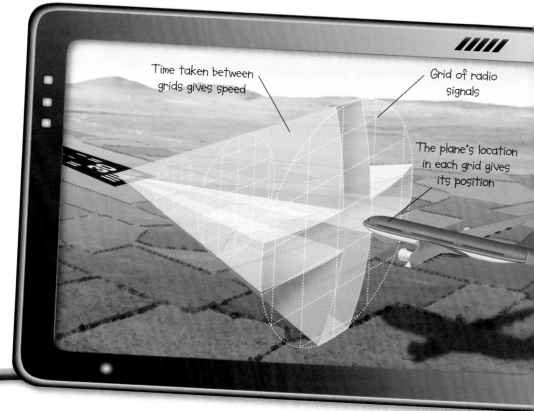

Time taken between grids gives speed

Grid of radio signals

The plane's location in each grid gives its position

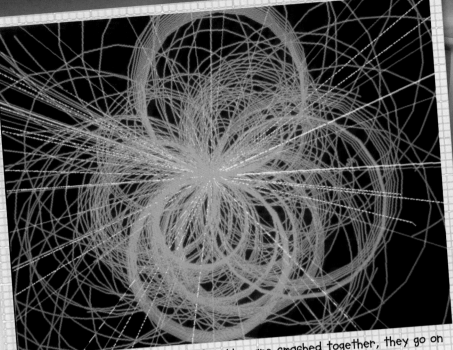

▲ When the smallest particles of matter are smashed together, they go on amazingly complicated curved pathways or tracks. These show their size, speed, and structure.

672 On the huge scale of space travel, knowing about speed and direction, and so velocity, is vital. As a space probe sets off for a distant planet it must aim exactly in the right direction. Otherwise, after a journey of perhaps 10 years, it could be millions of miles off course. Space scientists continually check its path to keep it on target.

673 On the tiniest scale, velocity helps us to understand the world of atoms and their parts. These particles are smashed together with incredible force, such as in the world's largest machine, the LHC (Large Hadron Collider). The velocity of the resulting bits—their speed and direction—gives clues to their most basic makeup.

◄ An Air Force jet fighter watches space shuttle *Atlantis* on its final blastoff in 2011. The jet plane is capable of 1,600 miles per hour. As the shuttle docks with the orbiting International Space Station, both the shuttle and the station will be traveling ten times faster. And both in the same direction—and so with the same velocity.

QUIZ

1. Rather than heading north, then the same distance east, what would be a quicker direction?

2. What is the name of the world's largest machine?

3. "The car's velocity was 70 kilometres per hour." What is wrong with this statement?

Answers:
1. Head northeast
2. Large Hadron Collider
3. You need to give the car's direction as well as its speed

Speed and energy

674 Something that moves has not only speed, but also a form of energy—the ability to cause changes and make things happen. Energy due to movement or motion is called kinetic energy. You can see it at work everywhere—it is used to generate electricity from rushing river water and it is the reason that we have air bags and seat belts in our cars.

675 Massively heavy things are more difficult to speed up. They have high inertia, which means they need lots of energy to give them motion. The heavy flywheel in an engine needs great force to get it going, but once it's spinning, it helps the engine run smoothly.

▶ One very strong human—Mikhail Sidorychev—can gradually overcome the inertia of a huge plane, giving it kinetic energy to get it moving.

676 Kinetic energy depends on two main features— an object's speed, and its mass (amount of matter). The faster something goes, the more kinetic energy it has, and the more mass it has, the more kinetic energy it has. So a very fast motorbike could have the same kinetic energy as a very slow truck.

HOW FAR?

You will need:

tennis ball   stiff card about 25 in long
pen   measuring tape

1. Draw a scale on the card, marking every one inch. Prop up one end of the card at an angle of about 30° to make a ramp.
2. Release the ball from each mark in turn. Measure how far it rolls each time. The ball gains more speed from each higher mark, and so has more energy to roll farther.

677 Once an object is moving with speed, it has lots of kinetic energy, or high momentum. Then it resists losing speed— being slowed down. A huge, speedy ship such as an oil tanker has so much momentum that it may take 30 miles to slow down.

▼ Racing bikers have to learn how to slow down and lean into corners.

▼ On a "Wall of Death," fast-circling riders produce enough outward force to overcome gravity and rise at right angles up the wall.

678 As an object goes around a bend or curve, it has different forces acting on it, and this affects its speed. A motorcycle can go fast in a straight line, but around a bend it must slow down as the rider leans to one side so that its tires don't lose grip and skid.

679 Spinning at speed causes another set of forces. One is felt as a pull away from the center of the spin. This is known as centrifugal force, and is used in machines called centrifuges. A medical centrifuge spins tubes of blood so fast, the heaviest parts sink to the bottom of the tube. This helps to separate blood into its different parts.

Natural speeds

680 The natural world has a huge range of speeds, from incredibly slow to ultra fast. Some of the slowest movers are the world's landmasses or continents. They drift around the planet's surface by a few centimeters each year. Glaciers are thick "rivers" of snow and ice. They slide slowly downhill, mostly by several feet each year. The Jakobshavn Glacier in Greenland sped along at more than 7 miles per year, probably as a result of global warming.

681 Rivers vary in speed from upward of 30 feet per second down steep rapids to slower than 3 feet per minute in other places. The giant Amazon River's average flow speed is about 1.2 miles per hour. One of the fastest ocean currents is the Agulhas Current in the Indian Ocean, at 6 miles per hour.

▼ Where a river flows through a narrow gorge, it speeds up as rapids. The same amount of water passes every second as in places where the river is less restricted.

30 ft/second

17 mi/year

▼ A scientist using an instrument called a theodolite. This records the exact position of marker poles at certain times to determine a glacier's speed.

682 In 1980, the eruption of Mount St. Helens in the Pacific northwest caused an avalanche and rockfall that traveled at more than 250 miles per hour. This was one of the fastest ever measured. Even a small avalanche can reach 75 miles per hour, which is much too fast to outrun.

▼ "Storm chasers" follow storms, partly for thrills. Many will record a storm's track. Here a storm chaser drops a weather probe (red) in the path of an oncoming tornado.

683 Violent winds such as hurricanes and tornadoes can reach speeds of more than 250 miles per hour. Even faster, at 430 miles per hour, is a pyroclastic flow—a cloudlike surge of superheated gas and rock particles from a volcano. The tsunami wave from an underwater earthquake goes even faster in the open ocean, up to 620 miles per hour.

430 mph

QUIZ

1. What is a theodolite?

2. Which volcanic eruption in 1980 was one of the fastest ever measured?

3. What is the top speed of a tsunami wave?

Answers:
1. An instrument used to measure the speed of a glacier
2. Mount St. Helens
3. 620 miles per hour

Pyroclastic flow

▶ Pyroclastic flows can pick up even more speed as they spread down steep hills under the pull of gravity.

684 The speed of sound in air varies with air's pressure and temperature. Near the ground it has an average speed of 770 miles per hour, or around 1,115 feet per second. So the boom from a thunderstorm 2 miles away takes around nine seconds to arrive.

Life in the fast lane

685 An animal's speed depends on the environment in which it is moving. The sailfish cuts through water at 68 miles per hour. The cheetah sprints on land at about the same speed. The peregrine falcon is the fastest of all animals—its stoop or "power dive" through the air can reach speeds of over 185 miles per hour.

185 mph

Part-folded wings lower air resistance

686 Cheetahs are famously fleet footed, but there are lots of other speedy creatures. The fastest reptile is the spiny-tailed iguana lizard, which runs at 22 miles per hour. The speediest shark—the shortfin mako—swims at more than 37 miles per hour, while the fastest mammal swimmer is the orca or killer whale at 34-plus miles per hour.

Small head for streamlining

Flexible backbone

Powerful muscles in shoulders and hips

68 mph

Tail works as an air rudder to change direction

▲ The cheetah's long, slim, flexible body and long legs allow it to cover 26 feet in each bound.

687 Animal adaptations for speed on land include long legs for lengthy strides, and powerful muscles in the shoulders and hips. In water, fast fish such as marlin have stiff, crescent-shaped tails that they thrash from side to side so fast, they look like they are quivering.

Stiff, narrow, curved tail

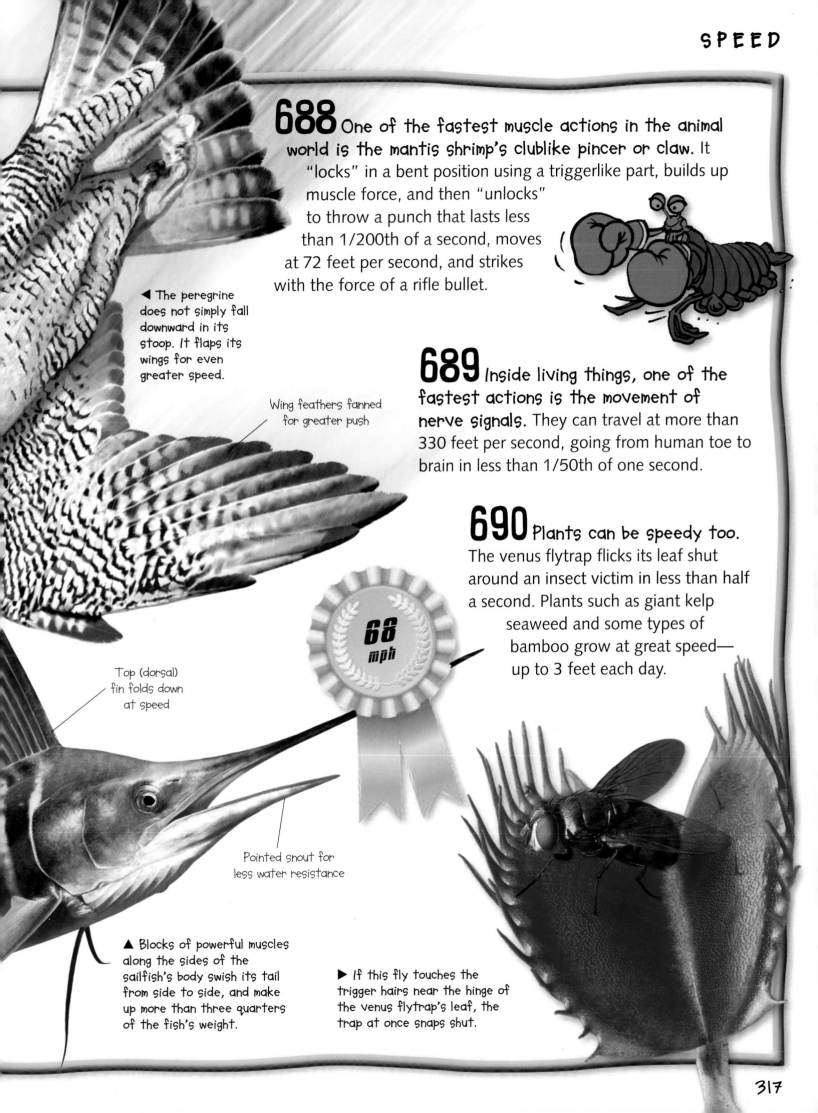

688 One of the fastest muscle actions in the animal world is the mantis shrimp's clublike pincer or claw. It "locks" in a bent position using a triggerlike part, builds up muscle force, and then "unlocks" to throw a punch that lasts less than 1/200th of a second, moves at 72 feet per second, and strikes with the force of a rifle bullet.

◄ The peregrine does not simply fall downward in its stoop. It flaps its wings for even greater speed.

Wing feathers fanned for greater push

689 Inside living things, one of the fastest actions is the movement of nerve signals. They can travel at more than 330 feet per second, going from human toe to brain in less than 1/50th of one second.

690 Plants can be speedy too. The venus flytrap flicks its leaf shut around an insect victim in less than half a second. Plants such as giant kelp seaweed and some types of bamboo grow at great speed—up to 3 feet each day.

Top (dorsal) fin folds down at speed

68 mph

Pointed snout for less water resistance

▲ Blocks of powerful muscles along the sides of the sailfish's body swish its tail from side to side, and make up more than three quarters of the fish's weight.

► If this fly touches the trigger hairs near the hinge of the venus flytrap's leaf, the trap at once snaps shut.

Breeding the best

691 People have held races to find the speediest animals and people for more than 5,000 years. Early races involved horses, camels, dogs, and humans. Running and chariot racing were among the most popular events at ancient Greece's Olympic Games, 2,500 years ago.

693 People can select the fastest animals of each kind, and breed them together to produce even speedier ones. This process is called selective breeding. It has produced the fastest type of dog, the greyhound. It races at almost 65 feet per second (45 miles per hour)—nearly twice as fast as a human sprinter.

692 Some of the biggest prizes are given for the fastest racehorses. Perhaps the quickest was Secretariat, an American thoroughbred that raced in the 1970s. He set records that still stand today, winning the 1973 Kentucky Derby at 54.7 feet per second (just over 37 miles per hour).

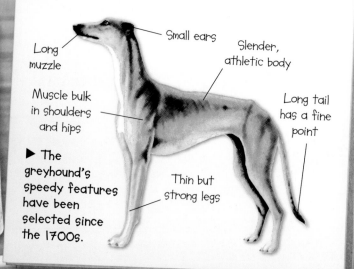

Small ears

Long muzzle

Slender, athletic body

Muscle bulk in shoulders and hips

Long tail has a fine point

Thin but strong legs

▶ The greyhound's speedy features have been selected since the 1700s.

▼ Fast-action photos show how the muscles that move a racehorse's leg are concentrated in the shoulder and buttock areas. Most of the leg is slim and easy to swing fast.

▲ The fastest camels are almost as rapid as racehorses, reaching speeds of over 34 miles per hour.

696 Training a champion animal speedster is a complicated business. Trainers pay great attention to diet and exercise, working out a series of activities that build gradually to the day of the big race. Some racehorses only run well if they have their "best friend" stable companion with them on the day—which might be a donkey!

694 Many animals are raced for speed and stamina (endurance). Strange races include camels, ferrets, maggots, elephants, sled–pulling husky dogs, hamsters in wheeled cars, and pigs with teddy bear "jockeys." Elephants weigh over 5 tons yet they can reach speeds of 22 feet per second (15 miles per hour).

695 Breeders look for several features in racing animals. These include a slim but muscular build, strong bones (especially in the legs), no spare fat, a strong heartbeat, and clear breathing to take in the oxygen in air needed by hardworking muscles.

WORM OLYMPICS
You will need:
earthworms   A4 paper
sticky tape

1. Roll and tape sheets of A4 paper into tubes about 0.5 inches wide.
2. Tape the paper rolls side by side.
3. Carefully gather garden earthworms and put each one into a tube at the "Start" end.
4. The worm that is first to emerge completely at the "Finish" end is the winner!

Note: After your race, put the worms back in the soil where you found them and wash your hands.

Out in front

697 **Human speeds improve year by year.** In 1912 the record time for the 100 meters sprint was 10.6 seconds. Today it is more than one second less. This is partly because people have generally become healthier, with better food and fewer illnesses, especially in childhood. We also understand more about exercise and how the body works.

698 **Human speeds have also increased for money reasons.** Modern sport is big business that attracts the best brains to train athletes. Coaches devise incredibly detailed training programs covering everything from building muscle and improving breathing, to planning an athlete's mental approach to each race.

▶ From 2008, Jamaica's Usain Bolt shattered sprint records and became World and Olympic champion at 100 and 200 meters, at speeds of up to 23.3 miles per hour.

Strong bone structure

Efficient lungs and heart

Slim arms

Narrow hips and slim legs

Minimal body fat

699 **Some people have innate (inbuilt) features, which help them to run fast.** Being tall and muscular with long legs is ideal for short distance sprinting. A smaller, slimmer, lighter build is more suited to long distances.

◀ Britain's Paula Radcliffe has the narrow, lightweight shape of a long distance runner. She took the world marathon record in 2003 at an average speed of 11.6 miles an hour.

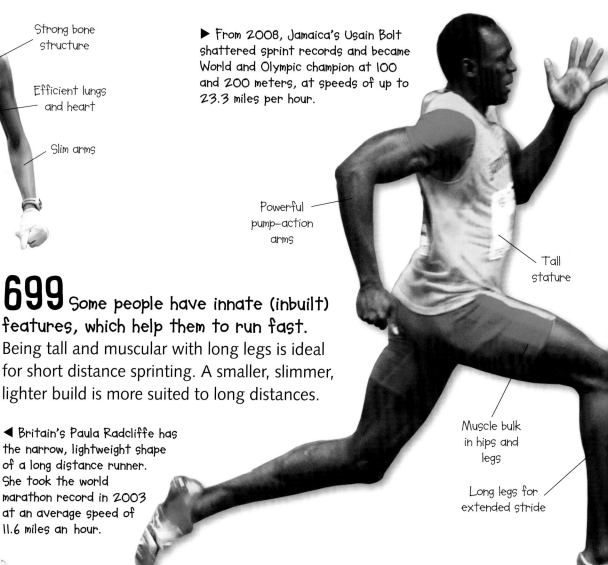

Powerful pump-action arms

Tall stature

Muscle bulk in hips and legs

Long legs for extended stride

700 Every so often, a great landmark or "milestone" is reached in human speed. In 1954 English runner Roger Bannister was the first person to run a mile in less than four minutes—which many people had said was impossible. In 1968 the USA's Jim Hines broke the "10-second barrier" and ran the 100 meters sprint in 9.9 seconds.

▶ When Bannister broke the four-minute mile, people doubted the time could reduce much more. Today's runners are 15 seconds faster.

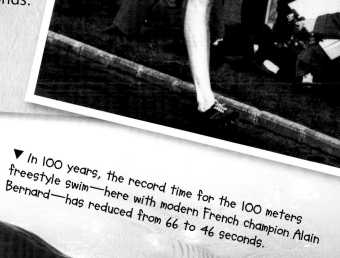

▼ In 100 years, the record time for the 100 meters freestyle swim—here with modern French champion Alain Bernard—has reduced from 66 to 46 seconds.

701 There are many different human speed records. These range from the 60-meter "flying start" and sprints at 100, 200, and 400 meters, to middle-distance 800 and 1,500 meters, and long distance 5,000 and the marathon (26.2 miles). If sprint swimmers in a 50 meters front crawl race could maintain their speed over 1,500 meters, they would cut the record time for that race (currently 14 minutes and 30 seconds) by four minutes!

Designed for speed

702 The quest for speed has led people to design, build, and operate all kinds of speed machines. From soapbox carts and penny-farthing bicycles to racing cars, powerboats, jet trucks, bullet trains, and rocket planes—as with human speed, machine speed keeps improving through the years.

Contoured helmet

Slippery body suit fabric

Arms and hands together

Spokeless disk wheels

▲ Track cyclists use every design trick to reduce air resistance or drag.

703 One important feature of a speed machine is its overall size. Bigger is usually faster, but only up to a certain point. A larger machine can have a bigger, more powerful engine, but the weight of the machine itself, with its frame and working parts, increases greatly and speed becomes slower again.

▶ Air is pushed over a car smoothly, rather than being allowed to go underneath and lift it at high speed.

Bonnet "flows" into windscreen

Mirrors close to body

Low sloping front

Rounded front wheel arches

◀ A hydrofoil lifts up at speed to reduce drag on its hull.

704 "Drag" is the enemy of speed. Drag is the resistance—the force that pushes back from air or water as an object shoves between its tiny particles or molecules. A speed machine is shaped to be streamlined or "slippery" with a pointed front, smooth surfaces and curves, a tapering rear end, and no parts that stick out.

705 Before building a speed machine, design models can be tested in wind tunnels or water tanks. This shows how the air or water flows past the vehicle. It reveals any swirls, eddies (circular movements), or vortexes (unsteady movements), which may increase drag and have a slowing effect.

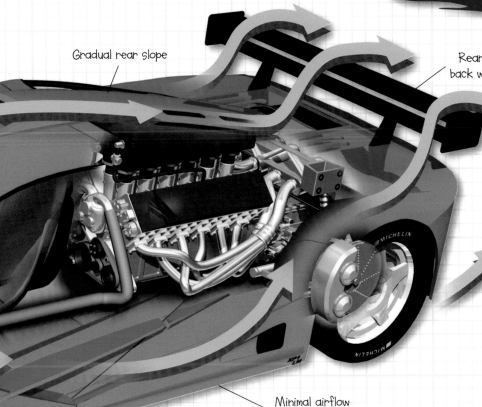

Gradual rear slope

Rear wing presses down back wheels for better grip

Minimal airflow under car

706 Speed machines cannot be totally smooth and streamlined, because they need to move in a steady, stable, safe way. So they may have ridges, fins, or wings that act like wings in reverse, pushing the car's wheels down onto the ground for extra traction (grip).

707 Computers also help to design speed machines. A virtual design, existing only in the computer, can be put into a virtual wind tunnel or water tank, also in the computer, to see how it performs. By pressing a few keys the designers can redesign a part to try and improve performance.

▶ Computer modeling shows how swirling air currents are "thrown off" the rear parts of a fast plane, slowing it down.

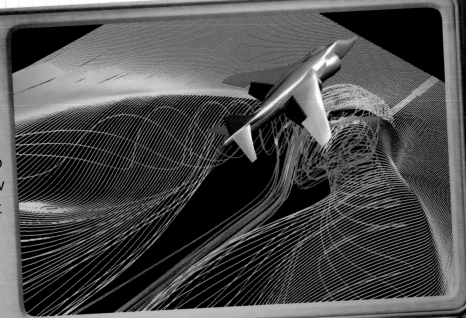

Making a breakthrough

708 Through history, different types of speed machines have got faster by small amounts. A big leap in performance is usually the result of a new invention or development, such as a new engine, better materials that save weight, or a new control method, such as a computer.

709 In the early 1950s a new kind of propeller–driven speedboat made a huge splash. *Slo-Mo-Shun IV* used a method called prop-riding, where the boat's hull rose at speed to lift the top parts of the propellers above the surface. This reduced their pushing force but reduced drag even more. It improved the water speed record by 37 miles per hour in two years, to 178 miles per hour.

▼ *Railton Mobil Special*, driven by John Cobb, was the last piston engined vehicle to hold the world land speed record.

▼ *Spirit of America* became the first jet car to take the land speed record, powered by an old GE J47 engine from a Sabre jet fighter plane.

SPIRIT OF AMERICA

GOOD YEAR

710 In the late 1940s the world land speed record was held by John Cobb in *Railton Mobil Special*, at 394 miles per hour. This vehicle had piston engines that turned the wheels, like an ordinary car. By 1965 the record had shot up to almost 621 miles per hour with Craig Breedlove in *Spirit of America*, due to the arrival of the jet engine.

FASTEST OR FARTHEST?
You will need:
computer   printer   A4 paper
1. Go to the Kids' Activity Corner on www.mileskelly.net and click on the link for this book.
2. Make two planes—the Condor is like Concorde and the Bullet is like the X-15.
3. Test outdoors on a calm day. Notice which goes faster and which one stays up longer— it's not always fastest that goes farthest.

711 In 1938 the steam locomotive *Mallard* set the speed record for railed vehicles, at 125.9 miles per hour. Then along came electric trains, which soon pushed the record higher, and by 2007 it was over 354 miles per hour. Maglev trains, which "float" above rails, go even faster.

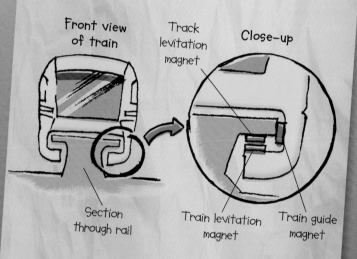

Front view of train

Track levitation magnet

Close-up

Section through rail

Train levitation magnet

Train guide magnet

▲ Maglev trains use magnetic levitation—magnetic forces that suspend the train over the track, removing the problem of wheels and friction.

▲ Concorde was the fastest ever passenger aircraft. But fuel costs, noise, and old age led to it being retired in 2003.

712 The invention of the jet engine had a huge effect on aircraft speed records. The fastest propeller plane was probably the Russian Tu-114 passenger aircraft of the 1960s, at 541 miles per hour. By 1969 jet-powered Concorde had more than doubled this to 1,350 miles per hour. Today jet fighters reach 2,050 miles per hour.

713 The fastest of all powered machines have rocket engines. In 1967 the USA's X-15 rocket plane reached 4,519 miles per hour, which is still a record for any manned vehicle or craft—apart from in space. Returning from the Moon in 1969, Apollo astronauts reached 24,855 miles per hour.

▲ The X-15 was launched in mid air from a giant bomber aircraft. Two X-15 flights zoomed for a few seconds to the edge of space, over 320 miles high.

Modern speed machines

714 Apart from kitesurfers and windsurfers, the fastest sailing craft is *Hydroptère*. It has one main hull and two smaller outer hulls, and is a hydrofoil, rising up at speed on winglike struts. The craft took the record in 2009 with a speed of 60.8 miles per hour.

▲ *Hydroptère* made several failed attempts on the water speed record—during one of which it almost sank—before its 2009 success.

715 In 1997 the U.K.'s jet car *Thrust SSC* roared across Black Rock Desert in Nevada to set the land speed record of 763 miles per hour. It was driven by fighter pilot Andy Green, with former record holder Richard Noble as team boss. "SSC" stands for Supersonic Car, because the vehicle also broke the sound barrier as it set the record.

▲ *Thrust SSC* caused a sonic boom as it scorched across Black Rock Desert on its record breaking two-way run.

716 In 1978 the world water speed record of 317.6 miles per hour was set by Ken Warby in his homemade, jet powered craft, *Spirit of Australia*. It was on Bowering Dam, Australia, with perfect conditions of wind and water surface. This record is one of the most dangerous, and two attempts to break it have killed the pilots. Warby's record still stands.

▲ Warby built *Spirit of Australia* in his garage, using a secondhand jet engine given by air force friends.

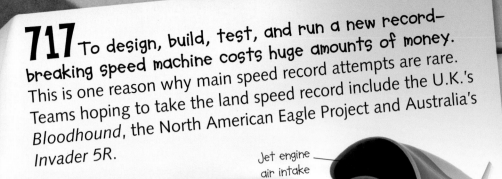

717 To design, build, test, and run a new record-breaking speed machine costs huge amounts of money. This is one reason why main speed record attempts are rare. Teams hoping to take the land speed record include the U.K.'s Bloodhound, the North American Eagle Project and Australia's Invader 5R.

Jet engine air intake

Stabilizer wing

Nose wheel

Pointed nose

▶ *Bloodhound* aims to attempt the land speed record by 2016, depending on how much money is raised.

QUIZ

1. Which is faster, a jet-powered car or one with an ordinary engine?

2. Which country holds the land speed record with Thrust SSC?

3. Where were the first "bullet trains"—Peru, Japan, or Barbados?

Answers:
1. A jet-powered car
2. UK 3. Japan

718 Apart from trains specially altered to break records, there are also records for the fastest regular or scheduled railway service. In 2011 a new type of train—called a "bullet train" because of its shape and speed—linked the Chinese cities of Beijing and Shanghai. It carries 500 people and can reach 298 miles per hour.

719 To get away from the vast cost of breaking the all out best speed, there is increasing interest in human-powered craft and vehicles. There are records in the air, on land and water, and even underwater. The human-powered submarine *Omer 5* set the underwater record in 2007, at 9.3 miles per hour.

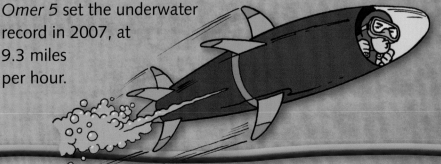

Reaching the limit

720 Speeds cannot keep increasing forever. To break the land speed record, *Thrust SSC* needed an incredibly flat surface and a straight course of more than 12 miles. Faster cars will probably need longer courses, until the Earth's landscape is the limit.

◀ Skydivers move their arms, legs, and body position to speed up or slow down. The belly-to-earth position gives a fall speed of 118 miles per hour.

721 As an object goes faster, the opposing drag or resistance rises too, at an ever increasing rate. Eventually, resistance equals forward force, and the speed limit (terminal velocity) is reached. As parachutists freefall to Earth, they are pulled by gravity but slowed by air resistance. When these forces balance the parachutist has terminal velocity, which is about 124 miles per hour.

722 Speeds are limited for safety reasons. On roads in built up areas, the speed limit is usually 30 miles per hour. Accident information shows that at this speed, about one person in ten hit by a car dies. At just 10 miles per hour more, nine in ten die.

▼ Stopping distance increases in proportion. At 60 miles per hour, it is over three times more than 30 miles per hour, not twice.

SPEED	THINKING DISTANCE	BRAKING DISTANCE	STOPPING DISTANCE
20 mph	20 feet	20 feet	40 feet
30 mph	30 feet	46 feet	76 feet
40 mph	40 feet	78 feet	118 feet
50 mph	50 feet	125 feet	175 feet
60 mph	60 feet	180 feet	240 feet
70 mph	70 feet	246 feet	316 feet

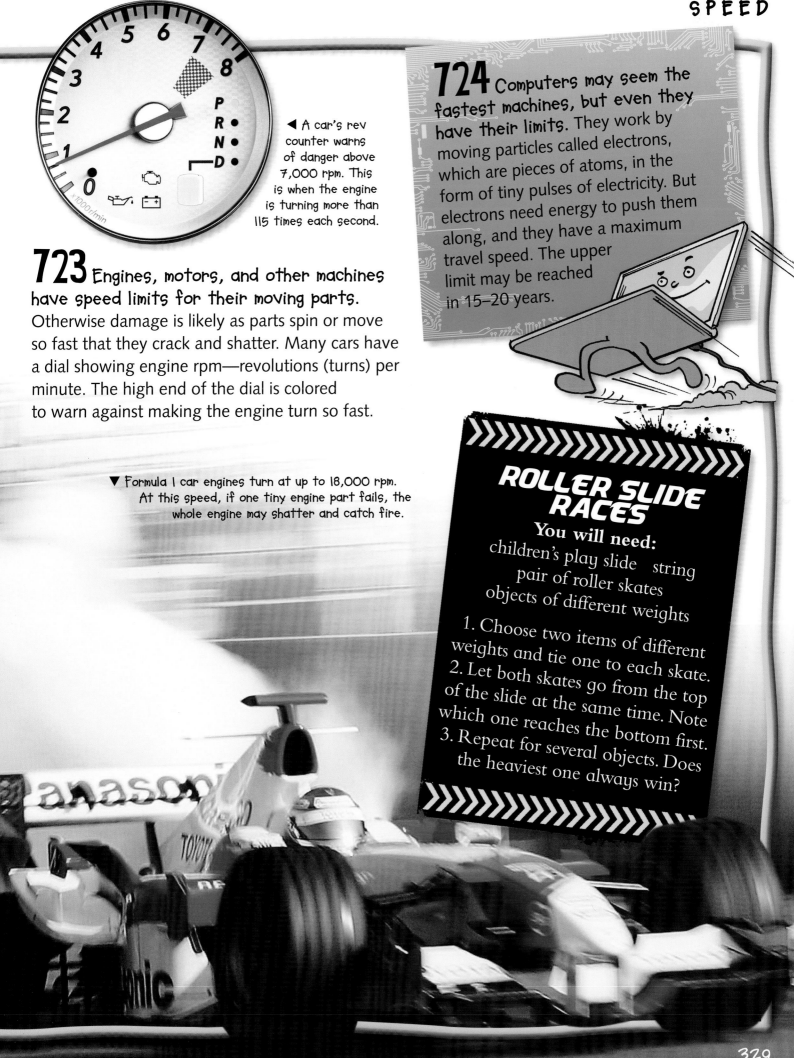

◀ A car's rev counter warns of danger above 7,000 rpm. This is when the engine is turning more than 115 times each second.

723 Engines, motors, and other machines have speed limits for their moving parts. Otherwise damage is likely as parts spin or move so fast that they crack and shatter. Many cars have a dial showing engine rpm—revolutions (turns) per minute. The high end of the dial is colored to warn against making the engine turn so fast.

724 Computers may seem the fastest machines, but even they have their limits. They work by moving particles called electrons, which are pieces of atoms, in the form of tiny pulses of electricity. But electrons need energy to push them along, and they have a maximum travel speed. The upper limit may be reached in 15–20 years.

▼ Formula 1 car engines turn at up to 18,000 rpm. At this speed, if one tiny engine part fails, the whole engine may shatter and catch fire.

ROLLER SLIDE RACES

You will need:
children's play slide   string
pair of roller skates
objects of different weights

1. Choose two items of different weights and tie one to each skate.
2. Let both skates go from the top of the slide at the same time. Note which one reaches the bottom first.
3. Repeat for several objects. Does the heaviest one always win?

Speeding up, slowing down

725 Hardly anything goes at a steady speed—not even planets traveling around the Sun. The Earth's speed varies by more than 2,200 miles per hour between the fastest and slowest part of its orbit. Movement always involves speeding up, called acceleration, and slowing down, or deceleration.

▼ Top Fuel dragsters are the fastest-accelerating cars. From standstill, they cover a one-quarter-mile track in five seconds, finishing at a top speed of over 310 miles per hour.

726 The rate of change for speed is measured by how the distance covered in a certain time changes with time. A car starts from standstill, goes 3 feet per second after one second, 6 feet per second after two seconds, and so on. Its rate of acceleration, or speeding up, is 3 feet per second per second. This is usually written as ft/s^2.

▲ This car speeds up from standstill to 60 miles per hour in ten seconds. So its average rate of acceleration is 6 miles per second per second, or 6 miles/sec^2.

727 Speeding up and slowing down are caused by a change in force, such as an engine turning faster or wind blowing harder. A familiar example is when something falls to Earth's surface under the force of gravity. In theory, this causes an acceleration of 9.81 m/s^2, often known as the "g force." In reality, air resistance reduces this acceleration.

▶ Lieutenant Colonel John Paul Stapp experiences extreme g forces during a rocket-propelled acceleration and deceleration exercise in which he reached 632 miles per hour in five seconds.

At standstill

Early acceleration

728 Bigger planets than Earth have much stronger forces of gravity, so their g forces are higher. On the largest planet, Jupiter, falling objects would accelerate at 25 m/s². On the Moon, which is much smaller, this would be 1.6 m/s².

729 Accelerometers measure how fast things speed up or slow down. Most contain small crystal-like parts that change shape slightly as their rate of movement alters, producing tiny amounts of electricity. Two of these devices at right angles can track the direction of a movement, as well as acceleration.

▲ If a micro accelerometer (seen on the hand at the front of the image) detects a car's sudden slowdown, the safety airbag inflates in one tenth of one second.

730 Accelerometers are used in hundreds of everyday objects, from airbags in cars to the handheld controllers for computer games and cell phones. They are also used to detect motion in volcanoes and cliffs that might warn of eruptions, earthquakes, and rockfalls.

Greatest acceleration

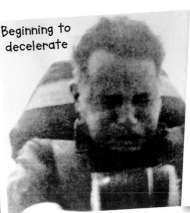

Top speed

Beginning to decelerate

Greatest deceleration

731 What speeds up, eventually slows down. Less speed, or deceleration, is a vital part of working machines, motors, and engines. To save time and stay safe, many of them have specially designed ways of slowing down.

733 Brakes are a common way to slow down. Most use rubbing or friction, which converts kinetic energy (the energy of movement) into heat energy. Many cars have disk brakes, in which stationary pads on the car rub against a disk attached to the road wheel. In many types of electric saw the spinning blade is "grabbed" by a friction device to slow it down fast when the motor is switched off.

732 Some kinds of brakes use drag or resistance. Fast planes have air brakes—flaps on the wings or body that fold out into the passing air to increase drag. Very fast planes release a parachute at the rear when they need to slow down fast, for example when landing on an aircraft carrier.

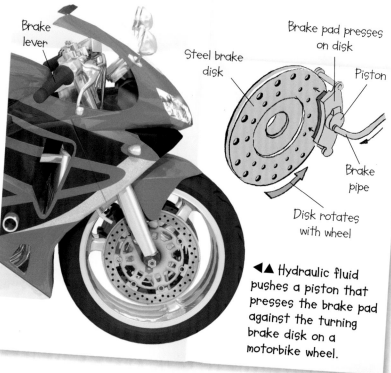

Brake lever

Steel brake disk

Brake pad presses on disk

Piston

Brake pipe

Disk rotates with wheel

◀▲ Hydraulic fluid pushes a piston that presses the brake pad against the turning brake disk on a motorbike wheel.

▶ On a short runway, the F-117 Nighthawk stealth fighter uses a parachute as an airbrake, to help it slow down when landing. This saves wear on the wheels, tires, and brakes.

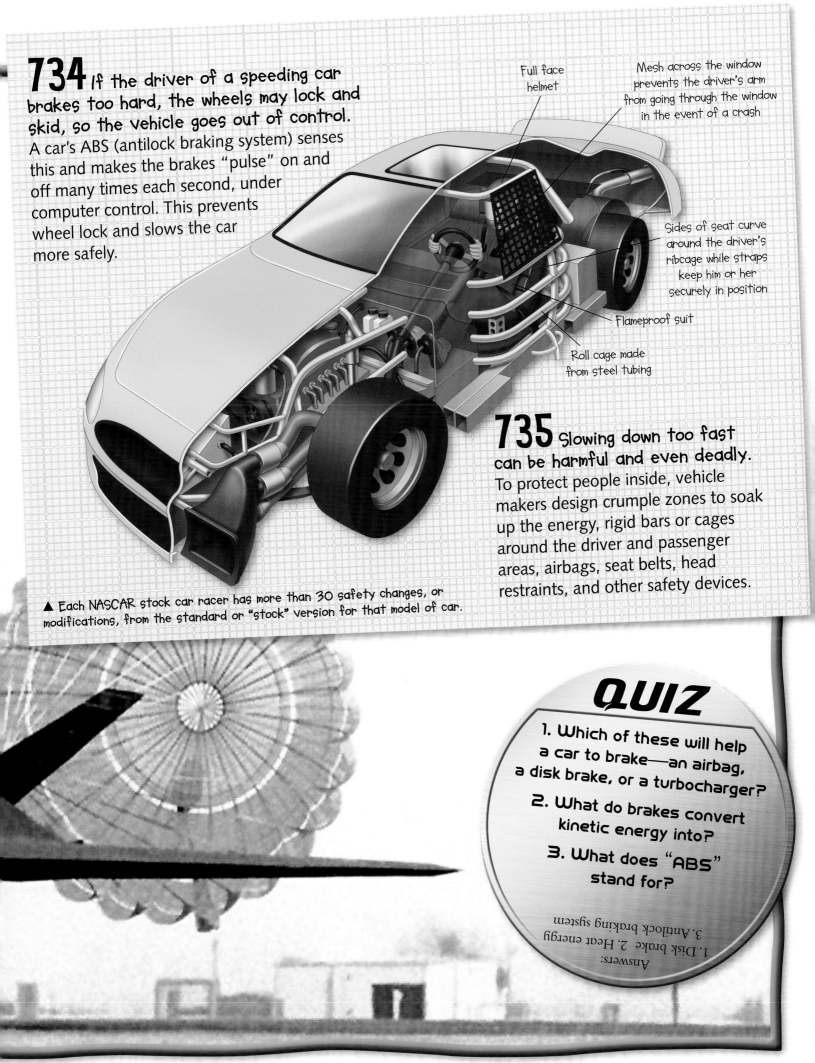

734 If the driver of a speeding car brakes too hard, the wheels may lock and skid, so the vehicle goes out of control. A car's ABS (antilock braking system) senses this and makes the brakes "pulse" on and off many times each second, under computer control. This prevents wheel lock and slows the car more safely.

Full face helmet

Mesh across the window prevents the driver's arm from going through the window in the event of a crash

Sides of seat curve around the driver's ribcage while straps keep him or her securely in position

Flameproof suit

Roll cage made from steel tubing

▲ Each NASCAR stock car racer has more than 30 safety changes, or modifications, from the standard or "stock" version for that model of car.

735 Slowing down too fast can be harmful and even deadly. To protect people inside, vehicle makers design crumple zones to soak up the energy, rigid bars or cages around the driver and passenger areas, airbags, seat belts, head restraints, and other safety devices.

QUIZ
1. Which of these will help a car to brake—an airbag, a disk brake, or a turbocharger?

2. What do brakes convert kinetic energy into?

3. What does "ABS" stand for?

Answers:
1. Disk brake 2. Heat energy 3. Antilock braking system

Special speeds

736 Speed crops up where many people would not think about it. These special uses and examples of speed range from making music to catching people who are driving over the speed limit, to predicting the weather.

0 Calm Chimney smoke rises straight up

1 Light air Smoke drifts gently

3 Gentle breeze Washing flutters

2 Light breeze Leaves rustle

4 Moderate breeze Paper blows around

737 Fast aircraft may measure their speed in Mach numbers. These compare the speed of an object to the speed of sound under the same conditions of air temperature and pressure. The speed of sound is always Mach 1. An aircraft flying at Mach 0.9 is traveling at nine tenths of the speed of sound. At sea level this is about 690 miles per hour. Very high, in cold thin air, it is 618 miles per hour.

▶ A shock wave of air (area of very high pressure) forming around this F-18 Super Hornet shows it is close to going faster than sound.

738 Speed is part of how things vibrate, or move to and fro. This is known as frequency, measured in Hertz (Hz). Twenty Hz is 20 vibrations per second, the lowest or deepest sound human ears detect. A piano's highest or top note is 4,186 Hz.

▼ High pitched or high frequency sounds have shorter waves than low or deep ones.

High pitch (short wave)   Low pitch (long wave)

▼ The Beaufort Scale does not measure the actual speed of the wind in miles per hour or knots, but what the wind does to its surroundings.

5 Fresh breeze Small trees sway

6 Strong breeze Hard to control an umbrella

7 Near gale Whole trees start to sway

8 Gale Difficult to walk into wind

9 Severe gale Small branches, tiles and chimneys blown off

10 Storm Houses damaged; trees blown down

11 Severe storm Serious damage

12 Hurricane Widespread damage

739 The Beaufort Scale for wind speed goes from 1, no wind, to 12, hurricane, and describes the wind's effects. For example, at 4 on the scale, dust and loose paper are raised and blown about, and small branches begin to move.

740 The speed of the shock or seismic waves from an earthquake or volcano shows its strength and how far damage will spread. These waves travel at 2–4 miles per second through rocks near the Earth's surface, but much faster—over 7 miles per second—through the middle of the planet.

741 "Speed guns" that check vehicle speeds use a feature of speed called the Doppler effect. The gun beams pulses of radio or similar waves and detects them as they bounce back off the vehicle. The faster the vehicle, the more it moves toward the gun between pulses, so the closer the bounced-back pulses are.

I DON'T BELIEVE IT!

Tornadoes on Earth have wind speeds of around 220 miles per hour. On the planet Neptune, storm winds blow over six times faster, at 1,360 miles per hour!

742 Modern science tells us that the fastest possible speed is the speed of light. It is about 186,000 miles per second (precisely 299,792,458 meters per second). This means light could go around the Earth seven times in less than a second. As far as we know, nothing can travel faster.

743 The speed of light is usually written as the symbol *c*. It is so important that it is the only speed that is fixed or constant, everywhere at any time. In fact, it is more constant than time itself. Scientists explain weird events in deep space by saying that time can go faster or slower, but the speed of light cannot.

▼ The fastest ever human-made objects, capable of reaching 157,078 miles per hour, were two *Helios* spacecraft sent to study the Sun in 1974.

744 Light speed is not only for light waves. It is for all similar kinds of waves, known as electromagnetic waves. These include radio waves, microwaves, infrared and ultraviolet rays, X-rays, and gamma rays. Also the speed of light is usually measured in a vacuum (a space empty of matter). It is slightly slower in air, and even slower in water.

▲ Like all forms of light, laser light beams—such as those seen here at a concert—go as fast as radio, X-rays, and all other waves made of electrical and magnetic energy.

745 Will it ever be possible to exceed light speed? Some experts suggest ideas such as "warp drive." Instead of light passing through space, space is bent or warped to pass around the light beam.

746 Going faster than the speed of light would lead to many strange events. One idea is that as you approach light speed, time slows down. At light speed, time stops. So faster than light could allow you to travel back in time. Then you could read this book all over again and be just as amazed!

▲ In science fiction on TV and in movies, craft such as Star Trek's *Enterprise* sometimes go faster than light— perhaps when being pulled into a massive black hole.

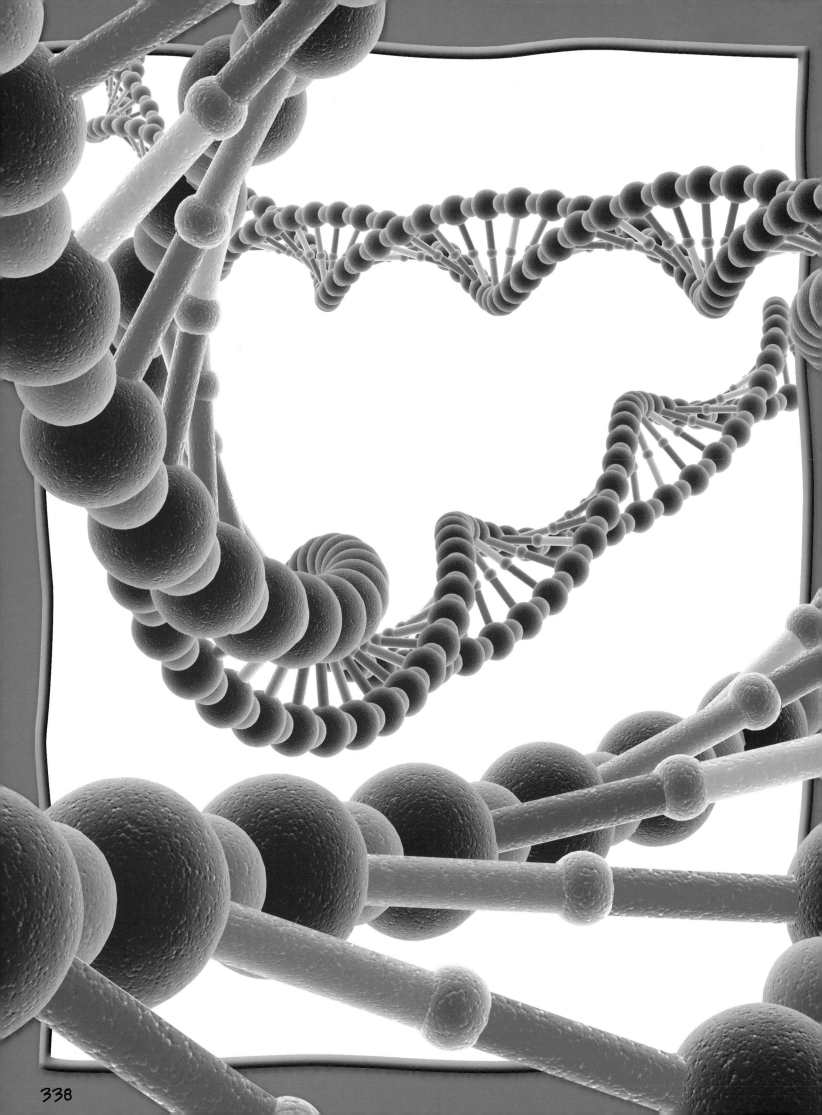

EVOLUTION

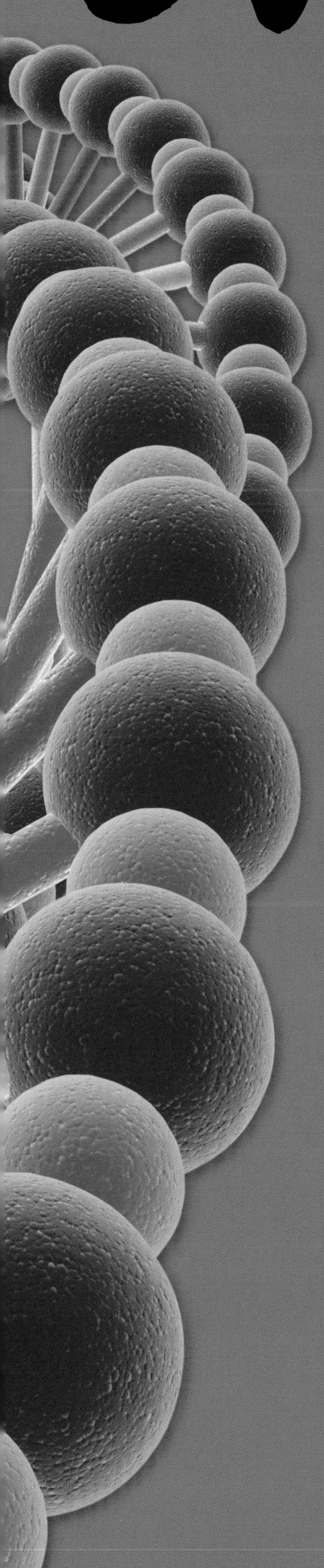

- Charles Darwin
- Classifying species
- Natural selection
- Studying fossils
- The evolutionary clock
- The first animals
- Reptiles and dinosaurs
- The rise of mammals
- Human evolution
- Artificial selection

How old was Darwin when he sailed around the world?

Where would you find a lemur?

What animal group do humans belong to?

How small were the smallest dinosaurs?

Life on Earth

747 Earth is about 4,600 million years old. At first our planet could not support life. It was a mass of red-hot, liquid rock often battered by meteorites (rocks from space). Over millions of years Earth cooled down and conditions changed, making it possible for life to exist. The first organisms (lifeforms) appeared on Earth about 3,500 million years ago.

▼ We don't know for certain what Earth looked like more than 3,000 million years ago before life began. There were many volcanoes, but no oceans.

748 The first organisms were very simple—just a single cell. Cells are the tiny, basic building blocks of all living things. Over millions of years life has become incredibly varied and complex, adapting to Earth's ever-changing environments. For example, the animal kingdom includes birds, insects, fish, reptiles, and mammals. This amazing development is called "evolution."

749 Evolution has been studied for more than one hundred years. In the 18th century, scientists such as Charles Darwin (1809–1882) started forming theories to explain the vast changes in life over time. Since then, scientists have continued to examine living things and fossils—the remains of once-living organisms preserved in rocks—to explain how evolution works.

Darwin's travels

750 Charles Darwin was one of the world's greatest scientists. His work on evolution changed people's ideas about life on Earth and it is still important today, influencing modern scientists.

▶ Charles Darwin joined HMS *Beagle* and sailed around the world when he was just 22 years old.

Despite its great weight, *Megatherium* could stand upright on two legs

751 The young Charles Darwin was a keen collector of beetles and fossils. He didn't do well in school and stopped studying medicine because he hated working on dead bodies. Darwin later went to Cambridge University to train to become a Christian priest, but some of his professors encouraged him to study living things instead.

▶ While at university, Darwin collected beetles, a popular craze of the time. These are some of the ones he gathered.

752 In 1831, Darwin joined HMS *Beagle* as the ship's naturalist. Naturalists are scientists that study animals and plants. Over the next five years, Darwin found many unknown species (types) of animals and plants. When HMS *Beagle* explored South America, Darwin saw volcanic eruptions, experienced earthquakes, and discovered ancient animal remains.

▶ In Argentina, South America, Darwin found a complete fossil of an animal that he had never seen before. It was a giant ground sloth named *Megatherium*.

753 While on HMS *Beagle*, Darwin visited the Galápagos Islands off the coast of South America. Here he discovered animals that were found nowhere else on Earth, such as giant tortoises.

754 After Darwin returned to England he spent years working on his theory of evolution. He studied his notebooks and the examples (specimens) of animals and fossils he had gathered during his travels. Darwin also discussed his ideas with other scientists. Despite illness, he lived to 73 years old, a good age for the time.

◀ Darwin's notes show his idea that life is linked in an evolutionary tree.

343

The riddle of life

▼ Each of these butterflies is a different species. They do not breed with each other and look different.

755 A species is a type of living thing. All the individuals of a species have a similar appearance. They can breed with each other to produce offspring (babies). There are millions of different species alive today, as well as millions that have become extinct (died out completely).

Brown argus

Purple emperor

Clouded yellow

Adonis blue

Green hairstreak

756 Darwin was not the first scientist to write about evolution. French scientist Jean-Bapiste Lamarck (1744–1829) had a theory that if an animal adapted to its environment during its lifetime, the changes would be passed on to its offspring. Although not entirely correct, his ideas sparked interest. Other scientists also began to question whether God had created species as they now exist.

◄ Lamarck falsely believed that if a giraffe stretched its neck to reach the highest leaves on a tree, its neck would get longer—and its offspring would have longer necks too.

757 For centuries, people thought that a species could not change. Darwin examined mockingbirds from the Galápagos Islands and found differences between the specimens. He had an idea that the birds may have adapted to the islands' different environments. Darwin showed that a species could change over time and does not have a "fixed" appearance.

► As Darwin explored the Galápagos Islands, he noticed small differences between the mockingbird species on each separate island.

758 In 1858, Alfred Russel Wallace (1823–1913), a fellow scientist, wrote to Darwin about his ideas on evolution. Darwin was horrified to discover that Wallace had similar theories to his own. This spurred Darwin into publishing his book, *On the Origin of Species* in 1859. Some people were very interested by its ideas, but others were outraged.

◀ This cartoon of Darwin with the body of an ape appeared in 1871 after he wrote that humans and apes had a common ancestor (relative from the past).

759 In 1871 Darwin published a second book entitled *The Descent of Man*. He wrote about the similarities and differences between humans and other apes, as well as the differences between humans from different cultures. Many people did not approve of the fact that Darwin had linked the evolution of people to that of chimpanzees.

▼ Darwin's theories about humans being related to other apes, such as chimps, are now accepted by most scientists.

760 Lots of people disagreed with Darwin, believing instead that God created all living things. This belief is called Creationism. Creationists believe that living organisms cannot produce new forms of life, and that only God can do this.

Classifying species

761 All living organisms are related and are linked in a huge web of life. To keep track of the vast number of species, living things can be classified (put into groups).

762 One method of classifying life is called cladistics. A clade is a group made up of an ancestor (a relative from the past) and all its living and extinct descendants, which developed from them.

763 A clade is based on features that have been inherited, or passed on, from the ancestor. Usually, only the descendants have the specific feature.

COMMON ANCESTOR

Animals with stalks attached to the sea floor. Crinoids have cup-shaped bodies and many feathery arms

Large central disk and four or more radiating arms

Crinoids

Star-shaped body with central disk and radiating

Starfish

Smaller central disk than starfish and snakelike arms

Brittlestars

Moving animals with mouths on the underside of their bodies

▲ ECHINODERM CLADE
Echinoderms are a unique group of animals, which have a spiny skin and five or more arms that radiate (branch) out from a body made up of five equal parts.

Round body shape with no arms

Body covered in long spines

Sea urchins

Elongated body with leathery skin

Sea cucumbers

CLASSIFYING SHOES

You will need:
pen   notepad   lots of shoes

1. Divide the shoes into groups such as trainers, boots, sandals.
2. Separate each group into smaller groups, using features such as heels, laces, and so on.
3. Keep dividing the groups until each shoe has its own group. Draw a chart to show how you classified the shoes.

764 All humans are related to the very first human beings. These first humans shared an ancestor with chimpanzees. If we look back further still, all primates—the animal group that includes monkeys and apes such as chimps and humans— share the same shrewlike, mammalian ancestor.

765 The scientist Carolus Linnaeus (1707–1778) classified organisms in a clear, scientific way. He arranged species into groups according to their body features and gave each species a unique Latin name. Each name is made up of two words, for example, the tiger is *Panthera tigris*.

SPECIES Tiger
A species is a particular type of living thing. There are six living and three extinct subspecies of tiger, each with a unique appearance.

GENUS Panthera
Related species are placed together in a genus. The lion, tiger, leopard, and jaguar belong to this genus. They are the only cats that can roar.

Lion   Tiger

FAMILY Felidae
The members of a family are closely related. There are 41 members of the felidae cat family.

Caracal   Domestic cat   Tiger   Cheetah

Red fox   Tiger   Sea lion   Wolf

Weasel

ORDER Carnivora
In an order, species are grouped together due to shared characteristics. Animals in the carnivora order are all meat-eating mammals.

CLASS Mammals
There are five vertebrate classes—birds, amphibians, reptiles, fish, and mammals. All mammals have hair, breathe air, and feed their young milk.

Bat   Whale   Gorilla   Tiger   Koala   Rabbit   Polar bear

Frog   Sailfish

Hummingbird   Tiger   Crocodile

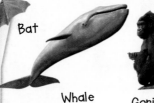

PHYLUM Chordates
Animals are grouped in different phylums depending on their body structure. Chordates have a spinal cord. Most are vertebrates (backboned animals).

766 Scientists used to classify different species purely by their appearance. For example plants were grouped according to leaf shape, or the color and number of their petals. The study of DNA (see pages 92–93) made scientists change their ideas about evolution and reclassify many species.

Dragonfly   Toad   Tiger   Snail   Eagle

Starfish   Jellyfish   Shark   Snake   Crab

KINGDOM Animalia
All living things are placed into five main groups, including animals, plants, and fungi.

The struggle for survival

767 Many things can affect an animal's survival. For example, food supply, disease, and climate. If there is a change, some individuals may survive the new conditions. The survivors pass on their favorable genes to their young— this is natural selection.

◄ Predators such as polar bears target their hunts at weak or sick animals. The healthier, fitter animals tend to survive and reproduce.

768 Natural selection can cause changes within a species. The ancestors of modern tigers may have had fewer stripes. Stripes give good camouflage as they help the animal blend in with its surroundings. The ancestors with the gene for more stripes may have been the most successful hunters, and so would have raised more offspring, passing on the genes for stripy coats.

▼▶ These are three of the different ways animals have evolved to ensure their genes are passed on.

APPEARANCE
A camouflaged appearance gives this tiger a natural advantage while hunting.

SEXUAL SELECTION
Stags with the biggest antlers and best fighting technique are more likely to win females and have young.

LOTS OF OFFSPRING
Some animals, such as toads, have to have lots of young as many won't survive to adulthood.

769 When species change due to natural selection, evolution takes place. This process of selection has led to all the different species alive today. It is also one reason species can become extinct, as the least successful animals die out.

770 If a species is separated and isolated this too can cause evolution. When a group of individuals is cut off from others of the same species, they can only breed with each other. As they adapt to the new local conditions they evolve into a new species, unable to breed with the original group they were separated from.

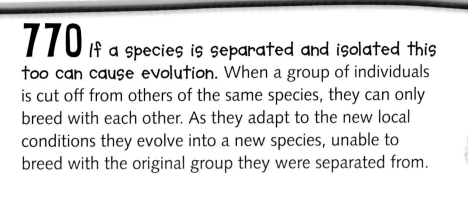

771 A group of animals can be isolated by a river, an ocean, or a mountain range. The Galápagos Islands are isolated from South America by the Pacific Ocean. Thousands of years ago, a few finches were blown there by strong winds. They stayed on the islands and bred, evolving separately from the mainland birds.

▼▶ The Galápagos Islands provided a range of environments to which the finches adapted.

SOUTH AMERICA

Galápagos Islands

▼▶ There are about 14 different finch species on the Galápagos Islands. Each has a different beak shape suited to its particular diet.

Common cactus finch
Beak Long and pointed
Diet Nectar of cactus flowers

Large ground finch
Beak Large and thick
Diet Nuts, seeds, and cactus fruits

Vegetarian tree finch
Beak Short, thick, parrotlike
Diet Plant buds, flowers, leaves

Woodpecker finch
Beak Pointed and narrow
Diet Insects and grubs

349

Looking for evidence

772 To show how species evolve, scientists look for evidence. They can examine and compare rocks, fossils, and DNA (a substance inside most cells that carries all the genes for a living thing) for clues to back up their theories.

773 The study of rocks can tell us about the climate on Earth millions of years ago. Rocks that are rich in corals and the skeletons of other marine animals were formed when there were tropical oceans covering the land.

▼ Coelacanths (say "seel-uh-kanths") were thought to be extinct until a living specimen was found in 1938. They are descended from the group of fish that evoved into amphibians.

Bony scales for protection not found on other live fish

Long, limblike fins are used to "walk" through the water

774 Fossils tell us what plants and animals looked like millions of years ago. Scientists compare living species with fossils of extinct species to see how much they have evolved over time.

775 Scientists can extract DNA from living cells to read their genetic code. The DNA of different organisms is compared to see how closely related they are. The most closely related have similar DNA.

◀ This fossil coelacanth shows that the fish has changed little over time.

Tenrecs are small, spiny animals found mostly in Madagascar. Their closest relatives are elephants and aardvarks

Prickly hedgehogs are found in Europe, Africa, parts of Asia, and New Zealand

The echidna from Australia uses its long snout to find ants and termites

776 Some unrelated species have evolved similar traits. Animals in different parts of the world have evolved spines for protection, while hummingbirds, butterflies, and possums all have long tongues for probing into flowers to reach nectar. This is called convergent evolution.

▲ Tenrecs, hedgehogs, and echidnas are unrelated species, yet they have each evolved similar body features because they live in similar environments.

777 Where animals are found in the world tells us about how they evolved. When Madagascar became separated from Africa, lemurs (a type of primate) became isolated, and evolved separately from other African primates.

AFRICA

Madagascar

▲ Madagascar split from the coast of Africa about 165 million years ago.

▲ Lemurs, such as these ring-tailed lemurs, are found only in Madagascar.

Fossil clues

778 Fossils are the remains of living organisms that have been preserved in the ground. Most fossils are of animals, but plants can be fossilized too. The oldest fossils are of cyanobacteria (simple, single-celled organisms) that lived more than 3,000 million years ago.

779 Fossil formation is a slow process. Some fossils can form in just 10,000 years, but most take much longer—usually hundreds of thousands, or even millions of years.

780 When an animal dies, its body might be buried under a layer of mud and sand. The soft body parts rot away but the hard parts, such as the bones, remain and become rocklike.

▼ The fossil magnolia (left) looks almost identical to the fruit from a living magnolia plant.

TRUE OR FALSE?

1. Fossils can be millions of years old.
2. The deeper the rock the younger the fossil.
3. Fossils helped Darwin work out his theory of evolution.

Answers:
1.True 2. False, usually the deeper the rock the older the fossil 3.True

▲ These paleontologists (scientists who study the history of life on Earth) are working on an excavation or "dig" in Wyoming in the United States, where dinosaur fossils have been found.

► These fossils were found in the La Brea Tar Pits near Los Angeles, United States. In the past, animals became trapped in the tar and died.

As we complete each piece, we fill it in. Keep checking back to watch our progress!

American lion (Panthera atrox) skeleton

Right Side Elements
Left Side Elements
Central Elements

781 Scientists can learn how an extinct species lived by studying its fossil. For example, the structure and joints of an animal's legs shows how the animal walked, and how its muscles were attached to its skeleton.

782 The study of fossils helped Darwin work out his theory of evolution. He noticed that animal fossils found on islands such as the Cape Verde Islands and Falkland Islands in the Atlantic Ocean looked different from those he found on the South American mainland, giving him ideas about separation and isolation (see page 349).

783 Fossils can be dated to find out when they lived on Earth. One way is to work out of the age of the rock in which they were found. Usually, the deeper the rock, the older the fossil. To work out a fossil's absolute age, scientists make use of carbon-dating. All living things contain natural radioactivity, which leaks away at a steady rate. The amount remaining helps date the fossil.

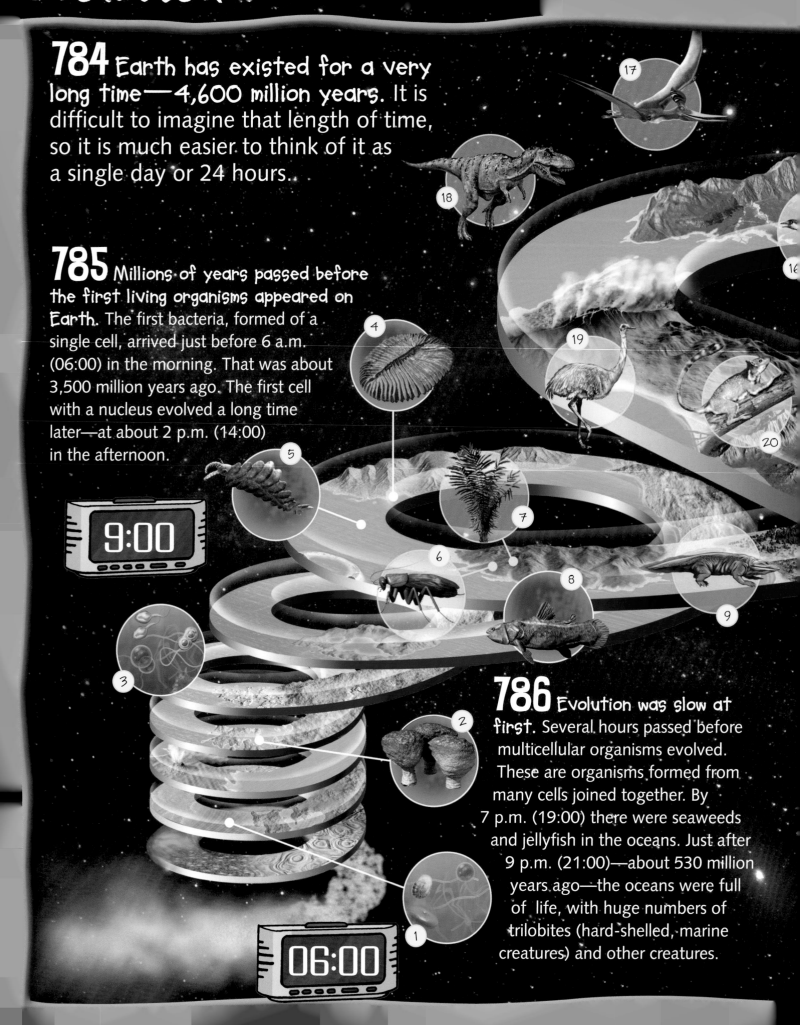

784 Earth has existed for a very long time—4,600 million years. It is difficult to imagine that length of time, so it is much easier to think of it as a single day or 24 hours.

785 Millions of years passed before the first living organisms appeared on Earth. The first bacteria, formed of a single cell, arrived just before 6 a.m. (06:00) in the morning. That was about 3,500 million years ago. The first cell with a nucleus evolved a long time later—at about 2 p.m. (14:00) in the afternoon.

786 Evolution was slow at first. Several hours passed before multicellular organisms evolved. These are organisms formed from many cells joined together. By 7 p.m. (19:00) there were seaweeds and jellyfish in the oceans. Just after 9 p.m. (21:00)—about 530 million years ago—the oceans were full of life, with huge numbers of trilobites (hard-shelled, marine creatures) and other creatures.

9:00

06:00

787 Animals moved onto land and by 10 p.m. (22:00) there were insects flying in the sky. The dinosaurs ruled the Earth from about 11 p.m. (23:00), while the first small, furry mammals appeared soon afterward.

11:00

EVOLUTION THROUGH TIME KEY

1 Simple cells
2 Cyanobacteria
3 Chidarians (soft-bodied animals)
4 Ediacaran (early marine animals)
5 Anomalocaris (arthropod—animals with segmented bodies and no backbone)
6 Cockroach (insect)
7 Cycad (cone-bearing plant)
8 Coelacanth (fish)
9 Diadectes (reptilelike amphibian)
10 Dimetrodon (small, early reptile)
11 Plesiosaur (marine reptile)
12 Lilienstennus (dinosaur)
13 Pteranodon (flying reptile)
14 Brachiosaur (large dinosaur)
15 Magnolia (flowering plant)
16 Archaeopteryx (early bird)
17 Quetzalcoatlus (pterosaur—flying reptile)
18 Tyrannosaurus rex (dinosaur)
19 Moa (flightless bird)
20 Plesiadapis (early mammal)
21 Indricotheres (rhinoceros-like mammal)
22 Saber-tooth (carnivorous mammal)
23 Macrauchenia (hoofed mammal)
24 Wolf (carnivorous mammal)
25 Homo sapiens (modern man)

11:59

▲ This diagram shows the evolution of life from the very first organisms that appeared more than 3,000 million years ago to modern humans.

788 It's difficult to believe that humans have been around for a relatively short time. Modern man arrived on Earth at just one minute to midnight, about 200,000 years ago.

789 Understanding the evolutionary clock helps scientists work out the speed at which evolution takes place. Over the last 4,600 million years, species have appeared and then disappeared, to be replaced by other species more suited to the changing environments.

The start of life

790 For a few hundred million years, Earth was a hot mass of molten rock and gases. The atmosphere—the layer of gases that surrounds the Earth—contained water vapor, carbon dioxide, and nitrogen but no oxygen. Gradually, the surface cooled, clouds formed, and water vapor fell as rain. Rain poured onto the land to create the oceans.

Frequent volcanic activity

◄ The Earth looked very different 3,000 million years ago, during a period known as the Archaean. Much of the planet was covered by oceans.

Deep sea vents

Stromatolites

791 Once there were oceans, conditions became more suited to the evolution of living things. The first building blocks of life appeared—amino acids, proteins, and DNA. There are many theories about how these chemicals were created and how they joined up to form cells, but nobody knows for sure. It is one of the greatest mysteries.

792 The cooling continued and by about 3,500 million years ago the first cells had evolved. These first cells were cyanobacteria. They grew in the sunny parts of the ocean and used sunlight to make food. During this process, cyanobacteria released oxygen into the atmosphere.

▼ Stromatolites, a type of cyanobacteria, are among the earliest fossils. They can still be seen at Shark Bay, Australia.

793 For the next 2,500 to 3,000 million years, life was very simple. There was bacteria, simple animals, and plants, but no animals with a head, body, and tail.

Jellyfish

▶ The first animals were soft bodied like jellyfish. *Charnia* was a strange animal that looked more like a plant.

Charnia

794 About 570 to 600 million years ago, evolution took off. Within a hundred million years or so, there were thousands of new species. There were seaweeds in the oceans, which—like the cyanobacteria—used light to make food, and there was an abundance of animals in the oceans.

Early animals

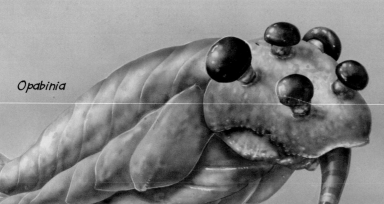

795 Fossils show that there were some very unusual animals living in the oceans about 500 million years ago. Some had several heads, trunks like elephants, backward-facing mouths, and many other odd features.

Opabinia

▼ Animals from the Cambrian Period died out when conditions on Earth changed. There are no living relatives.

Pikaia

796 Thousands of fossils have been found at the Burgess Shale deposits in Canada. The site was discovered in 1909 by Charles Walcott (1850–1927). He dug up more than 65,000 fossils. Amazingly, some were of soft-bodied animals such as jellyfish.

Ottoia

Pirania

▼ These scientists are working on a dig in the famous Walcott Quarry in the Burgess Shale deposits, Canada.

797 The oceans were full of life during the Cambrian Period (545–495 million years ago). There were mollusks, echinoderms, trilobites, worms, jellyfish, and some early fish. Fish were different from the other animals as they had backbones—they were the first vertebrate animals.

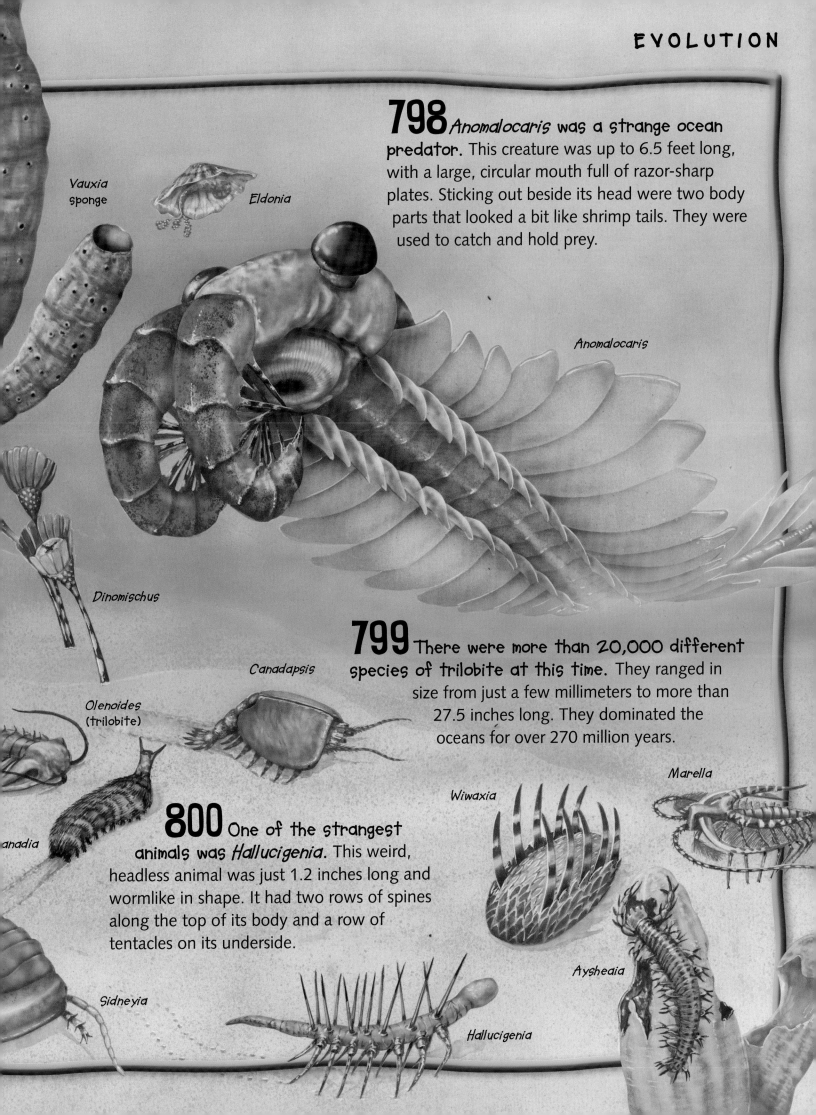

798 *Anomalocaris* was a strange ocean predator. This creature was up to 6.5 feet long, with a large, circular mouth full of razor-sharp plates. Sticking out beside its head were two body parts that looked a bit like shrimp tails. They were used to catch and hold prey.

799 There were more than 20,000 different species of trilobite at this time. They ranged in size from just a few millimeters to more than 27.5 inches long. They dominated the oceans for over 270 million years.

800 One of the strangest animals was *Hallucigenia*. This weird, headless animal was just 1.2 inches long and wormlike in shape. It had two rows of spines along the top of its body and a row of tentacles on its underside.

Vauxia sponge

Eldonia

Anomalocaris

Dinomischus

Canadapsis

Olenoides (trilobite)

anadia

Sidneyia

Wiwaxia

Marella

Aysheaia

Hallucigenia

Moving onto land

801 Simple plants first appeared about 400 million years ago. Mosses are primitive plants that can only grow in damp areas. Ferns are more highly evolved—they appeared 350 million years ago. By around 300 million years ago much of the land was covered conifer forests and swamps.

▲ This scene shows some early tree and plant species in a flooded forest during the Carboniferous Period (359–299 million years ago).

802 Most of the first land animals were plant eaters. One was *Arthropleura*, the largest ever millipede-like animal. Although it was related to arthropods such as insects and crabs, it grew to the size of a crocodile, with a body up to 6.5 feet in length.

803 Imagine a scorpion larger than you! This was *Pterygotus*, a fearsome predator that hunted fish more than 400 million years ago. Some of its relatives were among the first animals to crawl onto land. Sea scorpions are extinct, but they were the ancestors of the arachnid animal group that includes spiders and scorpions.

▼ Fossil footprints of *Arthropleura* have been found in rocks, showing the animals moved quickly over the ground.

EVOLVING ANIMALS

You will need:
pencil   notepad   tracing paper

1. Draw a simple outine of an animal.
2. Make a copy using tracing paper, but change one body part.
3. Trace the second picture. This time change something else.
4. Do this ten times, then look at your drawings to see how the animal evolved.

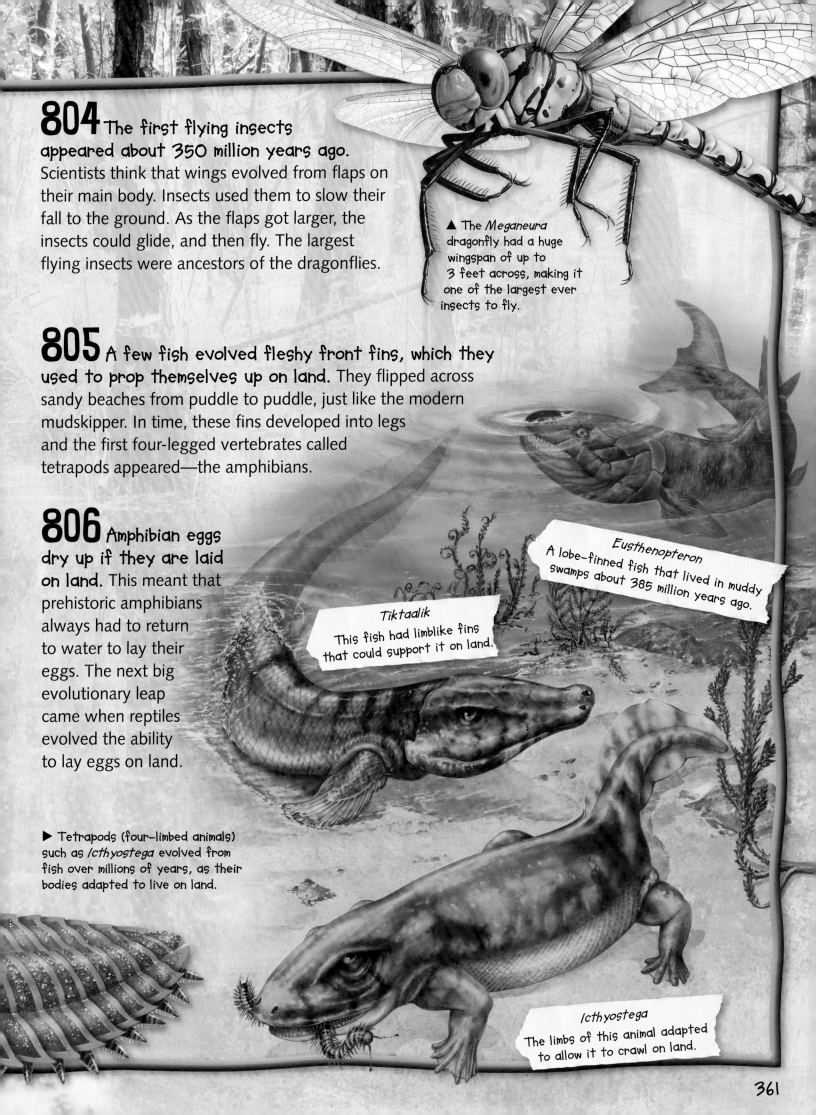

804 **The first flying insects appeared about 350 million years ago.** Scientists think that wings evolved from flaps on their main body. Insects used them to slow their fall to the ground. As the flaps got larger, the insects could glide, and then fly. The largest flying insects were ancestors of the dragonflies.

▲ The *Meganeura* dragonfly had a huge wingspan of up to 3 feet across, making it one of the largest ever insects to fly.

805 **A few fish evolved fleshy front fins, which they used to prop themselves up on land.** They flipped across sandy beaches from puddle to puddle, just like the modern mudskipper. In time, these fins developed into legs and the first four-legged vertebrates called tetrapods appeared—the amphibians.

806 **Amphibian eggs dry up if they are laid on land.** This meant that prehistoric amphibians always had to return to water to lay their eggs. The next big evolutionary leap came when reptiles evolved the ability to lay eggs on land.

Eusthenopteron
A lobe-finned fish that lived in muddy swamps about 385 million years ago.

Tiktaalik
This fish had limblike fins that could support it on land.

▶ Tetrapods (four-limbed animals) such as *Icthyostega* evolved from fish over millions of years, as their bodies adapted to live on land.

Icthyostega
The limbs of this animal adapted to allow it to crawl on land.

Reptiles and dinosaurs

807 The very first reptiles developed from amphibians around 315 million years ago. They were small, lizardlike animals that laid eggs with a leathery shell. This adaption meant that they could live in dry habitats. They moved onto land where few animals had ventured before.

▲ One of the first reptiles was *Hylonomus*, a small, lizardlike animal. It laid eggs on land.

▲ Over millions of years, more than 1,000 different dinosaur species evolved as they adapted to Earth's changing environments.

808 Dinosaurs evolved about 230 million years ago from a group of crawling reptiles. Dinosaurs ruled the Earth for about 170 million years, outnumbering the many other backboned creatures that lived at the same time.

809 The first dinosaurs, such as *Eoraptor*, were small, upright, and ran on their back legs. Their upright posture was possible because they developed different hips from other reptiles. They could place their legs directly under their body to raise it off the ground. This allowed them to move faster.

810 The smallest dinosaurs weighed just a few pounds, but there were some giants too. One of the largest was *Argentinosaurus*, which scientists think was about 130 feet long and weighed up to 50 tons. It is difficult to be sure as complete skeletons are rarely found.

▼ For about 100 million years enormous dinosaurs called sauropods, including *Argentinosaurus*, roamed the planet.

▶ *Giganotosaurus* was one of the largest carnivorous dinosaurs. Like *Argentinosaurus*, it lived in South America.

811 One of the most well known dinosaurs is *T rex*. It was one of the largest land carnivores that ever existed. *T rex* stood up on its hind legs and used its long tail to balance. It was 13 feet high at the hips and about 42 feet long. Despite its size, it was not quite as large as its relative *Giganotosaurus*.

▲ Near the end of the dinosaur's reign, sauropods were replaced by the plant-eating *Triceratops* (1), *Ankylosaurus* (2), and the duck-billed dinosaurs (3).

QUIZ

1. When did the first reptiles appear?
2. Was *Triceratops* a plant or meat eater?
3. For how long did dinosaurs rule the land?

Answers:
1. 315 million years ago
2. A plant eater. 3. About 170 million years

812 About 65 million years ago a huge number of living things died out in a short time. This was probably caused by a meteor smashing into Earth, throwing up vast amounts of dust into the atmosphere and causing a global winter. More than half of the world's species could not survive the sudden changes and became extinct, including nearly all large land animals.

The first birds

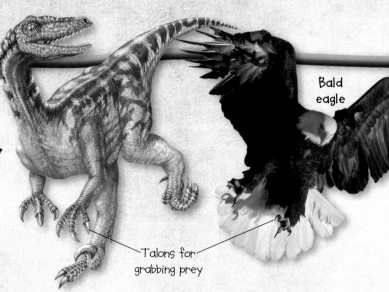

813 About 150 million years ago a small type of dinosaur evolved feathers and the ability to fly. Many scientists believe this dinosaur became the first bird. Birds are more closely related to the dinosaurs than dinosaurs are to modern-day crocodiles because they share a common ancestor.

Bald eagle

Talons for grabbing prey

Velociraptor

▲ *Velociraptor* had hands and feet with curved claws, similar to the talons of modern-day birds of prey.

Long tail

▶ Scientists are not sure whether *Archaeopteryx* could flap its wings or just glide from tree to tree.

814 Darwin suspected that birds and dinosaurs were linked. In 1861, just two years after *On the Origin of Species* was published, the fossil skeleton of a birdlike creature, *Archaeopteryx*, was discovered. It had features of both dinosaurs, such as teeth and a bony tail, and birds, such as wings.

815 Birds share many features with reptiles. Reptiles have scaly skin, and scales can still be seen on the legs of birds. Both birds and reptiles lay eggs with a shell. Birds are thought to be descended from small, raptorlike dinosaurs called "maniraptorans," which includes the *Velociraptor*.

Long flight feathers

Wing claws

Lightweight body

Toothed beak

◀ The feathers, claws, and skull of *Archaeopteryx* can be seen clearly on fossils of this prehistoric creature.

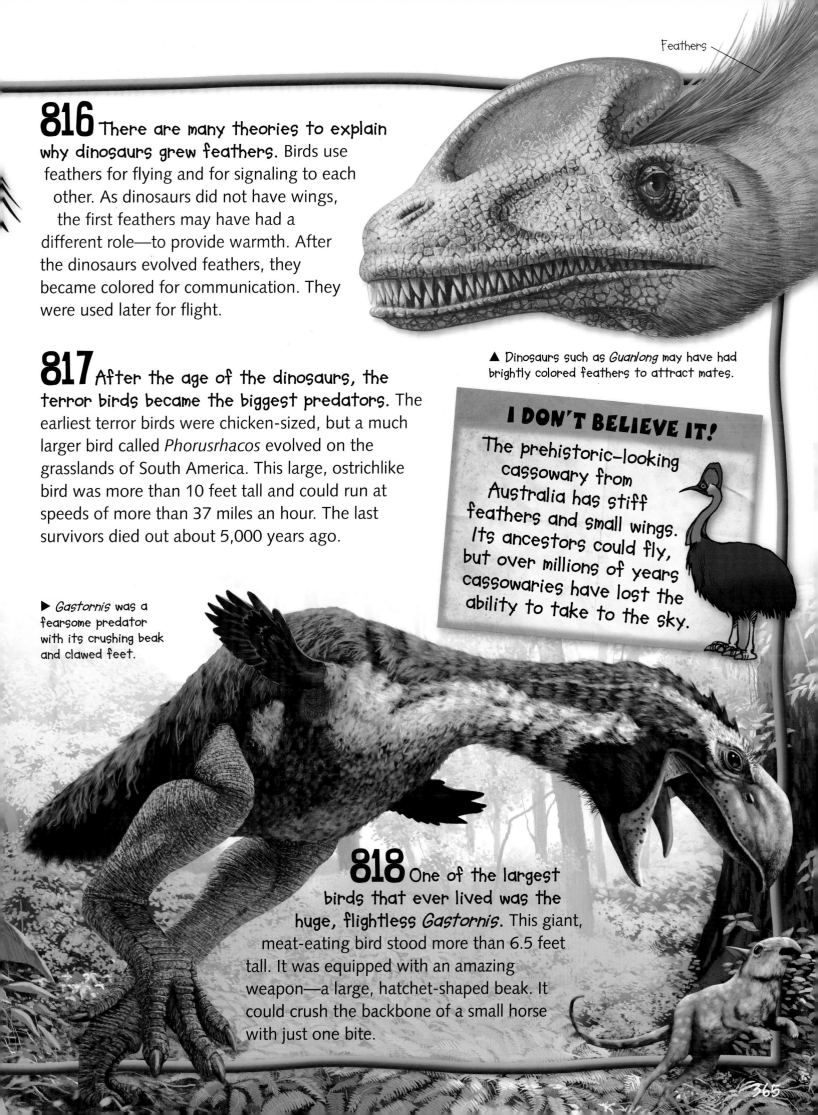

816 There are many theories to explain why dinosaurs grew feathers. Birds use feathers for flying and for signaling to each other. As dinosaurs did not have wings, the first feathers may have had a different role—to provide warmth. After the dinosaurs evolved feathers, they became colored for communication. They were used later for flight.

Feathers

▲ Dinosaurs such as *Guanlong* may have had brightly colored feathers to attract mates.

817 After the age of the dinosaurs, the terror birds became the biggest predators. The earliest terror birds were chicken-sized, but a much larger bird called *Phorusrhacos* evolved on the grasslands of South America. This large, ostrichlike bird was more than 10 feet tall and could run at speeds of more than 37 miles an hour. The last survivors died out about 5,000 years ago.

I DON'T BELIEVE IT!

The prehistoric-looking cassowary from Australia has stiff feathers and small wings. Its ancestors could fly, but over millions of years cassowaries have lost the ability to take to the sky.

▶ *Gastornis* was a fearsome predator with its crushing beak and clawed feet.

818 One of the largest birds that ever lived was the huge, flightless *Gastornis*. This giant, meat-eating bird stood more than 6.5 feet tall. It was equipped with an amazing weapon—a large, hatchet-shaped beak. It could crush the backbone of a small horse with just one bite.

Mammals take over

819 The first mammals evolved about 220 million years ago, and existed alongside the dinosaurs. They evolved from a different group of reptiles to dinosaurs and birds, called therapsids. The first mammals were small and weasel-like, and they probably hunted insects.

▶ The small, early mammal *Leptictidium* used its long snout to sniff out prey such as this cicada.

820 The rise of mammals was not quick—it took millions of years for them to develop and become more varied. Just like the dinosaurs before them, mammals evolved to suit many different habitats. Some returned to the sea in the form of whales and dolphins, others evolved long legs and roamed the grasslands, while bats developed wings and took to the air.

821 All mammals have the same arrangement of bones in their limbs. This is called the pentadactyl limb. The basic plan in the arm is a single bone in the upper limb (the humerus), which is jointed to two bones in the lower limb (the radius and the ulna). Each limb ends in five digits.

▼ The pentadactyl limb in each of these mammals has evolved so that it is adapted to suit their lifestyle.

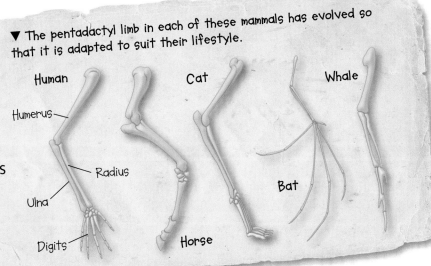

Human
Humerus
Radius
Ulna
Digits

Cat

Whale

Bat

Horse

822 Around 50 million years ago the first horselike animal appeared—*Hyracotherium*. These forest animals were the size of dogs. When grasslands replaced the forests, animals such as *Miohippus* took over from the *Hyracotherium*. *Miohippus* had large, ridged teeth for chewing tough grasses.

▲ *Miohippus* lived from about 36 to 25 million years ago. Its fossils have been found in North America.

823 Some amazing mammals lived during the last Ice Age, about 70,000 years ago. They adapted to survive in the extreme cold, as much of the land was covered in ice. Woolly mammoths lived alongside the saber-tooth. This big cat was more like a bear in size and hunted bison and small mammoths.

QUIZ

Which of the following mammals is the odd one out?

Tiger   Seal   Horse   Echidna
Bat   Whale   Dog   Horse

Answer:
Echidna, the rest are placental mammals

824 There are almost 5,500 species of mammal alive today. The most primitive are the egg-laying monotremes, such as the echidna, which share many characteristics with their reptilian ancestors. Marsupials such as the kangaroo and koala give birth to tiny babies that they care for in their pouch. The biggest group is the placental mammals, which give birth to well-developed young.

▶ Seals are placental mammals. The females are pregnant for one year and feed their young on milk.

▶ Marsupial mammals such as kangaroos carry their young around in a pouch.

▶ There are only two monotreme mammals, the echidna (right) and the duck-billed platypus.

The human story

825 Humans belong to the primate mammal group. All primates have a large brain for their size, with forward-facing eyes that give 3D vision. Most primates have fingers with nails that are used for manipulating and grasping objects.

Forward-facing eyes

Large brain

▶ Primates include lemurs, monkeys, and apes such as gibbons, chimps, and gorillas (shown here).

Fingers with nails

Ardipithecus ramidus
4.4 million years ago

826 The first primates appeared about 75 million years ago. Humans have a common ancestor with chimps that lived in Africa about six million years ago. Then the line splits, with chimps evolving separately to humans. Four million years ago, our human ancestors were still tree dwellers that tottered on two legs.

Australopithecus afarensis
3.9–2.9 million years ago

▶ This timeline shows how various human groups have evolved, from very early kinds that lived in Africa over four million years ago, to modern humans.

Australopithecus africanus
2–3 million years ago

▼ A human's pelvis is shorter and wider than a gorilla's. It allows humans to stand upright.

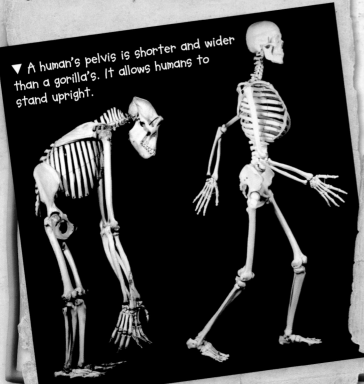

827 Two-and-a-half million years ago, the first human ancestor to use tools appeared. *Homo habilis* had a large brain and was very adaptable. It ate a varied diet, scavenging meat rather than eating grasses and learned to use stone tools to smash bones to get at the rich marrow inside.

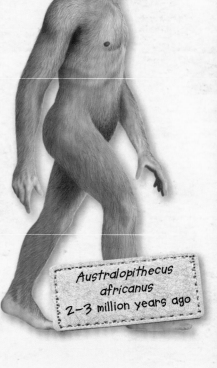

828 Two million years ago, one group of early humans moved out of Africa, and populated other regions of the world. This ancestor was *Homo erectus*, and it had a more humanlike appearance. It lived in a variety of different habitats and learnt how to use fire and cook food.

I DON'T BELIEVE IT!

In 1974, scientists found fossilized bones in Ethiopia, Africa. The bones were 3.2 million years old and belonged to a small female creature. Scientists called her Lucy but her Latin name is *Australopithecus afarensis*.

829 Neanderthal people lived in Europe about 130,000 years ago. Europe was still in an Ice Age at this time. The Neanderthals had a short, stocky body, which was adapted for living in the cold. They hunted animals and ate a mostly meat diet. Then about 30,000 years ago, the climate got warmer, humans from Africa arrived, and the Neanderthals died out.

Homo habilis 2.5–1.4 million years ago

Homo erectus 1.8–1.3 million years ago

Homo sapiens neanderthalensis 150,000–30,000 years ago

Homo sapiens sapiens 200,000 to present

830 The modern human, with a highly developed brain, originated in Africa about 200,000 years ago. Like many other early humans, modern humans proved to be highly adaptable. They developed a culture and language, and learned to depend on tools to alter their environment.

Designer evolution

831 People can alter evolution through artificial selection. This is similar to natural selection, but it involves people selecting the parents of the next generation. Over time, artificial selection can lead to new types of plants and animals.

832 The pet dog is related to the wolf. About 15,000 years ago, people started to tame the wolves that were found around their settlements. Over time, the appearences of the tamed animals changed as people selected parent dogs with particular features.

▼ Dogs can be grouped according to their appearance and the purpose for which they were bred.

GUNDOG
Irish setter

HOUND
Irish wolfhound

TERRIER
Jack Russell

TOY
Chihuahua

UTILITY
Bulldog

WORKING
Old English sheepdog

▲ Wolves are ancestors of all dog breeds. Wolves and dogs still have many features in common such as howling and barking.

833 The many different dog breeds look very different, but they are all the same species. This means they can breed with each other. There are different breeds of pet cats too, each bred for a particular appearance.

834 Artificial selection has developed crops and livestock too. By choosing parent plants with high yields or disease resistance, scientists have changed crop plants, such as wheat and rice. Dairy cows are now producing more milk, as farmers breed from cows that produce the most milk.

835 The most beneficial characteristics are chosen during artificial selection. As most living things have two parents, they show variation—new features that have developed as a result of their parental genes being shuffled. This gives some individuals an advantage. For example, some plants' genes make them grow taller, allowing them to reach sunlight more easily than other plants.

836 Clones—individuals that are genetically identical to each other—can also be made by artificial selection. They are at an evolutionary disadvantage, however, because there is no variation between the individuals. If a group of cloned animals or plants are affected by disease, they could all be wiped out.

▲ Plant breeding can produce crop plants with more flavor, greater yields, and more resistance to disease.

▼ Modern varieties of rice have greater yields. The latest types have been genetically altered so they survive in drought and salt water conditions.

Evolution in action

837 **Evolution never stops—it is taking place around us right now.** Usually, it occurs slowly, over millions of years. It took modern humans six million years to evolve from forest-dwelling animals. But sometimes evolution can happen in just a few years—or even less.

838 **By understanding evolution, scientists have a better chance of fighting diseases.** Humans can be vaccinated against influenza ('flu), a disease caused by a virus. The virus can evolve quickly, meaning scientists must keep developing new vaccines to keep up.

◄ Influenza vaccines no longer work when mutations change the surface of the influenza virus.

839 **Farmers use weedkillers on their crops, but some weeds are becoming resistant.** When a crop is sprayed, any weed that has a gene for resistance to the weedkiller survives, while the others die. This survivor produces seeds and soon there are more resistant weeds.

▶ The excessive use of weedkillers can cause some weeds to evolve a resistance to the chemicals.

▲ Mosquitoes carry parasites that cause malaria. The rise in global temperatures means they can now survive in more places.

840 The world's climate is changing and this is affecting evolution. Species with more variation can adapt to the changes and survive, while those that can't keep up are in danger of dying out. Climate change is also affecting the arrival of the seasons—in many places, spring is starting earlier. This is causing problems for plants and animals that depend on each other for survival.

841 Some lizards are changing their appearance to escape ants. Fire ants are small but aggressive and can kill the small fence lizard. Lizards that live close to these ants have longer legs than those that live in areas without the ants. Genes for long legs have been inherited to help the lizards escape.

▲ Long-legged fence lizards are more likely to survive and breed than the short-legged ones.

▼ The Hadza tribe of Africa are one of the few remaining hunter–gather tribes living in a way similar to our ancient ancestors.

842 Humans have evolved over the last few thousand years. Many adults cannot drink milk due to the lactose (sugar) it contains. About 5,000 years ago, Europeans began keeping cattle. A mutation occured that allowed adults to digest the lactose. Human beings are an adaptable species— our ability to change may help us to survive in an ever-changing world.

PLANT LIFE

- The plant kingdom
- Photosynthesis
- Parts of a flower
- Pollination
- Seed dispersal
- Meat-eating plants
- Plants and animals
- Habitats
- Forests and jungles

How do plants make food?

Which plant smells of rotting meat?

Why are some seeds prickly?

Do roots always grow underground?

How do desert plants survive?

Our green planet

843 Our planet is the only place in the known Universe where plants can grow. It is thanks to these living things that we have air to breathe and food to eat. They make the Earth an exciting, dynamic home to an enormous variety of animals and billions of people.

844 Most plants have leaves, stems, roots, and flowers. However, there are many exceptions, such as cacti, pine trees, ferns, and cushions of moss that grow on rocks. No one knows exactly how many different species (types) of plants there are, but the number is thought to be around 450,000. Scientists are discovering new species every day.

845 The first plants to grow on land appeared more than 500 million years ago. That's more than three billion years after the first signs of life on Earth. Today, plants survive in many different environments, from the icy Arctic to hot, dry deserts and steamy tropical forests.

▼ A forest is much more than just a collection of trees. It is home to millions of plants and animals, as well as people.

What is a plant?

846 Plants are living things that, like animals, are able to do seven important things. They can move, grow, breathe, feed, reproduce (make new plants), make waste products, and react to their surroundings.

847 While animals have to find food, plants are able to make their own. They use energy from sunlight to turn carbon dioxide and water into a sugary food. This process is called photosynthesis (say: foto-sin-the-sis) (see page 382).

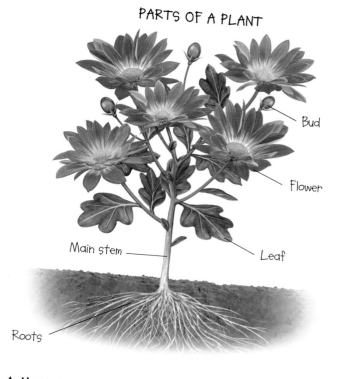

PARTS OF A PLANT

Bud

Flower

Main stem

Leaf

Roots

▲ Most plants have the same basic form, with roots, stems, and leaves. Some plants, known as angiosperms, also grow flowers.

▼ The oval leaflets on a mimosa plant move and fold inward when they are touched.

848 Plants are able to find out about their environment, and react to it. Animals use eyes, ears, and other organs to sense their surroundings, but the way plants do this is much simpler. Their roots can sense water in the soil, and their leaves move toward sunlight when they detect it.

▼ Here, squash seedlings grow toward light to receive as much energy as possible.

◀ Bamboo is a type of grass, and one of the fastest-growing plants on the planet.

849 In the right circumstances, some plants never stop growing. Bamboo shoots can grow more than 12 inches in a single day, and may reach 100 feet in a single growing season. Slow-growing lichens may take 50 years to grow just 0.2 square inches!

▶ Reindeer lichen can reach 100 years of age. When conditions are harsh it can stop growing completely and wait for warmer weather to return.

850 All plants are able to make new plants by a process called reproduction. Many plants grow flowers, which contain reproductive organs where seeds develop. Some flowers produce one seed, others produce millions.

851 People used to think that fungi, such as mushrooms, were plants. Now, scientists know they belong to a different group of living things. Fungi have some similarities to plants, but they lack the ability to make their own food.

▼ The most well-known fungi—mushrooms and toadstools—can be identified by their size, shape, and color.

Fairy ring mushroom

Field mushroom

Parasol

Devil's boletus

Fly agaric

Wood blewit

Many-zoned bracket fungus

Dryad's saddle

Death cap

Mealy tubaria

The family tree

852 If you could go back in time several million years you would see many plants different from those alive today. Plants change, or adapt, to suit changes in their habitat (natural home), and the ones that survive best are able to reproduce. This process is called evolution.

Mosses

Mostly small, simple plants without tubes that transport water and food around.

FUNGI KINGDOM

ANIMAL KINGDOM

▶ Living things can be put into groups called kingdoms depending on their characteristics. Here, the Plant Kingdom is explained.

PLANT KINGDOM

EARLY LIFE

853 The first plants probably lived in oceans, and were closely related to simple plants called algae (say: al-gee). Plants that existed long ago have lots in common with plants that evolved more recently. For example, all plants have a tough material called cellulose in their cell walls.

Green algae

Red algae

I DON'T BELIEVE IT!

Big plant-eating dinosaurs needed lots of food to survive. They trampled trees, and probably stripped entire forests clean.

ALGAE

Algae are similar to plants because they use the Sun's energy to make food. However, they do not have roots, leaves, or stems. We call them seaweeds, and there are three main groups of algae: green, red, and brown.

Brown algae

854 Mosses and liverworts are simple plants that grow in damp, shady places. They rarely grow more than a few inches tall, but gain height by growing on other plants. They do not have flowers, but reproduce using special cells called spores.

Liverworts

855 The first trees existed long before the dinosaurs and were similar to today's large ferns. Some ferns are only a few inches high, but the tallest grow into 65-foot-tall trees. Like mosses and liverworts, ferns reproduce by spores, which grow on the underside of each frond (leaf).

Seedless plants that reproduce by means of spores.

Ferns

Plants with tubes that transport food and water around. They can grow larger and are more complex.

Seed-producing plants that have reproductive parts. Seeds develop after fertilization (when a male cell and a female cell join together).

Conifers

856 Plants evolved seeds around 390 million years ago. These structures contain food reserves, which help new plants to grow. Early seed plants gave rise to a group called gymnosperms. Conifers, such as the huge giant sequoia, are gymnosperms.

857 Flowering plants, known as angiosperms, evolved at least 130 million years ago. At this time dinosaurs roamed the land and winged insects had existed for more than 175 million years. Humans evolved two million years ago.

Flowering plants

Sun catchers

858 **Plants flourish all over the planet.**
They can even be found in places where no
animal can survive. This success is thanks to
plants' special ability to photosynthesize—
make their own food using sunlight.

▶ Leaves are green
because of a green
substance in their cells
called chlorophyll that
helps them to make food.
Under a microscope, a
leaf's different cells and
tissues can be identified.

859 **Photosynthesis
happens in leaves and it
is one of nature's most
incredible processes.** Plants
use the energy from sunlight to turn
carbon dioxide and water into sugar
for food. Excess sugar is turned into a
substance called starch, which is
stored as reserve food supplies.

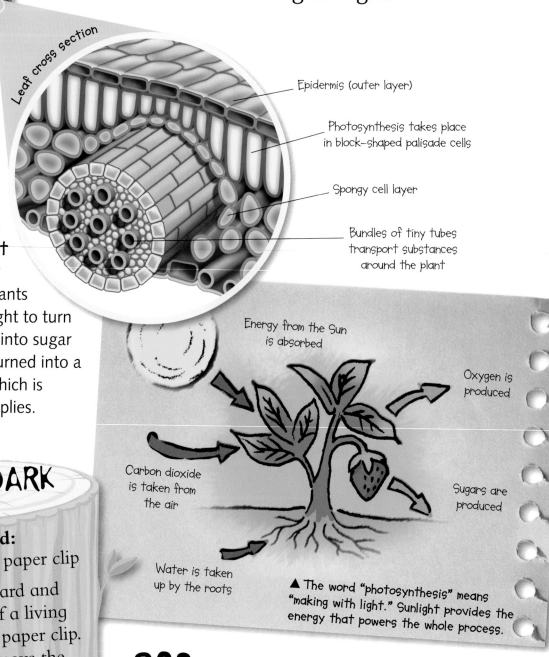

Leaf cross section

Epidermis (outer layer)

Photosynthesis takes place
in block-shaped palisade cells

Spongy cell layer

Bundles of tiny tubes
transport substances
around the plant

Energy from the Sun
is absorbed

Oxygen is
produced

Carbon dioxide
is taken from
the air

Sugars are
produced

Water is taken
up by the roots

▲ The word "photosynthesis" means
"making with light." Sunlight provides the
energy that powers the whole process.

LIGHT AND DARK

You will need:
piece of card   scissors   paper clip

Cut a circle in the card and
place it on the leaf of a living
plant. Secure with the paper clip.
After a few days, remove the
card. The covered area will have
faded. Why do you think this is?

Day one   Day four

860 **Plants need water, light, chlorophyll,
and carbon dioxide to photosynthesize.** Carbon
dioxide gas, which is in air, enters the plant through
tiny holes mainly on the underside of a leaf. During
photosynthesis, oxygen—the gas that all animals
breathe—is released as a waste product.

Needle

Round

Long

Oval

Compound

Pinnate

◀ Special words are used to describe leaf shapes. The largest leaves usually grow on trees that live in wet regions.

861 Leaves are sun catchers. Most leaves are flat and broad so they can catch lots of light. Plants that grow in cold, windswept places and receive less sunlight have tough, needle-shaped leaves. They lose less water, which helps them to photosynthesize in winter.

▼ Beetles chomp their way through leaves, and can quickly strip plants bare.

862 Plants have stems that raise their leaves up toward the light. They have roots that grow below the ground and absorb water (see page 384). From its roots, water travels up through a plant's stem and into its leaves through tubes called xylem tubes.

863 The sugary food that plants make is the fuel that many of the world's animals depend on. Some animals eat plants, and this gives them energy. Those animals may be eaten by other animals, and so the Sun's energy is passed along the food chain.

Going underground

864 One of the most amazing parts of a plant—the roots—usually lies hidden from view, underground. Roots look like white sprawling threads and they have four important jobs to do for the plant.

865 Roots take up water from soil for use in photosynthesis. They also absorb minerals that are essential for the plant's growth. Roots help to anchor a plant in the soil and stop the soil blowing away, and they store food for the plant.

◀ In Mexico, the roots from a tree growing above ground have reached through a natural sinkhole to find water below.

▼ Most roots are long, white, and slender, but they can grow in different ways, and in different forms.

Tuberous
Parts of the roots swell with stores of food

Adventitious
These roots are unusual because they grow down from the stems, branches, or leaves of a plant

Fibrous
Many branching roots grow as a thick clump

Taproot
One main, thick root grows vertically downward

866 Roots grow many smaller side roots and these are covered in millions of tiny "hairs" that are excellent at absorbing water. A scientist studied one rye plant (a type of grass) and discovered that if all its 13 million side roots were laid end to end they would stretch for 310 miles!

▼ Waves and currents push and pull mangrove trees, but their prop roots help them to stay upright.

867 Some roots grow above and below the ground. These are called prop roots and they give a plant extra strength to grow tall and sturdy. Mangrove prop roots trap mud, helping to support the trees and protect coastal areas from storms.

868 Some orchids grow on rain forest trees, a long way above the soil. They have fleshy green roots that grow along branches or dangle downward. These are called aerial roots.

Aerial roots

▲ An orchid's aerial roots absorb water straight from the air.

TRUE OR FALSE?

1. Roots grow toward light.
2. Mangrove trees have prop roots.
3. Roots can be good to eat.

Answers:
1. False 2. True 3. True

869 Some plants store water and energy as starch in their roots—and we use these roots as food. Carrots, beetroots, and sweet potatoes are all formed from roots, or parts of roots, and grow underground. They are packed full of fiber and vitamins—both essential parts of a healthy diet.

Blooming marvelous

870 Flowers are often spectacular blooms that are colorful and perfumed to entice animals to come to them. They put on a showy display not to please our senses, but in a fierce bid to survive and reproduce.

Petal

The ovary contains ovules (female sex cells)

Sepals

▲ When a flower is cut in half, its sex organs can be seen. The ovary is normally hidden from view.

871 The petals of a flower surround a plant's sex organs. These parts produce and protect sex cells, which must come together before seeds can develop. A flower stays closed until the sex organs are fully mature, then the petals unfurl to attract insects and other animals to pollinate them (see page 388).

872 Bright yellow grains of pollen contain male sex cells. Pollen is produced on anthers, which are attached to stalks called filaments. Female sex cells are called ovules and they are produced in the flower's ovary.

◄ Vibrant pink petals help insects to find pollen at the centers of these cosmos flowers.

I DON'T BELIEVE IT!

Sweet-smelling rose petals are used to make perfume, skin creams, and bath oils. In ancient Rome, women used to wash in baths full of rose petals!

Filament

Anthers contain
pollen grains
(male sex cells)

Stigma

873 Delicious smells and colorful petals help bring insects, or other animals, to a flower. Some petals have patterns that help to guide insects toward the flower's center. As well as pollen, there is often a sweet liquid called nectar there.

In UV light

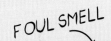

In natural light

◄▲ In ultraviolet light a silverweed flower appears as a bee would see it. The red shading is called a nectar guide—it guides the bee to pollen at the center and a reward of nectar.

874 During their long history on Earth, flowering plants have evolved in many different ways to help reproduction. Some flowers are as big as dustbin lids, others are smaller than a pea. Some flowers stink of rotting flesh, while others resemble bees, slippers, bells or even trumpets!

 ▶ Flowers grow in many different colors, shapes, and sizes to attract insects and other pollinating animals.

BUILT-IN PERCH

FOUL SMELL

The bird of paradise flower provides a handy perch for its bird pollinators

IMITATION

An orchid looks like a female bee to attract male bees carrying pollen from other flowers

The titan arum flower smells of rotting meat to attract flies

Perfect pollination

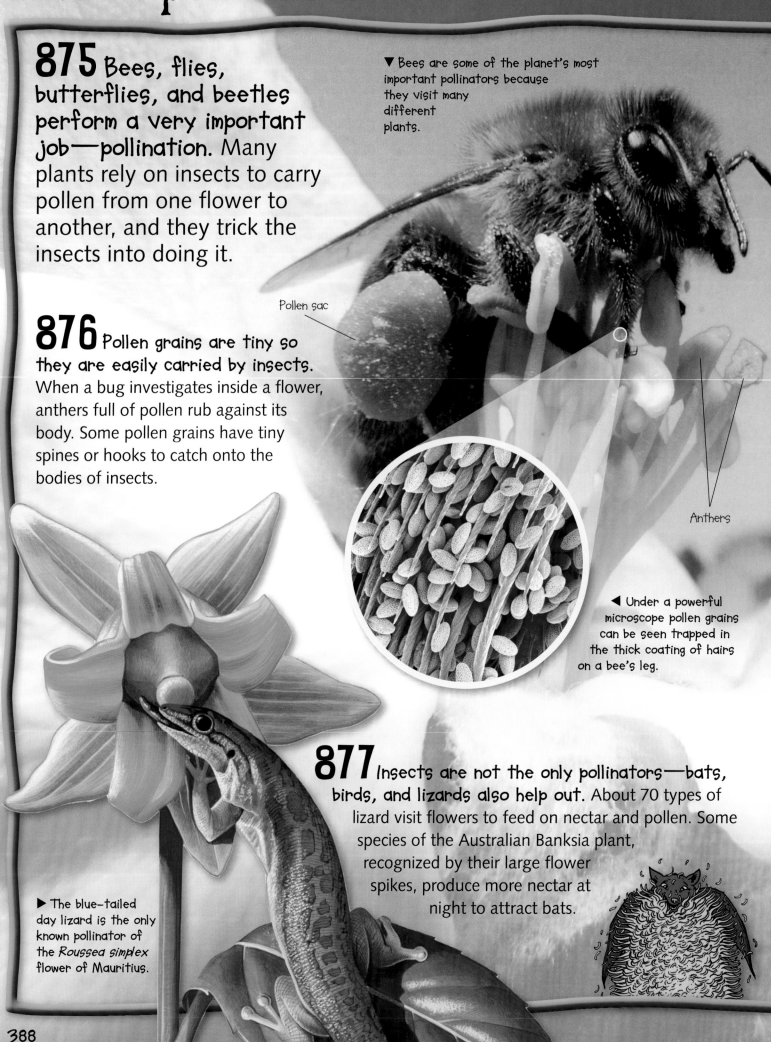

875 Bees, flies, butterflies, and beetles perform a very important job—pollination. Many plants rely on insects to carry pollen from one flower to another, and they trick the insects into doing it.

876 Pollen grains are tiny so they are easily carried by insects. When a bug investigates inside a flower, anthers full of pollen rub against its body. Some pollen grains have tiny spines or hooks to catch onto the bodies of insects.

▼ Bees are some of the planet's most important pollinators because they visit many different plants.

Pollen sac

Anthers

◀ Under a powerful microscope pollen grains can be seen trapped in the thick coating of hairs on a bee's leg.

877 Insects are not the only pollinators—bats, birds, and lizards also help out. About 70 types of lizard visit flowers to feed on nectar and pollen. Some species of the Australian Banksia plant, recognized by their large flower spikes, produce more nectar at night to attract bats.

▶ The blue-tailed day lizard is the only known pollinator of the *Roussea simplex* flower of Mauritius.

388

878 Not all flowers bother with fine looks and sweet smells to attract pollinators. Grasses don't rely on insects to carry their pollen, they let the wind do the job. These plants often have small flowers without petals or scent.

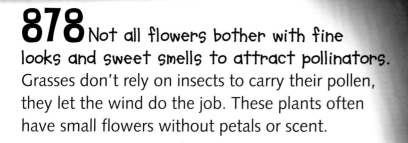

▲ A cloud of cocksfoot grass pollen is carried on the wind.

PARTS OF A FLOWER

Pollen grains on the stigma

Stigma

Style

Ovary

A pollen grain (male) joins with an ovule (female)

Pollen tube

► When a pollen grain lands on the stigma of a plant of the same species, it grows a tube down to the ovary.

879 When a pollen grain lands on a flower's stigma, pollination has taken place. The grain contains the male sex cell, which will fertilize an ovule (female sex cell). Only a fertilized ovule can grow into a seed.

Flower

Proboscis

Spur

880 Many animals have evolved alongside flowering plants, and they depend on each other to survive. Without pollination, most plants could not reproduce, and this would mean a shortage of food for land animals.

► The Morgan's Sphinx hawk moth is the only animal able to feed from the long spurs (tubes that contain nectar) of the comet orchid.

► Here, the moth's 10-inch-long proboscis (sucking mouthpart) is rolled up.

389

Traveling far

881 Plants are able to travel great distances, sometimes across entire oceans. That may come as a surprise because most plants are firmly rooted to the spot. However, when they are still seeds, some species make incredible journeys as they begin new lives.

▼ Protected by its buoyant waterproof outer case, a coconut can travel across an ocean to germinate on a new shore.

CANDELABRA LILY
NATIVE TO AFRICA

The spherical seed heads dry and then snap off. They are rolled along by the wind, scattering seeds as they travel.

HIMALAYAN BALSAM
NATIVE TO THE HIMALAYAS

The 0.3-inch-long seed pods explode when touched, propelling seeds up to 23 feet away.

▶ Seeds can be spread by a variety of methods, including by wind or animals.

882 Plants want their seeds to grow far away from them. That way, the seedlings will not fight with their parent plants for light, water, and space. So plants have developed ingenious ways to send their offspring far away.

I DON'T BELIEVE IT!

Squirting cucumbers can shoot their seeds 16 feet away. Their seedpods are full of water and explode at the slightest touch.

The lightweight seeds have tufts of silky hair and are carried by the wind, traveling like tiny parachutes.

883 Some plants have shaped seed cases that help seeds "fly" through the air. They act like parachutes, helicopters, or gliders, carrying their seeds to new places. Some seed cases explode, propelling their seeds through the air and away from the parent plant.

884 Fruit seeds are often wrapped in sweet, juicy flesh to tempt animals to eat them. The seeds are tough enough to pass through the animals' bodies unharmed and come out in droppings. The droppings contain nutrients, which help the seeds to grow into plants.

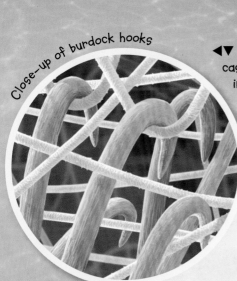

Close-up of burdock hooks

◀▼ It's easy to see why burdock seed cases were the inspiration behind the invention of Velcro, the hook-and-loop fastening system.

Bur in wool

885 Seeds with prickles, called burs, can hitch a lift on animals. Tiny hooks on burdock seed cases become attached to the fur of animals as they pass by. Eventually, some burs fall out of the animals' fur and may grow into new plants in new places.

Starting again

886 When a seed comes to rest in a suitable place with suitable conditions, it starts to grow. This is called germination and it marks the beginning of a new plant's life. All seeds need water and oxygen to germinate, and some need warmth too.

▼ Each sorus (spore-producing spot) on a fern can release thousands of tiny spores when ripe.

887 The first part of a plant to grow from the seed during germination is a special root called a radicle. A stem grows next, with leaflike structures called cotyledons. Then tiny leaves appear and an adult plant develops.

▼ A seed needs the right conditions to germinate.

① The radicle tip breaks through the seed casing

② Root hairs develop on the radicle

③ The radicle begins to grow downward

④ The leaflike cotyledons grow upward

▶ Despite the barren-looking landscape, a coconut has germinated in a lava field.

888 Mosses, liverworts, ferns, and fungi don't have seeds, but produce tiny cells called spores instead. Spores grow on the underside of a fern's leaves, inside round "spots" called sori. When the spores are released, they are carried on the wind.

889 Huge numbers of acacia tree seed pods are devoured by African elephants. Acacia seeds travel through an elephant's digestive system and are excreted in waste called dung. Many of the acacia seeds germinate, and grow into trees in new places.

◄▲ Most of the acacia seeds in this dung will germinate because they are in a warm, wet, and nutritious fertilizer.

Spring

890 Starting again doesn't always mean growing from seed. Some plants, such as strawberries, produce "baby" plants on long stems called runners. New potato plants can grow from "eyes"—small spots on the potato's skin where shoots grow. Pieces of stems or leaves may also grow into new plants.

Winter

▲► Bluebells flower in spring. Then they die down and survive the winter as bulbs underground, until the following spring.

891 When plants disappear over winter, they do not always die. Many survive just as roots, or as special structures called bulbs. The new shoots that grow in spring sprout from dormant roots or bulbs, which have stored food ready for the plant to grow again when the conditions are right.

SOWING SEEDS

You will need:
saucer   cotton wool
mustard and cress seeds

1. Put some cotton wool on a saucer and moisten it.
2. Sprinkle mustard and cress seeds on top of the damp cotton wool and leave in a warm, sunny spot.
3. Within a day, the seeds will begin to germinate.

Snaps, traps, and sticky bits

892 In places where there is little light or few nutrients in the soil, some plants have developed extraordinary ways to feed. Although these plants can still photosynthesize, they break the rules because they also get energy from "eating" insects and small organisms. These are the green, mean meat-eaters!

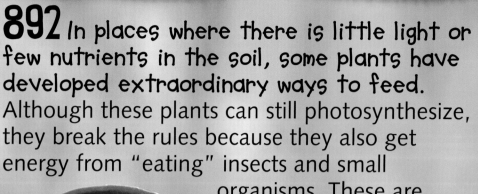

① A fly touches sensitive trigger hairs as it crawls along the trap

893 The Venus flytrap is the most famous of all meat-eating plants. Equipped with touch-sensitive trigger hairs, the flytrap's leaves sense when a bug crawls inside, and snap shut. Strong juices called enzymes are then poured over the bug so it can be digested (broken down).

▶ Venus flytraps grow naturally in bogs and other wet habitats in the United States.

894 Pitcher plants catch prey using sweet-smelling, slippery-sided deathtraps. Pitchers look like upturned trumpets, and they hold pools of water in their bases. Insects are attracted by perfume and nectar, but when they land they slip down the trumpet's waxy sides and drown in the pool. Strong acids hasten their death.

◀ A fly cannot clamber out of a pitcher plant, because of its slippery sides.

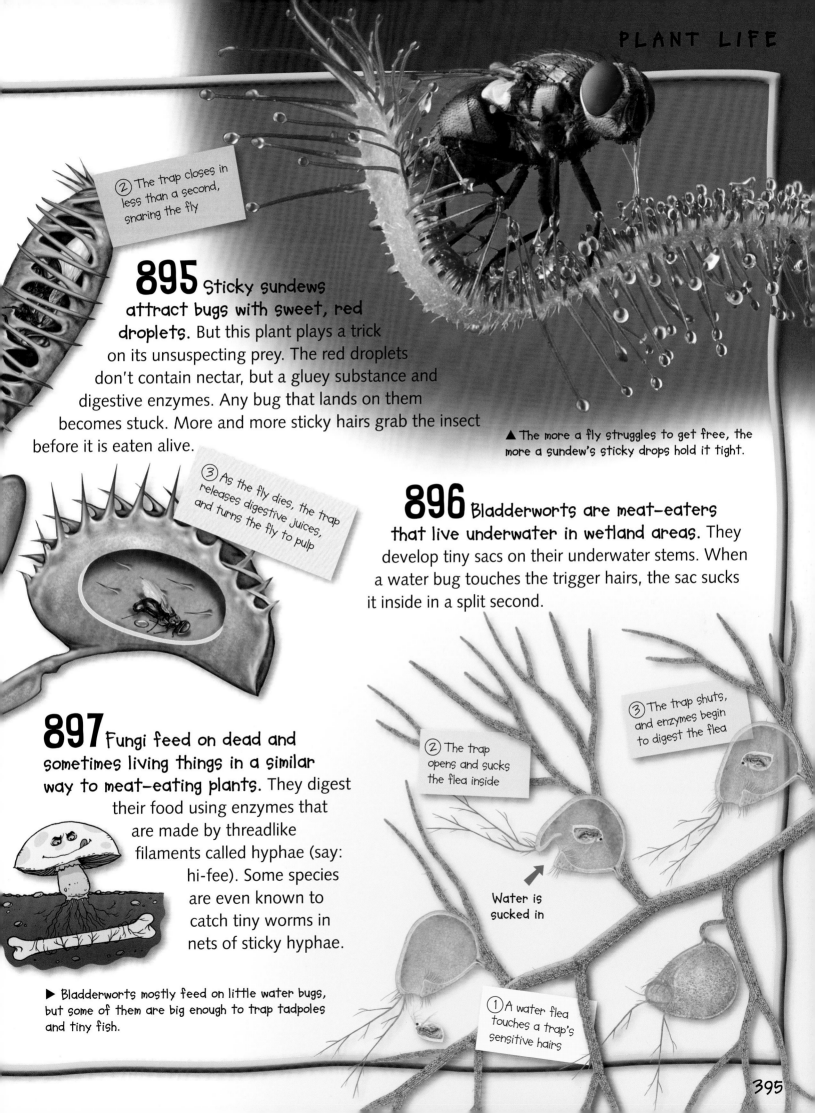

② The trap closes in less than a second, snaring the fly

895 Sticky sundews attract bugs with sweet, red droplets. But this plant plays a trick on its unsuspecting prey. The red droplets don't contain nectar, but a gluey substance and digestive enzymes. Any bug that lands on them becomes stuck. More and more sticky hairs grab the insect before it is eaten alive.

▲ The more a fly struggles to get free, the more a sundew's sticky drops hold it tight.

③ As the fly dies, the trap releases digestive juices, and turns the fly to pulp

896 Bladderworts are meat-eaters that live underwater in wetland areas. They develop tiny sacs on their underwater stems. When a water bug touches the trigger hairs, the sac sucks it inside in a split second.

③ The trap shuts, and enzymes begin to digest the flea

② The trap opens and sucks the flea inside

897 Fungi feed on dead and sometimes living things in a similar way to meat-eating plants. They digest their food using enzymes that are made by threadlike filaments called hyphae (say: hi-fee). Some species are even known to catch tiny worms in nets of sticky hyphae.

Water is sucked in

▶ Bladderworts mostly feed on little water bugs, but some of them are big enough to trap tadpoles and tiny fish.

① A water flea touches a trap's sensitive hairs

395

Friends and enemies

898 **Plants and animals depend upon one another.** But the relationship is not always one of cooperation—it's a battle for survival. Sometimes the best way to survive is to get along, but at other times, the fight is on!

899 **Arolla pine trees grow in high mountains thanks to alpine nutcrackers.** These birds gather the seeds and hide them in the ground as food stores. Some seeds germinate and new forests grow.

▼ Ants work hard to defend their acacia home.

▶ In the South American rain forest, sloths are camouflaged well thanks to the green algae that grows in their fur. Sloths also play host to moths, which feed on the green algae and lay eggs in the sloths' dung.

Moth in fur

900 **Some ants make nests in the thorns of acacia trees, but the trees tolerate this invasion.** The ants defend the tree by stinging browsing animals and cutting through tendrils of nearby plants. In return, the tree rewards the ants with food packets that grow on its leaflet tips.

Ants bite browsing animals

Ant nest inside a hollow thorn

Nectar glands provide ants with a sweet drink

▼ Goats don't mind climbing spiny Argan trees to reach the leaves and fruit, but this can cause a lot of damage.

901 There is fierce competition for light in dense tropical forests. Strangler figs wrap their roots and stems around trees and, over many years, eventually kill them. The strangler fig's roots take all the water from the soil, and its leaves block light from the host tree.

◀ A strangler fig germinates on a tree's bark, and its roots then grow down to the soil.

902 Plants have several ways to defend themselves against animals. Spines, stinging hairs, thorns, and foul-tasting parts are good ways to deter animals from eating leaves or flowers. Unripe fruit often tastes bad to prevent animals from eating it before the seeds inside are ready.

▶ Plants need to attract animals for pollination, but too much damage by plant-eaters can be harmful, so defenses are essential.

Ants gather nutritious food packets and take them back to the nest

PLANT DEFENSES

Horse chestnuts have tough, prickly seed cases.

Stinging nettles have sharp hairs that inject a burning chemical.

Roses have thorns that catch and tear skin.

Unripe persimmon fruits taste too bitter for most animals.

Ragwort's yellow flowers are poisonous to horses and other animals.

Thrive and survive

903 Plants are able to adapt. They can live on cliff faces, and inside giant clams in the sea. Plants can even survive under feet of snow, in rivers, or beneath the hot desert Sun. They have evolved to exist in almost every habitat on Earth.

▼ The fat stems of a cactus store water when it rains for use in dry times.

▼ The flowers of the Arctic poppy move to follow the Sun across the sky, which makes them warmer and more attractive to pollinating insects.

904 Many desert-living plants can store water—a handy adaptation in hot, dry environments. A giant saguaro cactus may hold several tons of water in its stems. Quiver trees can lose whole branches to save water when conditions get too dry.

905 Summer at the Earth's polar regions may last no more than a few days, and there is little warmth or sunshine through the year. Even water is a problem because it is locked up as ice. Despite this, plants survive—tiny algae have been found living inside rocks.

QUIZ

1. What spiny plants live in deserts?
2. How do cushion plants stay out of the wind?
3. What habitat is home to many grazing animals?

Answers:
1. Cacti 2. They grow low to the ground 3. Grasslands or plains

398

906 Fierce winds and cold air make life tough for plants living on mountains or high plains. Plants that survive are mainly low-growing and some form dense mats. These are called cushion plants, and scientists have found the temperature in their centers to be a few degrees higher than the surrounding air.

▼ A cushion plant survives cold winds by growing close to the ground. Its dense green surface absorbs and traps lots of heat from the Sun.

▼ The enormous prairies of North America cover 1.2 million square miles. Many animals, including bison, graze on them.

907 Grass often grows on huge plains where there is too little rain for trees to survive. In North America these are called prairies and they are home to many types of grazers—animals that feed on grass. Shoots of grass grow from the ground, and keep growing after the tops have been eaten. Grasses also have complex root systems that spread out in wide networks to absorb water.

908 When scientists discovered some 2,000-year-old magnolia seeds they decided to try and grow one—and succeeded! When conditions are difficult, plants can survive as seeds. These small packages contain all the information a plant needs to germinate and grow when the time is right..

Life underwater

909 Plants that live in ponds, rivers, and seas have plenty of nutrients and water—but lack of light can be a problem. Light doesn't travel through water as easily as it does through air. Giant water lilies combat this problem by growing enormous sun-catching leaves.

◀ Long stalks raise the water lily's leaves and flowers to the surface.

910 Water lilies keep their leaves above water, but some flowering plants live most of their lives entirely submerged. Their leaves are able to absorb gases from the water, so they can still photosynthesize. However, flowers must still poke above the water so insects or the wind can pollinate them.

911 Algae, including seaweed, are not true plants but are similar in that they share the extraordinary ability to photosynthesize. Some algae consist of a single cell and are only visible under a microscope. Others are huge—fronds of giant kelp can reach 150 feet in length.

▶ A raft of kelp drifting in the sea provides shelter for small fish, making it difficult for predators to catch them.

912 Beautiful coral reefs are home to billions of sea creatures, but they would not exist without the help of tiny algae. These algae live inside the bodies of coral polyps, which build the reef. The polyps provide a safe home for the algae, and the algae supply the polyps with food and the oxygen they need to breathe.

I DON'T BELIEVE IT!

Sea otters wrap strands of giant kelp around themselves so they don't float away while feeding on sea urchins or resting.

913 There are about 10,000 species of seaweed in the world. Most of them are red, but there are brown and green types too. Seaweeds have holdfasts, rather than roots, which enable them to stick firmly to rocks even when waves thrash them around.

▼ There are thousands of different types of algae, and many of them are seaweeds.

SEAWEED TYPES

Bladderwrack

Dulse

Knotted Wrack

Sea Lettuce

Oarweed

Kelp

▼ In the right conditions, microscopic algae can suddenly grow into huge groups called blooms.

914 Microscopic green algae in the oceans play an important part in supporting life on Earth. There are billions and billions of them, and they are food for many animals. They also produce much of the oxygen that goes into our atmosphere.

Forests of the world

915 Trees are long-living plants with stems that become thick and woody with age. A trunk can support heavy branches and thousands of leaves. Many trees growing in one place create a forest.

▼ As a tree grows it produces more layers of cells, or rings, in its trunk. These can provide clues about past climates.

Fast growth in warm or rainy season

First year growth

Slow growth in dry or cold season

Scar from forest fire

916 A forest is an ecosystem. This is a place where animals and plants live together, and depend on each other. A single tree provides a home for many animals, from the dead leaves around its base, to its branch tips. Some bugs and fungi live beneath a tree's bark.

KEY

1 Badger	4 Mole
2 Beetle	5 Hedgehog
3 Worm	6 Fox
	7 Butterfly

8 Squirrel
9 Chipmunk
10 Tawny owl
11 Jay

▶ Deciduous forests grow throughout Europe and in eastern U.S. They provide a range of habitats for a huge diversity of wildlife.

DECIDUOUS FOREST

CANOPY

UNDERSTORY

GROUND LEVEL

917 Forests can grow wherever there is enough warmth and water for trees to live. There are different types of forest, and each type requires different climatic conditions (temperature, winds, and rainfall) to grow.

918 Temperate forests grow in mild climates. Types of temperate forest include deciduous, where trees lose their leaves in the fall in preparation for winter, and temperate rain forest, where there is high rainfall.

▲ Unlike tropical rain forests, temperate rain forests have seasons and less variety of plant species. This type of forest can be found in western U.S.

919 Coniferous forests generally grow in cool places, often close to the Arctic region. The trees here are conifers, which have thin, needlelike leaves, and reproduce using cones. They are adapted for life in harsh conditions of snow, frost, and wind.

▼ Tropical rain forests grow in a narrow zone north and south of the Equator (an imaginary line around the center of the Earth). They receive rain and heat all year round.

CONIFEROUS
FOREST

▲ Coniferous forests grow where there are cold winters and warm summers.

TROPICAL
RAIN FOREST

QUIZ
1. What type of forest grows near the Equator?
2. What type of trees grow cones?
3. Where do worms live—in leaf litter or a forest canopy?

Answers:
1. Tropical rain forest
2. Conifers 3. Leaf litter

Lush jungles

920 Rain forests grow in places where there is at least 70 inches of rain each year. There needs to be rain most days, not just at certain seasons. Generally, rain forests grow in the warm region of the world known as the tropics, near the Equator.

RAIN FOREST LAYERS

Emergent layer

Canopy

Understory

Forest floor

▲ Scientists divide a rain forest and its plants into layers. Each layer provides a habitat for different animals.

Orchid

Passionflower

Heliconia

▲ An orangutan feasts on the fruit of a tree in the rain forest in Borneo.

◄ Rain forest flowers are often described as exotic. They have vivid colors and unusual shapes.

921 Tropical rain forests are lush, green places that benefit from both heavy rainfall and heat all year round. They are sometimes called jungles. Without seasons, plants grow all year round, which means there is an endless supply of flowers and fruit for animals to eat.

Vanilla orchid

Coffee berries

Banana palm flower

Cocoa pods

Rubber tree

Vanilla pods

Coffee beans

Bananas

Chocolate

Rubber tire

◄ Rain forest plants such as bananas have been grown in large quantities as crops, and their products are sold around the world.

922 Cloud forests grow high in hills and near mountaintops. The air in these rain forests is especially damp, and mist and low-level cloud cover the treetops. There are cloud forests in South America, Indonesia, and parts of Africa, where mountain gorillas live in these damp habitats.

924 Many natural materials and foods come from the rain forest. Rubber, chocolate, bananas, coffee, vanilla, cinnamon, and chicle (which is used to make chewing gum) all come from plants that grow in tropical forests. Precious woods, such as mahogany and ebony, also grow there.

923 Rain forests provide food and shelter for many people. Families of the Korowai and Kombai tribes of Papua New Guinea live in treehouses to stay safe from attack by other tribes. They find everything they need in the forest, and hunt, fish, and collect plants to eat.

► The air is thick and damp with mist in a Costa Rican cloud forest. Water drips from leaves and steam rises from the ground.

All around us

925 Plants are all around us—not just in our fields and gardens, but in our homes too. We breathe the oxygen they make, we eat them, we build with them, and we enjoy watching them grow.

▲ Central Park in the middle of New York city covers more than 1.2 square miles.

926 From bulbs and tubers to leaves and beans, the energy, fiber, and vitamins in plants keep our bodies healthy. Wheat, soya, corn, and rice are staples—they provide most of the energy we need.

▼ As well as food, materials such as cotton come from plants. Cotton has been used by humans for over 5,000 years.

927 Growing plants for our own use is called agriculture, and humans have been doing it for 10–15,000 years. The first plants people grew probably included barley and beans. With advances in technology and farming methods, farms today produce a wide variety of crops.

Cotton plant

928 Beautiful flowers are used to decorate homes, people, and even animals in some cultures. They play an important part in many festivals and ceremonies. Growing flowers for sale is called floriculture, and people who sell flowers are florists.

▼ The Netherlands is known for its huge flower farms where beautiful blooms—especially tulips—are grown.

929 Coal is a solid fuel that helped the modern world to develop steam power, factories, and transport systems. It was formed millions of years ago, when ancient forests died and turned into a black rock that is packed with energy.

930 For thousands of years people have used plants to treat diseases. Now scientists are discovering ways that plants can help us to develop better medicines. They also know that some plants harm us: tobacco, which is in cigarettes, comes from the leaves of tobacco plants and causes lung and heart diseases.

▶ Plants are still used in many medicines and treatments today.

Mint
This herb is traditionally used to treat stomach problems and pains

Pomegranate
Scientists think this fruit may help fight cancer

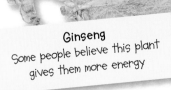

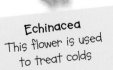

Echinacea
This flower is used to treat colds

Willow bark
This was used to develop aspirin, which treats pain

Ginseng
Some people believe this plant gives them more energy

Plants in peril

931 When plants photosynthesize they produce oxygen—the gas that all animals need to breathe. Plants also absorb carbon dioxide. This changes the climate since extra carbon dioxide in the atmosphere makes our planet warmer.

932 When large areas of plants are destroyed, the way that energy, water, and gases move through the world's systems is affected. The removal of many trees is called deforestation. This process releases carbon dioxide into the air, ruins the soil, and can even change local weather systems.

▼ Rain forests in Borneo are being cut down at an alarming rate. Orangutans, which live in these rain forests, will soon be homeless.

933 In some countries people have to cut down trees for fuel. Without the money to buy other kinds of fuel, they build fires for cooking, boiling water, and to keep their families warm. It is also common for natural habitats to be turned into farmland, or grazing areas for animals.

I DON'T BELIEVE IT!

Nearly half of all the trees that are cut down are used to make paper—more than 330 million tons every year.

935 When plants are removed from an ecosystem there are no roots to hold the soil in place. Wind and rain sweep the soil away, leaving bare rocks or sand as a desert develops. Very few types of plant can survive in these new desert areas.

◄ The welwitschia is one of the few plants that survive in the deserts of Africa, even when there is no rain for months.

▼ The devastating effects of acid rain can turn a green forest into a dry, barren land.

934 The survival of some plants is threatened by acid rain. This is caused by pollution, such as carbon dioxide in the air, which changes rain water and makes it harmful. It pollutes lakes and ponds, poisoning fish and other animals, and it can kill trees.

▼ Scientists closely monitor how pollution in the air and in the soil affect the way that plants grow.

936 Scientists believe that one in five types of plants is in danger of becoming extinct—dying out forever. Humans are mostly to blame for this because we cut down trees and remove natural habitats to farm or graze our animals on. The building of houses and roads in these areas increases pollution levels.

The future is green

937 Scientists are helping people to understand how precious plants are. If we care for our planet today, future generations will be able to enjoy it. We must use the planet's resources responsibly.

938 Some farmers who used wood for fuel now use other sources of **energy.** Solar lamps use energy from the Sun, and biogas from dung or rotting food is used to power ovens, lights, and even machinery.

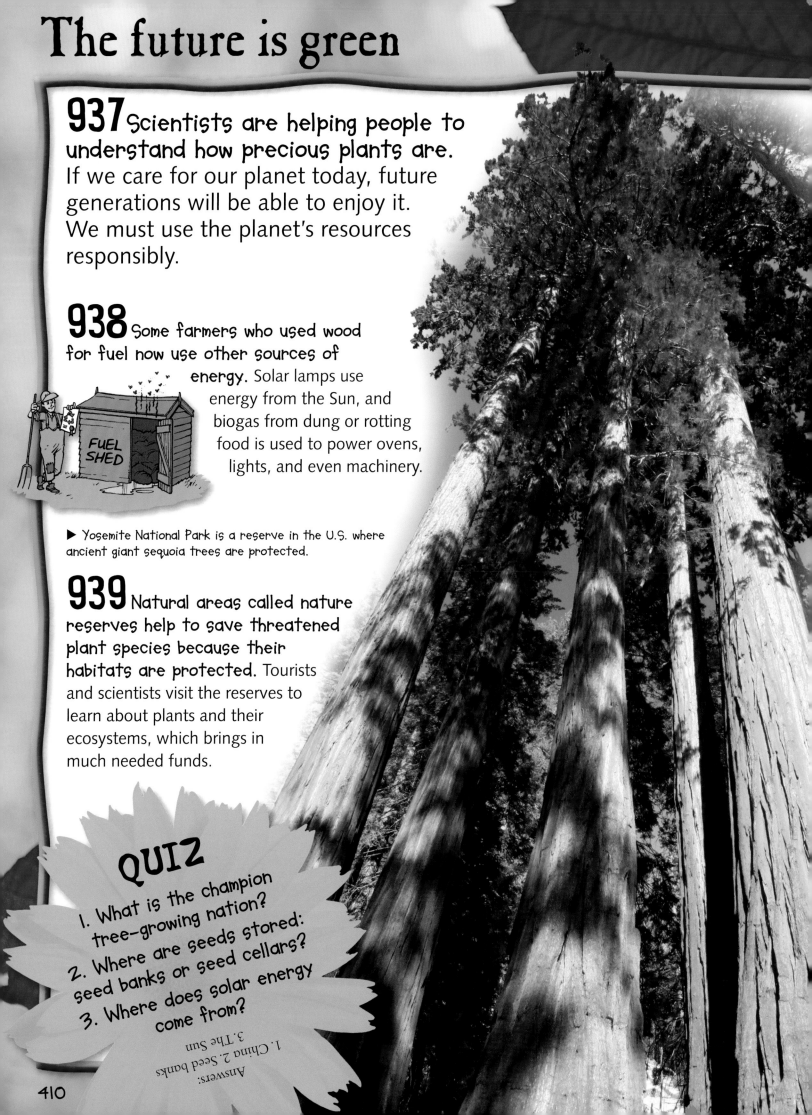

▶ Yosemite National Park is a reserve in the U.S. where ancient giant sequoia trees are protected.

939 Natural areas called nature reserves help to save threatened plant species because their habitats are protected. Tourists and scientists visit the reserves to learn about plants and their ecosystems, which brings in much needed funds.

QUIZ

1. What is the champion tree-growing nation?
2. Where are seeds stored: seed banks or seed cellars?
3. Where does solar energy come from?

Answers:
1. China 2. Seed banks
3. The Sun

940 China is the champion tree-growing nation. Many nations hope to halt deforestation. With China leading the way, ten percent more trees are expected in the world by 2050—enough to cover an area the size of India.

▶ More than 25,000 new trees were planted during this reforestation project in Haiti, in 2010.

◀ Seeds are carefully labeled and kept safe in this seed bank in Germany.

941 Saving seeds stops some plant species becoming extinct. Worldwide, scientists are collecting seeds from native plants, especially rare species, and storing them in seed banks. These huge seed collections are protected and studied to ensure that these plants are conserved for the future.

▼ The world's largest greenhouse is at the Eden Project in the UK. Many plants from around the world are grown here.

942 Plants are part of our everyday lives, and how we choose to live plays a part in the planet's future. Protecting and growing plants in our habitats—homes, parks, gardens, and schools—is a great way to begin a lifetime's journey into the world of plants.

ANIMAL LIFE

- Anatomy
- Movement
- Food chains
- Attack and defense
- Social animals
- Communication
- Reproduction
- Metamorphosis
- Habitats and homes
- Endangered animals

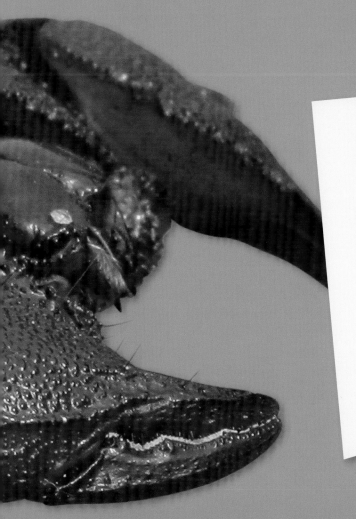

Why do rattlesnakes rattle?

Which animal group is the most intelligent?

Why do birds lay eggs?

How does a snake's tongue help it to pick up scents?

Why are rhinos in trouble?

Animal planet

943 Our planet is full of animals. They live almost everywhere, from the tops of mountains to the darkest depths of oceans. The greatest variety of animals live in places such as rain forests or coral reefs, where there is plenty of food and shelter.

▼ African animals gather round a waterhole in the dry season. The great grasslands of Africa are one of the last places where huge herds of grazing animals still survive.

944 Animals come in all shapes and sizes. Some, such as elephants, are giants, while others, such as fleas, are almost too small to see. There are at least five million different kinds of animals alive today. Scientists discover new kinds every day.

945 For at least 650 million years, animals have been living on our planet. Sponges are among the oldest known animals. They live in oceans today, but remains of sponges that lived 650 million years ago have been found preserved in Australia.

What is an animal?

946 Animals are living things that need to eat food, such as plants or other animals. This gives them the energy they need to survive. Animals use their senses to detect food and react to their surroundings.

▶ Animals can be divided into groups according to their features. Each group has certain characteristics in common.

947 An animal's body is usually made of many cells, which are grouped into tissues. Tissues may be joined together to form organs, such as the brain, heart, or lungs, which have different jobs to do.

▼ The organs inside a chimpanzee are very similar to those inside a human being.

Animal families

Invertebrates are usually small creatures, such as crabs and insects. Some have a hard shell, others are soft.

Fish live in the waters of oceans, rivers, and lakes. They breathe in oxygen from the water through flaps called gills.

Amphibians, such as frogs, live partly in water and partly on land. Most lay eggs in water.

Reptiles, such as snakes and lizards, usually live on land in warm places. Most baby reptiles hatch out of eggs.

Birds have wings instead of arms, and most can fly. All birds lay eggs that have a hard shell.

Mammals, such as bears, dolphins, and humans, are covered in fur or hair. They breathe air, even if they live in water.

Lungs for breathing

Kidneys to process wastes

Intestines to digest food

Brain (inside skull) to control the body

Heart to pump blood around the body

948 Well over 90 percent of all animals are invertebrates. These animals do not have an internal backbone to support their bodies. They rely on the support of their body fluids or a hard outer casing, called an exoskeleton.

949 Animals with a backbone are called vertebrates. Their backbone forms part of an internal skeleton, which is usually made of bone. However, sharks and rays have a skeleton made of rubbery cartilage. A skeleton supports the body, helps it to move, and protects the internal organs.

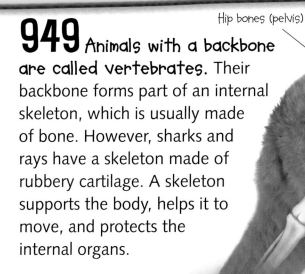

Hip bones (pelvis)

Cage of ribs protects organs

Backbone (spine)

Shoulder blade

Long neck

Skull

Strong jaw bone

Leg bones

Foot bones

950 Vertebrates have different coverings on the outsides of their bodies. Fish and reptiles have scales made from hard skin or bone. Frogs usually have smooth skin. Birds are the only animals with feathers, and mammals are the only animals with fur or hair.

▲ A polar bear has a short, strong backbone and powerful leg and hip bones. Its skull is long and slim to help it swim.

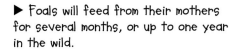
▶ Foals will feed from their mothers for several months, or up to one year in the wild.

951 Humans are mammals. Mammals are the most intelligent of all animals. Female mammals feed their young on milk, which they produce themselves. There are about 5,500 different kinds of mammals and up to one-quarter of them are bats!

On the move

952 Most animals move around to find food, water, or shelter, or escape from danger. Many use muscles to pull their skeleton into different positions. Others are carried along by wind or water currents.

▶ The powerful swimming muscles of the striped marlin make it one of the fastest fish in the ocean. It can swim at speeds of up to 50 miles an hour.

954 Eels are long fish that swim by wriggling their bodies from side to side. Penguins and turtles use flippers to propel themselves through the water. Most fish use their tails to move forward and their fins to steer, balance, or slow down.

955 Squid and octopuses move around by jet propulsion. They draw water into an internal chamber called a mantle cavity. Then they force the water out of their body through a narrow, bendy funnel called a siphon.

953 Some invertebrates, such as corals or sponges, spend all (or part) of their lives in one place. These are called sessile animals and they usually live in water.

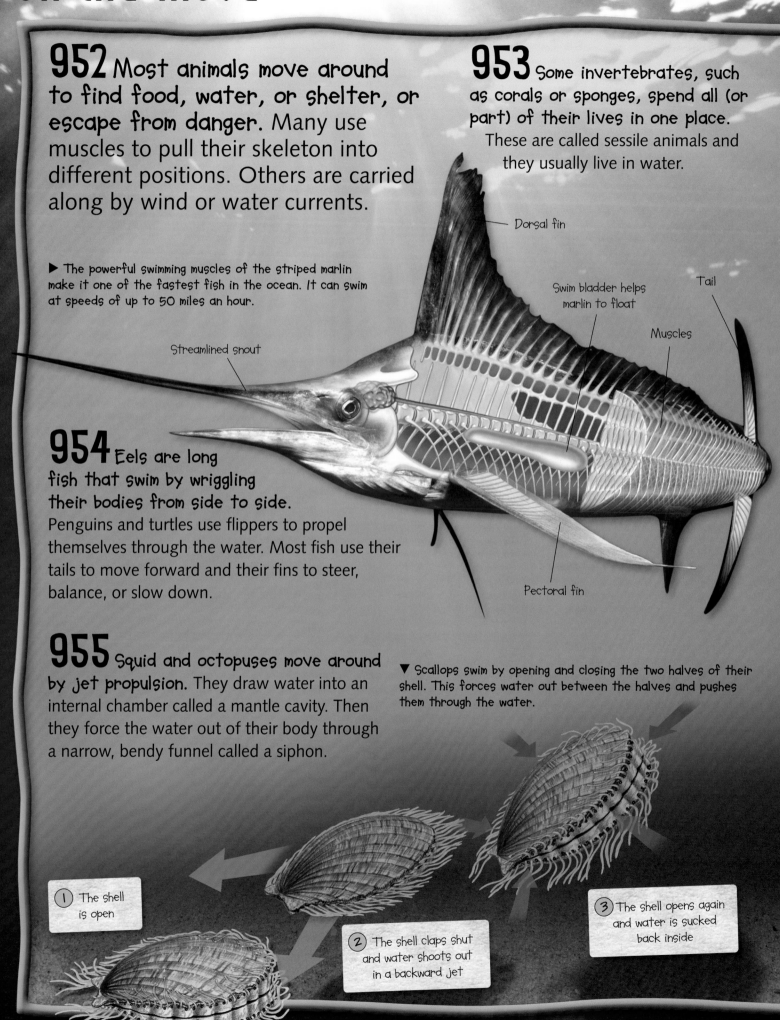

Dorsal fin

Swim bladder helps marlin to float

Tail

Muscles

Streamlined snout

Pectoral fin

▼ Scallops swim by opening and closing the two halves of their shell. This forces water out between the halves and pushes them through the water.

① The shell is open

② The shell claps shut and water shoots out in a backward jet

③ The shell opens again and water is sucked back inside

▼ An eagle's powerful chest muscles are joined to a large, flat part of its breastbone called the keel. These muscles pull its huge wings up and down as it soars through the sky.

Arm bones

Tail feathers

Chest muscles

Keel

Wing feathers

Wing covers (elytra)

Flying wings

◄ A ladybug protects its delicate flying wings under two wing covers, called elytra.

956 Birds, insects, and bats are the only animals capable of powered flight. They have lightweight bodies and powerful muscles to flap their wings. A bird's wings are arm bones covered in feathers. A bat's wings are made of skin stretched between finger bones.

957 Most amphibians, reptiles, and some mammals walk with their feet flat on the ground. Some animals, such as ostriches, cats, and dogs, walk and run on their toes, allowing them to move more quickly. A horse's hooves are at the tips of its toes.

I DON'T BELIEVE IT!

The peregrine falcon is the fastest animal in the world. It dives down to catch its prey at speeds of up to 200 miles an hour!

► Strong claws help wolves to grip slippery ground so they can cover long distances quickly.

Super senses

958 Animals sense the world around them through seeing, hearing, smelling, touching, and tasting. An animal's senses also supply information about its own body, such as whether it is too hot or too cold.

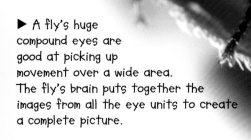

Sight

▶ A fly's huge compound eyes are good at picking up movement over a wide area. The fly's brain puts together the images from all the eye units to create a complete picture.

Hearing

Ears move backward and forward to detect danger

959 Many animals have eyes to detect light. Insects have compound eyes made up of hundreds of tiny eyes with one or more lenses. Animals with bigger eyes may have a slit in the middle of the eye called a pupil, which controls the amount of light entering the eye.

960 Mammals are the only animals with ear flaps that funnel sounds into the ear. The sounds hit an eardrum, which vibrates. Tiny bones pass on the vibrations to a fluid-filled chamber in the inner ear. Receptors in the inner ear send signals to the mammal's brain, which "hears" the sound.

◀ A rabbit's big ears can be turned in different directions to locate the source of a sound, or even listen to two sounds at the same time.

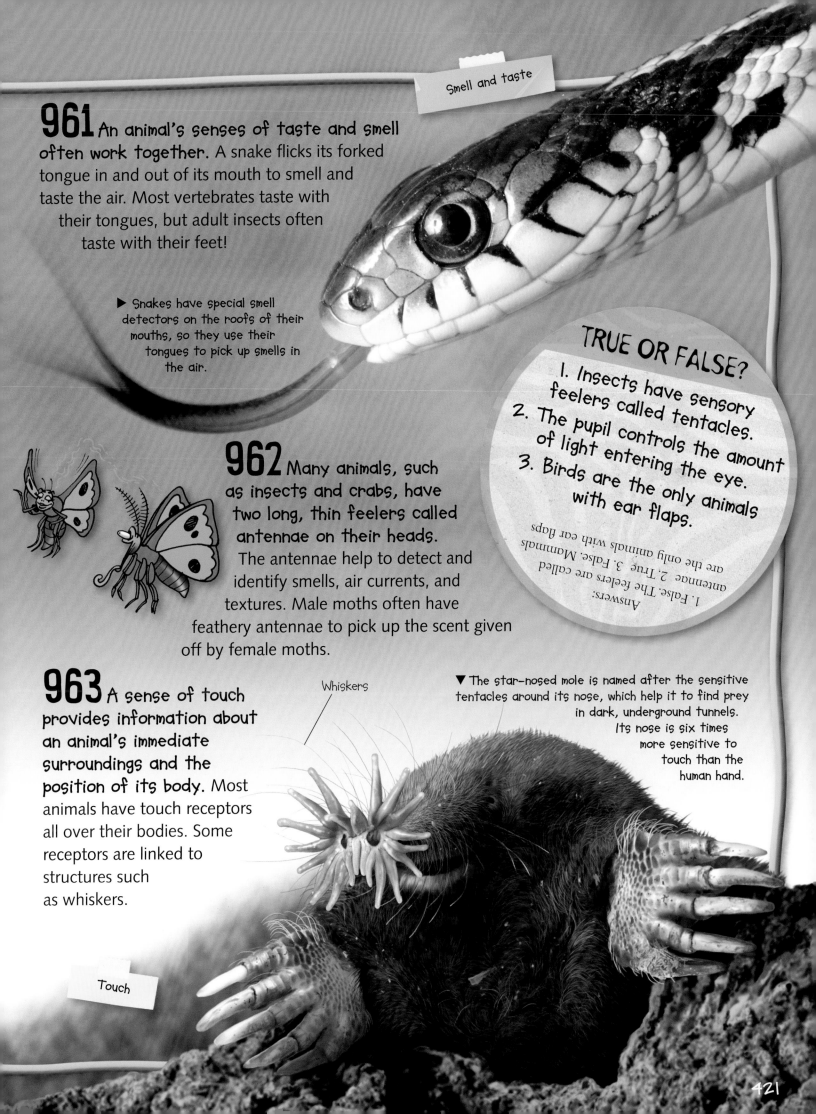

961 An animal's senses of taste and smell often work together. A snake flicks its forked tongue in and out of its mouth to smell and taste the air. Most vertebrates taste with their tongues, but adult insects often taste with their feet!

▶ Snakes have special smell detectors on the roofs of their mouths, so they use their tongues to pick up smells in the air.

962 Many animals, such as insects and crabs, have two long, thin feelers called antennae on their heads. The antennae help to detect and identify smells, air currents, and textures. Male moths often have feathery antennae to pick up the scent given off by female moths.

TRUE OR FALSE?

1. Insects have sensory feelers called tentacles.
2. The pupil controls the amount of light entering the eye.
3. Birds are the only animals with ear flaps.

Answers:
1. False. The feelers are called antennae 2. True 3. False. Mammals are the only animals with ear flaps

963 A sense of touch provides information about an animal's immediate surroundings and the position of its body. Most animals have touch receptors all over their bodies. Some receptors are linked to structures such as whiskers.

Whiskers

▼ The star-nosed mole is named after the sensitive tentacles around its nose, which help it to find prey in dark, underground tunnels. Its nose is six times more sensitive to touch than the human hand.

Touch

421

Food and eating

964 Animals eat a range of food, including plants, other animals, and dead remains. Some have a varied diet. Others eat a narrow range of food—koalas eat mainly eucalyptus leaves.

965 There are three main groups animals can be divided into. Plant-eaters are called herbivores, meat-eaters are called carnivores and animals that eat plants and meat are called omnivores. Food chains show how animals are linked together by what they eat.

FOOD CHAIN

Fox

Mouse

Grasshopper

Grass

◀ Food chains link animals together according to what they eat. Food chains always start with plants, because they can make their own food using the Sun's energy.

FOOD WEB

Fox

Owl

Mouse

Snake

Grasshopper

Frog

Rabbit

Grass

▲ Animals are usually part of several different food chains. This means that two or more food chains can be linked together into a network called a food web.

966 Food is easier to digest in small pieces. Many animals have teeth to tear, chew, or grind up their food. Some animals without teeth, such as spiders and scorpions, inject digestive juices into their food and then suck up the "soup" this produces.

▶ Carnivores have pointed teeth to seize and tear prey, and sharp cheek teeth to slice up meat or crack bones. Herbivores have lots of grinding teeth to mash up tough plants.

Carnivore (fox)

Herbivore (camel)

► The shape of a bird's bill is suited to its diet and where it finds food.

Toucans use their long bills to reach fruit

Puffins carry small fish in their bills

Coal tits probe for insects with their thin, pointed bills

967 Birds have a lightweight, toothless bill instead of a heavy jaw bone and teeth. The shape and size of a bird's bill depends on the kind of food it eats. Birds swallow their food whole and grind it up in a muscular part of their stomach, called the gizzard.

968 Filter-feeders collect tiny particles of food from the water. They use special body parts that work like sieves to trap the food. These include the baleen plates of some whales, the fringed bills of flamingos, and the feathery gills of peacock worms.

► Humpback whales strain fish and plankton from the water using fringed plates of baleen in their gigantic jaws.

MAKE A FOOD CHAIN

You will need:
pencil paper colored pens scissors tape ribbon

Draw and color a picture of a plant, a herbivore, and a carnivore. Cut them out. Stick each of your pictures to a length of ribbon, with the carnivore at the top and the plant at the bottom, to make your food chain.

Predators and prey

969 An animal that hunts and eats other animals is called a predator. Its victim is known as its prey. Predators have to find, catch, and kill their prey. They need strength, keen senses, quick reactions, and lethal weapons.

970 After dark, many predators rely on their excellent sense of hearing to find prey. Some bats hunt insects at night by producing high-pitched squeaks. They listen for the echoes that bounce back from their prey.

▼ Bats have large ears to pick up the sound echoes bouncing back from their prey.

Sounds made by bat

Echoes from prey

971 Some predators hide and wait for their prey to come to them. They may build traps, such as the webs of spiders, or lure their prey within close reach. The alligator snapping turtle has a false "worm" on its tongue to make fish swim right into its open jaws.

"Worm"

◄ The alligator snapping turtle wriggles the "worm" on its tongue to make it look alive. It stabs larger prey with the hooked tips of its strong jaws.

I DON'T BELIEVE IT!

A great white shark has about 300 razor-sharp teeth in its mouth. Its jaws open wide enough to swallow a whole seal in one big gulp!

◄ ► A cheetah can only run at top speed for a few hundred feet before it gets too hot and exhausted, and has to stop. If this warthog keeps running, it might get away.

972 Active predators need a set of weapons for attacking and killing their prey without being injured themselves. These weapons range from pointed teeth and powerful jaws, to curved claws, sharp bills, and poisonous stings or fangs.

◄ Ospreys use their strong, needle-sharp claws, called talons, to snatch fish from the water. Spines under their toes help them to hold their slippery prey.

973 Many spiders are agile, fast-moving hunters that stalk their prey. Jumping spiders prowl around, using their eight eyes to spot a meal. They pounce on their prey and kill it with a bite from their poisonous fangs. Some predators save energy by sneaking up on their prey, then attacking suddenly at the last minute. Many are well camouflaged (see page 426) so they can creep close to their prey.

▶ Chameleons creep very slowly along branches, but they shoot out their long, sticky tongues at lightning speed to catch insects.

425

Survival skills

974 The world is a dangerous place for animals, and they have different ways of staying alive. Many move fast to escape an attack. Others are protected by armor-plating, thick shells, horns, tusks, or spines.

975 Animals may have colors, patterns, or shapes that help them to blend in with their surroundings. Some disguise themselves by looking like twigs, thorns, or leaves. This is called camouflage.

▲ The striped skunk raises its tail, stamps its feet, and sprays smelly liquid at an attacker. Predators usually decide to leave the skunk alone!

▼ A poison arrow frog makes poison in its skin. Just a few drops of this poison are strong enough to kill an animal as big as a horse.

▲ A rattlesnake shakes the "rattle" on its tail to warn predators to keep away.

976 Brightly colored animals are often poisonous. Their colors are a warning message, which means "I am dangerous, don't eat me!" Predators learn to leave these animals alone. Harmless animals may copy these warning colors to protect themselves. This is known as mimicry.

Bony plates covered by horny keratin

977 Slow-moving animals often rely on body armor for protection. Tortoises and turtles can pull their soft body parts inside their shells. Armadillos, pangolins, and pill millipedes roll up into a ball to protect their soft undersides.

1 Armadillo curls into a ball if it senses danger

▲ A three-banded armadillo has body armor on its back, but not underneath. When it rolls up into a tight ball, its body armor protects its soft underparts.

Underside of body is soft and hairy

2 Armadillo starts to uncurl when it is safe again

Flexible skin between bands of armor

978 Predators prefer to eat living prey, so some animals survive an attack by pretending to be dead. Snakes such as the grass snake are good at playing dead. They roll onto their backs, open their mouths, and keep still. The snake starts to move again when the predator goes away.

3 Armadillo is protected by body armor even when walking

979 Some animals can break off parts of their bodies to escape from predators. Lizards may break off a tail tip, which wriggles about on the ground. This distracts an attacker, giving the lizard time to escape.

▲ The bright blue tail of this skink, a type of lizard, breaks at special fracture points between the bones inside the tail.

427

Living in groups

980 Many animals, including some insects, fish, birds, and mammals, live in groups with others of their kind. They are called social animals and may have female or male leaders.

▼ Cape fur seals gather on shorelines in colonies of up to 270,000 individuals to breed and look after their pups.

981 Other animals, such as bears, tigers, and orangutans, live on their own. They do not have to share their food and are able to have young if they find a mate. In a group of social animals, such as wolves, only one pair of animals may have babies.

982 Some animals live in groups just for the breeding season. Penguins and seals form large breeding colonies with hundreds, or even thousands, of members. They warn each other of nearby predators and parents may leave their young in "nurseries" when they go to find food.

▲ Flamingos live in colonies that may contain thousands of birds. This helps them to avoid predators and find food.

▲ Male lions (far right) are bigger than females. Their thick manes of hair make them look even bigger and more frightening to their enemies.

983 Lions are one of the few social cats. They
live in groups called prides, which consist of several related lionesses, their cubs, and one or more adult males. The males protect the pride from predators and rival lions, while the females do most of the hunting.

984 The young of most insects have
to fend for themselves. However, ants and termites, some types of bees, and a few wasps live in giant family groups. One or more females lay eggs, while other members of the group care for the young and defend the nest.

▶ Honeybees form a tightly-packed ball of bees, called a swarm, when they leave their nest to start a new colony.

Signals and signs

985 Animals give each other information by means of a variety of signals and signs. This is called communication. It usually involves giving a warning, telling each other where food is, or attracting a mate.

▶ Meerkats take turns to watch for predators. They give a sharp bark or a whistle to warn members of their group.

986 Many animals show off colorful body parts to find a mate. To impress females, male frigate birds puff out their bright red throat sacs, and male anole lizards flash their colorful throat flaps. Other visual signals that attract mates include the flashing lights of fireflies.

▼ Howler monkeys have a special voice box and throat pouch that make their calls loud. Males have louder, deeper calls than females and can be heard up to 3 miles away.

◀ Blue-footed boobies lift and spread their bright blue feet to impress their partners.

987 Sound signals are often used by a group of animals to tell others of their kind to keep out of their area, or territory. Howler monkeys claim their territories in thick rain forests using loud calls. Even though they can't see each other, the calls can still be heard.

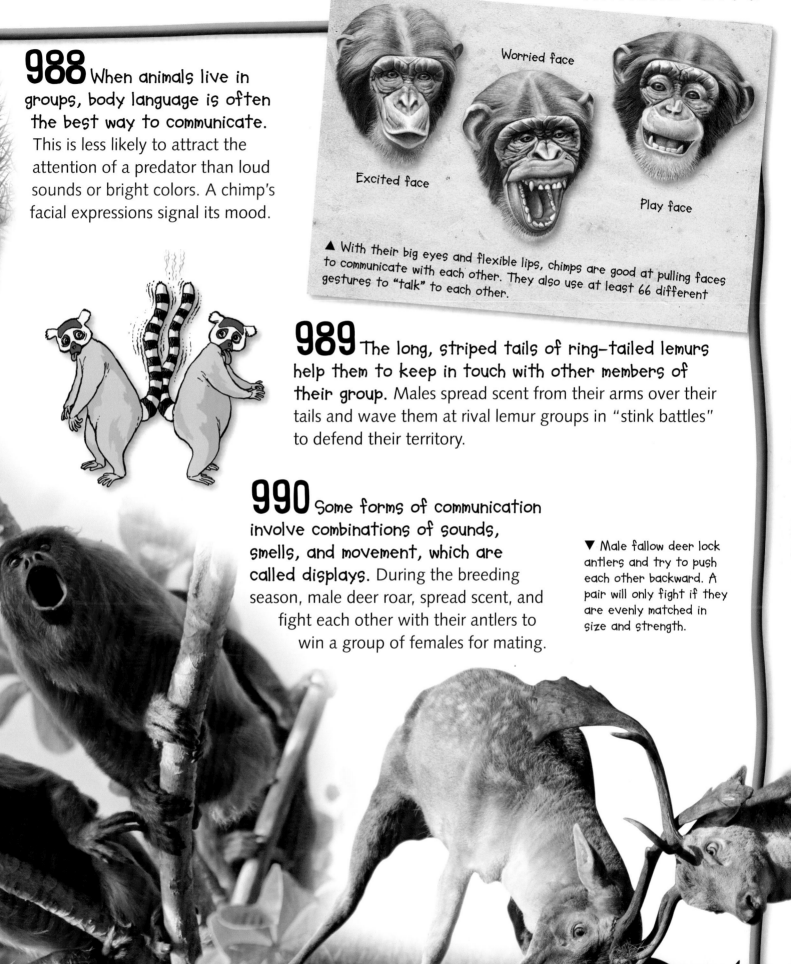

988 When animals live in groups, body language is often the best way to communicate. This is less likely to attract the attention of a predator than loud sounds or bright colors. A chimp's facial expressions signal its mood.

Excited face

Worried face

Play face

▲ With their big eyes and flexible lips, chimps are good at pulling faces to communicate with each other. They also use at least 66 different gestures to "talk" to each other.

989 The long, striped tails of ring-tailed lemurs help them to keep in touch with other members of their group. Males spread scent from their arms over their tails and wave them at rival lemur groups in "stink battles" to defend their territory.

990 Some forms of communication involve combinations of sounds, smells, and movement, which are called displays. During the breeding season, male deer roar, spread scent, and fight each other with their antlers to win a group of females for mating.

▼ Male fallow deer lock antlers and try to push each other backward. A pair will only fight if they are evenly matched in size and strength.

Eggs and babies

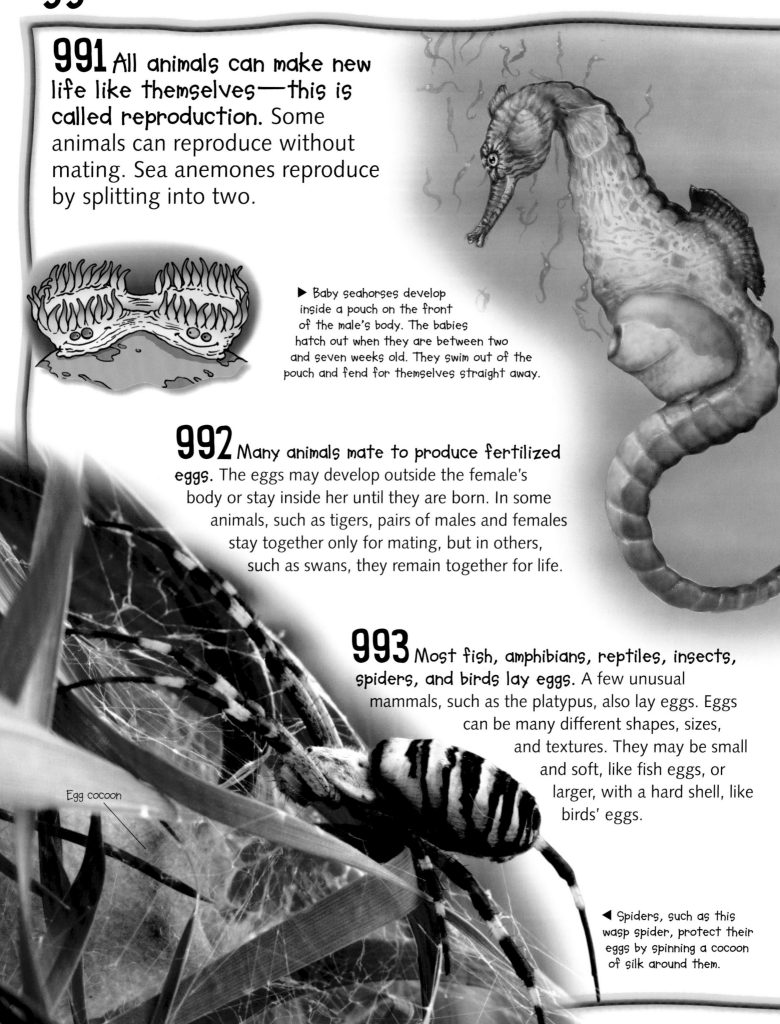

991 All animals can make new life like themselves—this is called reproduction. Some animals can reproduce without mating. Sea anemones reproduce by splitting into two.

▶ Baby seahorses develop inside a pouch on the front of the male's body. The babies hatch out when they are between two and seven weeks old. They swim out of the pouch and fend for themselves straight away.

992 Many animals mate to produce fertilized eggs. The eggs may develop outside the female's body or stay inside her until they are born. In some animals, such as tigers, pairs of males and females stay together only for mating, but in others, such as swans, they remain together for life.

993 Most fish, amphibians, reptiles, insects, spiders, and birds lay eggs. A few unusual mammals, such as the platypus, also lay eggs. Eggs can be many different shapes, sizes, and textures. They may be small and soft, like fish eggs, or larger, with a hard shell, like birds' eggs.

Egg cocoon

◀ Spiders, such as this wasp spider, protect their eggs by spinning a cocoon of silk around them.

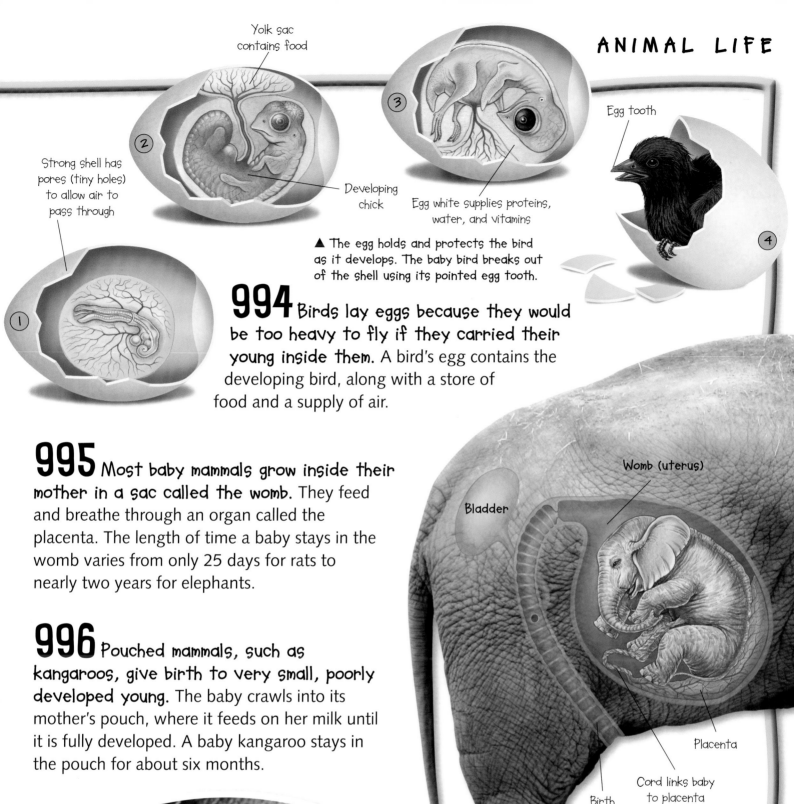

Yolk sac contains food

Strong shell has pores (tiny holes) to allow air to pass through

Developing chick

Egg white supplies proteins, water, and vitamins

Egg tooth

▲ The egg holds and protects the bird as it develops. The baby bird breaks out of the shell using its pointed egg tooth.

994 Birds lay eggs because they would be too heavy to fly if they carried their young inside them. A bird's egg contains the developing bird, along with a store of food and a supply of air.

995 Most baby mammals grow inside their mother in a sac called the womb. They feed and breathe through an organ called the placenta. The length of time a baby stays in the womb varies from only 25 days for rats to nearly two years for elephants.

996 Pouched mammals, such as kangaroos, give birth to very small, poorly developed young. The baby crawls into its mother's pouch, where it feeds on her milk until it is fully developed. A baby kangaroo stays in the pouch for about six months.

Womb (uterus)

Bladder

Placenta

Cord links baby to placenta

Birth canal

▲ A baby elephant develops inside a protective sac of liquid inside its mother's womb.

◄ A tiny red kangaroo feeds from a teat inside its mother's pouch.

Growing up

997 A series of changes take place during an animal's life—it grows, produces young and dies. This is called a life cycle. The life cycle of some insects lasts for only a few weeks, but the life cycle of a giant tortoise may last over 100 years.

▲ A mother tiger carries her cubs by the loose skin at the scruff of the neck to move them to a safe place.

QUIZ

1. How many stages does a butterfly have in its life cycle?

2. What is the name for the process of an animal losing its body casing?

3. How soon can a baby giraffe stand up after it is born?

Answers:
1. Four 2. Moulting
3. About one hour

▲ Under the cover of darkness, baby turtles race down to the sea as soon as they hatch out of their eggs on the beach. Many are caught by predators.

998 Animals that produce lots of young, such as fish, do not usually look after them. The large numbers mean that some of the young will manage to survive. Animals with fewer babies, such as mammals, almost all birds, and some reptiles, often feed and protect their young during early life.

999 Some animals, such as bear cubs and baby owls, are helpless when they are born. Others, such as zebras, deer, and ducklings, can run around soon after birth. This helps them to escape from predators and keep up with other members of their group.

1,000 Some young animals, such as tadpoles and caterpillars, look very different from their parents. They change their body shape as they mature into adults. Tadpoles change into frogs and caterpillars change into butterflies.

▼ A baby giraffe, or calf, can stand up and walk about one hour after it is born. When the calf grows bigger, its mother will leave it with other young giraffes in a "nursery" with an adult "babysitter."

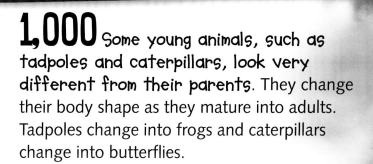

① Egg

② Caterpillar

③ Pupa

④ Adult butterfly

▲ Butterflies have four stages in their life cycle. The pupa goes through a dramatic change called metamorphosis as it changes into an adult butterfly.

1,001 Animals with a hard outer body casing, such as insects, spiders, and crabs, have to shed their body casing in order to grow. This is called molting. The soft skin underneath quickly expands and hardens to form a new, bigger casing.

1,002 Baby animals grow and learn at different rates. Mice are ready to leave the nest when they are only two or three weeks old, while orangutans, gorillas, tigers, and elephants spend many years raising their young.

◄ Some birds have chicks that are blind when they hatch. Their parents feed them and they grow fast.

Animal homes

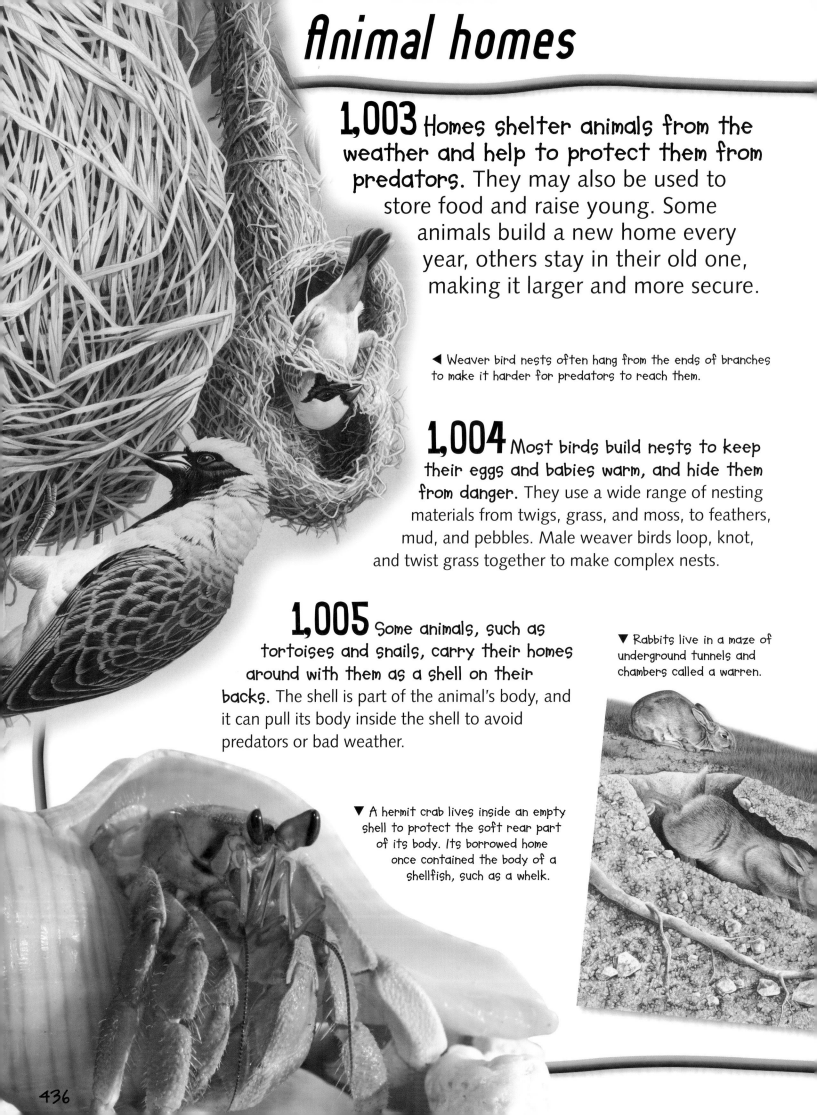

1,003 Homes shelter animals from the weather and help to protect them from predators. They may also be used to store food and raise young. Some animals build a new home every year, others stay in their old one, making it larger and more secure.

◀ Weaver bird nests often hang from the ends of branches to make it harder for predators to reach them.

1,004 Most birds build nests to keep their eggs and babies warm, and hide them from danger. They use a wide range of nesting materials from twigs, grass, and moss, to feathers, mud, and pebbles. Male weaver birds loop, knot, and twist grass together to make complex nests.

1,005 Some animals, such as tortoises and snails, carry their homes around with them as a shell on their backs. The shell is part of the animal's body, and it can pull its body inside the shell to avoid predators or bad weather.

▼ Rabbits live in a maze of underground tunnels and chambers called a warren.

▼ A hermit crab lives inside an empty shell to protect the soft rear part of its body. Its borrowed home once contained the body of a shellfish, such as a whelk.

I DON'T BELIEVE IT!

A queen termite may lay 30,000 eggs each day—that's one egg every few seconds!

1,006 Termites build huge mounds of rock-hard soil above their nest, which is home to millions of termites. Inside their nest are stores of food, nurseries for the eggs and young, and a chamber for the queen, who lays all the eggs. Chimneys inside the mound let hot air escape and keep the nest cool.

▶ Termite towers as large as this one may take ten, or even as long as 50 years to build! These mud skyscrapers help the tiny termites to survive in hot, dry places.

1,007 Many small mammals and a few birds live in narrow tunnels underground, where predators find it hard to follow them. These animals use their strong claws for digging. Their tunnels include lots of entrances and exits, so they can escape easily.

Living in water

▼ Dolphins have to come to the water's surface to breathe air through a blowhole on the top of their heads. Their streamlined shape helps them to swim fast.

1,008 The water of oceans, rivers, lakes, and swamps supports an animal's body. Many animal giants, such as whales, live in the oceans for this reason. Watery habitats are good places for animals to live because they contain plenty of food and places to shelter.

1,009 Some animals, such as crocodiles, surface to breathe in oxygen from the air. Others, such as fish, absorb oxygen directly from the water into their blood through thin flaps, called gills.

▲ A basking shark swims along with its huge mouth wide open. Tiny floating creatures are trapped on bristles in front of the gills.

Webbed feet

1,010 Water animals usually have a smooth, streamlined shape and a slippery body that slides through water easily. Many, such as frogs, otters, and hippos, have webs of skin between their toes to help them swim. Leeches have suckers to cling onto rocks in fast-flowing rivers.

◄ An otter's long, flexible body and webbed feet give it power and maneuvrability in the water. Its strong, thick tail helps it to steer.

1,011 Most deep-sea animals have watery flesh to help them resist the crushing water pressures. Prey is scarce, so predators have huge mouths and stomachs to eat as much as possible whenever they find a meal.

▼ The huge, pointed teeth of the fangtooth grab and hold other fish in the deep sea. Its teeth are no good for chewing, so the fangtooth swallows its prey whole.

1,012 On shorelines, shellfish, such as whelks, have thick shells to withstand pounding waves. At low tide on sandy or muddy shores, worms and crabs burrow underground so their bodies will not dry out.

▼ A coral reef is made from the skeletons of dead corals, which are tiny animals related to sea anemones. Living corals perch on top and use their stinging tentacles to catch food.

1,013 Coral reef animals often have bright colors and patterns, which may help them to recognize others of their kind. Colors may also help to attract a mate or provide camouflage for both predators, such as coral groupers, and prey, such as weedy sea dragons.

Desert survivors

1,014 The greatest challenge to animals in deserts is the lack of water. Scorpions and reptiles have watertight body coverings, which lose little water. Kangaroo rats get all the water they need from their food.

◄ Scorpions can survive without water for several months.

1,015 To avoid the daytime heat, many desert animals sleep in underground burrows or inside cacti. They come out when the temperature drops at night. Some animals use their bodies to stay cool. The giant ears of the fennec fox give off heat, and the ground squirrel uses its tail as a sunshade.

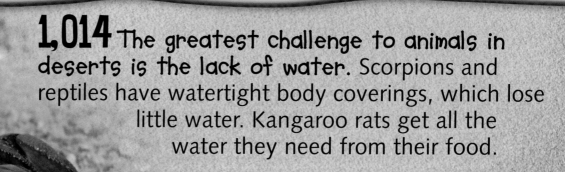

1,016 Feathers are good at keeping heat out, which stops birds overheating in the day. They are also good at keeping birds warm during the bitterly cold desert nights and winters. The poor-will avoids the desert winter altogether by going into a deep sleep, called hibernation.

◄ The fennec fox's huge ears help it to hear its small prey. Hairs inside the ears help to keep out the dust and sand of the desert.

QUIZ

1. What does a camel store inside its humps?
2. Why does a fennec fox have big ears?
3. How long can a scorpion last without water?

Answers:
1. Fat 2. To give off heat and to hear its small prey
3. Several months

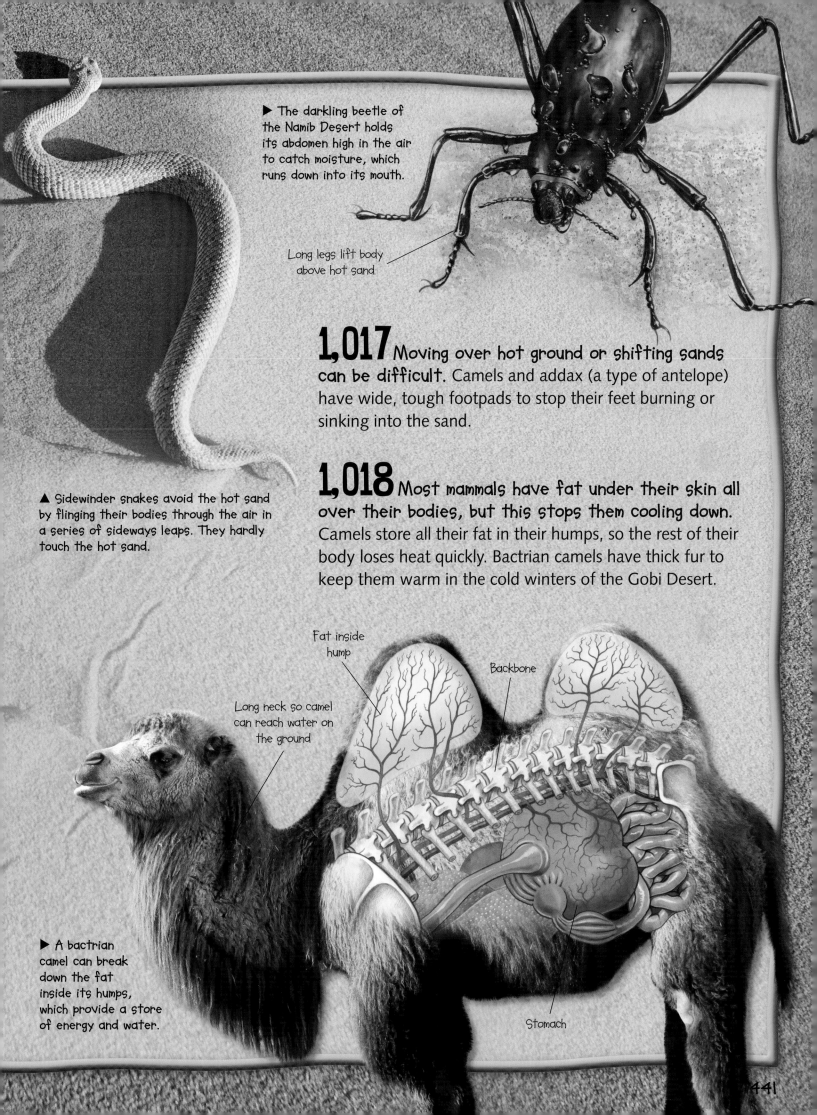

▶ The darkling beetle of the Namib Desert holds its abdomen high in the air to catch moisture, which runs down into its mouth.

Long legs lift body above hot sand

1,017 Moving over hot ground or shifting sands can be difficult. Camels and addax (a type of antelope) have wide, tough footpads to stop their feet burning or sinking into the sand.

▲ Sidewinder snakes avoid the hot sand by flinging their bodies through the air in a series of sideways leaps. They hardly touch the hot sand.

1,018 Most mammals have fat under their skin all over their bodies, but this stops them cooling down. Camels store all their fat in their humps, so the rest of their body loses heat quickly. Bactrian camels have thick fur to keep them warm in the cold winters of the Gobi Desert.

Fat inside hump

Backbone

Long neck so camel can reach water on the ground

▶ A bactrian camel can break down the fat inside its humps, which provide a store of energy and water.

Stomach

Life in the trees

1,019 Rain forests make good habitats (places to live) because they are warm and wet all year round. However, animals living there have to compete for living space and avoid the many predators. In temperate forests, animals have to cope with cold winters.

▼ Wallace's flying frog spreads its webbed feet to slow down its fall as it jumps from tree to tree.

1,020 Predators lurk at all levels of the rain forests. There are fierce birds of prey such as hawks and eagles in the canopy (treetops). Snakes and woodpeckers make their homes in the branches. The forest floor is inhabited by tigers, bears, and spiders.

▼ A spider monkey has a strong prehensile tail, which allows it to hang from branches.

1,021 Forest animals are good at climbing, swinging, and gliding through the trees. Gibbons have long arms to swing from branch to branch, while some monkeys and snakes have special prehensile (gripping) tails. Some animals, such as flying frogs or sugar gliders, glide from tree to tree on flaps of thin skin.

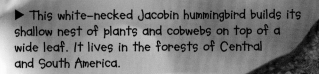

▶ This white-necked Jacobin hummingbird builds its shallow nest of plants and cobwebs on top of a wide leaf. It lives in the forests of Central and South America.

1,023 Forests provide a good choice of nesting places for birds. Parrots, toucans, and owls nest inside tree holes. Many birds nest high in the trees to keep their eggs and young out of reach of most predators.

1,022 Many forest animals are nocturnal (come out at night). Their senses are specially adapted to help them thrive in the dark. They may have huge eyes and ears, or extra-sensitive noses. Snakes such as pit vipers can sense the heat given off by birds and mammals and track their prey in total darkness.

▼ The greater musky fruit bat of the Philippines eats the fruit of rain forest trees. It spits out the seeds, which may grow into new trees.

MONKEY MASK

You will need:
coloring paints and pencils
paper plate   paper   scissors
glue   ribbon or string
Paint a paper plate brown. On the paper, draw two eyes, a nose, a mouth, and two ears. Cut them out and glue them onto the paper plate. Carefully cut holes in the eyes. Then make holes in the sides of the plate and use ribbon or string to tie the mask to your face.

1,024 Forest animals are closely linked with plants, helping to spread pollen and seeds. Brightly colored birds called quetzals spread the seeds of avocado trees. Brazil nut trees rely on guinea piglike agoutis to break open their tough seed cases with their strong teeth.

Out in the cold

1,025 Many animals have to survive in the coldest environments on Earth. Land animals living there rely on thick fur or feathers to keep them warm. Small, round ears and muzzles help to reduce heat loss.

1,026 Some animals live in cold oceans. Walruses and seals rely on a thick layer of fat, called blubber, under their skin to keep them warm. This is because fur and feathers are not so good at trapping heat when they are wet.

1,027 Animals living in places where it snows in winter sometimes turn white for camouflage. The Arctic fox, snowshoe hare, ptarmigan, and stoat all have white coats in winter to help them blend in with their snowy surroundings. When the snow melts, they turn brown or gray to match the summer landscape.

▲ The walrus has a layer of fatty blubber up to 4 inches thick. Its flat flippers support its heavy body on land.

1,029 Some animals, such as ice-fish, survive at temperatures well below freezing. This is because they have a chemical "anti-freeze" in their blood. The "anti-freeze" stops ice crystals from forming inside their bodies so they don't freeze solid.

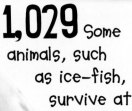

▲ The snowy owl's white feathers provide good camouflage as it hunts for small mammals to eat.

1,028 Slippery ice, deep snow, and steep mountain slopes can make it hard to get around. The long, furry back feet of snowshoe hares stop them sinking into the snow, while polar bears have non-slip soles.

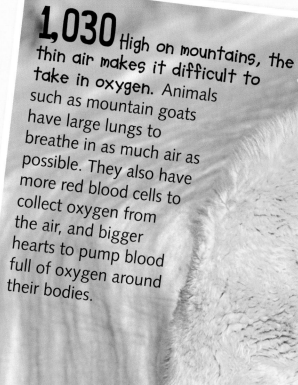

1,030 High on mountains, the thin air makes it difficult to take in oxygen. Animals such as mountain goats have large lungs to breathe in as much air as possible. They also have more red blood cells to collect oxygen from the air, and bigger hearts to pump blood full of oxygen around their bodies.

▶ Mountain goats have sharp, pointed hooves, with two toes that spread wide to improve their balance. Rough pads on the bottom of each toe provide good grip.

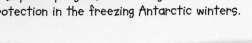

◀ Emperor penguins huddle together for warmth and protection in the freezing Antarctic winters.

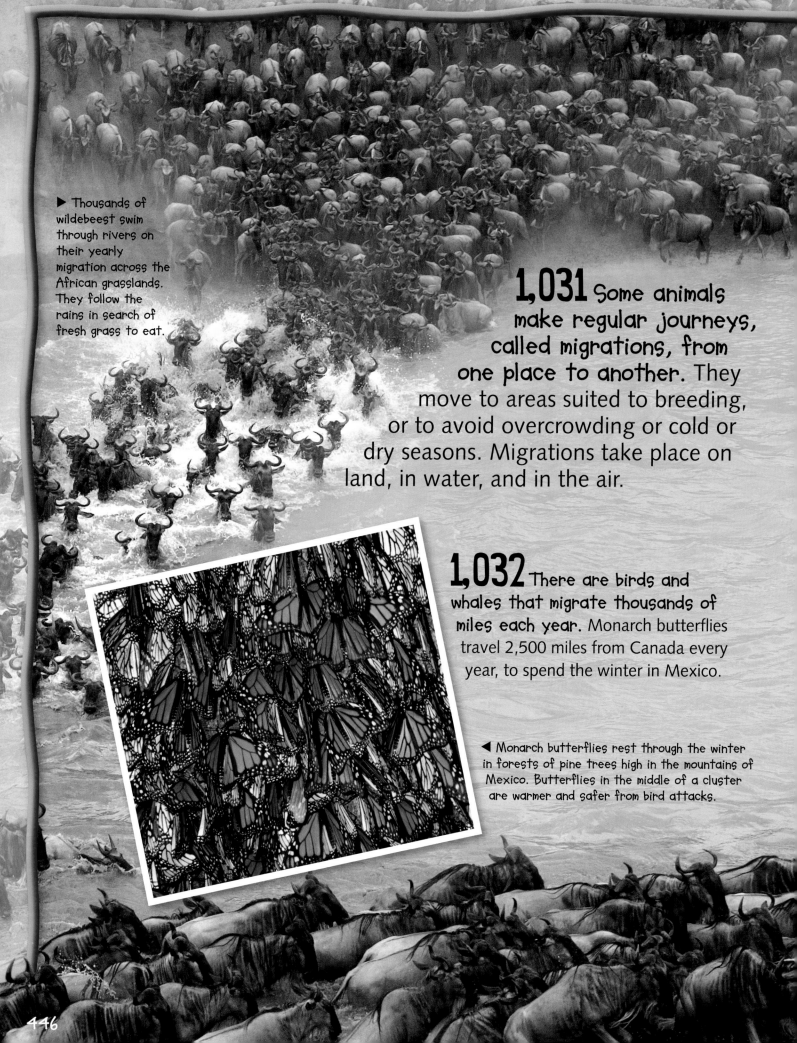

Incredible journeys

▶ Thousands of wildebeest swim through rivers on their yearly migration across the African grasslands. They follow the rains in search of fresh grass to eat.

1,031 Some animals make regular journeys, called migrations, from one place to another. They move to areas suited to breeding, or to avoid overcrowding or cold or dry seasons. Migrations take place on land, in water, and in the air.

1,032 There are birds and whales that migrate thousands of miles each year. Monarch butterflies travel 2,500 miles from Canada every year, to spend the winter in Mexico.

◀ Monarch butterflies rest through the winter in forests of pine trees high in the mountains of Mexico. Butterflies in the middle of a cluster are warmer and safer from bird attacks.

1,033 Fish such as salmon migrate at different stages in their lives. Adult salmon live in the oceans, where there is more food, but they migrate to rivers to breed. European eels migrate in the opposite direction: adults live in rivers, but they migrate to the Sargasso Sea to breed.

▶ Vast numbers of sockeye salmon swim from the sea to the rivers where they were born to lay their eggs. Ten million may migrate up one river in a single season.

1,034 Adult animals may show young ones which way to go on migration journeys. However many, such as eels, rely on instinct to find their way. Animals also navigate using familiar landmarks, sounds, scents, the positions of the Sun, Moon, and stars, and the Earth's magnetic field.

▼ Chemical reactions in the eyes of birds may help them to sense the Earth's magnetic field. This could help them to keep flying in the right direction during long migrations.

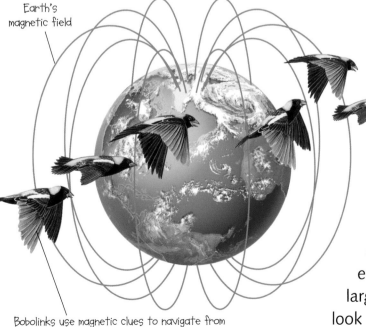

Earth's magnetic field

Bobolinks use magnetic clues to navigate from South America to North America each year

I DON'T BELIEVE IT!
Caribou make the longest trek of any land mammal. They travel more than 3,000 miles a year —roughly the distance from New York to London!

1,035 Lemmings make regular seasonal migrations between summer and winter areas. They also make more erratic journeys every few years when their numbers grow too large for their food supply. These animals set off to look for food on journeys that have no particular destination. Migrations like this are called irruptions.

Endangered animals

1,036 Endangered animals are in danger of dying out, or becoming extinct, in the near future. Many are threatened by the things people do, such as destroying their habitats or by hunting them.

◀ Some scientists are trying to protect rare tigers by fitting them with radio collars. They can track their movements in the wild and work out the best ways to save them.

1,037 Many endangered animals, such as Galapagos giant tortoises, live on small islands. They are specially adapted to survive in one small area, and are not good at surviving the rapid changes that happen when people settle on islands.

◀ Giant tortoises stand a better chance of survival now that people are protecting their eggs and babies.

1,038 There are now only about 1,600 giant pandas left in the wild in China, but numbers are slowly increasing. Panda reserves in bamboo forests are being linked together and illegal killing of pandas has been reduced.

▼ Several giant pandas bred in captivity have now been released into the wild.

RARE ANIMALS POSTER

You will need:
pen paper atlas glue pictures of rare animals

Using a pen and paper, trace a world map from an atlas. Write the names of the continents on your map. Stick pictures of rare animals in the places where they live.

1,039 Rhinos were once widespread in Africa and Asia, but today, most rhinos only survive inside national parks and reserves. They are endangered by habitat loss and illegal trade in rhino horn for traditional Asian medicines.

▲ Over 20,000 southern white rhinos survive in protected sanctuaries. This rhino has a particularly long front horn.

1,040 Albatrosses usually fish from the surface of the sea. When they see long lines of fishing hooks floating behind fishing boats, they fly down to steal the bait on the hooks. Unfortunately, some birds swallow the hooks, are dragged underwater and drown.

◄ Albatrosses can be saved by different fishing methods, such as sinking the lines deeper underwater.

1,041 Our closest living relatives are great apes, like us—bonobos, chimps, gorillas, and orangutans. Yet they are endangered by habitat loss, climate change, diseases, and illegal hunting. We need to work hard to save them.

► The money tourists pay to watch mountain gorillas in the wild provides funds for conservation and helps to create jobs for local people.

HUMAN BODY

- Babies and children
- Skin, hair, and nails
- Skeletons and muscles
- Lungs and breathing
- Food and digestion
- Circulation
- The heart
- Senses and nerves
- The brain
- Keeping healthy

Why do we sweat?

How many bones do I have?

What is hair made from?

How fast do nerve signals travel?

Where is my windpipe?

How do I learn new things?

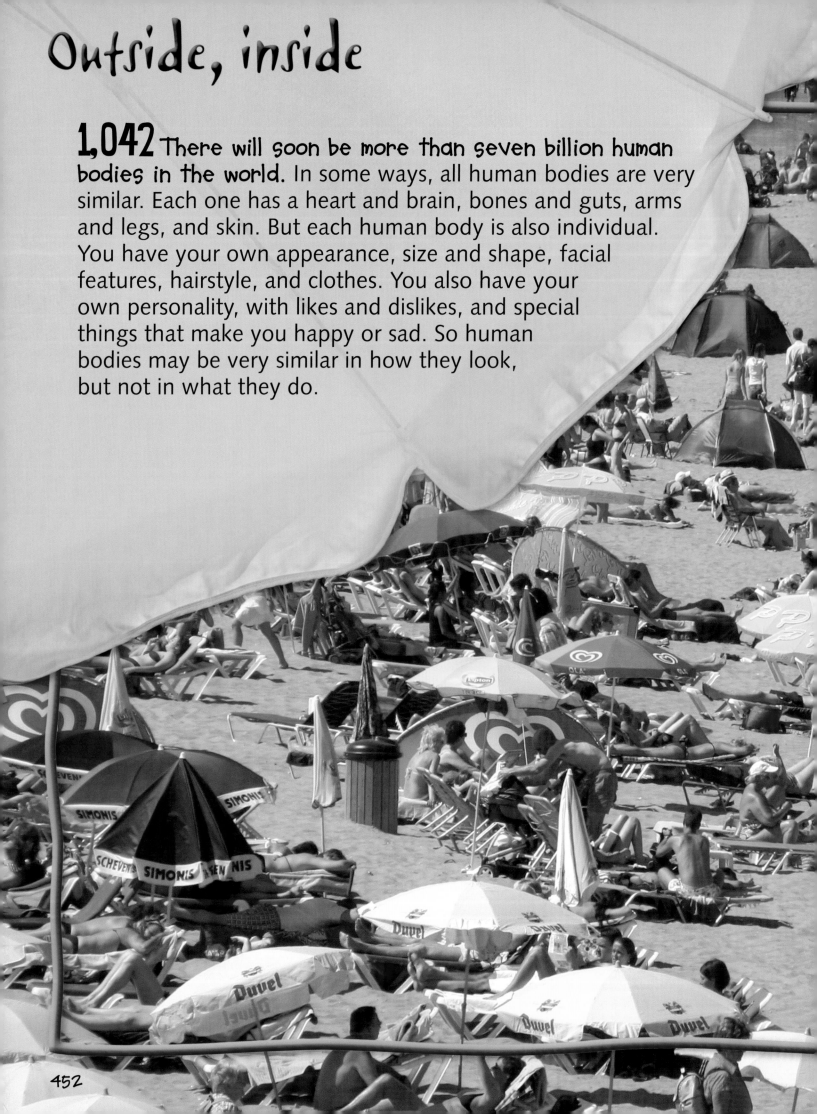

Outside, inside

1,042 **There will soon be more than seven billion human bodies in the world.** In some ways, all human bodies are very similar. Each one has a heart and brain, bones and guts, arms and legs, and skin. But each human body is also individual. You have your own appearance, size and shape, facial features, hairstyle, and clothes. You also have your own personality, with likes and dislikes, and special things that make you happy or sad. So human bodies may be very similar in how they look, but not in what they do.

▲ We tend to notice small differences on the outside of human bodies, such as height, width, hair color, and clothes. This allows us to recognize our family and friends.

453

Baby body

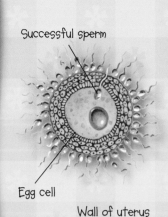

Successful sperm

Egg cell

1,043 A fully grown human body is made of billions of microscopic parts, called cells. But in the beginning, the body is a single cell, smaller than this period. Yet it contains all the instructions, known as genes, for the whole body to grow and develop.

Wall of uterus

Fluid around baby

Bones of skeleton start to form

Hair begins to grow on head

Placenta (afterbirth)

Two months

Face has taken shape

Three months

▲▶Thousands of sperm cells reach the egg (top), but only one is successful and joins with it, at fertilization. This starts the growth of the baby, shown here after two, three, five, seven, and nine months.

Baby begins to move and kick

Five months

Umbilical cord

Seven months

1,044 The body begins when an egg cell inside the mother joins up with sperm from the father. The egg cell splits into two cells, then into four cells, then eight, and so on. The bundle of cells embeds itself in the mother's womb (uterus), which protects and nourishes it. Soon there are thousands of cells, then millions, forming a tiny embryo. After two months the embryo has grown into a tiny baby, as big as your thumb, with arms, legs, eyes, ears, and a mouth.

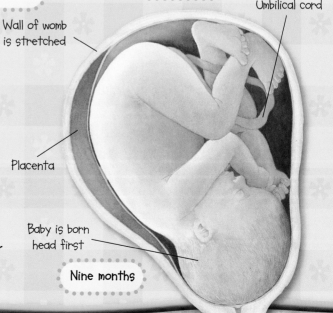

Wall of womb is stretched

Umbilical cord

Placenta

Baby is born head first

Nine months

Cervix (neck of womb)

1,045 After nine months in the womb, the baby is ready to be born. Strong muscles in the walls of the womb tighten, or contract. They push the baby through the opening, or neck of the womb, called the cervix, and along the birth canal. The baby enters the outside world.

1,046 A newborn baby may be frightened and usually starts to cry. Inside the womb it was warm, wet, dark, quiet, and cramped. Outside there are lights, noises, voices, fresh air, and room to stretch. The crying is also helpful to start the baby breathing, using its own lungs.

1,047 Being born can take an hour or two—or a whole day or two. It is very tiring for both the baby and its mother. After birth, the baby starts to feel hungry and it feeds on its mother's milk. Finally, mother and baby settle down for a rest and some sleep.

I DON'T BELIEVE IT!

The human body never grows as fast again as it does during the first weeks in the womb. If the body kept growing at that rate every day for 50 years, it would be bigger than the biggest mountain in the world!

▲ Once the baby is settled it is time for its mother to admire her newborn and rest.

The growing body

1,048 **A new baby just seems to eat, sleep, and cry.** It feeds on milk when hungry and sleeps when tired. Also, it cries when it is too hot, too cold, or when its nappy needs changing.

1,049 **A new baby is not totally helpless.** It can do simple actions called reflexes, to help it survive. If something touches the baby's cheek, it turns its head to that side and tries to suck. If the baby hears a loud noise, it opens its eyes wide, throws out its arms, and cries for help. If something touches the baby's hand and fingers, it grasps tightly.

1,050 **A new baby looks, listens, touches, and quickly learns.** Gradually it starts to recognize voices, faces, and places. After about six weeks, it begins to smile. Inside the body, the baby's brain is learning very quickly. The baby soon knows that if it laughs, people will laugh back and if it cries, someone will come to look after it.

WHAT HAPPENS WHEN?

Most babies learn to do certain actions in the same order. The order is mixed up here. Can you put it right?

walk, crawl, roll over, sit up, smile, stand

Answers:
smile, roll over, sit up,
crawl, stand, walk

▼ In the grasping reflex, the baby tightly holds anything that touches its hand or fingers. Its grip is surprisingly strong!

▼ Most babies crawl before they walk, but some go straight from sitting or "bottom-shuffling" to walking.

1,052 As a baby grows into a child, at around 18 months, it learns ten new words every day, from "cat" and "dog" to "sun" and "moon." There are new games such as piling up bricks, new actions such as throwing and kicking, and new skills such as using a spoon at mealtimes and scribbling on paper.

1,051 At about three months old, most babies can reach out to hold something, and roll over when lying down. By the age of six months, most babies can sit up and hold food in their fingers. At nine months, many babies are crawling well and perhaps standing up. By their first birthday, many babies are learning to walk and starting to talk.

1,053 At the age of five, when most children start school, they continue to learn an amazing amount. This includes thinking or mental skills such as counting and reading, and precise movements such as writing and drawing. They learn out of the classroom too—how to play with friends and share.

▼ Playing is lots of fun, but it's learning too, as children develop control over the muscles in their fast-growing bodies.

On the body's outside

1,054 Skin's surface is made of tiny cells that have filled up with a hard, tough substance called keratin, and then died. So when you look at a human body, most of what you see is "dead!" The cells get rubbed off as you move, have a wash, and get dry.

1,055 Skin rubs off all the time, and grows all the time too. Just under the surface, living cells make more new cells that gradually fill with keratin, die, and move up to the surface. It takes about four weeks from a new skin cell being made to when it reaches the surface and is rubbed off. This upper layer of skin is called the epidermis.

Hair

Oil gland

Epidermis

Dermis

Hair follicle

▲ This view shows skin magnified (enlarged) about 50 times.

▲ Lots of dead skin is removed without you realizing when you dry yourself after a shower.

1,056 Skin's lower layer, the dermis, is thicker than the epidermis. It is made of tiny, bendy, threadlike fibers of the substance collagen. The dermis also contains small blood vessels, tiny sweat glands, and microsensors that detect touch.

1,057 One of skin's important jobs is to protect the body. It stops the delicate inner parts from being rubbed, knocked, or scraped. Skin also prevents body fluids from leaking away and it keeps out dirt and germs.

1,058 Skin helps to keep the body at the same temperature. If you become too hot, sweat oozes onto your skin and, as it dries, draws heat from the body. Also, the blood vessels in the lower layer of skin widen, to lose more heat through the skin. This is why a hot person looks sweaty and red in the face.

1,059 Skin gives us our sense of touch. Millions of microscopic sensors in the lower layer of skin, the dermis, are joined by nerves to the brain. These sensors detect different kinds of touch, from a light stroke to heavy pressure, heat or cold, and movement. Pain sensors detect when skin is damaged. Ouch!

Safety helmet protects head and brain

Elbow pads cushion fall

Gloves save fingers from scrapes and breaks

Knee pads prevent hard bumps

▲ Skin is tough, but it sometimes needs help to protect the body. Otherwise it, and the body parts beneath, may get damaged.

SENSITIVE SKIN
You will need:
a friend   sticky-tack
two used matchsticks   ruler
1. Press some sticky-tack on the end of the ruler. Press two matchsticks into the sticky-tack, standing upright, about 0.4 inches apart.
2. Make your friend look away. Touch the back of their hand with both matchstick ends. Ask your friend: "Is that one matchstick or two?" Sensitive skin can detect both ends
3. Try this at several places, such as on the finger, wrist, forearm, neck, and cheek.

Hair and nails

1,060 There are about 120,000 hairs on the head, called scalp hairs. There are also eyebrow hairs and eyelash hairs. Grown-ups have hairs in the armpits and between the legs, and men have hairs on the face. And everyone, even a baby, has tiny hairs all over the body—5 to 10 million of them!

Blonde wavy hair is the result of carotene from an oval hair follicle

Black curly hair is the result of black melanin from a flat hair follicle

Straight red hair is the result of red melanin from a round hair follicle

◄ Hair contains pigments (colored substances)—mainly melanin (dark brown) and some carotene (yellowish). Different amounts of pigments, and the way their tiny particles are spread out, cause different hair colors.

1,061 Each hair grows from a deep pit in the skin, called a follicle. The hair is only alive where it gets longer, at its base or root, in the bottom of the follicle. The rest of the hair, called the shaft, is like the surface of the skin—hard, tough, dead, and made of keratin. Hair helps to protect the body, especially where it is thicker and longer on the head. It also helps to keep the body warm in cold conditions.

Straight black hair is the result of black melanin from a round follicle

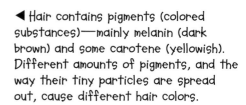

1,062 Scalp hairs get longer by about 0.1 inches each week, on average. Eyebrow hairs grow more slowly. No hairs live forever. Each one grows for a time, then it falls out, and its follicle has a "rest" before a new hair sprouts. This is happening all the time, so the body always has some hairs on each part.

1,063 Nails, like hairs, grow at their base (the nail root) and are made of keratin. Also like hairs, nails grow faster in summer than in winter, and faster at night than by day. Nails lengthen by about 0.02 inches, on average, each week.

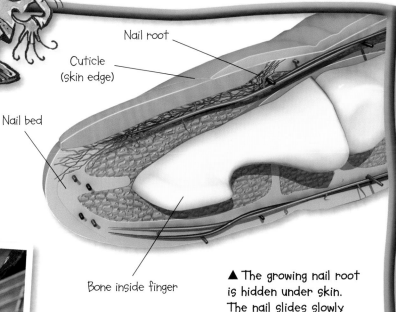

Nail root

Cuticle (skin edge)

Nail bed

Bone inside finger

▲ The growing nail root is hidden under skin. The nail slides slowly along the nail bed.

▲ Nails make the fingertips stronger and more rigid for pressing hard on guitar strings. Slightly longer nails pluck the strings.

1,064 Nails have many uses, from peeling off sticky labels to plucking guitar strings or scratching an itch. They protect and stiffen the ends of the fingers, where there are nerves that give us our sense of touch.

► Keeping your nails clean is very important. If you don't, germs can build up under your nails and make you ill.

I DON'T BELIEVE IT!

A scalp hair grows for up to five years before it falls out and gets replaced. Left uncut during this time, it would be about 3 feet long. But some people have unusual hair that grows faster and for longer. Each hair can reach more than 16 feet in length before dropping out.

The bony body

1,065 Without bones, the body would be as floppy as a jellyfish! Bones do many jobs. The long bones in the arms work like levers to reach out the hands. The finger bones grasp and grip. Bones protect softer body parts. The domelike skull protects the brain. The ribs shield the lungs and heart. Bones also produce blood cells, as explained on the opposite page.

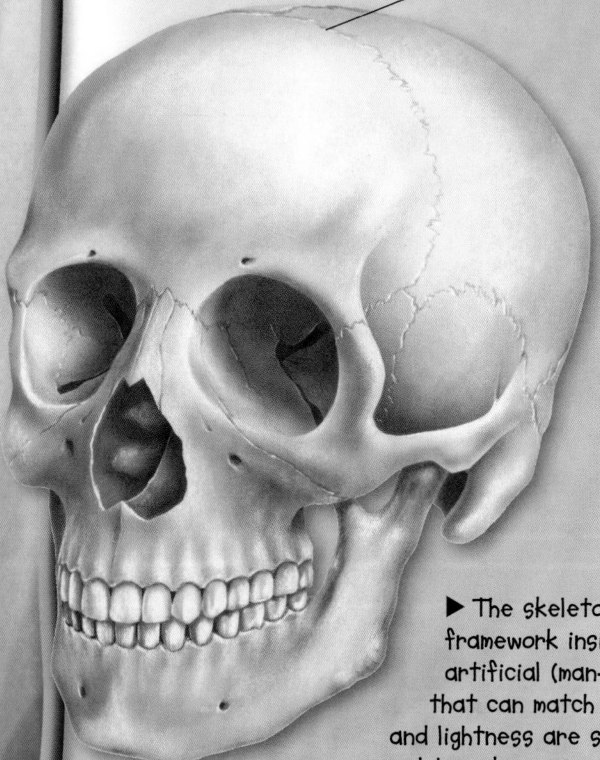

Suture

◀ The skull has deep bowls for the eyes, and small holes where nerves pass through to join the brain inside.

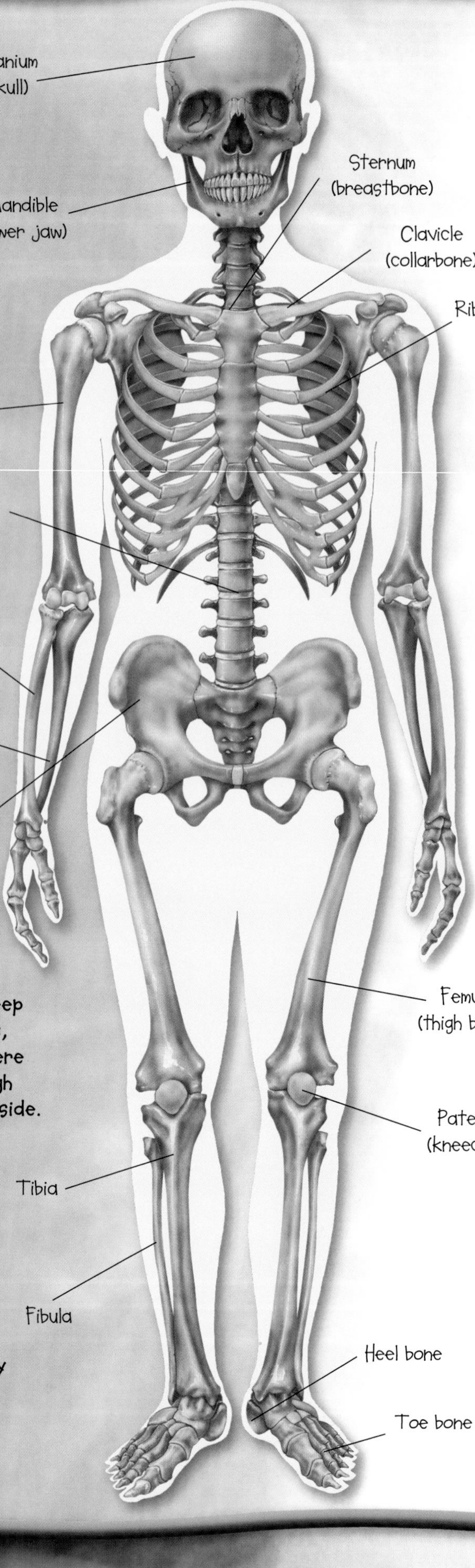

▶ The skeleton forms a strong framework inside the body. The only artificial (man-made) substances that can match bone for strength and lightness are some of the materials used to make racing cars and jet planes.

Cranium (skull)

Mandible (lower jaw)

Sternum (breastbone)

Clavicle (collarbone)

Rib

Humerus

Vertebra (backbone)

Ulna

Radius

Pelvis (hip bone)

Femur (thigh bone)

Patella (kneecap)

Tibia

Fibula

Heel bone

Toe bone

1,066 All the bones together make up the skeleton. Most people have 206 bones, from head to toe as follows:
- 8 in the upper part of the skull, the cranium or braincase
- 14 in the face
- 6 tiny ear bones, 3 deep in each ear
- 1 in the neck, which is floating and not directly connected to any other bone
- 26 in the spinal column or backbone
- 25 in the chest, being 24 ribs and the breastbone
- 32 in each arm, from shoulder to fingertips (8 in each wrist)
- 31 in each leg, from hip to toetips (7 in each ankle)

1,067 Bone contains threads of the tough, slightly bendy substance called collagen. It also has hard minerals such as calcium and phosphate. Together, the collagen and minerals make a bone strong and rigid, yet able to bend slightly under stress. Bones have blood vessels for nourishment and nerves to feel pressure and pain. Also, some bones are not solid. They contain a Jell-Olike substance called marrow. This makes tiny parts for the blood, called red and white blood cells.

Spongy bone

Marrow

Nerves and blood vessels

Compact (hard) bone

"Skin" of bone (periosteum)

End or head of bone

▲ Bone has a hard layer outside, a spongy layer next, and soft marrow in the middle.

NAME THE BONE!

Every bone has a scientific or medical name, and many have ordinary names too. Can you match up these ordinary and scientific names for various bones?

1. Mandible 2. Femur 3. Clavicle
4. Pelvis 5. Patella 6. Sternum

a. Thigh bone b. Breastbone
c. Kneecap d. Hip bone
e. Collarbone f. Lower jaw bone

Answers:
1f 2a 3e 4d 5c 6b

The flexible body

1,068 Without joints, almost the only parts of your body that could move would be your tongue and eyebrows! Joints between bones allow the skeleton to bend. You have more than 200 joints. The largest are in the hips and knees. The smallest are in the fingers, toes, and between the tiny bones inside each ear which help you hear.

1,069 There are several kinds of joints, depending on the shapes of the bone ends, and how much the bones can move. Bend your knee and your lower leg moves forward and backward, but not sideways. This is a hinge-type joint. Bend your hip and your leg can move forward, backward, and also from side to side. This is a ball-and-socket joint.

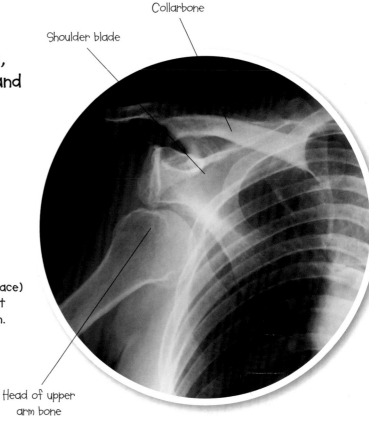

Collarbone

Shoulder blade

Head of upper arm bone

▶ This X-ray shows a dislocated (out of place) shoulder. The shoulder joint has the biggest range of movement, so this injury is common.

TEST YOUR JOINTS

Try using these different joints carefully, and see how much movement they allow. Can you guess the type of joint used in each one—hinge or ball-and-socket?

1. Fingertip joint (smallest knuckle)
2. Elbow
3. Hip
4. Shoulder

Answers:
1. ball 2. hinge
3. ball-and-socket 4. ball-and-socket

1,070 Inside a joint where the bones come together, each bone end is covered with a smooth, shiny, slippery, slightly springy substance, known as cartilage. This is smeared with a thick liquid called synovial fluid. The fluid works like the oil in a car, to smooth the movements and reduce rubbing and wear between the cartilage surfaces.

1,071 The bones in a joint are linked together by a baglike part, the capsule, and strong, stretchy, straplike ligaments. The ligaments let the bones move but stop them coming apart or moving too far. The shoulder has seven strong ligaments.

1,072 In some joints, there are cartilage coverings over the bone ends and also pads of cartilage between the cartilage! These extra pads are called articular disks. There is one in each joint in the backbone, between the spinal bones, which are called vertebrae. There are also two of these extra cartilages, known as menisci, in each knee joint. They help the knee to "lock" straight so that we can stand up without too much effort.

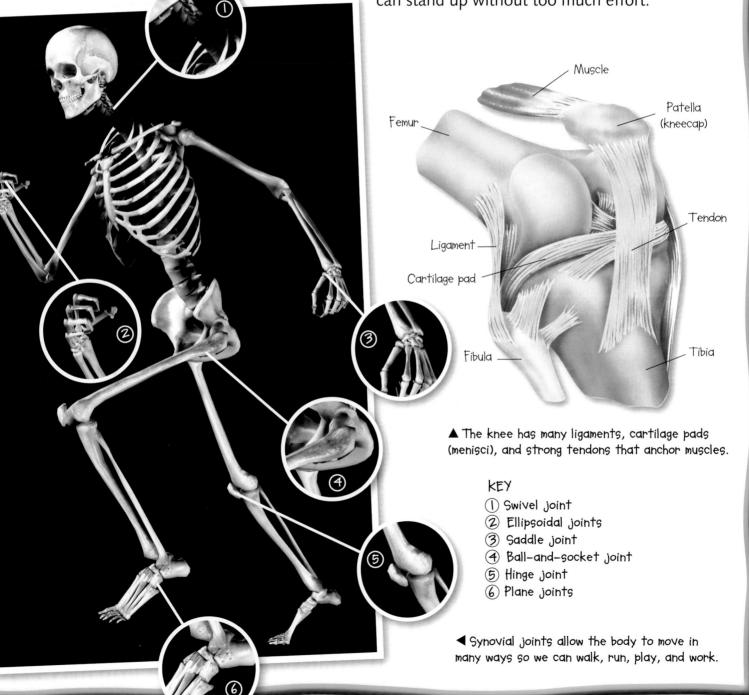

Muscle

Patella (kneecap)

Femur

Tendon

Ligament

Cartilage pad

Fibula

Tibia

▲ The knee has many ligaments, cartilage pads (menisci), and strong tendons that anchor muscles.

KEY
① Swivel joint
② Ellipsoidal joints
③ Saddle joint
④ Ball-and-socket joint
⑤ Hinge joint
⑥ Plane joints

◀ Synovial joints allow the body to move in many ways so we can walk, run, play, and work.

When muscles pull

1,073 Almost half the body's weight is muscles, and there are more than 640 of them! Muscles have one simple but important job, which is to get shorter, or contract. A muscle cannot forcefully get longer.

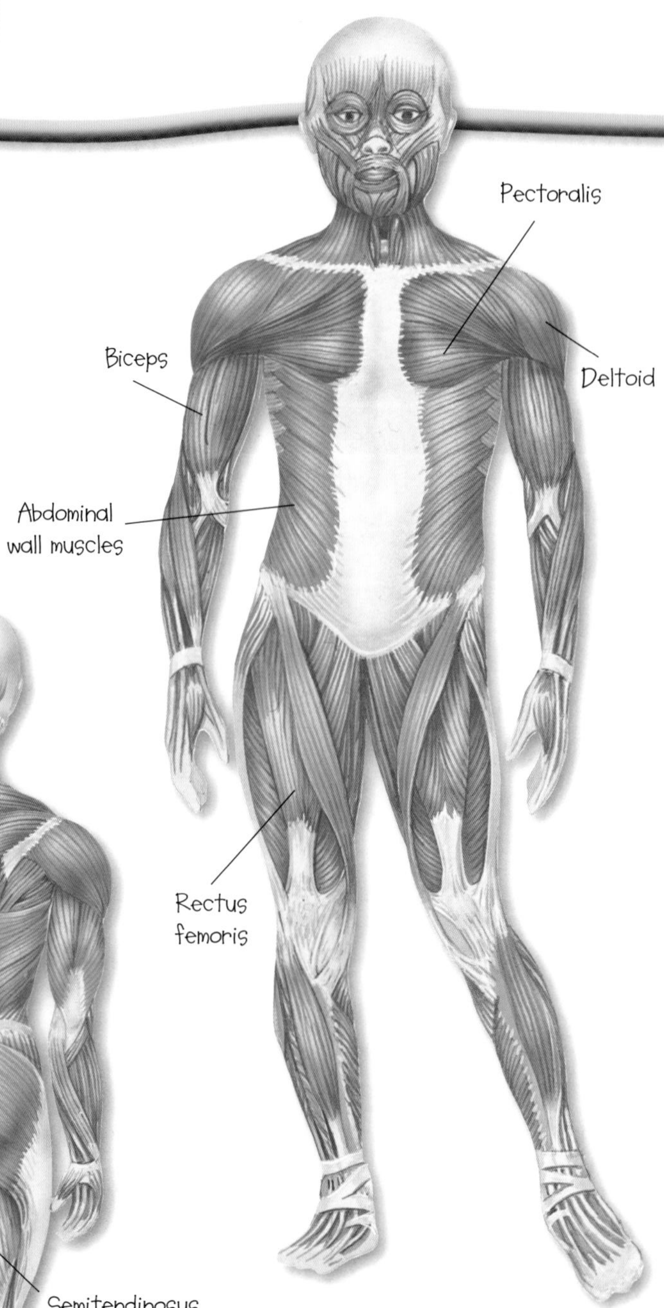

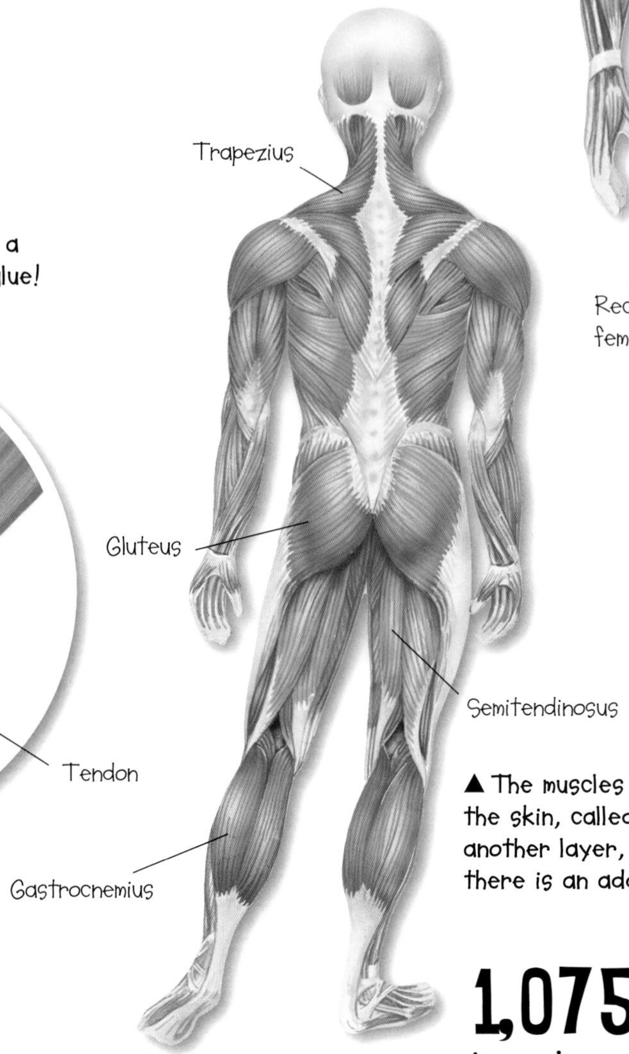

Pectoralis

Biceps

Deltoid

Abdominal wall muscles

▼ A tendon is stuck firmly into the bone it pulls, with a joint stronger than superglue!

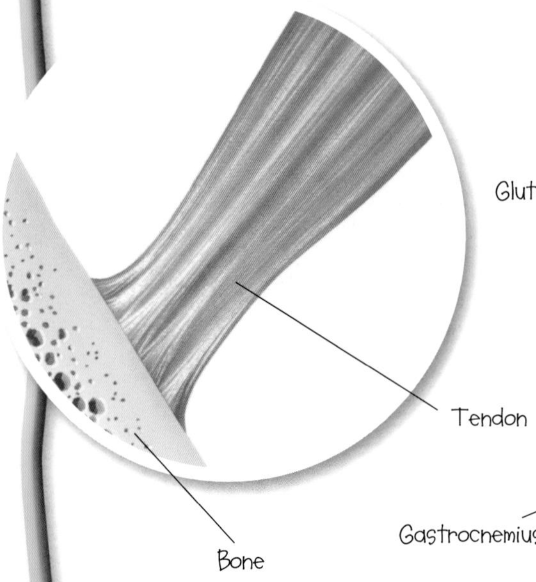

Trapezius

Rectus femoris

Tendon

Gluteus

Bone

Semitendinosus

Gastrocnemius

▲ The muscles shown here are those just beneath the skin, called superficial muscles. Under them is another layer, the deep muscle layer. In some areas there is an additional layer, the medial muscles.

1,074 A muscle is joined to a bone by its tendon. This is where the end of the muscle becomes slimmer or tapers, and is strengthened by strong, thick fibers of collagen. The fibers are fixed firmly into the surface of the bone.

1,075 Some muscles are wide or broad, and shaped more like flat sheets or triangles. These include the three layers of muscles in the lower front and sides of the body, called the abdominal wall muscles. If you tense or contract them, they pull your tummy in to make you look thinner.

1,076 Most muscles are long and slim, and joined to bones at each end. As they contract they pull on the bones and move them. As this happens, the muscle becomes wider, or more bulging in the middle. To move the bone back again, a muscle on the other side of it contracts, while the first muscle relaxes and is pulled longer.

1,077 Every muscle in the body has a scientific or medical name, which is often quite long and complicated. Some of these names are familiar to people who do exercise and sports. The "pecs" are the pectoralis major muscles across the chest. The "biceps" are the biceps brachii muscles in the upper arms, which bulge when you bend your elbow.

▶ A breakdancer needs endurance, strength, and control over their muscles to carry out moves such as this.

1,078 If you take plenty of exercise or play sport, you do not gain new muscles. But the muscles you have become larger and stronger. This keeps them fit and healthy. Muscles which are not used much may become weak and floppy.

Biceps gets shorter and bends the elbow

To move the forearm back down, the triceps shortens and the biceps gets longer

▶ Muscles work in two-way pairs, like the biceps and triceps, which bend and straighten the elbow.

Biceps

Triceps

Muscle power

1,079 Muscles have many shapes and sizes, but inside they are all similar. They have bundles of long, hairlike threads called muscle fibers, or myofibers. Each muscle fiber is slightly thinner than a hair. A big muscle has many thousands of them. Most are about 1.2 to 1.6 inches long. In a big muscle, many fibers of different lengths lie alongside each other and end-to-end.

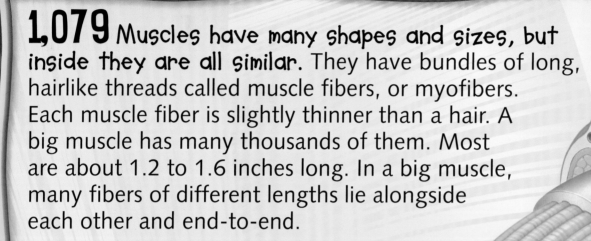

Muscle fiber

Nerve branches

Muscle fiber

Muscle fibril

▶ Male gymnasts need extreme upper body strength when using the rings. Many different muscles work together to hold the gymnast in the correct position.

1,080 Each muscle fiber is made of dozens or hundreds of even thinner parts, called muscle fibrils or myofibrils. There are millions of these in a large muscle. And, as you may guess, each fibril contains hundreds of yet thinner threads! There are two kinds, actin and myosin. As the actins slide past and between the myosins, the threads get shorter—and the muscle contracts.

Body of muscle

▶ Dozens of arm and hand muscles move a pen precisely, a tiny amount each time.

◀ The main part of a muscle is the body or belly, with hundreds of muscle fibers inside.

Actin

Myosin

1,081 Muscles are controlled by the brain, which sends messages to them along stringlike nerves. When a muscle contracts for a long time, its fibers "take turns." Some of them shorten powerfully while others relax, then the contracted ones relax while others shorten, and so on.

WHICH MUSCLES?

Can you match the names of these muscles with different parts of the body?

a. Gluteus maximus b. Masseter
c. Sartorius d. Cardiac muscle
e. Pectoralis major

1. Heart 2. Chest 3. Front of thigh
4. Buttock 5. Mouth

Answers:
a4 b5 c3 d1 e2

1,082 The body's biggest muscles are the ones you sit on—the gluteus maximus muscles in the buttocks. The longest muscle is the sartorius, across the front of the thigh. Some of its fibers are more than 12 inches in length. The most powerful muscle, for its size, is the masseter in the lower cheek, which closes the jaws when you chew.

The breathing body

1,083 The body cannot survive more than a few minutes without breathing. This action is so important, we do it all the time without thinking. We breathe to take air into the body. Air contains the gas oxygen, which is needed to get energy from food to power all of the body's vital life processes.

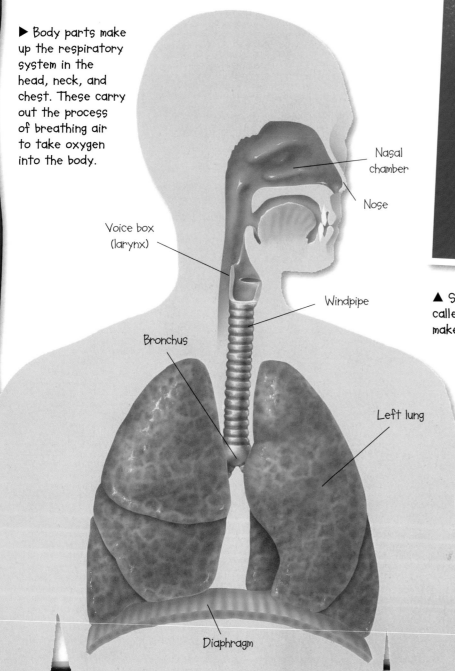

▶ Body parts make up the respiratory system in the head, neck, and chest. These carry out the process of breathing air to take oxygen into the body.

Nasal chamber

Nose

Voice box (larynx)

Windpipe

Bronchus

Left lung

Diaphragm

▲ Scuba divers wear special breathing apparatus called "aqua lungs." They control their breathing to make their oxygen supply last as long as possible.

1,084 Parts of the body that work together to carry out a main task are called a system—so the parts that carry out breathing are the respiratory system. These parts are the nose, throat, windpipe, the air tubes or bronchi in the chest, and the lungs.

1,085 The nose is the entrance for fresh air to the lungs—and the exit for stale air from the lungs. The soft, moist lining inside the nose makes air warmer and damper, which is better for the lungs. Tiny bits of floating dust and germs stick to the lining or the hairs in the nose, making the air cleaner.

▼ When playing the trumpet, the diaphragm and chest control the air flowing in and out of the lungs.

1,086 The windpipe, or trachea, is a tube leading from the back of the nose and mouth, down to the lungs. It has about 20 C-shaped hoops of cartilage in its wall to keep it open, like a vacuum cleaner hose. Otherwise the pressure of body parts in the neck and chest would squash it shut.

1,087 At the top of the windpipe, making a bulge at the front of the neck, is the voice box or larynx. It has two stiff flaps, vocal cords, which stick out from its sides. Normally these flaps are apart for easy breathing. But muscles in the voice box can pull the flaps almost together. As air passes through the narrow slit between them it makes the flaps shake or vibrate—and this is the sound of your voice.

HUMMMMMM!

You will need:

stopwatch

Do you think making sounds with your voice box uses more air than breathing? Find out by following this experiment.

1. Take a deep breath in, then breathe out at your normal rate, for as long as you can. Time the out-breath.

2. Take a similar deep breath in, then hum as you breathe out, again for as long as you can. Time the hum.

3. Try the same while whispering your favorite song, then again when singing.

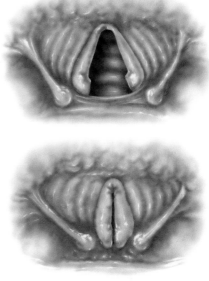

▲ The vocal cords are held apart for breathing (top) and pulled together for speech (bottom).

Breathing parts

1,088 The main parts of the respiratory (breathing) system are the two lungs in the chest. Each one is shaped like a tall cone, with the pointed end at shoulder level.

1,089 Air comes in and out of the lungs along the windpipe, which branches at its base to form two main air tubes, the bronchi. One goes to each lung. Inside the lung, each bronchus divides again and again, becoming narrower each time. Finally the air tubes, thinner than hairs, end at groups of tiny "bubbles" called alveoli.

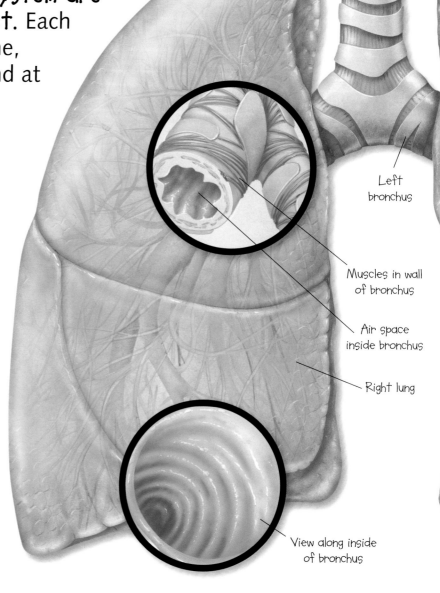

Left bronchus

Muscles in wall of bronchus

Air space inside bronchus

Right lung

View along inside of bronchus

1,090 There are more than 200 million tiny air bubbles, or alveoli, in each lung. Inside, oxygen from breathed-in air passes through the very thin linings of the alveoli to equally tiny blood vessels on the other side. The blood carries the oxygen away, around the body. At the same time a waste substance, carbon dioxide, seeps through the blood vessel, into the alveoli. As you breathe out, the lungs blow out the carbon dioxide.

1,091 Breathing needs muscle power! The main breathing muscle is the dome-shaped diaphragm at the base of the chest. To breathe in, it becomes flatter, making the lungs bigger, so they suck in air down the windpipe. At the same time, rib muscles lift the ribs, also making the lungs bigger. To breathe out, the diaphragm and rib muscles relax. The stretched lungs spring back to their smaller size and blow out stale air.

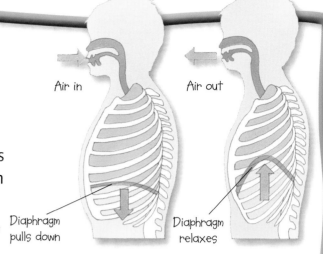

Air in   Air out

Diaphragm pulls down   Diaphragm relaxes

▲ Breathing uses two main sets of muscles, the diaphragm and those between the ribs.

▶ After great activity, the body breathes faster and deeper, to replace the oxygen used by the muscles for energy.

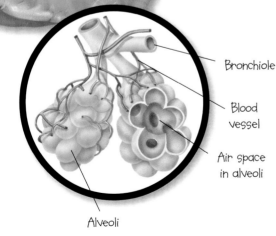

Bronchiole

Blood vessel

Air space in alveoli

Alveoli

▲ Inside each lung, the main bronchus divides again and again, into thousands of narrower airways called bronchioles.

1,092 As you rest or sleep, each breath sends about one pint of air in and out, 15 to 20 times each minute. After great activity, such as running a race, you need more oxygen. So you take deeper breaths faster—6 pints or more of air, 50 times or more each minute.

The hungry body

1,093 All machines need fuel to make them go, and the body is like a living machine whose fuel is food. Food gives us energy for our body processes inside, and for breathing, moving, talking, and every other action we make. Food also provides raw materials that the body uses to grow, maintain itself, and repair daily wear and tear.

1,094 We would not put the wrong fuel into a car engine, so we should not put unsuitable foods into the body. A healthy diet needs a wide variety of foods, which have lots of vital nutrients. Too much of one single food may be unhealthy, especially if that food is very fatty or greasy. Too much of all foods is also unhealthy, making the body overweight and increasing the risk of illnesses.

▶ It is important for children to learn how to cook healthily. Grilling or barbecuing food is much healthier than frying it.

▲ Fresh fruits such as bananas, and vegetables such as carrots, have lots of vitamins, minerals, and fiber, and are good for the body in lots of ways.

▼ Foods such as bread, pasta, and rice contain lots of starch, which is a useful energy source.

1,095 There are six main kinds of nutrients in foods, and the body needs balanced amounts of all of them.

- Proteins are needed for growth and repair, and for strong muscles and other parts.
- Carbohydrates, such as sugars and starches, give plenty of energy.
- Some fats are important for general health and energy.
- Vitamins help the body to fight germs and disease.
- Minerals are needed for strong bones and teeth and also healthy blood.
- Fiber is important for good digestion and to prevent certain bowel disorders.

◀ Fish, low-fat meats such as chicken, and dairy produce such as cheese all contain plenty of valuable proteins.

FOOD FOR THOUGHT

Which of these meals do you think is healthier?

Meal A
Burger and lots of fries, followed by ice cream with cream and chocolate.

Meal B
Chicken, tomato, and a few fries, followed by fresh fruit salad with apple, banana, pear, and melon.

Answer: Meal B

▲ Fats and oily foods are needed in moderate amounts. Plant oils are healthier than fats and oils from animal sources.

Bite, chew, gulp

1,096 The hardest parts of your whole body are the ones that make holes in your food—teeth. They have a covering of whitish or yellowish enamel, which is stronger than most kinds of rocks! Teeth need to last a lifetime of biting, nibbling, gnashing, munching, and chewing. They are your own food processors.

1,097 There are four main shapes of teeth. The front ones are incisors, and each has a straight, sharp edge, like a spade or chisel, to cut through food. Next are canines, which are taller and more pointed, used mainly for tearing and pulling. Behind them are premolars and molars, which are lower and flatter with small bumps, for crushing and grinding.

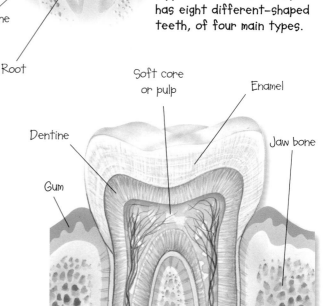

Incisor

Canine

Premolar

Molar

Jaw bone

Root

▲ In an adult, each side (left and right) of each jaw (upper and lower) usually has eight different-shaped teeth, of four main types.

▶ At the center of a tooth is living pulp, with many blood vessels and nerve endings that pass into the jaw bone.

Soft core or pulp

Enamel

Dentine

Jaw bone

Gum

1,098 A tooth may look almost dead, but it is very much alive. Under the enamel is slightly softer dentine. In the middle of the tooth is the dental pulp. This has blood vessels to nourish the whole tooth, and nerves that feel pressure, heat, cold, and pain. The lower part of the tooth, strongly fixed in the jaw bone, is the root. The enamel-covered part above the gum is the crown.

1,099 Teeth are very strong and tough, but they do need to be cleaned properly and regularly. Germs called bacteria live on old bits of food in the mouth. They make waste products which are acid and eat into the enamel and dentine, causing holes called cavities. Which do you prefer—cleaning your teeth after main meals and before bedtime, or the agony of toothache?

▶ Clean your teeth by brushing in different directions and then flossing between them. They will look better and stay healthier for longer.

▼ The first set of teeth lasts about ten years, while the second set can last ten times longer.

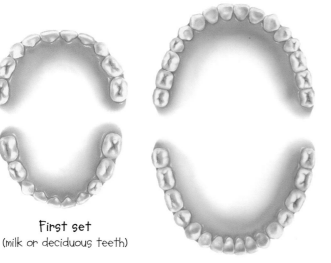

First set
(milk or deciduous teeth)

Second set
(adult or permanent set)

1,100 Teeth are designed to last a lifetime. Well, not quite, because the body has two sets. There are 20 small teeth in the first or baby set. The first ones usually appear above the gum by about six months of age, the last ones at three years old. As you and your mouth grow, the baby teeth fall out from about seven years old. They are replaced by 32 larger teeth in the adult set.

1,101 After chewing, food is swallowed into the gullet (esophagus). This pushes the food powerfully down through the chest, past the heart and lungs, into the stomach.

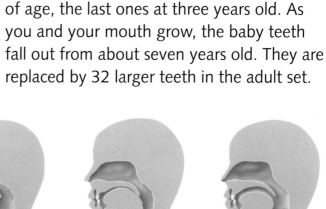

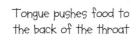

① Tongue pushes food to the back of the throat

② Throat muscles squeeze the food downward

③ The esophagus pushes food to the stomach

Food's long journey

1,102 The digestive system is like a tunnel about 30 feet long, through the body. It includes parts of the body that bite food, chew it, swallow it, churn it up, and break it down with natural juices and acids, take in its goodness, and then get rid of the leftovers.

1,103 The stomach is a bag with strong, muscular walls. It stretches as it fills with food and drink, and its lining makes powerful digestive acids and juices called enzymes, to attack the food. The muscles in its walls squirm and squeeze to mix the food and juices.

1,104 The stomach digests food for a few hours into a thick mush, which oozes into the small intestine. This is only 1.6 inches wide, but more than 16 feet long. It takes nutrients and useful substances through its lining, into the body.

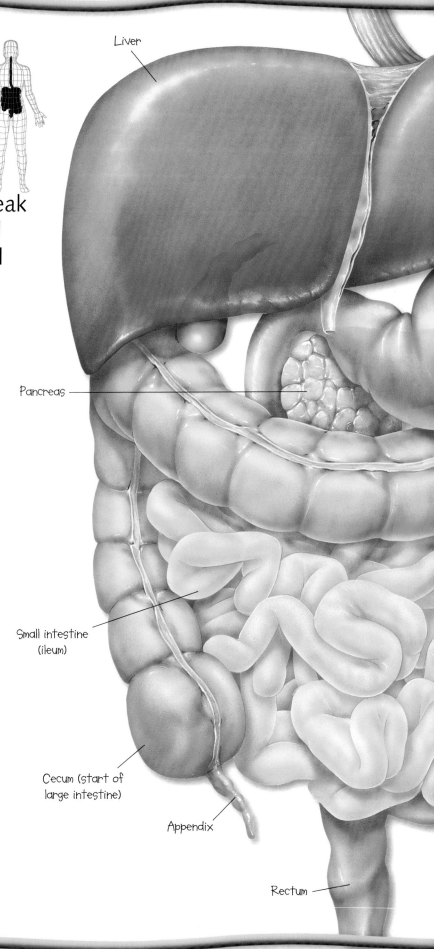

Liver

Pancreas

Small intestine (ileum)

Cecum (start of large intestine)

Appendix

Rectum

1,105 The large intestine follows the small one, and it is certainly wider, at about 2.4 inches, but much shorter, only 5 feet. It takes in fluids and a few more nutrients from the food, and then squashes what's left into brown lumps, ready to leave the body.

Stomach

Large intestine

Villus

Vessels inside villus

Vessels in intestine lining

▶ The lining of the small intestine has thousands of tiny fingerlike parts called the villi, which take nutrients from food into the blood and lymph system.

◀ The digestive parts almost fill the lower part of the main body, called the abdomen.

1,106 The liver and pancreas are also parts of the digestive system. The liver sorts out and changes the many nutrients from digestion, and stores some of them. The pancreas makes powerful digestive juices that pass to the small intestine to work on the food there.

I DON'T BELIEVE IT!

What's in the leftovers? The brown lumps called bowel motions or feces are only about one half undigested or leftover food. Some of the rest is rubbed-off parts of the stomach and intestine lining. The rest is millions of "friendly" but dead microbes (bacteria) from the intestine. They help to digest our food for us, and in return we give them a warm, food-filled place to live.

Blood in the body

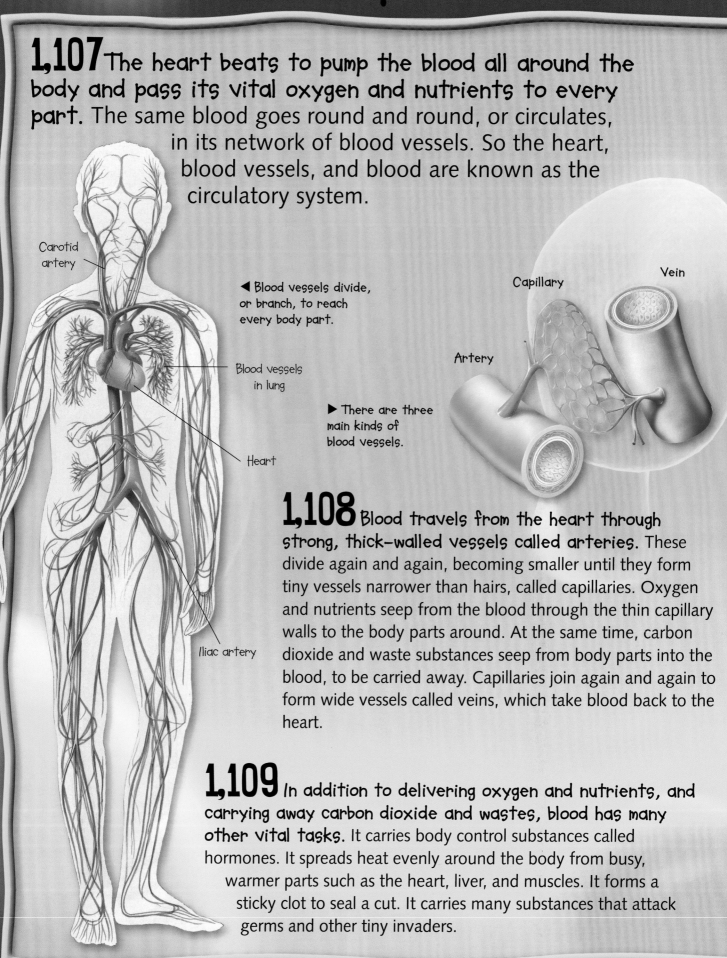

1,107 The heart beats to pump the blood all around the body and pass its vital oxygen and nutrients to every part. The same blood goes round and round, or circulates, in its network of blood vessels. So the heart, blood vessels, and blood are known as the circulatory system.

Carotid artery

◄ Blood vessels divide, or branch, to reach every body part.

Blood vessels in lung

▶ There are three main kinds of blood vessels.

Heart

Iliac artery

Capillary

Vein

Artery

1,108 Blood travels from the heart through strong, thick-walled vessels called arteries. These divide again and again, becoming smaller until they form tiny vessels narrower than hairs, called capillaries. Oxygen and nutrients seep from the blood through the thin capillary walls to the body parts around. At the same time, carbon dioxide and waste substances seep from body parts into the blood, to be carried away. Capillaries join again and again to form wide vessels called veins, which take blood back to the heart.

1,109 In addition to delivering oxygen and nutrients, and carrying away carbon dioxide and wastes, blood has many other vital tasks. It carries body control substances called hormones. It spreads heat evenly around the body from busy, warmer parts such as the heart, liver, and muscles. It forms a sticky clot to seal a cut. It carries many substances that attack germs and other tiny invaders.

1,110 Blood has four main parts. The largest is billions of tiny, saucer-shaped red cells, which make up almost half of the total volume of blood and carry oxygen. Second is the white cells, which clean the blood, prevent disease, and fight germs. The third part is billions of tiny platelets, which help blood to clot. Fourth is watery plasma, in which the other parts float.

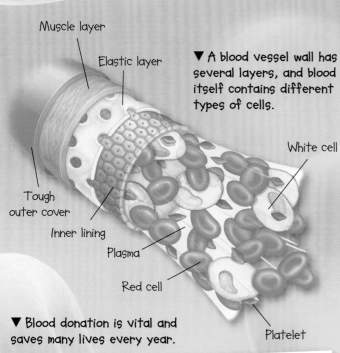

Muscle layer
Elastic layer
Tough outer cover
Inner lining
Plasma
Red cell
White cell
Platelet

▼ A blood vessel wall has several layers, and blood itself contains different types of cells.

▶ Each kidney has about one million tiny filters, called nephrons, in its outer layer, or cortex.

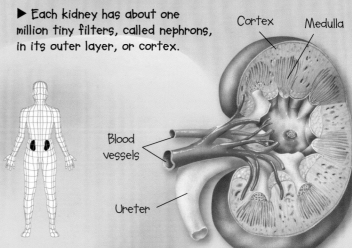

Cortex
Medulla
Blood vessels
Ureter

▼ Blood donation is vital and saves many lives every year.

A Positive

1,111 Blood is cleaned by two kidneys, situated in the middle of your back. They filter the blood and make a liquid called urine, which contains unwanted and waste substances, plus excess or "spare" water. The urine trickles from each kidney down a tube, the ureter, into a stretchy bag, the bladder. It's stored here until you can get rid of it—at your convenience.

The beating body

1,112 The heart is about as big as its owner's clenched fist. It is a hollow bag of very strong muscle, called cardiac muscle or myocardium. This muscle never tires. It contracts once every second or more often, all through life. The contraction, or heartbeat, squeezes blood inside the heart out into the arteries. As the heart relaxes it fills again with blood from the veins.

1,113 Inside, the heart is not one baglike pump, but two pumps side by side. The left pump sends blood all around the body, from head to toe, to deliver its oxygen (systemic circulation). The blood comes back to the right pump and is sent to the lungs, to collect more oxygen (pulmonary circulation). The blood returns to the left pump and starts the whole journey again.

From upper body

To upper body

Aorta (main artery)

Pulmonary artery to lung

To lung

From lung

Right atrium

Valve

Right ventricle

From lower body

To lower body

▶ The heart is two pumps side by side, and each pump has two chambers, the upper atrium and the lower ventricle.

1,114 Inside the heart are four sets of bendy flaps called valves. These open to let blood flow the right way. If the blood tries to move the wrong way, it pushes the flaps together and the valve closes. Valves make sure the blood flows the correct way, rather than sloshing to and fro, in and out of the heart, with each beat.

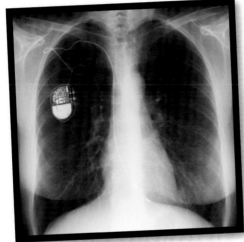

▶ This X-ray of a chest shows a pacemaker that has been implanted to control an irregular heartbeat.

1,115 The heart is the body's most active part, and it needs plenty of energy brought by the blood. The blood flows through small vessels, which branch across its surface and down into its thick walls. These are called the coronary vessels.

1,116 The heart beats at different rates, depending on what the body is doing. When the muscles are active they need more energy and oxygen, brought by the blood. So the heart beats faster, 120 times each minute or more. At rest, the heart slows to 60 to 80 beats per minute.

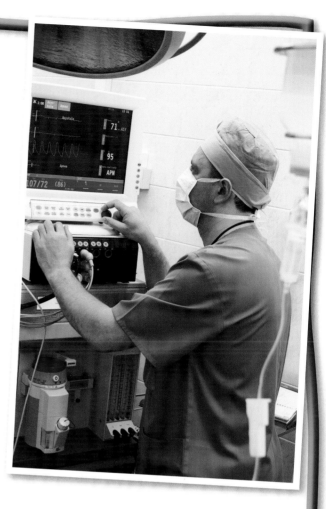

▲ Doctors use ECG machines to monitor the electrical activity of the heart.

HOW FAST IS YOUR HEARTBEAT?

You will need:
plastic funnel   tracing paper
plastic tube (like hose)   sticky-tape

You can hear your heart and count its beats with a sound-funnel device called a stethoscope.

1. Stretch the tracing paper over the funnel's wide end and tape in place. Push a short length of tube over the funnel's narrow end.

2. Place the funnel's wide end over your heart, on your chest, just to the left, and put the tube end to your ear. Listen to and count your heartbeat.

Looking and listening

1,117 **The body finds out about the world around it by its senses—and the main sense is eyesight.** The eyes detect the brightness, colors, and patterns of light rays, and change these into patterns of nerve signals that they send to the brain. More than half of the knowledge, information, and memories stored in the brain come into the body through the eyes.

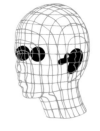

► The eye is moved by six tiny muscles, and inside, it is filled with a clear fluid, vitreous humor.

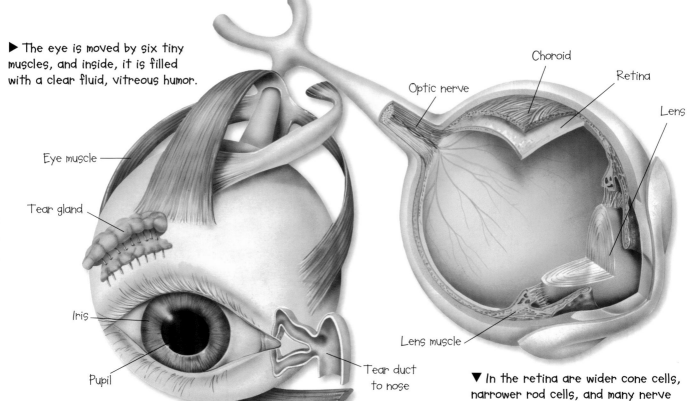

Eye muscle

Tear gland

Iris

Pupil

Choroid

Optic nerve

Retina

Lens

Lens muscle

Tear duct to nose

1,118 **Each eye is a ball about one inch across.** At the front is a clear dome, the cornea, which lets light through a small, dark-looking hole just behind it, the pupil. The light then passes through a pea-shaped lens, which bends the rays so they shine a clear picture onto the inside back of the eye, the retina. This has 125 million tiny cells, rods, and cones, which detect the light and make nerve signals to send along the optic nerve to the brain.

▼ In the retina are wider cone cells, narrower rod cells, and many nerve cells with long fibers connecting them.

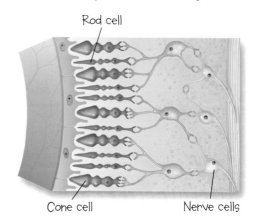

Rod cell

Cone cell

Nerve cells

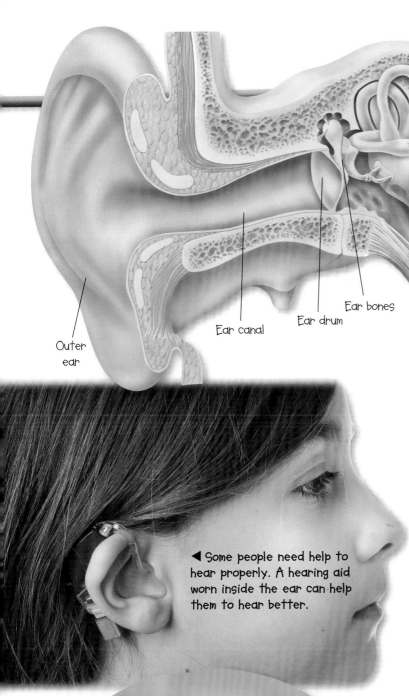

Semi-circular canal
(for balance)

Auditory
nerve

Cochlea

Air tube
to throat

Ear bones

Ear drum

Ear canal

Outer
ear

▲ Most of the small, delicate parts of the ear are inside the head, well protected by skull bones around them.

▶ The loudness, or volume, of sounds is measured in decibels (dB). Louder than about 90 dB can damage hearing.

Atom bomb 210 dB

Jet takeoff 140 dB

Thunder 100 dB

Talking 40 dB

Rustling leaves 10 dB

◀ Some people need help to hear properly. A hearing aid worn inside the ear can help them to hear better.

BRIGHT AND DIM

Look at your eyes in a mirror. See how the dark hole which lets in light, the pupil, is quite small. The colored part around the pupil, the iris, is a ring of muscle.

Close your eyes for a minute, then open them and look carefully. Does the pupil quickly get smaller?

While the eyes were closed, the iris made the pupil bigger, to try and let in more light, so you could try to see in the darkness. As you open your eyes, the iris makes the pupil smaller again, to prevent too much light from dazzling you.

1,119 The ear flap funnels sound waves along a short tunnel, the ear canal to the eardrum. As sound waves hit the eardrum it shakes or vibrates, and passes the vibrations to a row of three tiny bones. These are the ear ossicles, the smallest bones in the body. They also vibrate and pass on the vibrations to another part, the cochlea.

1,120 Inside the cochlea, the vibrations pass through fluid and shake rows of thousands of tiny hairs that grow from specialized hair cells. As the hairs vibrate, the hair cells make nerve signals, which flash along the auditory nerve to the brain.

Smelling and tasting

▼ The parts that carry out smelling are in the roof of the large chamber inside the nose.

Olfactory cells

Nasal cavity

Mucus lining

1,121 You cannot see smells, which are tiny particles floating in the air—but your nose can smell them. Your nose can detect more than 10,000 different scents, odors, and fragrances. Smell is useful because it warns us if food is bad or rotten, and perhaps dangerous to eat. That's why we sniff a new or strange food item before trying it.

1,122 Smell particles drift with breathed-in air into the nose and through the nasal chamber behind it. At the top of the chamber are two patches of lining, each about the area of a thumbnail and with 5 million olfactory cells. The particles land on their sticky hairs, and if they fit into landing sites called receptors there, like a key into a lock, then nerve signals flash along the olfactory nerve to the brain.

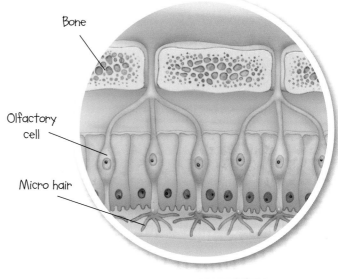

Bone

Olfactory cell

Micro hair

▶ Olfactory (smell) cells have micro hairs facing down into the nasal chamber, which detect smell particles landing on them.

486

1,123 The body's most flexible muscle is also the one which is coated with 10,000 microsensors for taste—the tongue. Each microsensor is a taste bud shaped like a tiny onion. Most taste buds are along the tip, sides, and rear upper surface of the tongue. They are scattered around the much larger flaps and lumps on the tongue, which are called papillae.

◄ The tongue is sensitive to flavors, texture, and temperature.

1,124 Taste works in a similar way to smell, but it detects flavor particles in foods and drinks. The particles touch tiny hairs sticking up from hair cells in the taste buds. If the particles fit into receptors there, then the hair cell makes nerve signals, which go along the facial and other nerves to the brain.

SWEET AND SOUR

The tongue detects a huge range of flavors, which can be categorized into several key flavor areas, such as sweet or salty. Which of these foods is sweet, salty, bitter, or sour?

1. Coffee 2. Lemon 3. Bacon
4. Ice cream

Answers:
1. bitter 2. sour 3. salty 4. sweet

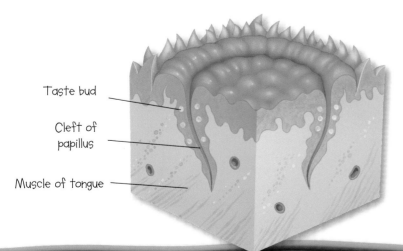

Taste bud

Cleft of papillus

Muscle of tongue

◄ The large pimplelike lumps at the back of the tongue, called papillae, have tiny taste buds in their deep clefts.

The nervous body

1,125 The body is not quite a "bag of nerves," but it does contain thousands of miles of these pale, shiny threads. Nerves carry tiny electrical pulses known as nerve signals or neural messages. They form a vast information-sending network that reaches every part, almost like the body's own Internet.

Brain

Spinal cord

Sciatic nerve

Tibial nerve

1,126 Each nerve is a bundle of much thinner parts called nerve fibers. Like wires in a telephone cable, these carry their own tiny electrical nerve signals. A typical nerve signal has a strength of 0.1 volts (one fifteenth as strong as a torch battery). The slowest nerve signals travel about 1.6 feet each second, the fastest at more than 328 feet per second.

Axon

◀ Nerves branch from the brain and spinal cord to every body part.

Dendrites

Synapse (junction between nerve cells)

1,127 All nerve signals are similar, but there are two main kinds, depending on where they are going. Sensory nerve signals travel from the sensory parts (eyes, ears, nose, tongue, and skin) to the brain. Motor nerve signals travel from the brain out to the muscles, to make the body move about.

▶ The brain and nerves are made of billions of specialized cells, nerve cells or neurons. Each has many tiny branches, dendrites, to collect nerve messages, and a longer, thicker branch, the axon or fiber, to pass on the messages.

1,128 Hormones are part of the body's inner control system. A hormone is a chemical made by a gland. It travels in the blood and affects other body parts, for example, making them work faster or release more of their product.

1,129 The main hormonal gland, the pituitary, is also the smallest. Just under the brain, it has close links with the nervous system. It mainly controls other hormonal glands. One is the thyroid in the neck, which affects the body's growth and how fast its chemical processes work. The pancreas controls how the body uses energy by its hormone, insulin. The adrenal glands are involved in the body's balance of water, minerals, and salts, and how we react to stress and fear.

▲ Sports such as snowboarding cause us to produce more adrenaline due to excitement and fear.

◄ Female and male bodies have much the same hormone-making glands, except for the reproductive parts—ovaries in the female (left) and testes in the male (right).

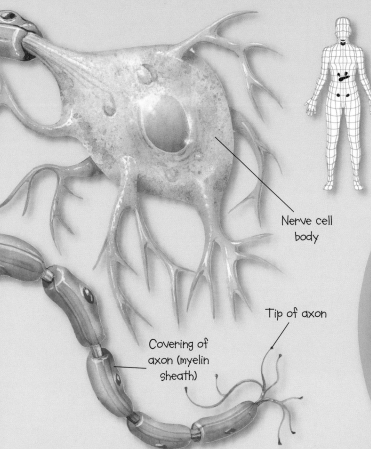

Nerve cell body

Tip of axon

Covering of axon (myelin sheath)

TIME TO REACT!

You will need:

friend ruler

1. Ask a friend to hold a ruler by the highest measurement so it hangs down. Put your thumb and fingers level with the other end, ready to grab.

2. When your friend lets go grasp it and measure where your thumb is on the ruler. Swap places so your friend has a go.

3. The person who grabs the ruler nearest its lower end has the fastest reactions. To grab the ruler, nerve signals travel from the eye, to the brain, and back to the muscles in the arm and hand.

The brainy body

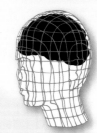

1,130 Your brain is as big as your two fists side by side. It's the place where you think, learn, work out problems, remember, feel happy and sad, wonder, worry, have ideas, sleep, and dream.

▶ The two wrinkled hemispheres (halves) of the cerebrum, where thinking happens, are the largest brain parts.

1,131 The brain looks like a wrinkly lump of gray-pink Jell-O! On average, it weighs about 3 pounds. It doesn't move, but its amazing nerve activity uses up one fifth of all the energy needed by the body.

▼ Different areas or centers of the brain's outer layer, the cerebral cortex, deal with messages from and to certain parts of the body.

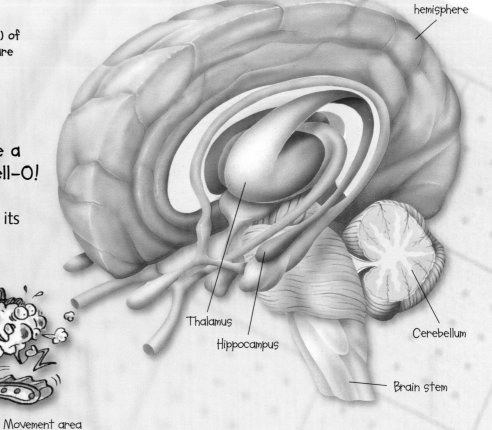

Cerebral hemisphere

Thalamus

Hippocampus

Cerebellum

Brain stem

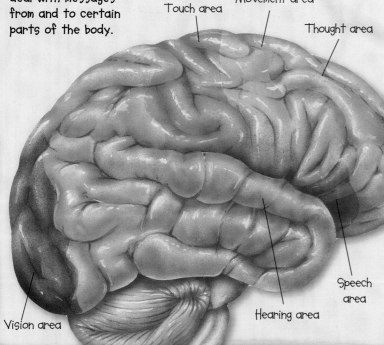

Touch area

Movement area

Thought area

Vision area

Hearing area

Speech area

1,132 The main part of the brain is its bulging, wrinkled upper part, the cerebrum. Different areas of its surface (cerebral cortex) deal with nerve signals to and from different parts of the body. For example, messages from the eyes pass to the lower rear part of the cerebrum, called the visual center. They are sorted here as the brain cells work out what the eyes are seeing. There are also areas for touch, hearing, taste, and other body processes.

1,133 The cerebellum is the rounded, wrinkled part at the back of the brain. It processes messages from the motor center, sorting and coordinating them in great detail, to send to the body's hundreds of muscles. This is how we learn skilled, precise movements such as writing, skateboarding, or playing music (or all three), almost without thinking.

1,134 The brain stem is the lower part of the brain, where it joins the body's main nerve, the spinal cord. The brain stem controls basic processes vital for life, like breathing, heartbeat, digesting food, and removing wastes.

▲ Our brains allow us to draw from memory, expressing emotions.

1,135 The brain really does have "brain waves." Every second it receives, sorts, and sends millions of nerve signals. Special pads attached to the head can detect these tiny electrical pulses. They are shown on a screen or paper strip as wavy lines called an EEG, electro-encephalogram.

▼ The brain's "waves" or EEG recordings change, depending on whether the person is alert and thinking hard, resting, falling asleep, or deeply asleep.

I DON'T BELIEVE IT!

The brain never sleeps! EEG waves show that it is almost as busy at night as when we are awake. It still controls heartbeat, breathing, and digestion. It also sifts through the day's events and stores memories.

The healthy body

1,136 No one wants to be ill—and it is very easy to cut down the risk of becoming sick or developing disease. For a start, the body needs the right amounts of different foods, especially fresh foods like vegetables and fruits. And not too much food either, or it becomes unhealthily fat.

1,137 Another excellent way to stay well is regular sport or exercise. Activity keeps the muscles powerful, the bones strong, and the joints flexible. If it speeds up your breathing and heartbeat, it keeps your lungs and heart healthy too.

1,138 Germs are everywhere—in the air, on our bodies, and on almost everything we touch. If we keep clean by showering or bathing, and especially if we wash our hands after using the toilet and before eating, then germs have less chance to attack us.

1,139 Health is not only in the body, it's in the mind. Too much worry and stress can cause many illnesses, such as headaches and digestive upsets. This is why it's so important to talk about troubles and share them with someone who can help.

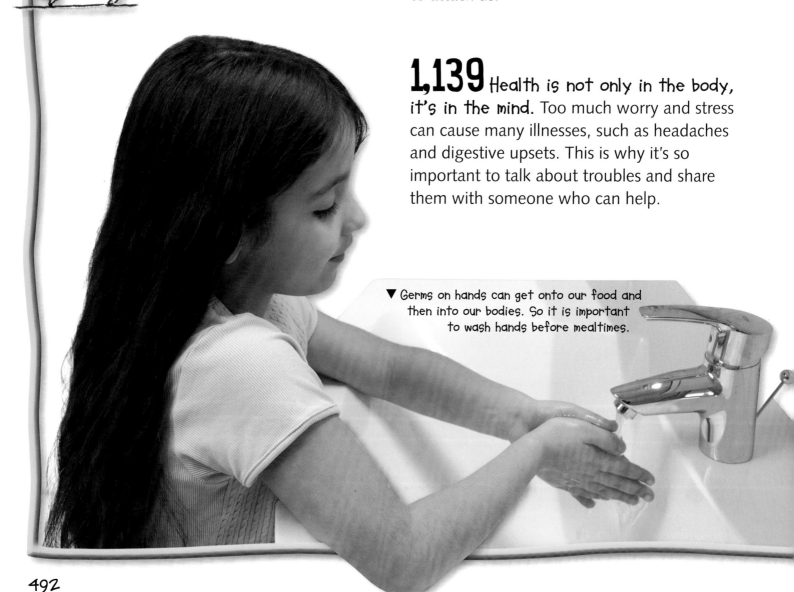

▼ Germs on hands can get onto our food and then into our bodies. So it is important to wash hands before mealtimes.

1,140 Doctors and nurses help us to recover from sickness, and they also help prevent illness. Regular checkups at the dentist, optician, and health center are vital. For most people immunizations (vaccinations) also help to protect against diseases. It is good to report any health problem early, before they become too serious to treat.

▼ In some immunizations, dead versions of a germ are put into the body using a syringe, so the body can develop resistance to them without suffering from the disease they cause.

1,141 Old age is getting older! More people live to be 100 years or more and for many of them, their bodies are still working well. How would you like to spend your 100th birthday?

▼ Exercise keeps the body fit and healthy, and it should be fun too. It is always best to reduce risks of having an accident by wearing a cycle helmet for example.

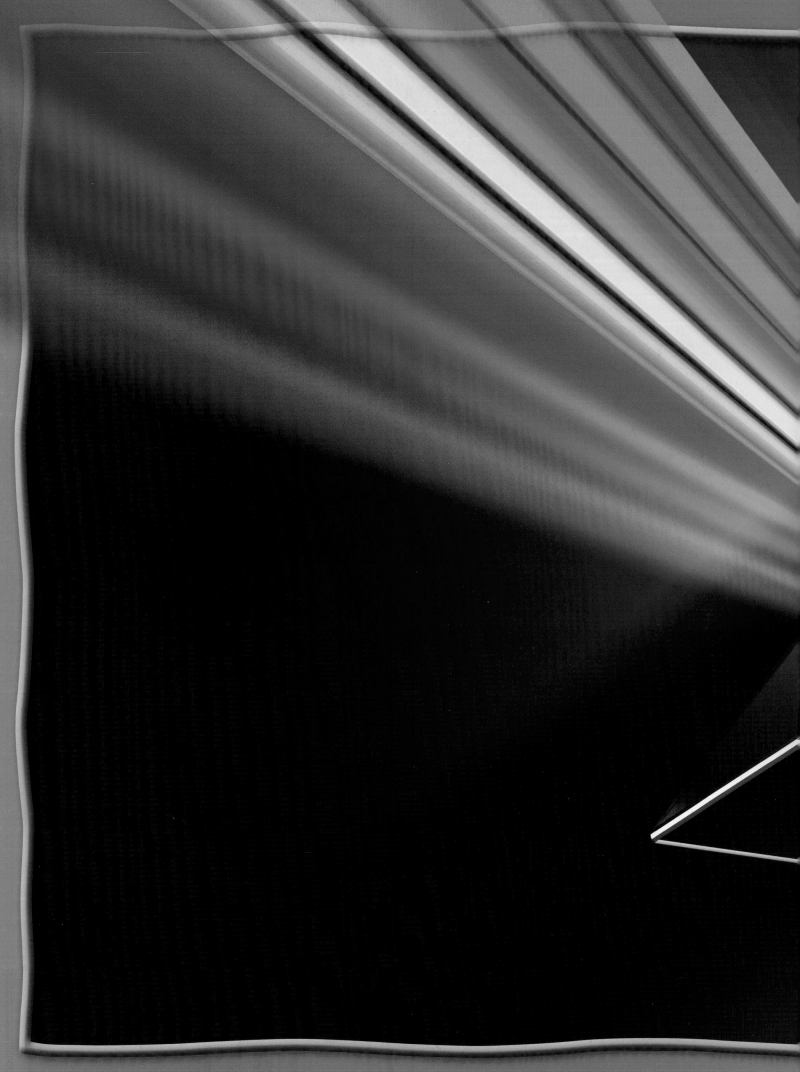

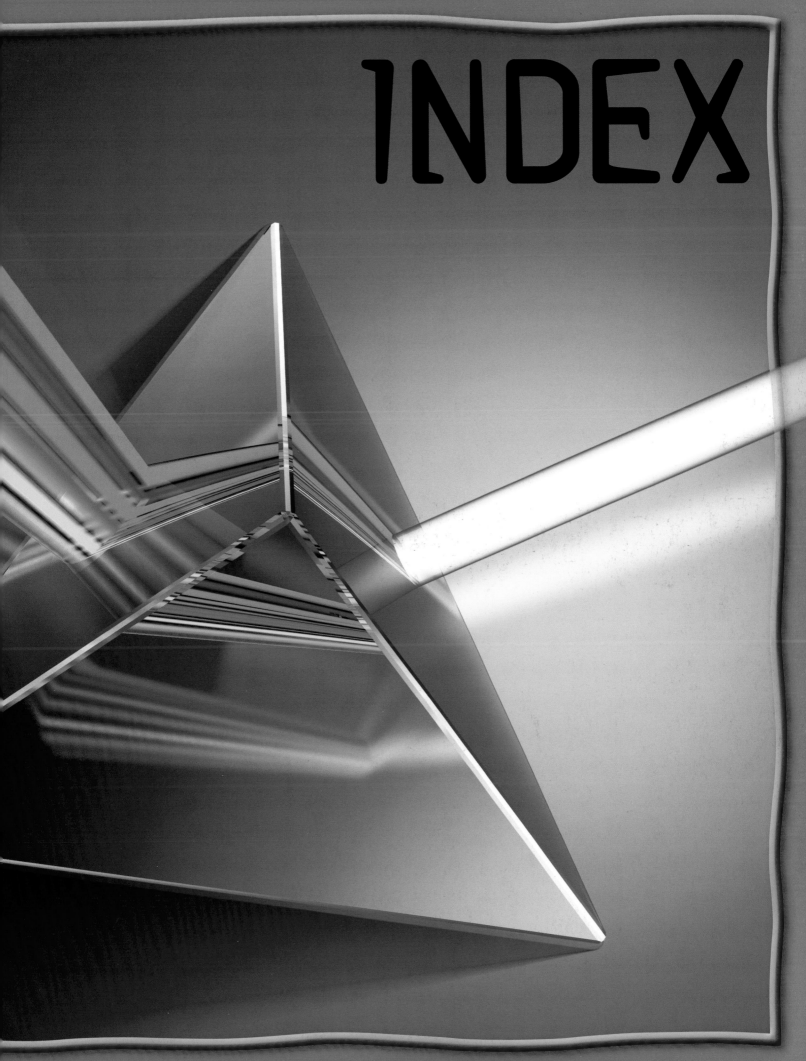

INDEX

Index

Entries in **bold** refer to main subject entries. Entries in *italics* refer to illustrations.

A

abacuses 123, *123*
acacia trees 393, *393*, 396, *396*
acceleration **330–331**
acid rain 409, *409*
acids 38, 49, *49*, 60, *60*
acoustics **30–31**
adaptive optics 236
aerial roots 385, *385*
agriculture 406
ailerons *267, 270, 271, 277*
air 136, 147
airbags 312, 331, *331*, 333
air brakes 332, *332, 333*
air traffic controllers 273, *273*, 279, 286
Airbus A380 264, *264*, 277
Airbus Super Transporter Beluga 298, *298*
aircraft carriers *285*, 292, *292*
air currents *323*
airliners 258, 262, 263, *263, 264, 265, 267, 269, 272, 274, 275*, **276–277**, *297*, 298
airports *28, 29*, 272, 277, **278–279**, *278, 279*, 292
airships 262, *262*, **282–283**, *283*
albatrosses **449**, *449*
alchemy 75
Alcock, John 261
Aldrin, Buzz 182
algae 380, *380*, 396, 398, 400, 401, *401*
algebra **69**
alkalis 49, *49, 51*
al-Kharizmi **69**
alpine nutcrackers 396
aluminum *46*, 51, *51*
alveoli **472**, *473*
amateur astronomy **252–253**

Amazon River 314
amphibians *355*, 361, *361*, 362, **416**, *416*, 419, 432
Andromeda galaxy *232*
animals
   displays **431**
   homes 402, *402* **436–437**
   mating **432**
   mimicry **426**
   molting **435**
   offspring 344, *344*, 348, *348*
   relationship with plants **396–397**, *396, 397*
   signals **496–497**, *496, 497*
   speed 305, **316–317**, *316, 317*
Ankylosaurus 363
Anning, Mary **77**, *77*
Anomalocaris 355, 359, *359*
antennae, animal **421**
antennas, spacecraft *189, 191*
antibiotics **83**, *83*
Antonov AN-225 272, 288, *288*
ants 396, *396*
apes 345, *345*, 346, *368*
Apollo 11 mission 170–171
Apollo missions **182–183**
Arber, Werner 93
Archaeopteryx 355, 364, *364*
Archimedes **66**, **67**, *67*
Arctic poppies *398*
Ardipithecus ramidus 368
Ares rocket 297
Argentinosaurus 363, *363*
Ariane 5 rocket **162**, *187, 296*
armadillos 427, *427*
Armstrong, Neil 182
arrows 98, 108, 109, 119
arteries **480**, *480*, 482
Arthropleura 360, *360*
artificial selection **370–371**
asphalt 48, *48*
asteroid belt 153

asteroids 141, **149**, *176–177*, **208–209**, *208–209*
astrolabe **68**
astronauts 136,164–165, 166, 182
   floating/no weight 165
   journey to Mars 145
   and Moon **143**, 170–171
   sleeping bags 165, *165*
Atacama Desert 239
Atacama Large Millimeter Array (ALMA) 254
Atlantis space shuttle *311*
atmospheres 196
atoms 36, 38, *38*, 50, *50*, 51, *51*, **52–53**, *52, 53*, *65*, **79**, **86–87**, 94, *95*, 311, 329
   scientists 52
Australopithecus afarensis 368
Australopithecus africanus 368
Avery, Oswald 92
axes 101, *101*, 110, *110*
axles 22, *22*, 27, 46, *53*
Aztec worship of Quetzalcoatl 223

B

babies
   animal *432*, 433, *433*, 436
   human **454–455**, *456*
backbone *462*, 463, 465
bacteria 73, 83, *83*, 354, 357, 477, 479
bagpipes 127, *127*
Baird, John Logie 129
ballistae 118
balloons 260, *260*, 262, 268, **282–283**, *282, 283*, 291
bamboo 379, *379*
Bannister, Roger 321, *321*
bases 49, *49*
bats *31*, 388, 417, 419, 424, *424, 443*
batteries 27, 38, *38*, 49, **80**, **81**

Index

Index

Index

Index

Index

Index

Acknowledgments

All artworks are from the Miles Kelly Artwork Bank

The publishers would like to thank the following sources for the use of their photographs:
Key: t = top, b = bottom, c = center, l = left, r = right, m = main, bg = background

Cover (front, tl) Tsekhmister/Shutterstock.com, (tr) Benjamin Albiach Galan/Shutterstock.com, (b) NASA/Science Photo Library, (spine) Arsgera/Shutterstock.com, (back, tl) Kjpargeter/Shutterstock.com, (cr) SARANS/Shutterstock.com, (bl) Leigh Prather/Shutterstock.com

Alamy 66(l) Guy Bell; 85(c) Photo Researchers; 90(bl) Pictorial Press Ltd; 199(tr) Keith Morris; 273(b) Antony Nettle; 379(tl) Derek Harris; 390(b) Science Photo Library; 400(b) Stephen Frink Collection; 432(bl) Antje Schulte – Spiders and Co.; 448(tr) Aditya "Dicky" Singh

Ardea 368(bl) Jean Michel Labat

Corbis 68(b) Blue Lantern Studio; 185 Roger Ressmeye; 195(t) Michael Benson/Kinetikon Pictures; 204(t) Bill Ingalls/NASA/Handout/CNP; 205(t) Roger Ressmeyer; 223(c) Araldo de Luca; 237(tl) IAC/GTC; 266 Bettmand; 273(t) Ron Watts; 274 Arne Dedart/dpa; 281(t) Michel Setboun; 283(b) Lowell Georgia; 285; 288(t) George Hall, (b) George Hall; 289 Charles O'Rear; 314–315 Thilo Brunner; 320(bl) PCN Photography; 321(tr) Hutton-Deutsch Collection; 324(bc) Bettmann; 330–331(c) Leo Mason; 334–335 Christopher Pasatieri/Reuters; 352–353 Louie Psihoyos; 398(bl) Wayne Lynch/All Canada Photos; 402(c) David Ponton/Design Pics; 408 Martin Harvey

Dreamstime 32 Silverstore; 33(bg) Adam1975; 35(t) Paha_l; 48(tr) Zoom-zoom; 232(c) Kramer-1; 240(t) Silverstore; 345(crab) Mailthepic; 379(tr) Surz01; 397(persimmon) Carla720, (ragwort) Rmorijn; 402(br) Egonzitter; 405(rubber tree) Braendan, (tyre) Chuyu; 416(fish) Goodolga; 455(b) Alangh; 456(b) Velkol; 471 Tobkatrina; 477 Kati1313

European Space Agency (ESA) 174 Mars Express; 188(r) D. Ducros; 203 Mars Express D. Ducros; 204–205(b); 207(bl) 2007 MPS/DLR-PF/IDA; 213(tl) ESA/NASA/JPL/University of Arizona; 215(t) C. Carreau, (tr) AOES Medialab

FLPA 348(t) Rob Reijnen/Minden Pictures; 349(vegetarian free finch, woodpecker finch) Tui De Roy/Minden Pictures; 351(br) Thomas Marent/Minden Pictures; 370 Paul Sawer; 391(br) Wayne Hutchinson; 398(tr) Hiroya Minakuchi/Minden Pictures; 399(tr) Grant Dixon/Minden Pictures, (c) Tim Fitzharris/Minden Pictures; 405 Konrad Wothe/Imagebroker; 424–425 Elliott Neep; 428(c) Chris Stenger/Minden Pictures; 429(t) ImageBroker/Imagebroker; 430(r) Piotr Naskrecki/Minden Pictures; 431(br) Paul Sawer; 433(b) Mitsuaki Iwago/Minden Pictures; 435(b) Claus Meyer/Minden Pictures; 441(b) ImageBroker/Imagebroker; 443(t) Robin Chittenden; 446 Suzi Eszterhas/Minden Pictures, (bl) Frans Lanting; 447(tr) Yva Momatiuk & John Eastcott/Minden Pictures; 448(c) Pete Oxford/Minden Pictures, (b) Gerry Ellis/Minden Pictures; 449(t) Colin Marshall, (b) Thomas Marent/Minden Pictures

Fotolia.com 27(tl) Paul Heasman, (cr) Dariusz Kopestynski; 35(b) photlook; 48(third from tr); 70(m) MalDix; 70(t, bg) Alexey Khromushin; 100–101(tc) Alexey Khromushin; 106(b) Rafa Irusta; 117(b); 123(cr); 125(t); 126(cl); 178(bl) D.aniel; 229(tl) Georgios Kollidas, (r) Konstantin Sutyagin; 232(tc) pdtnc; 232–233(bg) Jenny Solomon; 252(clockwise from bl) Stephen Coburn, Petar Ishmeriev, pelvidge, Mats Tooming; 265 sharply_done; 267(b) Chris Fourie; 281(b) Jetpics; 282(b) IL; 322–323(bg) Sharpshot; 340(c); 341(bl) Kirsty Pargeter; 353, 356, 357, 366, 367, 368, 369 (paper) Alexey Khromushin; 383(round leaf) AndreyTTL; 402(butterfly) Dmytro Fomin, (squirrel) Dave Timms; 405(banana) Darren Hester, (cocoa pod) Shariff Che'Lah, (chocolate) Maksim Shebeko; 416(reptile) Paul Murphy; 465 chrisharvey; 467 Alexander Yakovlev; 485(r) Andres Rodriguez

Getty Images 12(c) Stocktrek Images; 66(t) Will & Deni McIntyre; 74(t) Mark Ralston, (c) Barcroft Media/Contributor; 82(tr) Gaston Melingue; 201(br) Time & Life Pictures; 200–201(bg) SSPL via Getty Images; 212 Time & Life Pictures; 302–303(c) Getty; 308(tr); 309(br); 311 Barcroft Media; 313(tr) AFP; 315(tc) Carsten Peter; 318–319 Dennis O'Clair; 321(b) AFP; 322(tr) AFP; 324(cl) Time & Life Pictures; 325(b) National Geographic; 326(tr) AFP; 328–329(b); 344(l) Jim Zuckerman; 372 Spencer Grant; 373(b) Ariadne Van Zandbergen; 404(c) Visuals Unlimited, Inc./Thomas Marent

iStockphoto.com 30–31(bg) Kevin Smith; 110–111(bg) Sander Kamp; 119(br) Duncan Walker; 128(br) HultonArchive; 130(tl) hohos; 130(bl) James Steidl; 184–185(bg) Nicholas Belton; 192(r) Jan Rysavy; 228–229(bg) Duncan Walker; 229(br) Steven Wynn; 230(cr) Steven Wynn; 231(br) Steven Wynn; 232(tl) HultonArchive; 233(tc) Duncan Walker; 357(tr) Jouke van der Meer; 376(bl), 377(tr) spxChrome; 387(cr) Sergey Chushkin, (titan arum) Tim Messick; 392(b) JPhilipson, (l) Ruud de Man; 397(horse chestnut) Marko Roeper; 402(badger) Chris Crafter; 406(t) Terraxplorer; 418(bg) Miguel Angelo Silva; 457(b) Rosemarie Gearhart

NASA 90(c) NASA/JPL/California Institute of Technology; 91(c) NASA/JPL-Caltech; 94(t) NASA/JPL-Caltech; 138(t) NASA-JPL, (c) Goddard Space Flight Center Scientific Visualization Studio; 139(tl); 140–141 NASA-JPL; 143 JPL-Caltech; 148 NASA-HQ-GRIN; 152 T. Rector (University of Alaska Anchorage), Z. Levay and L.Frattare (Space Telescope Science Institute) and National Optical Astronomy Observatory/Association of Universities for Research in Astronomy/National Science Foundation; 155(t) NASA-GSFC, (b) GReatest Images of NASA (NASA-HQ-GRIN); 157; 158 NASA-JPL; 159 NASA/STScI; 161 X-ray: NASA/CXC/ M.Markevitch et al. Optical: NASA/STScI; Magellan/U.Arizona/ D.Clowe et al. Lensing Map: NASA/STScI; ESO WFI; Magellan/ U.Arizona/D.Clowe et al.; 162 NASA/Tony Gray & Robert Murray; 162–163(b); 163; 165; 167; 172(l) NASA-

JPL; 179(b) JPL-Caltech; 183(bl); 184(c) JPL-Caltech, (t) NASA Langley Research Center (NASA-LaRC); 184–185(b); 188(bl); 188–189(t) Johns Hopkins University Applied Physics Laboratory/Southwest Research Institute; 190 JPL/University of Arizona; 192(c); 193 Saturn JPL, Borrelly photograph JPL, Uranus, Neptune, Voyager 2 gold disk, Voyager 2 JPL-Caltech, Deep Space 1; 194(bl) STEREO; 195; 197(bl), (br); 199 NASA/JPL/Cornell University/Maas Digital; 200(bl) JPL/Cornell; 202–203(bg) JPL/ Cornell; 202(bl) Goddard Space Flight Center Scientific Visualization Studio, Mariner 4 JPL, Mariner 9 JPL, Mars 3 Russian Space Research Institute (IKI), Viking lander, Mars Global Surveyor; 203 Sojourner JPL-Caltech, Spirit/Opportunity rover JPL, Mars Reconnaissance Orbiter JPL; 204–205(bg); 209(br); 211(c), (b); 214(bl) Johns Hopkins University Applied Physics Laboratory/ Southwest Research Institute; 215(br); 216–217(bg) JPL-Caltech/T. Pyle (SSC); 230(bl) NASA-JPL; 232(cl) NASA-HQ-GRIN, (bc) NASA-JPL, (br) NASA-JPL; 237(br) NASA-JPL; 242–243(c) NASA-JPL; 243(tr) NASA Marshall Space Flight Center (NASA-MSFC), (bl) NASA-JPL; 246 NASA-JPL; 249; 250(br) NASA-JPL; 251(cr) NASA-JPL, (br) NASA-JPL; 299(b); 336(br) NASA Kennedy Space Center (NASA-KSC)

National Geographic Stock 376–377 Frans Lanting; 400(br) James P. Blair

Nature Picture Library 310(cl) Robin Chittenden; 345(b) Andy Rouse; 388 Solvin Zankl; 390–391 Jurgen Freund; 390(cl) Neil Lucas; 400 Tim Fitzharris/Minden Pictures; 418(c) Brandon Cole; 423(b) Brandon Cole; 427(b) Nature Production; 434 Jurgen Freund; 435(r) Anup Shah; 444–445 Fred Olivier; 445(r) Shattil & Rozinski

NHPA 350 Gerard Lacz; 352(cl) Theodore Clutter; 393(tr) Anthony Bannister

Newscom 345(tl) Album/Prisma; 411(tr) www.westend61.de/Westend61/Florian Kopp

Photolibrary 33(b) Laguna Design; 226–227 Steve Vidler; 385(t); 389(tr); 394 Ed Reschke; 397(r) Natalie Tepper

Photoshot 312–313 UPPA; 425(l) Woodfall; 440–441 NHPA

Reuters 179(t) Kimimasa Mayama

Rex Features 93(cr) Jason Rasgon; 127(c); 197(tl); 205(br) NASA; 216(tl) Everett Collection, (c) Paramount/Everett; 217(b) KeystoneUSA-ZUMA; 235(cr) Nils Jorgensen; 308–309 Sipa Press; 314(bl) Ashley Cooper/SpecialistStock/ SplashdownDirect; 319(tl) Claire Leimbach/Robert Harding; 326–327 Charles M. Ommanney; 327(t) Curventa; 332–333(b); 336–337 Everett Collection; 342–343(c); 343(b) Sipa Press; 353(tr) KeystoneUSA-ZUMA; 411(b) Dean Houlding

Shutterstock.com 1 TebNad; 18–19 Alexander Raths; 20–21 ssguy; 22–23 Sergey Lavrentev; 23(t) Ljupco Smokovski; 24(bg) Deymos, (tr) Vakhrushev Pavel, (b) Ivonne Wierink; 25(t) w shane dougherty; 26(tr) yuyangc; 28(m) yxm2008, (bl) ARENA Creative; 29(b) Tatiana Makotra; 34(bg) asharkyu, (cr) Eimantas Buzasl; 36–37(m) vadim kozlovsky; 38–39(bg) Gunnar Pippel; 38(b) Smileus; 39(c) Ray Hub; 40(c) Sebastian Crocker; 41(b) Hywit Dimyadi; 42–43(bg) archibald, (c) ifong; 43(tl) Viktor Gmyria; 44–45(bg) Redshinestudio; 45(all) Annette Shaff; 46 Jaggat; 47(c) michael rubin; 48(second from tr) Maksim Toome; (from fourth from tr) Balazs Toth, CaptureLight, Jaochainoi; 54(tl) Kurhan, (br) Tamara Kulikova; 55(t) Alexander Raths, (b) Kirsty Pargeter; 57(t) wim claes, (b) indiangypsy; 58(m) beerkoff, (bl) Smit; 61(tr) Morgan Lane Photography, (b) ssuaphotos; 62–63 iDesign; 64–95 throughout paper labels by kanate; white paper by nuttakit; lined paper by happydancing; 65(b) Cameramannz; 69(bg) pixeldreams.eu, (br) Maridav; 70(tr) c., (tl) Janaka Dharmasena; 71(bl) Suzan Oschmann; 72(bg) basel101658, (tl) D. Kucharski & K. Kucharska, (c) Jubal Harshaw; 73(b) argus; 74(bg) Chepko Danil Vitalevich, (b) testing; 75(tr), (bl) koya979; 76(cl) Gerasia, (bl) vovan, (bg) beboy; 77(tr) thoron; 78(tl) JonMilnes, (c) Mazzzur; 79(c) omer cicek, (t) bonchan, Arturo Limon, Denis Selivanov, (br) fzd.it; 80(bg) Molodec, (bl) Gunnar Pippel; 81(tr) Gunnar Pippel; 83(t) Fotocrisis; 84(bg) Stephen Aaron Rees; 86(bl) MrJafari, Stephen Aaron Rees; 89(br) wanchai; 92(bl) Lisa F. Young; 93(t) Andrey Yurlov, (b) Linda Z Ryan; 96 Julien Tromeur; 100–101(bg) Mark Carrel; 101(cr) Richard Peterson, (br) Fedorov Oleksiy; 102(tr) Marijus Auruskevicius; 103(tr) Maksym Gorpenyuk; 105(tl) Bernd Juergens, (br) Michael Stokes; 107(b) Orientaly; 109(br) Julija Sapic; 111(c) Oleg - F, (r) Kjersti Joergensen; 113(br) Darren Baker; 114(tl) Irafael; 115(tr) Thirteen; 116(l) Alex Staroseltsev; 119(bl); 120(bl) Geoffrey Kuchera; 121(t) Alexandru Chririac; 123(tl) marekuliasz, (bl) Lim Yong Hian; 124(tl) alexnika; 125(m) Caitlin Mirra; 126(violas) Milan Vasicek, (conductor) HitToon.com; 127(br) Stephen Meese; 128(l) EW CHEE GUAN, (cr) Barry Barnes, (b) Pakhnyushcha; 129(br) Alexandr Kolupayev; 131(cl) Gordan, (bl) drfelice; 133(t) Maksym Bondarchuk, (bl) steamroller_blues, (br) Slaven; 134–135 1971yes; 142(t) Andrea Danti; 172(t–b) Elisei Shafer, javarman; 178–179(c) pio3; 180–181(bg) Phase4Photography; 182–183(bg) SURABKY; 189(l) jamie cross; 188–189(bg) plavusa87; 192–193(bg) plavusa87; 218 Rafael Pacheco; 222(cl) caesart; 223(br) Gordon Galbraith; 227(cr) Alex Hubenov; 232(tl frame) RDTMOR; 233(l) jordache; 235(bg) Vlue; 239(b) H. Damke; 249(tr) Dmitry Nikolajchuk; 256–257 William Attard McCarthy; 300–301 DSPA; 304(br) papkin; 304–305 Max Earey; 305(t) JetKat; 306–307(bg) Brian Weed; 306 nuttakit; 306–307(paper bg) somchaij; 307(br) Picsfive; 308(bc) Garsya, (bl) Edgaras Kurauskas; 309(tr) piyato; 313–314(c) Ahmad Faizal Yahya; 315(br) exclusive studio; 316–317 Kraska; 316(cl) vesna cvorovic; 317(br) Cathy Keifer; 320(br) Andrey Yurlov; 321(t) alexkar08; 322(bl) Ralf Siemieniec; 325(tr) Graham Bloomfield; 328(tl) Germanskydiver, (br) MustafaNC, Péter Gudella, (bl) sabri deniz kizil; 329(tl) Pavel Kapish, (tr) dicogm; 332(tl) Andrei Marincas; 333(t) somchaij; 334(cl) helissente; 337(tr) bedecs; 338 Benjamin Albiach Galan; 342–343(bg) Mark Carrel; 342(tr), (br); 343(br) Andy Lidstone; 342–343 (c/bg) MalDix; 343(cr) donatas1205; 344(br) Brandelet; 345(t) Ragnarock, (bg) Mark Carrel, (caption bg) sharpner, (tiger, lion, caracal, cat, cheetah, fox, sea lion, gorilla, koala, frog) Eric Isselée, (weasel) Ronnie Howard, (wolf) Maxim Kulko, (bat) Kirsanov, (whale) Computer Earth, (rabbit) Stefan Petru Andronache, (polar bear) Ilya Akinshin,

ACKNOWLEDGMENTS

(hummingbird) Steffen Foerster Photography, (sailfish) holbox, (crocodile) fivespots, (dragonfly) Subbotina Anna, (frog) Arek Rainczuk, (snail) Sailorr, (eagle) Steve Collender, (starfish) Mircea Bezergheanu, (jellyfish) Khoroshunova Olga, (shark) Rich Carey, (snake) fivespots; 346(clade bg) kanate, (t–b) Rostislav Ageev, Christopher Elwell, FAUP, NatalieJean, Philip Lange, (bl) donatas1205; 348(tiger) Uryadnikov Sergey, (stags) Mark Bridger, (tadpoles) Paul Broadbent, (caption bg) U.P.images_vector; 349(tr) donatas1205, (map) AridOcean, (globe) Anton Balazh, (large ground finch, common cactus finch) Stubblefield Photography; 351(globe) Anton Balazh; 352(bl) donatas1205; 355(panel) illustrart; 360–361(bg) Andre Mueller; 360(bl) donatas1205; 362–363 Pakhnyushcha; 363(bl) donatas1205; 364(bg) Lucy Baldwin, (tr) FloridaStock; 367(cr) donatas1205, (caption bg) sharpner; 368–369(bg) Mark Carrel; 368–369(leather panels) saiko3p; 371 Dudarev Mikhail; 373(t) Pasi Koskela; 374–375 Tungphoto; 376(tl) Iurii Konoval; 377(br) PhotoHappiness; 378–379(bg) Scapinachis; 378(t) Terric Delayn, (b) WendellandCarolyn, (mud) Ultrashock, (lined paper) Katrina Brown; 379(yellow paper) Kanate; 380–381(bg) Pablo H Caridad; 380(tr) Imageman; 381(tl) Dr. Morley Read, (c) Vaclav Volrab, (cr) Anna Kucherova, (br) Sergii Figurnyi; 382(bl) Valentina_G, (paper) Happydancing; 383(oval and long leaves) Maxstockphoto, (compound leaf) SlavaK, (needle) Oleksandr Kostiuchenko, (b) Ron Rowan Photography; 384(tl) Ales Liska; 385(bl) Irin-k; 386–387(bg) T. Kimmeskamp; 387(bird of paradise flower) Steve Heap, (bee orchid) Witchcraft; 391(t) Richard A. McGuirk; 392(bl) Konstanttin; 393(c) Clinton Moffat; 395(t) Cathy Keifer; 397(border) Nyasha, (stinging nettle) Marilyn Barbone, (thorns) Mexrix; 398–399(bg) AlessandroZocc; 398(tl) Ronstik, (bl) Hank Frentz, (stamp) AlexanderZam; 399(tl) Irena Misevic; 400(cl) Shi Yali; 402–403(globes) Anton Balazh; 402 Inga Nielsen, (bluejay) Mike Truchon, (chipmunk and fox) Eric Isselée, (hedgehog) Ok.nazarenko, (mole) Tramper, (owl) Tomatto, (worm) Dusty Cline; 403(tr) Natalia Bratslavsky; 404(bg) Szefei; 405(r) Quang Ho, (banana flower) Tungphoto, (coffee berries) Matuchaki, (vanilla pods) LianeM; 406(b) Alaettin YILDIRIM, (bl) Mark Winfrey; 407(r) Erperlstrom, (echinacea) Elena Elisseeva, (pomegranate) Viktar Malyshchyts, (willow bark) Marilyn Barbone, (ginseng) Sunsetman; 409(cr) 3355m, (paper) Stephen Aaron Rees; 410–411(bg) Tania Zbrodko; 410(r) Urosr; 412–413 EcoPrint; 414–415 Igor Janicek; 416(invertebrate) Richard Waters, (amphibian) Audrey Snider-Bell, (bird) Steve Byland; 417(t) Thomas Barrat, (b) Rita Januskeviciute; 419(t) FloridaStock, (b) gillmar; 420(t) Pan Xunbin, (b) wim claes; 421(t) Ivan Kuzmin; 422(paper and notebook) nuttakit; 425(br) Cathy Keifer; 426(t) Geoffrey Kuchera, (c) Audrey Snider-Bell, (bl) Dirk Ercken; 428–429 Anna Omelchenko; 429(c) Steven Russell Smith Photos; 433(r) Norma Cornes; 434(t) Eric Gevaert; 436(bl) Nancy Kennedy; 437(r) Neale Cousland; 438–439 Krzysztof Odziomek; 439(b) Specta; 440(tl) EcoPrint; 442 worldswildlifewonders; 444(c) Ecostock; 445(tl) Wayne Duguay; 448–449(bg) House @ Brasil Art Studio; 448(paper and tape) sharpner; 449(c) Janelle Lugge; 450–451 Pete Saloutos; 452–453 jan kranendonk; 452(tl and br) Fotoluminate LLC; 457(t) Kozlovskaya Ksenia; 458 Lilya Espinosa; 459 Stanislav Fridkin; 460(blonde) Jeanne Hatch, (straight black) wong sze yuen, (curly black) Felix Mizioznikov; 461(l) Steven Chiang, (r) Carmen Steiner; 464 konmesa; 468–469 PiLart; 468 Taranova; 469 Jaren Jai Wicklund; 470 JonMilnes; 473 Lawrence Wee; 474–475 Elena Schweitzer; 474(bl) Yuri Arcurs; 477 Kati1313; 480–481(bg) Sebastian Kaulitzki; 483(tr) beerkoff; 485(l) Paul Matthew Photography; 487 Elena Elisseeva; 491 Sebastien Burel; 492 picturepartners; 493 Monkey Business Images; 494–495 XYZ

Science Photo Library 64(c) Anakao Press/Look at Sciences; 70(c) Christian Jegou Publiphoto Diffusion; 78(br) Sheila Terry; 81(br) Peter Menzel; 82(c) Jacopin; 86(c) U.S. Navy; 89(t) Mikkel Juul Jensen, (bl) Lawrence Livermore, (tr) Harvard College Observatory; 95(t) Thomas Deerinck, NCMIR, (b) David Parker; 181(b) NASA; 186–187 David Ducros; 189(r) David Parker; 197(tr) NASA; 198 Detlev Van Ravenswaay; 200–201(c) NASA/JPL/ UA/Lockheed Martin; 203(b) NASA/JPL-Caltech, (tl) NASA/JPL/UA/Lockheed Martin; 206(t) SOHO/ESA/NASA; 207(tl) NASA; 208 Chris Butler; 211(t) NASA/JPL; 220–221 J-P Metsavainio; 224(bl) Royal Astronomical Society; 225(tl) Detlev Van Ravenswaay; 226(tr) Eckhard Slawik; 228(bc) Dr Jeremy Burgess, (br) Royal Astronomical Society; 228–229(t) NYPL/Science Source; 229(cl); 230–231(tc); 232(tr) Richard J. Wainscoat, Peter Arnold inc.; 234–235(tc) J-P Metsavainio; 238 David Nunuk; 239(tr) Adam Hart-Davis; 240–241(b) Christian Darkin; 241(tr) Dr Jean Lorre; 244–245 Peter Menzel; 245(br) NRAO/AUI/ NSF; 249(br) NASA; 248–249(bl) Mark Garlick, (tl) NASA/WMAP Science Team, (cr) NASA/ESA/STSCI/R.Williams, HDF-S Team; 252–253 Frank Zullo; 253(tl) Detlev Van Ravenswaay, (tr) Tony & Daphne Hallas; 254(r) NASA/Regina Mitchell-Ryall, Tom Farrar; 255(tr) European Space Agency, (cr) European Space Observatory; 305(tr) NASA; 311(tr) David Parker; 323(br) NASA; 330–331(b) NASA; 331(cr) Peter Menzel; 340–341 Mark Garlick; 342–343(t); 354–355 Jose Antonio Peñas; 356–357 and 360 Christian Jegou Publiphoto; 358 Alan Sirulnikoff; 365(b) Jaime Chirinos; 366(t) Christian Darkin; 371(cl) Philippe Psaila; 372(cl) Russell Kightly; 378(cl) Martin Shields; 387(cl) Bjorn Rorslett; 388(c) Susumu Nishinaga; 392(r) Power and Syred; 409(b) Simon Fraser

Topfoto.co.uk 72(bl) The Granger Collection; 75(c) The Granger Collection; 80(tr) The Granger Collection; 83(b) The British Library/HIP; 85(t) World History Archive; 260 Roger-Viollet; 283(t) Star Images; 287(b) ImageWorks; 294; 298(b) keystone; 326(bl) Topham/UPP

All other photographs are from:

Corel, digitalSTOCK, digitalvision, ImageState, John Foxx, PhotoAlto, PhotoDisc, PhotoEssentials, PhotoPro, Stockbyte

Every effort has been made to acknowledge the source and copyright holder of each picture.
Miles Kelly Publishing apologizes for any unintentional errors or omissions.